Flash 5!

Creative Web Animation

Derek Franklin
Brooks Patton

macromedia®
PRESS

Flash 5! Creative Web Animation

Derek Franklin and Brooks Patton

Published by Macromedia Press, in association with Peachpit Press,
a division of Addison Wesley Longman

Macromedia Press

1249 Eighth Street
Berkeley, CA 94710
(510) 524-2178
(800) 283-9444
(510) 524-2221 (fax)

http://www.peachpit.com
http://www.macromedia.com

Editor	Jill Marts Lodwig
Copyeditor	Jill Simonsen
Production Coordinators	Kate Reber, Lisa Brazieal
Compositor	Rick Gordon, Emerald Valley Graphics; Myrna Vladic, Bad Dog Graphics; and Deborah Roberti, Espresso Graphics
Interior Design Modifications	Owen Wolfson
Cover Design	TMA Ted Mader Associates
Indexer	James Minkin
Macromedia Tech Readers	Erika Burback, Jeremy Clark, Peter Davey, Jonathan Duran, and Lisa Young

Notice of Rights

Trademark Notice

Notice of Liability

ISBN 0-201-71969-X

9 8 7 6 5 4 3 2 1

Printed and bound in the United States of America.

Dedication

To the awesome Flash community who made the previous edition of this book such a huge success. The support and feedback I continue to receive from you is truly inspirational. I hope this edition helps take your ambitions further and that you derive as much joy using Flash as I have.

—Derek

———————

To my wife, Leslie; my son, Brooks Jr.; my mother, Jane; my sister, Melissa; my brothers, Leland and Wendell; my good friend, Gary; and my mother-in-law and father-in-law. Finally, to my father, whom I will forever miss and love.

—Brooks

Acknowledgments

Despite my exhaustion after grinding through the arduous schedule for this book, I have looked forward to writing this page. It gives me an opportunity to thank my friends at Peachpit, who have had every bit as much to do with this book as I have, and my family, who have been incredibly understanding and supportive during this seemingly unending marathon.

I am very much indebted to one of the most organized, motivated, and skilled editors in the business, Jill Marts Lodwig. There was never a moment when she wasn't able to make this project even better. Special thanks also to Kate Reber, production coordinator, whose patience and incredible skill has made this book one I am very proud of. Thanks to Jill Simonson, copy editor, whose ability to take my words and actually make them sound intelligent continually boggles my mind, and to compositors Rick Gordon, Myrna Vladic, and Deborah Roberti for their consummate skill and attention to detail. And finally, thanks to Marjorie Baer, executive editor, and Nancy Runzel, publisher, to whom I will be forever grateful for their faith and confidence in me.

I'm also very much indebted to my awesome wife, Kathy, for putting up with my 18-hour workdays, and to my daughter, Ashlie Russell, for her maturity, which gives me one less thing to worry about. Thanks also to my brother Eddie, for providing the laughs when I needed them most, and to my brother-in-law Jackie, whose curiosities about Flash were inspirational. And finally, special thanks to my two moms—my real one and my adoptive one, Sue Stailey (my favorite mother-in-law). These ladies continue to be my biggest fans. I love you both.

—Derek

Contents

Introduction

Over the years, Macromedia Flash has developed into a tool that far exceeds its designers' original vision. What started, in 1996, as a program for creating interactive, animated GIFs has evolved into a full-scale Web development tool. Today, in addition to Web site design, developers are using Flash to create everything from product demos to e-commerce front ends to CD-ROM-based presentations—and the list continues to grow.

While Macromedia Flash has improved and evolved with each update, the latest version is more revolutionary than evolutionary. By far the most ambitious update yet, Flash 5 represents a mature platform for creating sophisticated interactive applications for the Web and CDs. If, as a Web developer, you only have time to learn one program, Flash is your ticket: As a drawing, animation, and interactivity powerhouse, Flash can take care of all your needs, and then some.

Like most things worth doing, though, Flash takes some study and practice to master. That's where we enter the picture. Drawing on our years of experience teaching and working with Flash, our goal with this new book is to help you maximize the program's potential while avoiding the pitfalls that can beset new users.

If you're familiar with the last edition, you'll notice we've made some changes—most of which are based on your feedback. The book is now divided into sections that break down the development process into its various parts. And we've added chapters on Flash's new Movie Explorer and ActionScripting engine. One thing that hasn't changed, however, are the QuickTime tutorials: They still form the heart of this book—though there are now more of them, and they've all been updated. In these tutorials, we'll teach you some tricks and techniques, as well as introduce you to the new user interface. Best of all, by watching us use the program, you'll be able to see how you can make it all come together to create your own movies and presentations.

The Parts

Before you begin, we should explain some terminology. First, the terms *movie, presentation, content,* and *project* all refer to basically the same thing: the Flash file you create to show to the world. *Animation* in this context means any kind of onscreen movement you intentionally create. *Interactivity* refers to anything you create in Flash that reacts to viewer input—via keyboard or mouse. Finally, *multimedia* is where all of these things, including sound, come together.

Now take a look at the following list of chapters to see what's in store:

Chapter 1 — Why Flash? As if you had to ask. Here you'll find out why Flash 5 is the tool of choice for creating high-impact Web sites and multimedia presentations.

Chapter 2 — Getting Started. If you want to find out what's new in Flash 5 as well as familiarize yourself with the redesigned authoring environment and its enhancements, this is the place to go.

Chapter 3 — Graphics. Although some people find Flash's drawing tools limited, we believe just the opposite to be true. Here we'll show you why as well as provide an in-depth discussion of the program's powerful tool set, including Flash 5's newly designed interface for drawing and color tools and the powerful new Pen tool. If you work with FreeHand and Fireworks, this is where you can learn how to import files that you create with those programs directly into Flash.

Chapter 4 — Text. Although text is far from the most exciting part of a movie, it doesn't have to be boring. In this chapter, we'll show you how to use text to receive user input and liven up your presentation. You'll also learn about Flash 5's new support for HTML tags as well as font symbols.

Chapter 5 — Sound. Visual effects are great, but their impact is even greater if you use them in conjunction with sound. Here we show you how to harness the power of audio.

Chapter 6 — Bitmaps. When you add bitmap elements (or photos) to your Flash presentations, there's no limit to the visual effects you can achieve. Here, we'll show you how, and then detail some great uses for bitmaps.

Chapter 7 — Symbols. These "do all" elements represent the heart of Flash's Web multimedia capabilities. If you can master the use of symbols, you're halfway to handling most of what you'll encounter in Flash.

Chapter 8 — *Working with Elements on the Stage.* Learn how to move, align, flip, skew, and transform your movie elements in almost every way imaginable. In this chapter, you'll find out how to create new movie elements and edit existing ones on Flash's stage.

Chapter 9 — *Using Layers to Separate Content and Functionality.* Learning how to use layers is the first step in creating an interactive presentation. Here we'll show you how to use them to separate the content and functionality within your movie, and how they help give it dimension and depth.

Chapter 10 — *Using Animation to Build Movement.* Bring your movie to life with frame-by-frame and tweened animation. In this chapter, we'll describe techniques, as well as teach you how to create flowing transitions and deal with processor issues that may hinder the playback of your movie.

Chapter 11 — *Basic Actions for Building Interactivity.* Learn how to engage your viewer by creating dynamic, interactive presentations.

Chapter 12 — *Using ActionScript for Advanced Interactivity.* Want to take your presentations to the next level? With an understanding of Flash 5's new professional scripting capabilities, you'll be able to create complete Web applications, printable movies, games, and more.

Chapter 13 — *Using the Library to Manage Your Assets.* A movie contains many elements; Flash's library is where you keep track of them all. In this chapter we'll show you how to organize your movie assets in the library as well as describe Flash 5's new shared libraries—the answer to easy updates to your content, as well as revision control issues that can arise from working on group authoring projects on multiple machines.

Chapter 14 — *Using Movie Explorer to Manage Structure.* If you want a blueprint of your movie project, this is your tool. In this chapter we'll show you how to use Flash 5's new Movie Explorer to analyze and manage your project.

Chapter 15 — *Testing.* With so many things to consider when creating a Flash movie, things can sometimes slip through the cracks. Here, we'll show you how to use Flash's testing tools to create compact, smooth-running, error-free movies.

Chapter 16 — *Publishing.* All your hard work is for naught if you're unable to share the final product. Here we'll familiarize you with the many formats in which Flash allows you to present your work, and describe the potential and appropriate uses of each. You'll also learn about how to place a Flash movie on an HTML page and how to deal with plug-ins.

How to Use This Book

We've tried to organize this book so that it echoes a Flash presentation's stages of development, first discussing the elements that make up a movie, then proceeding on to discuss movie management, movie production, and movie distribution. Although we recommend that you go through this book from front to back, sections are organized so that you can easily reference them in the future. The book also includes plenty of tips, tricks, warnings, and other learning aids to keep you on track. And the CD-ROM contains the QuickTime video tutorials that accompany most chapters (as well as a QuickTime installer so that you can view the movies). The CD also contains the tutorials' associated source files, which you can open in Flash to see what makes them tick.

With this revision, we've worked hard to make this book as easy, enjoyable, and informative as possible. Now it's up to you to take the information and run with it. We'd love to hear of your successes as well as view what you've created. Contact us at flash5@derekfranklin.com or flash5@crazyraven.com. Although we may not be able to respond to all of your emails, we'll certainly do our best. Tell us what you think of the book and what you'd like to see in future editions. We'll be listening.

Why Flash?

A better question might be Why *not* Flash? As an increasingly popular standard, Macromedia Flash is ubiquitous these days. From the Web, to cell phones, to Internet-enabled appliances and personal digital assistants (PDAs), businesses the world over are using Flash to market their products and to do e-commerce right. The reason the Web development community is so crazy about Flash? There's simply nothing that compares when it comes to creating interactive, high-impact content. And it doesn't hurt that Flash is cool, hip, and fun to use, too!

The key to Flash's popularity, though, is its powerful multimedia capabilities—features that have enabled Flash to transform the Web from the text/graphics medium that it was a few years ago into the multisensory, interactive experience it has become today. A painstakingly produced Flash movie can be as enjoyable as a well-orchestrated symphony. And like a symphony, it brings together a number of elements—sound, movement, interaction— to produce some extraordinary results.

Need more convincing? Probably not. But read on anyway to learn about some of the other aspects of Flash that make it such an appealing tool for creating next-generation Web content.

Speed

One thing that makes Flash such an incredible Web development tool is its use of vector graphics as the default graphics mode. Vector graphics are objects defined by mathematical equations, or vectors, that include information about the object's size, shape, color, outline, and position. This efficient mode of handling graphics keeps files relatively small—even when you're dealing with complex drawings. What's more, because vector graphics are resolution independent, a vector graphic the size of a pinhead will retain the same file size—with no degradation in quality—even when enlarged to fit your entire screen **(Figure 1.1)**.

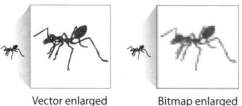

Vector enlarged   Bitmap enlarged

Figure 1.1
Comparison of an enlarged vector graphic with an enlarged bitmap graphic.

Traditionally (and on the Web in particular), graphics have been delivered primarily in the form of *bitmaps.* Although effective and often quite artistic, bitmaps are bandwidth intensive and share none of the benefits of vector graphics. Bitmap graphic files, for example, are almost always larger in size than their vector counterparts (even though they appear similar)—a fact that becomes more apparent as the physical dimensions of the graphic increase. The construction of bitmaps accounts for this difference.

Unlike vector images, which use mathematical equations, bitmaps are made up of a collection of dots, or *pixels,* placed in a grid formation, or pattern, one right next to another. These pixels are usually so small that from a distance, the pixels in the pattern that make up a bitmap blend seamlessly to form a picture. However, if you were to zoom in on this picture, the tiny square pixels would become apparent. Each pixel in a bitmap has associated information that relates to its color. Most images comprise thousands, hundreds of thousands, or even millions of pixels. Obviously, the larger the graphic, the more pixels it contains. Hence, even a small bitmap 100 pixels tall by 100 pixels wide would have to store information for 10,000 pixels. You can begin to see the benefits of using vector graphics wherever possible. Although vector graphics offer file size advantages, there are some graphic effects you can achieve only with bitmaps. Fortunately, Flash supports bitmap graphics, even direct import of Macromedia Fireworks 3 or later files. And because it uses the latest compression technologies, Flash helps you keep file size to a minimum even when using bitmaps.

Flash's development approach also facilitates the creation of complex multimedia presentations while still maintaining small file sizes. Because such elements as vectors, bitmaps, and sounds are usually employed more than once in a given movie, Flash allows you to make a single version of an object, which you can then reuse elsewhere rather than re-create the object each time you wish to use it—a capability that goes a long way toward conserving file size. For example, if you wanted to use a 10-KB bitmap graphic in 10 locations in your Flash presentation, it would *appear* to require 100 KB (10 KB used 10 times) of file space. However, Flash requires just one actual copy of the 10-KB graphic; the other nine instances are simply references to the main file. Although these "references" appear just as the actual file would, less than 100 bytes per instance are required to reference the actual file **(Figure 1.2)**. So, you would save nearly 90 KB in file size—a considerable amount on the Web. You can use this powerful capability with vectors, bitmaps, sounds, and more to create compelling yet compact multimedia productions.

10K   10K

Figure 1.2
A single graphic in Flash can be reused without increasing your movie's overall file size.

A final—and perhaps defining—factor in Flash's ability to create fast-loading multimedia over the Web is its ability to stream content. If it couldn't do this, Flash would probably not be practical for the Web.

Streaming content is another example of a technology born out of necessity on the Web. Before streaming, bandwidth issues prevented users from viewing or listening to files until all of their contents had been downloaded. Engineers, however, realized that users don't see or hear every byte in a file simultaneously: They understood that you could receive the full impact of the content by receiving it incrementally. For example, when reading a book, you view only a page at a time. So, if your book were delivered over the Web, you would probably appreciate being able to read the first few pages while the rest of the book was being downloaded in the background. If you had to wait for the whole book to be downloaded before you could begin reading, you might give up and click elsewhere **(Figure 1.3)**.

Flash's streaming capabilities mean that even large files with sound, animation, and bitmaps can begin playing almost instantaneously. If you plan your project precisely, your audience can view a 10- to 15-minute presentation over the Web without noticing that content is being downloaded in the background.

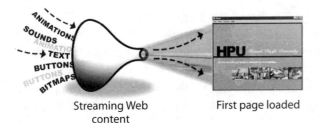

Streaming Web
content

First page loaded

Figure 1.3
Flash allows content to be streamed, which means users can view downloaded sections while other content continues to load.

Web Standard

As most Web developers will attest to, browser and software manufacturers frequently tout Web standards even as they continue to define their own *versions* of those standards. We all have our own ways of doing things, and nowhere is this more apparent than in the browser itself. Take the following scenario: After spending hours creating the perfect Web page, with graphics placed just so and perhaps some JavaScript added for a bit of simple interactivity, you view your work in your favorite browser, where it looks and functions just as it should. You feel pretty good until you decide to view the page through your *least favorite* browser: Now you're mortified. Besides not looking anything like it should, your Web page is producing JavaScript error after JavaScript error. Your beautiful interactive page has fallen victim to a compatibility problem between browsers—one that may well send you back to the drawing board.

Since the Web continues to evolve at a phenomenal rate, the lack of universal standards remains a roadblock to a number of powerful technologies. Many developers are sticking to the basics rather than running the risk of creating compatibility problems by including fancier features—a problem Macromedia addressed by creating the Flash Player, a plug-in that enables the program's content to be viewed consistently across browsers, operating systems, Web-enabled appliances, and even video game consoles (for example, Sega Dreamcast and Sony Play Station).

Now, in addition to proliferating on the Web and in electronic devices, Flash technology is turning up on many major companies' Web sites. In fact, 35 percent of the world's top 50 Web sites make use of the program. And more than 90 percent of the browsers in use today—or nearly 250 million users—are able to view Flash content without having to download the player. (However, rest assured: If you do need to download the plug-in, the process is quick and simple.) What's more, current (and future) versions of the major browsers include the Flash Player, and current versions of Windows and Macintosh operating systems ship with it preinstalled: If these facts doesn't make Flash a standard, we can't imagine what would.

The icing on the cake, though, came after Macromedia made the SWF (Flash movie) format available to the public last year, allowing any software developer to create products that export content in Flash's file format. In response to this action—and in tacit acknowledgement of Flash's market-leading position—Adobe has included support for the Flash format in its own Web content development product, LiveMotion: Instead of creating a proprietary multimedia tool that would require its own plug-in, Adobe is offering a product that can export the content it creates to the Flash format— great news for developers, who now have a choice of authoring tools (although LiveMotion's interactive capabilities do not compare to Flash 5's). What's more, a number of other third-party developers have also begun creating all sorts of animation, 3-D, and other production tools that export content to the SWF file format. And many popular graphics applications (including Adobe Illustrator and CorelDraw) can now export directly to the SWF format as well.

The bottom line for Flash developers is that they can create content once—with all the design and interactive wizardry they wish—and know that it will look and act the same, regardless of what platform, browser, or Web-enabled electronic appliance their viewers are using **(Figure 1.4)**. We don't need to tell you that *that's* good news for developers.

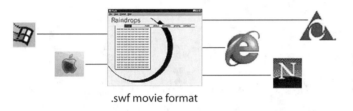

.swf movie format

Figure 1.4
A Flash movie will look the same regardless of the platform or device it is being viewed on.

Interactivity

Humans find few things as captivating as movement and interaction. As kids, a butterfly or a favorite animated show could hold our attention for hours. And while few of us enjoy staring at a rock, we could watch time and again a cartoon in which a rock was being obliterated by all kinds of explosions. We all like to provoke a response with our actions. Flash allows you to create this type of experience for users—one that's directly tied to the creativity you've expressed in producing your own interactive offering.

With Flash, you can create interactivity that makes your movie display data, print information, play sounds, take users to different points in your movie, and react to mouse events. In addition, users can drag around and manipulate elements of your movie. You can also create unique games or complete Web applications with built-in logic, and your movie can move along at a predefined pace or follow a path defined by viewer input. You can even incorporate HTML-based text and functionality **(Figure 1.5)**. The final touch, though, is Flash 5's new scripting language. Offering capabilities that rival or even surpass those found in JavaScript, it provides users with control over a wide range of

Figure 1.5
With Flash, you can incorporate dynamically generated and formatted HTML text into your project.

features (including cursor, object color, etc). Your movies will now do more; your users will have greater control; and the experience you provide will likely be unforgettable.

One final factor that will go far to enhance your Flash presentation is sound. Without it, even the most phenomenal visual display will seem lacking. Flash allows you to enhance the user experience by adding sound effects or synchronizing onscreen actions with a soundtrack. By letting the user control volume and panning (the amount of sound coming out of the left or right speaker), you can turn passive users into active participants. And the more you engage your users, the more likely they are to retain the message you're trying to convey.

Ease of Use

As cool as all of the above sounds, the icing on the cake is that all of these elements are easy to create: You can produce a full-blown multimedia extravaganza, complete with interactive controls and buttons, without opening another graphics program or scripting anything in an HTML editor. And your creation will look and work the same in any Flash-enabled device.

Flash uses a development metaphor of timelines, frames, and scenes that makes it easy to conceptualize animations and interactive content. In addition, Flash offers a number of tools for organizing content and assets, streamlining workflow, and analyzing and testing your project before distribution—all of which allow you to be more creative and ambitious with your productions.

Flash provides a wide range of tools that enable you to produce professional-looking designs without learning new skills or techniques. And with this version, Macromedia has made Flash's interface more intuitive and more similar to its other development products. (For example, if you're familiar with Dreamweaver or Fireworks, learning Flash should be relatively easily.) Although Flash's tool set shares a number of concepts with other vector drawing programs, it handles some drawing tasks in a unique fashion. If you've used an illustration program before, though, not to worry: You should be up and running with Flash's drawing tools in no time. And even if you haven't used a drawing program, the concepts are simple and easy to pick up.

When Flash's own drawing tools are insufficient (such as when you need a bitmap graphic), you can take advantage of the program's strong import capabilities. This way, you can create artwork in your favorite illustration or photo editing program and then import it into Flash for use in your movie. In addition, Flash can now import FreeHand and Fireworks files directly—further indication that creating great-looking presentations will never be a worry.

Design Capabilities

When the Web was first gaining popularity, layout and design were minor concerns. Most pages had colored backgrounds, a few centered graphics, and some text—not very engaging visually but effective (to some degree) nonetheless. Then came the introduction of frames and tables into browsers, and Web page creation became an art. Suddenly complex pages were the standard—and one that wasn't necessarily easy to live up to since methodology was tricky and browsers remained limited in their graphics presentation.

Designers learned that by chopping, slicing, and precisely positioning graphics, they could emulate the beauty of the printed page—a popular though limited approach to Web page design. Certain key elements—such as exact positioning and the use of layers to stack page elements on top of one another—were still missing.

Both major browsers tackled these issues in their 4.0 editions by introducing *Dynamic HTML,* or DHTML, which allows for exact positioning of elements, the incorporation of layers, and a number of other long-requested capabilities. Although these capabilities opened many doors, there are still associated challenges. For one, a thorough understanding of DHTML and scripting is a necessity. Some design tools make the process easier, yet even they are occasionally cryptic in themselves. And compatibility, too, remains an issue: Pre-4.0 browsers will not recognize DHTML (not to mention the fact that the browsers themselves handle DHTML differently); so your hard work will be unappreciated unless you take the time to create another version to accommodate these older browsers. And, as mentioned earlier, many designers simply choose to design for the least common denominator—that is, 3.x browsers.

In contrast, Flash-designed content has few design limitations. Graphic elements can be placed precisely—using grids, guides, and rulers—anywhere on the page. And you can stack elements on layers. You can also create online forms in Flash that can receive information from your users or display HTML-enhanced text blocks complete with formatting and hyperlinks. In addition, Flash's transparency capabilities give your layouts depth and make them more visually appealing. You can even use a background that doesn't tile across the screen **(Figure 1.6)**.

Tiled background

Flash background

Figure 1.6
With Flash's complete graphics control, you need never use another tiled background in your designs.

You can use Flash to easily achieve all the wonderful layout possibilities of printed material. Moreover, you can animate your material as well as make it interactive. You can even choose to forego Flash's multimedia capabilities altogether and use it simply as the most precise Web page layout tool available today: that's OK too.

The best thing about all of these capabilities is that they're not too complex for the average user. You simply place a graphic on the page, add some interactivity (if you wish), and then rest assured that it will look exactly as you created it—regardless of which browser or other Flash-enabled device your audience is viewing it with. For advanced users, this version includes many helpful and time-saving features, including a debugger, color-coded syntax within the Action panel, and the ability to easily import and export scripts for use in other projects.

Versatility

Flash can handle jobs of all sizes and proportions. You can use it to create a full multimedia Web site with tons of cool graphics, form elements, and interaction, or you may employ it simply to create a navigation bar or banner. The choice is yours. Listed below are just some of the things you can use Flash to create:

- Games
- Cartoons
- Interactive maps
- Single Web pages
- Full-blown multimedia-enhanced Web sites
- Interactive online forms
- Web database front ends
- Promotional or marketing tools
- Vacation presentations
- Banner ads
- Enhanced QuickTime movies
- Stand-alone applications
- Web jukeboxes
- Shopping cart systems

Widespread Viewability

The Internet represents the future of communications. Already, it allows us to view video from anywhere in the world, send messages with pictures, make Internet phone calls, and hold international meetings. However, not everyone has an Internet connection, and even if they do, it may not always be available to them.

Although Flash was designed to create compact, fast-loading multimedia—which makes it an ideal technology for the Web—you are not restricted to delivering your Flash content over the Internet. Any Flash-created content can be exported as a multimedia movie for use on the Web, as video that can be viewed on both Windows and Macintosh computers, and even as a stand-alone program that you can distribute on floppy disks. With the Flash player being integrated into nearly every type of digital informational or entertainment device, you can count on a growing audience for years to come.

With Flash, you no longer have an excuse for delivering boring, static content. It's easy to use, powerful, interactive, and just plain fun. If you're the least bit creative, you'll be amazed at what you can come up with—and seeing someone else enjoying your work is a feeling you won't soon forget.

Integration

Powerful as Flash is, it needs a bit of outside help for more advanced projects such as chat functionality or shopping-cart systems (for e-commerce). Flash can easily communicate with Web application servers such as ASP and Cold Fusion or work with CGI scripts written in Perl, PHP, or other Web scripting languages. And let's not forget about its ability to communicate with the browser via JavaScript. Flash's tight integration with these technologies makes it possible for you to process information within your movie (for example, entered into form elements), display dynamic text from a database, or make your movie react to information it receives from a Web server.

As if that weren't enough, Flash can now work with XML data as well. For developers, this ability to transmit and receive structured XML data over a constant open server connection is a dream come true, facilitating multiplayer games, real-time chat, and a wide range of other sophisticated applications in the Flash universe. In a word, *wow!*

What Is *XML?*

XML is a protocol that sets rules, guidelines, and conventions for structuring data in a way that produces unambiguous files which are easy to generate and read (by a computer). The following is a chunk of XML data:

```
<Person>
    <firstname>Derek</firstname>
    <lastname>Franklin</lastname>
    <age>30-something</age>
</Person>
```

Like HTML, XML makes use of tags (words bracketed by '<' and '>') and attributes (of the form name="value"), but while HTML specifies what each tag and attribute means, XML uses the tags only to delimit pieces of data, leaving the interpretation of the data to the application that reads it. Thus, the same piece of XML data can be used in a spreadsheet, an address book, and financial transactions across different platforms with minimal effort.

If you're looking to push Flash to its limits, XML is a language worth learning—and if you know how HTML works, XML should be a breeze.

For more information, visit the XML homepage at http://www.xml.com

Getting Started

One of the great things about Macromedia Flash is that it's not rocket science. With a little practice, you can be well on your way to creating fun, interactive movies. In the first part of this chapter, we'll help you gain a basic understanding of the way Flash works— a few simple concepts, without which you won't get far. Then we'll take a look at some of this version's many enhancements. Lastly, we'll let you get your feet wet with an interactive tutorial that helps you create your first Flash movie.

By the time you finish this chapter, you'll have mastered the basics you need to work through the rest of this book. Keep in mind, however, that you're building momentum as you go: Don't get discouraged if you get hung up somewhere down the line. It's impossible to become a Flash master overnight—especially with all the new features Macromedia has crammed into this update.

How Flash Works

Flash content is produced and distributed using two files: an authoring file, where you create content, animation, and interactivity, and a compressed and optimized version of this file, better known as a Flash movie.

The authoring file, which has an *.fla* extension, is your production file. This is where you store your work so that you can tinker with it later—it's the file you actually work on when Flash is open. It contains all the sounds, bitmaps, drawings, text, and interactivity you want your final movie to contain. The authoring file is your movie in its *preoptimized* state—which means it can balloon to well over several megabytes.

When you've gotten your authoring file to look and work the way you want, it's time to distribute it by turning it into a Flash movie. This is known as *exporting*. When you export your authoring file to a movie (which has an *.swf* file extension), Flash compresses and optimizes it so that the movie file is dramatically smaller than the original authoring file **(Figure 2.1)**. You place this smaller file on your Web page or distribute it on disk or CD. For the most part, the exported movie cannot be edited. If you wish to edit your movie's content, you must reopen the original authoring file, make your changes, and then re-export the authoring file to a Flash movie.

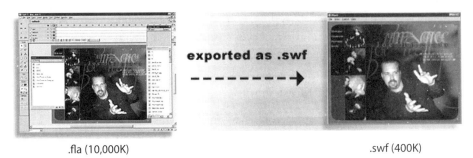

.fla (10,000K)   .swf (400K)

Figure 2.1
Exporting your authoring file to a Flash movie creates an optimized version that looks and acts similar to the authoring file but is actually a substantially smaller file size.

Many factors will affect the size of your Flash movie—most of which you can control. Getting the smallest file size for your final movie usually involves balancing the quality of your movie's elements (bitmaps, audio, and so on) against your movie's file size. Sometimes you'll need to compromise, sacrificing quality—such as sound clarity or picture sharpness—for a smaller exported movie. We'll strive to show you how you can use Flash's tools to produce the best-quality movie possible while still retaining a reasonable file size.

From your authoring files, you can not only create Flash movies but also export these same files to produce QuickTime movies, animated GIFs, and even static or non-animated graphics—and you can have Flash create all of these simultaneously! This means you can create once (the authoring file) and distribute many ways (Flash movie, QuickTime movie, animated GIF, JPEG, and so on).

Content Creation

Flash projects can take many forms, including presentations, tutorials, product demos, slide shows, and even games. Some Flash projects use interactivity but little or no animation, while others employ motion graphics but have little interactivity.

Regardless of your project's scope, your work will typically proceed as follows:

1. Draw or import graphics into Flash.

2. Transform buttons, independent animations, and any elements you intend to reuse into symbols.

3. Place your movie elements (including vector graphics, bitmaps, and symbols) on the stage.

4. Attach actions to buttons, movie clips, or frames on the timeline to make them interactive.

5. Select a frame, symbol, stroke, fill, or text block on the stage to adjust its properties via different panels.

A few things to keep in mind about the way Flash works: At any given time what you're viewing on the stage represents the contents of the current frame on the timeline. When you move the playhead to a different frame, the scene on the stage will change. Animation is created when content on the stage is rearranged from frame to frame, and the frames are viewed quickly and in a sequential order. To make it easier to work with the many frames your timeline will comprise, Flash allows you to break down the authoring file into *scenes*. Think of scenes as pages within your authoring file, each of which is unique. A single authoring file can have as many scenes as you wish; however, all of the scenes are part of a single exported movie. Scenes merely simplify content creation in the authoring environment by splitting the timeline into manageable parts.

Content Distribution

After you've created content in your authoring file, you must export it as a Flash movie and then decide what you want to do with the final optimized .swf file. One option is to embed your movie in a Web page, where it will appear as a regular graphic—only animated and interactive. You can, in fact, create an entire Web site based solely on a single Flash movie. If this is how you wish your audience to view your movie, however, be aware that they must have the Flash Player installed to view it.

Your Flash movie will be streamed over the Web, which means that viewers can begin playing it almost immediately while the rest of the movie is being downloaded in the background. You can tell Flash to open and close browser windows, accept information from your user (which can be processed by a CGI script), play sounds, interact with the user, and more while the movie is playing.

Another popular way of delivering your Flash movie is to turn it into a *projector*, or stand-alone player, which transforms it into a self-running application. This means you can put your movie on a disk or CD, and anyone can view it immediately just by opening it—even without the Flash plug-in. With Flash's new scripting engine and support for communication with Web servers, you can create full-blown, powerful Flash applications that you can distribute via projector file. In fact, you can create your Web site entirely in Flash, then put it on the Web *and* give it to your customers on disk or CD.

You can also turn your Flash project into a QuickTime movie, a Windows AVI file, or even a RealPlayer file. No matter what your requirements, Flash can probably handle the job with ease.

What's New in Flash 5

Macromedia has spared no expense in giving its loyal community of Flash developers a fresh new tool for creating next-generation multimedia content. While the general interface has undergone some changes (as you'll soon discover), most of the improvements take the form of new tools or enhancements to Flash's underlying capabilities.

Even if you're a long-time Flash user, you'll probably need some time to familiarize yourself with this latest version and find your groove in the new environment. Once you do, you're likely to find that most tasks can now be more quickly and efficiently accomplished.

The following summarizes the enhancements and additions to Flash 5 (all of which will be described in greater detail later in the chapter):

Common Macromedia interface. To make its various production tools easier to work with, Macromedia has updated Flash's interface so that it more closely resembles the company's other development tools (Dreamweaver, Fireworks, and so on).

Pen tool. Flash now comes with a Bezier Pen tool that resembles those found in professional vector drawing programs. The Pen tool will give users more precision in creating and editing vector graphics.

Panels. Representing one of the biggest changes to the overall interface, panels provide quick access to an element's options and parameters. As a replacement for a number of cumbersome dialog boxes, they go far to enhance work flow.

Draggable guides. If you've ever used another vector drawing program, you're sure to have fallen in love with the way draggable guides can help you place and arrange objects in your layout. This layout enhancement will come in especially handy in Flash's animation environment.

Selection highlights. A graphic element's selection box can now show the color of the layer on which it is located—helpful for quickly identifying the layer on which a selected element resides.

Better color support. Creating and editing colors and gradients is much easier now that Flash includes a professional-level Eyedropper tool for selecting and creating perfect color matches. A number of other color tool enhancements are included as well.

Shared libraries. If you are part of a work group that develops Flash content, or even if you just want an easy way to maintain version control over your movie's elements, shared libraries are for you. They allow you to place movie elements in a central library, where you can then link to them from any Flash project. If you edit an element in a shared library, any project that uses link elements from that library will reflect the edits as well.

Font symbols. Using font symbols, it's easy to change the font face of text elements used throughout your movie. This is similar to the functionality cascading style sheets provide in an HTML document.

Smart Clips. With Smart clips—movie clips that you assign functionality to via ActionScript—you can quickly create movie elements such as menus, drop-down boxes, and more.

Closer integration with Macromedia Freehand and Fireworks files. If you use FreeHand to create vector content for your movie and Fireworks to create bitmaps for import, you can now import these files directly so that layers and text blocks are maintained and objects remain editable.

Customizable keyboard shortcuts. Want complete control over keyboard shortcuts? Flash 5 gives it to you, allowing you to use various keyboard shortcut sets (such as those from Fireworks and PhotoShop) or to create you own from scratch.

MP3 import. Flash 4 gave us the ability to export our Flash project's audio to the MP3 format, but it didn't allow us to *import* an MP3 file. Now you can import MP3 files as well, which means you can make authoring files much smaller.

HTML-enhanced text blocks. Text blocks in Flash can now incorporate HTML 1.0 formatting, allowing you to format them with colors, font sizes and styles, and hyperlinks.

Movie Explorer. This new tool provides an at-a-glance view of your project's overall structure, allowing you to analyze your movie as well as quickly find and edit its elements.

Reinvented ActionScript. The Flash development team has completely transformed ActionScript, which now features a JavaScript-like syntax and a complete set of math functions. You can now give your audience even more control over your movies' elements.

XML support. Using XML, Flash can work with and manipulate structured data in a way that opens up a whole new set of possibilities in Flash application development, such as sophisticated shopping carts, multi-player games, and more.

Printable movies. Take your content beyond the digital medium and allow users to print individual frames or entire movies using a button or frame action inside your movie. Printable movies can be used for distributing coupons, product info, and more.

Debugger. With Flash projects growing ever more complex, a Flash design team needs to find a way to *debug,* or find mistakes, in ActionScripts and in the functionality of a project. The new debugger tool allows them to do this in the most efficient manner possible.

Interface

Macromedia has made Flash 5's new interface more approachable and intuitive, which means a shorter learning curve and more efficient work flow. If you've used other Macromedia products, you'll note the similarities between the programs, such as the Launcher bar, icons for tools on the toolbar, the organization of menu commands, and the use of panels for working within your project.

Let's get acquainted with and learn how to customize Flash 5's interface, including the toolbars, menu bar, context menus, panels, and so on **(Figure 2.2)**. We'll take a general look at the interface before we go on to examine each area in more detail. Some areas, such as the timeline and the layer interface, are covered in more depth in the chapters on animation and layers.

Toolbars

The Windows version of Flash has two primary toolbars (standard and drawing), while the Macintosh version has just one, a drawing toolbar. This is one of the few ways the program varies between operating systems.

The standard toolbar (Windows only) provides quick access to many of the functions that are otherwise available from the menus. This includes buttons for creating new

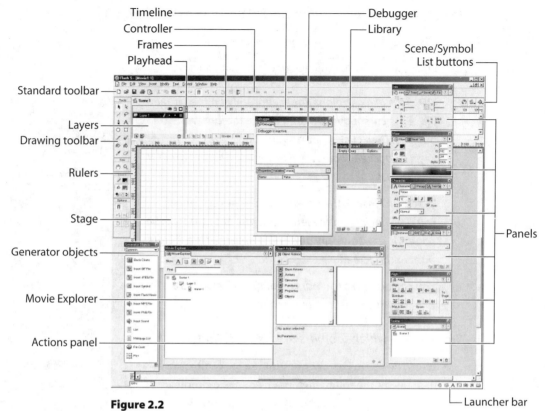

Figure 2.2
The various parts of the Flash interface.

projects and for common commands such as opening, saving, printing, cutting, copying, and pasting.

The drawing toolbar includes a complete set of Flash's creation tools.

Another toolbar, the controller, is a VCR-like control pad for playing, stopping, rewinding, and fast-forwarding your movie within the authoring environment **(Figure 2.3)**. In Windows, the standard, drawing, and controller toolbars can be docked to a screen edge or float above it. On Macintosh computers, the toolbars cannot dock to the interface—they must always remain floating.

Figure 2.3
The Controller lets you play, stop, rewind, and fast-forward your movie within the Flash authoring environment.

To dock a toolbar on another edge of the screen (Windows only):

1. Click and hold on an area on the toolbar with no buttons.

2. Drag the toolbar to an edge of the screen and release.

> **TIP** *To make a toolbar float separately on the screen, place the cursor over an area on the toolbar with no buttons. Then click while holding down the Control key. The docked toolbar will become a floating toolbar (Figure 2.4).*

> **NOTE** *In Flash 4, the drawing toolbar in Windows could be docked on the left, right, top, or bottom of the screen. It can now only be docked on either the left or right of the screen.*

> *You can also turn toolbars on or off to include them in or remove them from the interface.*

To configure which toolbars are visible (Windows):

◆ From the menu bar, choose Window > Toolbars > then one of the following options to make a toolbar visible (indicated by a check) or invisible (unchecked).

   Main. Check to display the standard toolbar.

   Status. Check to display the status toolbar.

   Controller. Check to display the controller.

To configure which toolbars are visible (Macintosh):

◆ From the menu bar, choose Window > Tools to make the drawing toolbar visible (indicated by a check) or invisible (unchecked), or Window > Controller to make the controller visible or invisible.

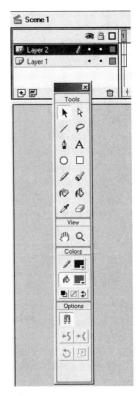

Figure 2.4
The Drawing toolbar can float above the Flash interface, so that you can work in the way that's most comfortable.

Menu Bar

Flash's menus provide access to many of the program's commands. An arrow to the far right of a selection in the menu bar indicates a submenu, and keyboard shortcuts for menu commands are shown to the right of some commands. For clarity, the terms

Flash project and *project* denote Flash-authoring documents—that is, the place where you create the content that you eventually export as a Flash movie.

File menu

Use the File menu to create, open, and save files **(Figure 2.5)**.

Open as Library. Opens another Flash project's library, which allows its items to be added and used in the currently opened project.

Open as Shared Library. Opens a shared library, which allows its items to be added and used in the currently opened project.

Import. Imports sounds, bitmaps, QuickTime video, and other files.

Export Movie. Exports the current Flash project to a Flash or QuickTime movie, an animated GIF, or another animated sequence.

Export Image. Creates a non-animated image from content on the stage.

Publish Settings. Adjusts settings for publishing your Flash project to HTML, QuickTime, and more.

Publish. Creates a file based on settings you've selected with the Publish Settings option.

Edit menu

The selections on the Edit menu help you work on your files **(Figure 2.6)**.

Paste in Place. Pastes content on the clipboard into the same relative position on the stage that it was cut or copied from.

Cut Frames. Cuts frames selected on the timeline and places them on the clipboard.

Copy Frames. Copies frames selected on the timeline and places them on the clipboard.

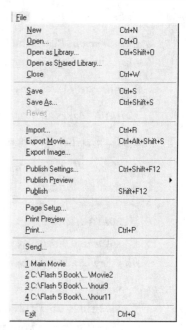

Figure 2.5
The parts of the File menu.

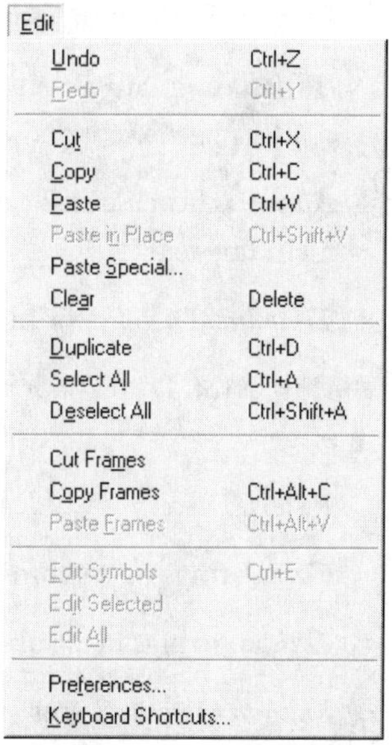

Figure 2.6
The parts of the Edit menu.

Paste Frames. Pastes frames from the clipboard onto the timeline.

Edit Symbols. Places the last edited symbol back into symbol-editing mode so that you may edit its stage and timeline. (Item changes to Edit Movie when editing a symbol.)

Edit Selected. Places a selected symbol into symbol-editing mode.

Edit All. Makes all content available for editing.

Preferences. Lets you personalize some of Flash's features.

Keyboard Shortcuts. Opens a dialog box for changing, editing, or creating your own Keyboard shortcuts.

View menu

You use the selections on this menu to control how you view your project as well as the various layout features that Flash provides **(Figure 2.7)**.

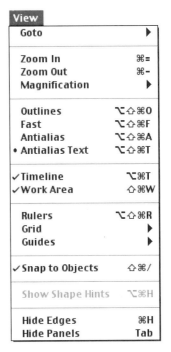

Figure 2.7
The parts of the View menu.

Goto. Brings up a submenu to help you navigate to frames or scenes in your movie.

Outlines. Turns all objects visible on the stage into outlines (no fills) for fast object redraw.

Fast. Turns off antialiasing for fast object redraw.

Antialiasing. Smoothes the edges of all objects visible on the stage except text.

Antialias Text. Antialiases all objects on the stage, including text.

Timeline. Displays or hides timeline.

Work Area. Displays or hides the work area around the stage.

Rulers. Displays or hides horizontal and vertical rulers.

Grid. Brings up a submenu for setting various grid options.

Guides. Brings up a submenu for setting various guide options.

Snap to Objects. Turns snapping on or off.

Show Shape Hints. Shows where shape hints are placed on shapes that are part of a shape tween.

Hide Edges. Hides or displays the selection box around selected elements on the stage.

Hide Panels. Hides or displays panels.

Insert menu

The Insert menu gives you control over frames and layers **(Figure 2.8)**.

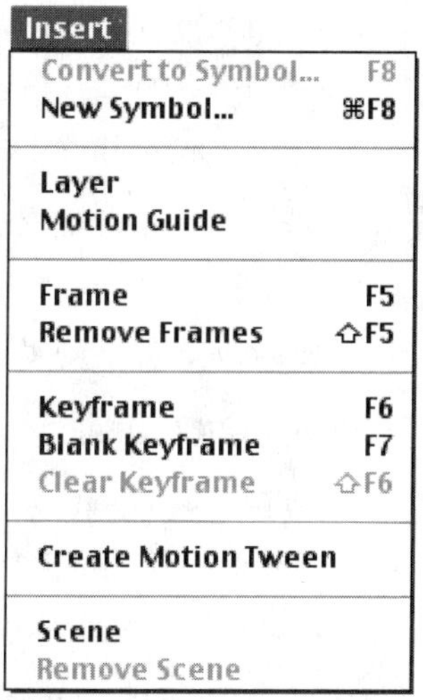

Convert to Symbol. Converts all selected elements on the stage into symbols.

New Symbol. Creates a new, empty symbol.

Layer. Creates a new, empty layer above the selected one on the timeline.

Motion Guide. Creates a new Motion Guide layer above the selected layer.

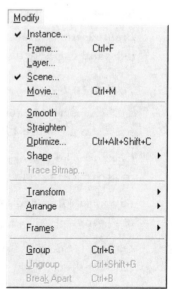

Figure 2.8
The parts of the Insert menu.

Frame. Creates a new, empty frame to the right of the selected one.

Remove Frames. Deletes the selected frame(s) on the timeline.

Keyframe. Converts the selected frame on the timeline to a keyframe, which contains the same content as the last keyframe on the layer.

Blank Keyframe. Converts the selected frame on the timeline into a blank keyframe.

Clear Keyframe. Converts the selected keyframe to a regular frame.

Create Motion Tween. Converts all elements on the selected layer and frame to a symbol so that they may be motion-tweened.

Modify menu

Use the Modify menu to edit or change the properties of various elements in your project **(Figure 2.9)**.

Instance. Opens the Instance panel, where you configure the properties of the selected instance.

Frame. Opens the Frame panel, where you set the properties for the selected frame.

Figure 2.9
The parts of the Modify menu.

Layer. Opens the Layer Properties dialog box, where you set the properties for the selected layer.

Scene. Opens the Scene panel, where you change the name of the current frame.

Movie. Opens the Movie Properties dialog box, where you set the properties of your movie.

Smooth. Smoothes the selected line(s) on the stage.

Straighten. Straightens the selected line(s) on the stage.

Optimize. Opens a dialog box that allows you to remove unnecessary points on a selected vector graphic(s) to make it more file-size efficient.

Shape. Opens a submenu with options for editing lines and shapes.

Trace Bitmap. Opens the Trace Bitmap dialog box, where you adjust the settings for turning the selected bitmap into a vector graphic.

Transform. Opens a submenu with options for transforming, editing, and reshaping the selected object or shape.

Arrange. Opens a submenu with options for changing the "stacking order" of objects and for locking and unlocking them.

Frames. Opens a submenu with options for modifying the selected frames on the timeline.

Break Apart. Converts selected text to shapes, breaks a selected symbol into its individual shapes, or turns a bitmap into an editable element.

Text menu

The Text menu lets you adjust various options for the currently selected text **(Figure 2.10)**.

Character. Hides or displays the Character panel for quick editing of all character options for currently selected text.

Paragraph. Hides or displays the Paragraph panel for quick editing of all paragraph options for currently selected text.

Options. Hides or displays the Text Options panel for setting properties for the currently selected text block.

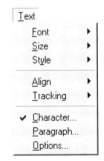

Figure 2.10
The parts of the Text menu.

Control menu

The Control menu lets you choose various options for how your movie works and plays in the authoring and testing environment **(Figure 2.11)**.

Test Movie. Exports a temporary version of the current movie to Flash's testing environment.

Debug Movie. Exports a temporary version of the current movie to Flash's testing environment for debugging purposes.

Test Scene. Exports a temporary version of your current scene to Flash's testing environment.

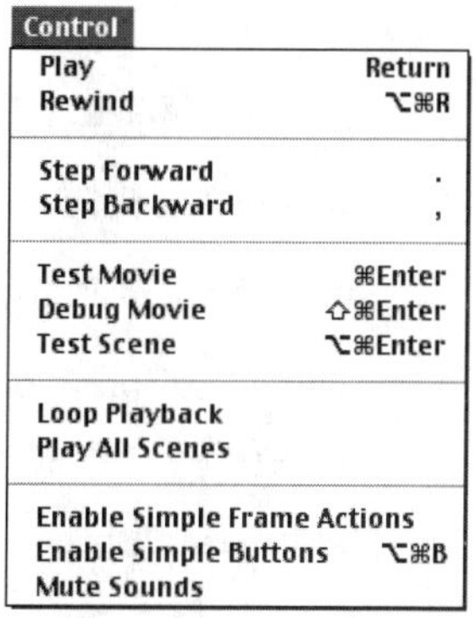

Figure 2.11
The parts of the Control menu.

Loop Playback. If playing your movie within the authoring environment, plays the timeline again when it has reached its last frame.

Play All Scenes. If playing your movie within the authoring environment, plays all scenes in the project. When turned off, playback will end on the last frame of the current scene.

Enable Frame Actions. If playing your movie within the authoring environment, lets the timeline react to any frame actions that have been set up.

Enable Buttons. Enables buttons in the authoring environment to reflect their Up, Over, Down, and Hit states in reaction to the cursor.

Window menu

The Window menu gives you access to the various toolbars and dialog boxes in Flash **(Figure 2.12)**.

Toolbars (Windows only). Opens a submenu that lets you select which toolbars to display or hide.

Tools. Displays or hides the drawing toolbar.

Controller (Macintosh only). Displays or hides the movie controller.

Panels. Opens a submenu that lets you select which panels to display or hide.

Panel Sets. Opens a submenu that lets you choose a previously saved panel arrangement.

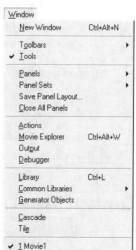

Figure 2.12
The parts of the Windows menu.

Save Panel Layout. Saves the current panel arrangement for later use.

Close All Panels. Closes all open panels.

Actions. Displays or hides the Actions panel.

Movie Explorer. Displays or hides the Movie Explorer.

Output. Displays or hides the Output window, which allows you to trace variable values within your project.

Debugger. Displays or hides the Debugger tool.

Library. Displays or hides the library window for working with reusable elements in your movie.

Common Libraries. Opens a submenu that displays a list of common libraries.

Generator Objects. This option is grayed out unless you have Macromedia Generator installed on your machine. If Generator is installed, it displays or hides the Generator Objects panel.

Help menu

Use the Help menu for guidance **(Figure 2.13)**.

Using Flash. Opens online help for Flash within the browser window.

ActionScript Reference. Opens the ActionScript Reference section of Flash online help within the browser window.

ActionScript Dictionary. Opens the ActionScript Dictionary section of Flash online help within the browser window.

Macromedia Dashboard. Opens a Flash-based module that connects you with the latest news about Flash.

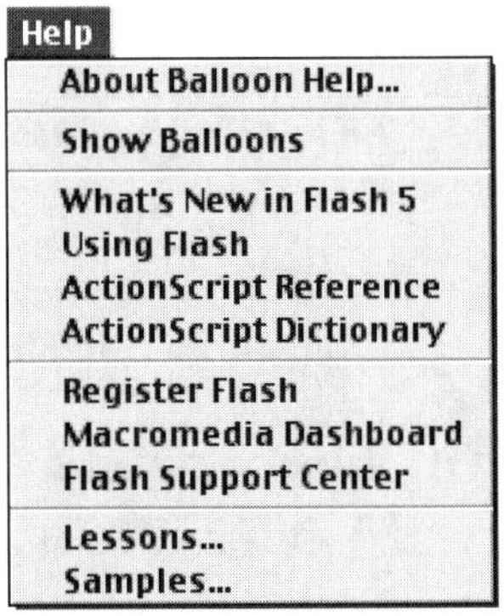

Figure 2.13
The parts of the Help menu.

Context Menus

Flash includes several additional menus that are not available from the main menu bar. Known as *context menus,* they provide commands determined by the cursor's position. If, for example, you access a context menu while your cursor is over a frame, you'll be able to access commands pertaining to that frame **(Figure 2.14)**. These menus are useful for quickly accessing appropriate commands without moving the mouse too much.

To access a context menu:

◆ Right-click (Windows) or Control-click (Macintosh) a toolbar, a timeline frame, a layer, the stage (or an element there), panel names, any area in Flash that can accept or display text, the library preview window, an item in the library or in the Action panel or Movie Explorer windows.

Timeline

The timeline is where you'll work with the layers and frames that make up your project's content and animation. Layers represent the "stacking order" of elements in your animation, and the row of frames associated with each layer represents the way in which that layer's elements move over time **(Figure 2.15)**. When you select a layer and then draw on the stage or import content there, that content becomes part of the selected layer. You move, add, change, and delete content from layers

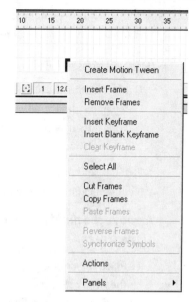

Figure 2.14
Placing your mouse over an item and then right-clicking (Windows) or Control-clicking (Macintosh) opens a context-sensitive menu relevant to the item clicked.

on various frames to create movement and animation. Using multiple layers allows you to stack content from top to bottom on the timeline to create depth in your animation—for example, objects that appear above a background. For more information about the timeline, see Chapter 12, "Building Movement Using Animation."

Figure 2.15
The way in which layers are "stacked" on the timeline relates directly to the way they appear on the stage.

You can resize the timeline to display as few or as many layers as you wish by adding or removing screen space allocated to the stage and work area. You can also move the timeline from its default position at the top of the authoring environment to any edge of the screen. Relocating it in this way lets you see either more frames or more layers of the timeline—whichever is most relevant to your current task **(Figure 2.16)**.

To resize the timeline:

1. Place your mouse over the line that separates the timeline from the stage. Your cursor will turn into a double-sided arrow.

2. Click and drag the separating bar to a new location, then release.

To move the timeline to another edge of the screen:

1. Place the cursor over the area above the time ruler, then click and drag. An outline of the timeline will appear as you drag **(Figure 2.17)**.

2. Once you've reached the edge of the screen, release the cursor. The timeline will dock there.

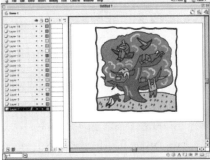

Figure 2.16
Moving the timeline to a different edge of the screen lets you see more frames or more layers of the timeline—whichever is more relevant to the task.

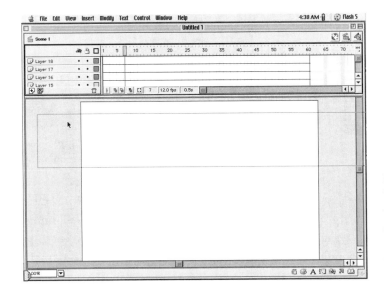

Figure 2.17
When moving the timeline, an outline representing the timeline appears as you drag.

TIPS *If you hold down the Control key as you drag, the timeline will be prevented from docking, even to areas where it normally would. This allows you to move it around freely to any point on the interface.*

You may turn the timeline docking feature off altogether if you find it interferes with the way you work. From the Edit menu choose Preferences and check the Disable Timeline Docking option that's located on the General Preferences tab.

Stage

The stage is the rectangular area of the screen where you draw and place the content that will go into your movie. Only content placed within this area is exported and visible in your final movie. What you see on the stage at any given time represents the contents of the current frame.

The stage—with its default color of white—also serves as the background for your movie and will be visible in any areas of your final movie that are not covered by a movie element. The background color remains the same throughout. By importing a bitmap and placing it on the bottom-most layer of a scene so that it completely covers the stage, this bitmap becomes a background.

To change the background color of the stage:

1. From the Modify menu choose Movie to open the Movie Properties dialog box.

2. Click the Background Color control button.

3. Using the Eyedropper tool, click a color on the palatte or click anywhere within the Flash authoring environment, then click OK **(Figure 2.18)**.

   The stage color will change to the color you selected.

Figure 2.18
The Eyedropper tool lets you select colors from anywhere within the authoring environment.

Work Area

The work area is the gray area surrounding the rectangle that represents the stage. You can draw and place experimental elements in this area, and they will not be exported to your final movie. The work area is commonly used as a starting or ending point of an animation where an object slides in or out of a movie.

> **TIP** *If you don't want to be distracted by elements in the work area, from the View menu choose Work Area. This will hide all elements except the stage and the uncluttered work area. Repeating this step will unhide the elements and place them back in view within the work area.*

Library

The library is where you manage the assets within your Flash project. For more detailed information about the library, see Chapter 9, "Using the Library to Manage Your Assets."

Panels

Flash comes with a number of panels that allow you to perform tasks for which you formerly had to use dialog boxes. Panels streamline work flow by providing a quick means of accessing the settings and parameters that need to be adjusted as you develop your project. Use them to modify frames, text blocks, symbols, instances, and other elements of your movie and feel free to organize, rearrange, and resize them to your heart's content—whatever makes your work process most efficient. We'll provide a more in-depth discussion of panels later in this chapter, but first let's take a look at the individual panels you'll be working with.

Info panel

The Info panel **(Figure 2.19)** shows the size, both vertical and horizontal, and the position, from the top and left sides of the stage, of the currently selected object. You can enter new values in the text boxes and press Enter/Return to resize or reposition selected objects.

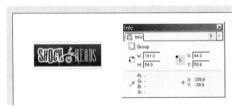

Figure 2.19
The Info panel contains information about the currently selected element.

The top-right corner of the Info panel indicates whether the currently selected item on the stage is a shape, instance of a graphic symbol, button or movie-clip symbol, or text.

If you place the cursor over a stroke or fill that's not part of a group or symbol on the stage, its color and alpha values will be displayed.

The Info panel always displays the current position of the mouse in relation to the top-left corner of the stage.

Fill panel

The Fill panel **(Figure 2.20)** allows you to set attributes when creating or editing fills with the Oval, Rectangle, Brush, or Paint Bucket tools, or when you're setting fill properties for shapes that are currently selected on the stage. A drop-down list provides various fill types to choose from, including None, Solid,

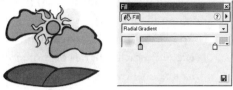

Figure 2.20
The Fill panel displays the fill used in the currently selected object (as this graphic demonstrates) or the fill that will be used when creating new graphic elements on the stage.

Linear Gradient, Radial Gradient, and Bitmap. You'll use this panel to create and edit gradients. (For more information on how to use this panel, see Chapter 3, "Graphics.")

Stroke panel

The Stroke panel **(Figure 2.21)** allows you to set attributes when creating or editing strokes with the Line, Pen, Pencil, or Ink Bottle tools, or when you're setting fill properties for shapes that are currently selected on the stage. A drop-down list provides various styles you can apply to a stroke. You can also use this panel to set or adjust a stroke's size and color.

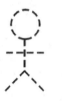 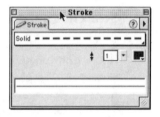

Figure 2.21
The Stroke panel displays the stroke used for the currently selected object (as this graphic demonstrates) or the stroke that will be used when creating new graphic elements on the stage.

Transform panel

The Transform panel **(Figure 2.22)** allows you to scale, rotate, and skew selected elements an amount determined by the value you enter into the appropriate text boxes. When you select an element on the stage, the values that initially appear in the Transform panel reflect how much the element has been transformed in relation to its original state. (For more information on how to use this panel, see Chapter 8, "Working with Elements on the Stage.")

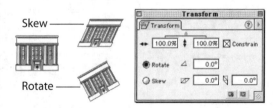

Figure 2.22
The Transform panel lets you rotate or skew selected elements on the stage.

Align panel

The Align panel **(Figure 2.23)** provides options for aligning, distributing, sizing, and spacing several selected elements in relation to each other. (For more information on how to use this panel, see Chapter 8, "Working with Elements on the Stage.")

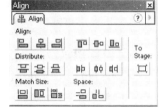

Figure 2.23
The Alignment panel has settings for precisely aligning selected elements on the stage.

Mixer panel

The Mixer panel **(Figure 2.24)** allows you to define new colors according to three different modes: RGB, HSB, or Hexadecimal. (For more information on how to use this panel, see Chapter 3, "Graphics.")

Swatches panel

The Swatches panel **(Figure 2.25)** allows you to choose colors from predefined or custom palettes that you've created or imported. (For more information on how to use this panel, see Chapter 3, "Graphics.")

Figure 2.24
The Mixer panel is where you edit and create new colors.

Character panel

The Character panel **(Figure 2.26)** allows you to set various attributes when creating or editing text, including font, font style, font color, and more. (For more information on how to use this panel, see Chapter 4, "Text.")

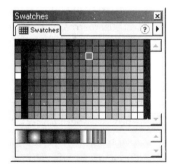

Figure 2.25
The Swatches panel contains all the colors and gradients available on the current palette.

Figure 2.26
The Character panel allows you to set character-level settings in text blocks, including font, font color, kerning, and more.

Paragraph panel

The Paragraph panel **(Figure 2.27)** allows you set various attributes when creating text or editing selected paragraphs within a text block, including margin sizes, alignment settings, and line spacing. (For more information on how to use this panel, see Chapter 4, "Text.")

 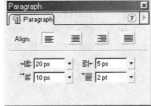

Figure 2.27
The Paragraph panel lets you adjust paragraph settings such as alignment and margins for selected paragraphs of text.

Text Options panel

The Text Options panel **(Figure 2.28)** allows you to set various attributes when creating or editing text blocks, including type of text box, its variable name, whether it's HTML enabled, and more. Settings made in this panel affect the entire text block, not just selected text within it. (For more information on how to use this panel, see Chapter 4, "Text.")

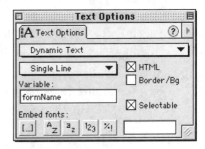

Figure 2.28
The Text Options panel has settings that affect the selected text block as a whole.

Instance panel

The Instance panel **(Figure 2.29)** allows you to set various attributes for any selected symbol instance on the stage. The options on this panel will vary according to the type of instance selected—that is, graphic, button, or movie clip. The graphic at the top-left corner of this panel indicates the type of symbol selected. (For more information on how to use this panel, see Chapter 7, "Symbols.")

Figure 2.29
The Instance panel lets you adjust instance settings of symbols on the stage.

Effects panel

The Effects panel **(Figure 2.30)** lets you apply color and alpha effects to a selected instance on the stage. If an effect has been previously applied to the selected instance, the previous setting will be automatically displayed. (For more information on how to use this panel, see Chapter 7, "Symbols.")

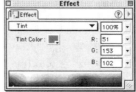

Figure 2.30
The Effect panel lets you apply a color or alpha effect to an instance on the stage. Applying different effects to several instances of the same symbol lets you use a single symbol in various ways throughout your movie.

Clip Parameters panel

The Clip Parameters panel **(Figure 2.31)** allows you to set parameters for a Smart Clip that's been selected on the stage. It also displays a description about the Smart Clip. (For more information on how to use this panel, see Chapter 14, "Building Advanced Interactivity with ActionScript.")

Figure 2.31
The Clip Parameters panel lets you set various parameters for Smart Clips.

Frame panel

The Frame panel **(Figure 2.32)** contains tweening options as well as allows you to assign a label or a set of comments to a frame. (For more information on how to use this panel, see Chapter 12, "Building Movement Using Animation.")

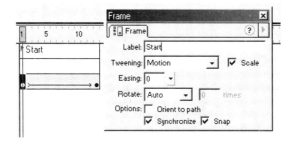

Figure 2.32
The Frame panel lets you set labels, comments, and tweening options for frames.

Sound panel

The Sound panel **(Figure 2.33)** lets you add sounds or adjust parameters for sounds attached to frames on the timeline. You can also open Flash's sound editing tools from this panel to edit a sound's length, volume, and pan settings. (For more information on how to use this panel, see Chapter 5, "Sound.")

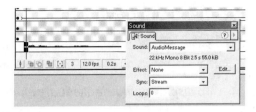

Figure 2.33
The Sound panel contains options for configuring the sounds used in your movie.

Scene panel

The Scene panel **(Figure 2.34)** helps you work with and organize scenes in your project, allowing you to create, delete, reorganize, and switch between scenes. (For more information on how to use this panel, see Chapter 12, "Building Movement with Animation.")

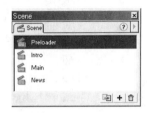

Figure 2.34
The Scene panel is where you create, delete, and organize scenes.

Generator panel

The Generator panel **(Figure 2.35)** is used to work with Macromedia Generator–related content. This panel is not functional unless you have Generator installed.

Actions panel

The Actions panel **(Figure 2.36)** is used for creating interactivity in your movie. Clicking a frame, button, or movie clip makes the options on the Actions panel available. It also has several options so that you can make this panel work in the way that best suits you. (For more information on how to use this panel, see Chapter 13, "Building Interactivity Using Basic Actions.")

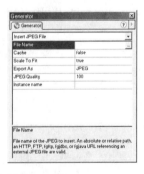

Figure 2.35
The Generator panel lets you set parameters for Generator objects you may use in your movie.

Figure 2.36
The Actions panel is where you work with ActionScript in order to add interactivity to your movie.

Working with Panels

Depending on how you work or how much screen space is available, customizing the various panels can greatly boost your productivity.

To display or hide individual panels:

- Choose Window > Panel. From the submenu that appears choose the panel you wish to display. (If a panel is already visible, these steps will hide it.)

- Click the close box on the panel located on the upper-left corner (Macintosh) or upper-right corner (Windows) of the panel.

- The Launcher bar **(Figure 2.37)** allows you to quickly hide and display various panels as well as the library and the Movie Explorer. The buttons on the Launcher are toggle buttons, which means that pressing one will display or hide the particular interface element, depending on its current state.

Figure 2.37
The Launcher bar provides quick access to many of Flash's panels. Clicking a button displays or hides a panel or group of panels.

To display, hide, or close all panels:

- Press the Tab key. This is a toggled command that either hides or displays all currently active panels, depending on their current state. This command is also available by choosing View > Hide All Panels.

- Choose Window > Close All Panels. This action closes all currently open panels.

Grouping panels allows you to attach panels with similar functions so that your mouse travels less when performing various edits on movie elements.

To group panels:

- Click the panel's name, drag it on top of another panel, and then release the mouse.

  The panel you dragged and the one you dragged to are now grouped. You can drag as many panels to a group as you wish.

To ungroup panels:

- Click the name of the panel you wish to ungroup, drag it away from the group, and then release the mouse **(Figure 2.38)**.

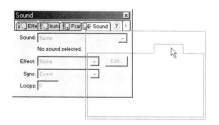

Figure 2.38
Clicking and dragging the tab on a panel lets you group it with and ungroup it from other panels.

The panel you just dragged is now separated from the group.

You can save custom groupings for use at a later date with just a simple click of the mouse. Called panel sets, these custom groupings are great for performing specific tasks.

To save a panel set:

- Choose Window > Save Panel Layout to open the Save Panel Layout dialog box.

- Give your panel set a name and click OK **(Figure 2.39)**.

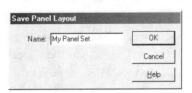

Figure 2.39
The Save Panel Layout dialog box.

To use a previously saved panel set:

- Choose Window > Panel Set to open a submenu listing the default panel layout along with any custom layouts you have created.

To delete a previously saved panel set:

- To delete a panel set, locate it in the Flash 5\Panel Sets folder and delete it. Flash will remove the panel set from its list of choices.

Movie Explorer

Figure 2.40
Clicking the Movie Explorer button on the Launcher Bar lets you toggle the Movie Explorer open or closed.

The Movie Explorer offers a snapshot of your entire Flash project, including its construction and the elements it contains. You can display or hide it by clicking the Movie Explorer button on the Launcher bar **(Figure2.40)**. (For more information on how to use the Movie Explorer, see Chapter 10, "Using Movie Explorer to Manage Structure.")

Grid, Rulers, and Guides

Flash offers several tools for helping you accurately place items on the stage as you're developing your project, including a grid (the digital world's answer to graph paper), rulers, and guides **(Figure 2.41)**. If you know how to make effective use of these tools, you can save numerous steps when laying out your design. (For more information on how to use these alignment tools, see Chapter 8, "Working with Elements on the Stage.")

Figure 2.41
This composite graphic shows you how the grid, guides, and rulers can help you place graphics accurately on the stage.

Scene and Symbols List Buttons

The Scene and Symbol buttons **(Figure 2.42)** provide pop-up menus that allow you to quickly navigate to and edit scenes or symbols in your project.

Figure 2.42
Clicking an item in the Scene/Symbol List takes you to the specific scene or to the symbol's editing window.

Options and Settings

No two people's work styles are identical. Thus, the reason for user-definable settings: You may feel a program is working too slowly under its current settings, or that you liked the features of an older version better, or that the "help" offered just gets in the way. Whatever the case, Flash 5 is easy to configure so that it works for *you*.

Preferences

By choosing Edit > Preferences, you bring up the Preferences settings dialog box **(Figure 2.43)**, which contains three tabs that let you control and set General, Editing, and Clipboard preferences. Let's take a look at each group of settings.

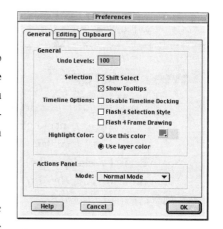

Figure 2.43
The Preferences dialog box.

General

Undo Levels. This setting allows you to set the levels of undo/redo available in Flash. The higher the setting, the more memory is required and thus the more performance degradation your computer may suffer. The maximum setting is 200. The default setting is usually more than reasonable unless you have memory to spare—in which case you may want to adjust it higher to get more breathing room for experimentation.

Printing Options—Disable Postscript (Windows only). This option enables or disables PostScript output when printing to a PostScript printer.

Selection Options—Shift Select. This option sets how you select elements on the stage and work area. If it is checked, selecting an element will deselect other elements and would require you to hold down the Shift key to select multiple objects. If it's not checked, you need only click once on any element to add it to the current selection.

Selection Options—Show Tooltips. Selecting this option will cause tooltips to appear when the mouse pauses on various parts of the interface. These tooltips contain information pertaining to the particular element that the mouse is paused over. If you find them annoying, deselect this option.

Timeline Options—Disable Timeline Docking. When you disable Timeline Docking, the timeline will detach from the Flash interface and remain free-floating (which is already the case on the Macintosh version)—a useful feature if you move the timeline much and don't want it to snap into place at the top of the screen as it usually would.

Timeline Options—Flash 4 Selection Style. Frame selection works a bit differently in this version of Flash. If you prefer Flash 4's style, select this option.

Timeline Options—Show Blank Keyframes. In Flash 4 a small, hollow circle identified a blank keyframe on the timeline. In Flash 5 the hollow circle is no longer used. (Don't ask us why—we liked it!) Selecting this option will bring that small circle back, causing it to appear on blank keyframes.

Highlight Color. When you select on-stage elements such as groups, text, and symbols, a colored box surrounds them to indicate that they have been selected. If you choose Use This Color as the highlight color, the color you select will be used to identify selected elements on *all* layers. If instead you choose Use Layer Color, the color of an element's selection box will reflect the color used to identify the layer on which it resides. By selecting the latter option, you can quickly identify the layer on which a selected element resides.

Action Panel Mode. The Action panel can operate in two modes: Normal and Expert. This option lets you set the default mode that the Option panel will use when creating new actions. (For more information on this setting, see Chapter 13, "Building Interactivity Using Basic Actions.")

Editing

These options are discussed in detail in Chapter 3, "Graphics."

Clipboard

(Windows Only) When you cut or copy a graphic from Flash, two versions of the graphic are placed on the clipboard: one based on Windows metafile information (useful for pasting vector-based graphics into other vector programs) and a bitmap version for pasting into a bitmap program.

Windows settings for bitmaps on the clipboard:

Color Depth. Sets the color depth. The higher the value, the larger the graphic file will be when placed on the clipboard. Choose 32-bit color w/alpha to maintain any transparencies in elements when they are placed on the clipboard.

Resolution. Sets the resolution of the bitmap. Once again, larger resolution results in a larger file size.

Size Limit. Allows you to set the maximum RAM you wish to allocate for placing the bitmap on the clipboard. (Higher resolutions require more RAM.) Choose None if you're computer has limited memory because this option will set aside the specified amount of memory regardless of use.

Smooth. Antialiases, or smoothes, the bitmap when it's placed on the clipboard.

Gradients. This option sets the quality of the gradients in files created by copying objects to the clipboard. Choose None for this setting if you will only be copying and pasting within Flash itself. This will speed the time it takes to copy complex, gradiated drawings.

FreeHand Text. If pasting text blocks from a Macromedia Freehand document, select this option to keep them editable within Flash.

Mac settings for bitmaps on the clipboard:

Type. Lets you choose whether to create a bitmap out of objects cut or copied from Flash or to just leave them as vectors when placing them on the clipboard.

Resolution. Sets the resolution of the bitmap. A larger resolution results in a larger file size.

Including PostScript. If you are exporting a PICT file as object- or vector-based, including PostScript information will optimize the graphic for PostScript printing.

Gradients. Sets the quality of the gradients in PICT files created by copying objects to the clipboard. You should choose None for this setting if you will only be copying and pasting within Flash itself. This will speed the time it takes to copy complex, gradiated drawings.

Display Options

Not all of us work on dual-processor Macintosh G4s. If we did, not only would the world be a happier place, this section would be largely unnecessary. Fact is, though, some of us do remain "processor challenged," so working on projects with numerous vector graphics can get in the way of productivity when you have to constantly wait for the screen to redraw after you've edited a graphic.

Flash gets around this problem by providing a number of options for how elements are displayed within the authoring environment. These are available by choosing View > and then selecting from the following options **(Figure 2.44)**:

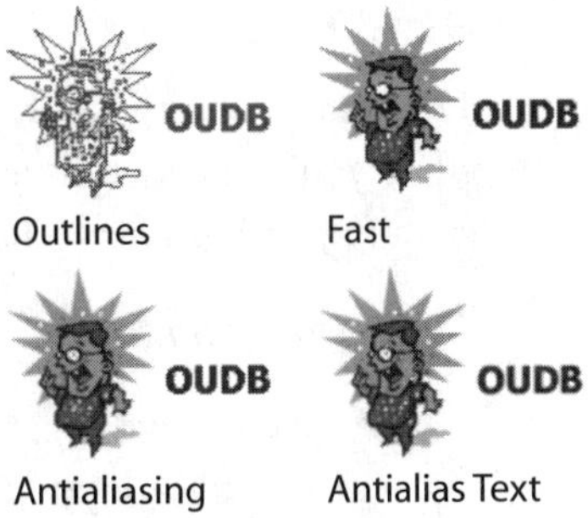

- *Outlines.* If you choose this option, fills will be removed and elements will be displayed with only their outlines (vector graphics) or bounding boxes (bitmaps), thus speeding the display of complex layouts.

- *Fast.* If you choose this option, all of a graphic's characteristics will be displayed, but smoothing (antialiasing) will be turned off.

- *Antialiasing.* This option smoothes graphics but not text—the reason being that very small text can be hard to read if antialiased.

- *Antialias Text.* This option smoothes everything, even text. Although this is the most processor-intensive option, it's also the one most developers prefer.

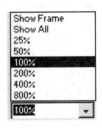

Outlines   Fast

Antialiasing   Antialias Text

Figure 2.44
A sampling of the various display options.

Viewing Options

In Flash, you can zoom in on the stage and work area for more detailed work or zoom out for an overall look at your layout. You can control both with the View pop-up menu **(Figure 2.45)**. Choose a percentage from the pop-up menu to enlarge or shrink the stage. The Show Frame option makes the entire stage visible, and the Show All option makes all objects on the stage and work area visible. All other options adjust the magnification of the stage and work area by a percentage.

Figure 2.45
The View pop-up menu lets you choose a magnification amount at which to view content on the stage.

> **TIP** *These same options are available from the menu bar by choosing View > Magnification, then selecting a setting from the submenu that appears.*

Hand Tool

The Hand tool serves only one purpose: to help you easily navigate the stage/work area when you're zoomed in to your layout and want to move to an area not currently in view. (You can use scroll bars to accomplish the same thing, though not as efficiently.)

To use the Hand tool:

1. Click the Hand tool button on the toolbar or press "H" on the keyboard. The cursor will turn into a small hand.

2. Place the cursor over any area on the stage or work area then click and drag to navigate around your layout.

   TIPS *For this tool to work, you must make the work area viewable by selecting View > Work Area.*

   Any time you are drawing with another tool, you can hold down the spacebar to activate the Hand tool. Releasing the spacebar returns you to the tool you were previously using.

Magnifier Tool

The Magnifier tool allows you to zoom in or out of your drawing to work on fine details or to get a good overall look.

The Magnifier tool has two options, or modifiers:

- *Enlarge.* Allows you click on the stage or work area to zoom in on your drawing, magnifying it by 200 percent.

- *Reduce.* Allows you to click on the stage or work area to zoom out on your drawing, reducing its current magnification by 50 percent.

TIP *To enlarge an area of the stage, select the Magnifier tool and then click and drag on the stage. The area you're defining will be identified by a thin, black outline. Release the mouse to complete your selection. Flash will automatically zoom in on the area you defined (**Figure 2.46**). (The maximum zoom amount is 2000 percent.)*

Figure 2.46
The Zoom tool lets you magnify the stage so you can edit elements more precisely.

Keyboard Shortcuts

While menus, toolbars, and buttons all make working in Flash easier, sometimes there's no quicker or more efficient way to perform a task than with a key-press or two. With Flash, you can use keyboard shortcuts to do all sorts of things, including cutting, copying, deleting, adding and removing scenes, adding and removing frames, hiding and displaying panels, and more.

Now, Flash has taken keyboard shortcuts to a new level by giving users the ability to create or assign their own: You can set up a number of custom shortcuts and save them together in a custom keyboard shortcut set. In fact, Flash comes with several sets already installed, including its default set and sets that are used in other programs, such as PhotoShop, Fireworks, Freehand 9, and Illustrator.

The process of creating and editing keyboard shortcuts is done through the Keyboard Shortcuts dialog box.

To open the Keyboard Shortcuts dialog box:

- ◆ Choose Edit > Keyboard Shortcuts.

Let's examine the interface first **(Figure 2.47)** and then look at the actual process of creating a keyboard shortcut set.

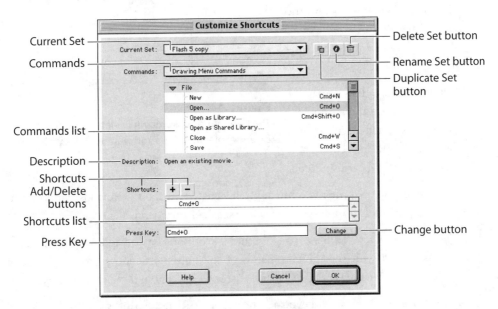

Figure 2.47
The Customize Shortcuts dialog box.

Current Set. When you open the Keyboard Shortcuts dialog box, this drop-down box shows the set of keyboard shortcuts in use. In addition, you use this box for selecting other shortcut sets.

Duplicate Set button. Creates a duplicate set of shortcuts based on the currently selected set, providing a starting point for creating a custom set.

Rename Set button. Opens the Rename dialog box, where you can rename the currently selected set of shortcuts. You cannot perform this action on the default set of Flash 5 shortcuts.

Delete Set button. Deletes the currently selected keyboard shortcuts. You cannot perform this action on the default set of Flash 5 shortcuts.

Commands. There are three categories of shortcut commands: Drawing Menu Commands, Drawing Tools and Test Movie Menu Commands (**Figure 2.48**). Selecting a category from the drop-down box will display all the available commands that can be set for that category. The Commands window below the Commands drop-down box will show a hierarchical list of commands for the selected category.

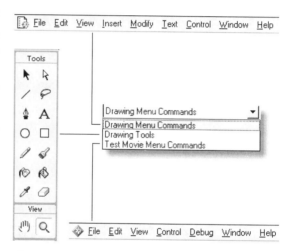

Figure 2.48
The Commands drop-down list lets you select the category of commands you want to work with.

Commands List. This hierarchical list, based on the Command category selected (see above), displays all available commands that can have keyboard shortcuts.

Description. When a menu command is selected from the Commands window, this area will provide a short description of the selected command.

Shortcuts Add/Delete buttons. The "+" and "−" buttons let you add or remove shortcuts associated with specific commands. The Shortcuts window provides a list of shortcuts associated with the command currently selected in the Commands window.

Shortcuts List. Displays all keyboard shortcuts associated with the currently selected command in the command list window.

Press Key. Displays either the key combination for the currently selected shortcut (as shown in the Shortcuts window) or any new key combination you have entered for the particular shortcut.

Change button. Associates the key combination displayed in the Press Key box with the shortcut currently selected in the Shortcut window.

Now that you're familiar with the interface, let's look at the process for creating a custom keyboard shortcut set.

To create a custom keyboard shortcut set:

1. With the Keyboard Shortcuts dialog box open, select an existing set from the Current Set drop-down box.

2. Press the Duplicate button. From the Duplicate dialog box that appears, give this duplicated set a name and press OK.

3. From the Commands drop-down box, select a command catagory. A hierachical list of available commands for that catagory will appear in the Commands list.

4. Select a command from the Commands list. A description of the command appears in the Description area of the dialog box.

5. To associate a new key combination with the currently selected command, press the Add (+) button. To change the key combination, select it from the Short-cuts list.

TIP *You may also remove a shortcut at this point by selecting it in the Shortcut list and pressing the Remove Shortcut button (Figure 2.49).*

Figure 2.49
Selecting a shortcut from the shortcut list and then pressing the Remove Shortcut button removes the selected shortcut.

6. Select the Press Key text box and then the key combination you want to associate with the currently selected command.

7. Click the Change button.

8. Repeat these steps to add or edit shortcuts associated with commands.

9. Click the OK button to close the dialog box and activate your new shortcut(s).

TIP *Several shortcuts can be associated with a single command.*

To remove a custom keyboard shortcut set:

1. With the Keyboard Shortcuts dialog box open, click the Delete Set button.

2. From the Delete Set dialog box that appears, select the set you wish to delete and click OK.

To rename a custom keyboard shortcut set:

1. With the Keyboard Shortcuts dialog box open, click the Rename Set button.

2. Enter a new name in the Rename dialog box that appears and click OK.

Setting Movie Properties

To begin a Flash project, you must specify the number of frames you want it to play per second (the frame rate) and its vertical and horizontal size. You should have a clear idea of what you want these settings to be right from the start because changing them halfway into your project can adversely affect everything you've already created. For example, animated movie elements that look just right when viewed at 12 frames per second (fps) probably won't look so good at another frame rate. Sure, you can re-edit to compensate, but that can take a considerable amount of time. Better to plan ahead and get it right the first time.

To set your movie's properties:

1. Choose Modify > Movie to bring up the Movie Properties box.

2. In the Frame Rate box, type the number of frames per second you would like your movie to play.

The default setting of 12 is sufficient for most projects. However, you can choose a higher or lower number if you wish. Remember, the higher the frame rate, the more difficult it will be for slower machines to play back your movie.

3. In the Dimension boxes, enter values for the width and height of your movie.

The minimum width or height is 18 pixels; the maximum is 2880 pixels.

4. Choose a background color using the Background color control.

The background color is also known as the stage color.

5. From the drop-down list, choose a ruler unit.

The ruler unit you choose will affect all areas of the program where dimensional values are used (for example, grid settings, Info panel settings, and so on).

Several other settings are available when you finally export your project to a movie. We'll look at these in more detail in Chapter 16, "Publishing."

Planning Your Project

Size Considerations

It's important to realize when setting your movie's dimensions that a larger movie usually means viewers' computer processors will have to work harder. Not that your movie will blow up their machines, mind you, but the animated content you worked so hard to create may play back much slower than you intended.

You can balance your craving for super-dazzling presentations with the limitations posed by processors by making your movie smaller: All you need to do is change its dimensions. A full-screen animated movie will play much slower than the same movie at half the size.

Once again, this isn't to say you can't create full-screen presentations. Sometimes it's more important to use a lot of screen space than it is to use a lot of animation.

If, for example, you're trying to showcase the beauty and craftsmanship of a product, you may want to adopt the full-screen approach and cut back on animation. However, if instead you want to evoke a sense of excitement through movement, you should probably employ smaller dimensions for your movie so that you can use animation without over-burdening your viewers' processors.

Another option would be to create a full-screen presentation with colorful, imaginative, and effective static (or nonmoving) content, and then just animate a portion of the screen at a time. If, for example, you wanted to display a big picture of your products that changed occasionally, you could simply animate some content next to each product picture, providing a workable compromise.

The QuickTime Interactive Tutorials

 Alright, it's initiation time: Time to get acquainted with the QuickTime video tutorials. The interactive tutorials included on the accompanying CD-ROM demonstrate the entire process of creating a Flash-based Web site and are the best way to apply what you've learned in the chapters. Watch the tutorial with the program open, and pause it to perform the same task on your own computer. Replay sections as many times as you need to feel you've grasped the concept and are ready to move on.

For information about the accompanying CD, how to use the tutorials, and the demo software included, see Appendix A in the back of this book.

The CD includes the following tutorials, along with their source files:

- ***Introducing Flash.*** This tutorial will introduce you to the Flash work flow and guide you through the steps of creating your first interactive Flash movie. You'll see how drawing works, create movement, assign variable names for interactivity, and test your project. This tutorial will give you a feel for authoring in the Flash environment.

- ***Creating a Custom Keyboard Shortcut Set.*** In this tutorial we'll guide you through the process of creating a custom keyboard shortcut set for use in our project.

Graphics

CHAPTER 3

What you'll learn...

Using and modifying the tools

Working with strokes and fills

Importing vector graphics

Optimizing graphics

Working with color

Ready to play the role of production designer? The person charged with the task of creating a project's look and feel plays an essential role in a movie's development. After all, without their spectacular visual effects, even such wildly successful films as *Jurassic Park* and *Independence Day* would be little more than exciting soundtracks—and we all know that a soundtrack alone does not a movie make.

In this chapter we'll show you how to use Flash's powerful drawing tools to create stunning animated, interactive works of art. With these tools, you can draw perfect squares and rectangles, paint with myriad colors, and erase your mistakes—in short, everything you can do with real-world drawing tools, and more. If you can point and click a mouse, you can create graphic elements in Flash. But don't be fooled: This ease of use does not come at the expense of graphic sophistication. The artwork you create with Macromedia Flash can be as complex as anything you could produce using the leading vector art tools on the market.

You may notice, however, that Flash handles some aspects of graphics creation differently than other drawing programs. Although this may seem awkward at first, once you've grown accustomed to the tool set, you may just decide that the Flash way is the *only* way.

As mentioned earlier, Flash drawing tools create *vector graphics*—mathematical equations that your computer translates and displays as drawn objects. This equation contains all the information your computer needs to display the object accurately, including its size, shape, and position; whether it has a fill (and if so, what color); and whether it has an outline (and if so, what type). The best part of this process is that you never see the mathematical equation; all *you* see is the *computer representation* of the equation. If only all math were so easy.

Let's take a look at the way Flash's tool set works.

Tools and Options

The Flash drawing toolbar is what you use to create graphic elements within Flash (bitmaps and graphics from other programs are imported). It consists of two areas: the toolbar buttons and their options (**Figure 3.1**). When you click a tool, it becomes active, displaying a set of options you can use to adjust its settings: Select the Eraser tool, for example, and only those options that apply to it will appear in the Options section of the toolbar. This type of context-sensitive interface makes numerous settings readily accessible without having to access the menu bar—a clutter-free and time-saving feature that surprisingly few other programs incorporate.

Most drawing tools are controlled by the Fill or Stroke panels. This means that any new graphic elements you create with the drawing tools reflect these panels' current settings. If the current fill is a red-to-blue gradient, any new graphic element created with a fill will have that same red-to-blue gradient. You can change these panel settings whenever you need to, and you can always edit elements to change their fill or stroke (more on this later).

The following examines the tools and their options in the order they appear on the toolbar; later, we'll explore drawing tasks in depth. Because the Text tool has so many unique settings and uses, we discuss it at length in the next chapter. For quick clarification, the term *simple shapes* refers to the initial state of the graphic elements (lines and fills) you create with the drawing tools. Groups, text, symbols, and bitmaps are considered *objects* (more on this later). Both simple shapes and objects make up what are known as *movie elements,* or just elements (**Figure 3.2**). Also, the terms *lines* and *strokes* are used interchangeably, as are the terms *fill, filled shape,* and *outline.*

The letter in parentheses following each tool name below represents a keyboard shortcut: Simply press that letter on the keyboard to quickly switch between tools.

Figure 3.1
Many tools have options that appear at the bottom of the toolbar when you click a tool's button.

Movie Elements

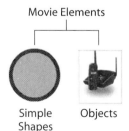

Simple Shapes   Objects

Figure 3.2
Simple shapes and objects make up all graphical movie elements.

Arrow Tool (V)

There's a reason this is the first tool in the toolbar: It's the one you'll use the most. Acting as your "hands" inside of Flash, the Arrow tool is what you use to grab, select, move, and reshape your graphics (**Figure 3.3**). However, you must select an object before you can do anything with it—and you usually do so by clicking it.

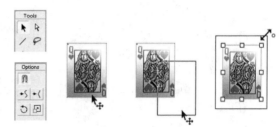

Figure 3.3
The Arrow tool is your hand within Flash. It allows you to move, scale, and edit graphics in various ways.

The Arrow tool includes the following five options:

- **Snap to Objects.** If you choose this option, objects that you draw, move, rotate, or resize will "snap" into position on the stage, making it easy to place your movie elements precisely. For more information on this feature, see Chapter 8, "Working with Elements on the Stage."

- **Smooth.** Allows you to smooth lines or simple shapes on the stage.

- **Straighten.** Allows you to straighten lines or simple shapes on the stage.

- **Rotate.** Allows you to rotate elements on the stage in any direction.

- **Scale.** Allows you to resize elements on the stage.

> **TIPS** *The smooth and straighten options can only be applied to simple shapes. They have no affect on objects such as groups, text, symbols, and bitmaps that have not been broken apart.*
>
> *All the Arrow tool options except Snap to Objects will be grayed out until you select an object.*

Subselect Tool (A)

The Subselect tool (**Figure 3.4**) is similar to the Arrow tool except that instead of selecting an entire object, the Subselect tool allows you to select and work with anchor points that exist along the shape's path. More on this later.

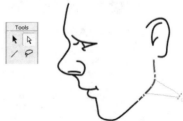

Figure 3.4
The Subselect tool is used for working with anchor points on a path.

Line Tool (N)

The Line tool is as straightforward as its name suggests: You use it to draw straight lines, which are initially simple shapes, employing the current settings on the Stroke panel (**Figure 3.5**).

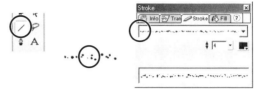

Figure 3.5
The Line tool and Stroke panel work in tandem when you draw lines.

> **TIP** To color a line with a gradient or even a bitmap fill, you must first convert it into a fillable area by selecting the line with the Arrow tool and then choosing Modify > Shape > Convert Lines to Fills.

Lasso Tool (L)

The Lasso tool is similar to the Arrow tool in that it's used for selecting simple shapes on the stage. It's a bit more specialized, however. With the Lasso tool, you define odd-shaped areas inside simple shapes to select them for editing. You also use this tool to select colors in bitmaps if they've been broken apart (**Figure 3.6**).

Figure 3.6
The Lasso tool lets you select odd-shaped areas in simple shapes.

The Lasso tool includes the following options:

- *Magic Wand.* Selected by default, it allows you to select odd-shaped areas inside simple shapes.

- *Magic Wand Properties.* Allows you to adjust Magic Wand tool settings.

- *Polygon Mode.* Allows you to select polygon-shaped areas in simple shapes.

Pen Tool (P)

This versatile tool allows you to precisely create a wide variety of open or closed shapes with straight or curved line segments, employing the current settings on the Stroke panel. If you draw a closed shape (that is, you connect the starting and ending point of a line segment), it will automatically be filled (**Figure 3.7**).

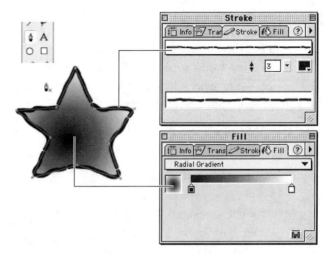

Figure 3.7
The Pen tool works in tandem with the Stroke and Fill panel when you create shapes.

Text Tool (T)

We cover the Text tool in detail in Chapter 4, "Text."

Oval Tool (O)

You use the Oval tool to create ovals—which are initially simple shapes—employing the current settings on the Stroke and Fill panels (**Figure 3.8**).

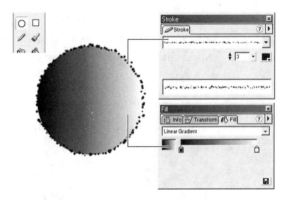

Figure 3.8
The Oval tool works in tandem with the Stroke and Fill panel when creating ovals.

Rectangle Tool (R)

You use the Rectangle tool to create rectangles—which are initially simple shapes—employing the current settings on the Stroke and Fill panels.

The Rectangle tool includes the following option:

- **Round Rectangle Radius.** Allows you to create rectangles with rounded corners. Clicking this button opens the Rectangle Settings dialog box, where you can set the amount of radius for the corners on newly created rectangles (**Figure 3.9**).

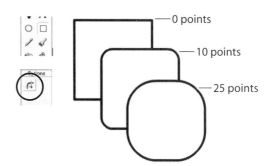

— 0 points

— 10 points

— 25 points

Figure 3.9
Use the Round Rectangle Radius button to round the corners of the rectangles you create.

Pencil Tool (Y)

Using the current settings on the Stroke panel, the Pencil tool lets you draw freehand straight or curved lines, which begin as simple shapes. The Pencil tool includes the pencil mode option (**Figure 3.10**), which allows you to designate how you want Flash to modify drawn lines:

- **Straighten.** Performs shape recognition, which means that if you draw a rough square, circle, straight line, or curve, Flash will perfect the shape based on what it thinks you're trying to draw.

- **Smooth.** Does just what its name implies: It smoothes jagged lines.

- **Ink.** Does nothing to your line, which means you can draw a line and be assured that Flash won't modify it.

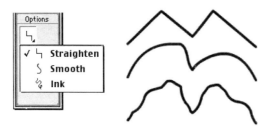

Figure 3.10
The effect of using the three Pencil modes.

Brush Tool (B)

Use the Brush tool to fill, or *brush,* areas with a solid color, bitmap, or gradient fill. When creating brush strokes—which begin as simple shapes— you employ the current settings on the Fill panel.

The Brush tool includes the following five options:

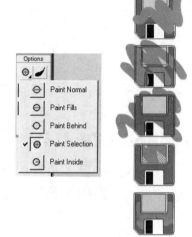

- **Brush Mode.** Several brush modes let you determine how brush strokes are applied to your drawing (**Figure 3.11**):

  Paint Normal paints over any area on the stage.

  Paint Fills paints filled areas but not lines.

  Paint Behind paints around simple shapes on the stage but not over them, giving the appearance of painting behind a shape.

  Paint Selection paints only inside filled areas that are selected.

  Paint Inside allows you to begin a brush stroke inside a filled area and there-after paint only within that area, without affecting any lines. If the point where you begin does not have a fill, your brush stroke will not affect previously filled areas.

- **Use Pressure.** Available only for pressure-sensitive graphics tablets, this option lets you create pressure-sensitive brush strokes. (A mouse can't make use of this feature.)

- **Brush Size.** Lets you set the size of the brush stroke. Employed with the Use Pressure option, it defines the maximum size of the pressure-sensitive stroke.

- **Brush Shape.** Lets you set the shape of your brush so you can create all sorts of interesting effects.

- **Lock Fill.** Allows you to control how Flash paints areas with gradients. When turned off, each stroke will be distinct and display the entire gradient. When turned on, all brush strokes that use the same gradient will appear to be part of one large gradient stretching across the stage (**Figure 3.12**).

Figure 3.11
The effect of the different Brush modes.

Figure 3.12
The Lock Fill option determines how fills are painted on the stage.

Ink Bottle Tool (S)

The Ink Bottle tool allows you create and modify the color, size, and style of the stroke surrounding a shape, employing the current settings on the Stroke panel (**Figure3.13**).

Figure 3.13
The Ink Bottle tool can quickly change the attributes of multiple shapes.

Figure 3.14
The Paint Bucket tool can quickly change the fill attributes of multiple shapes.

Paint Bucket Tool (K)

You use the Paint Bucket tool (**Figure 3.14**) to add a fill to a shape made up only of a stroke or to change a shape's existing fills, employing the current settings on the Fill panel.

The Paint Bucket tool includes the following three options:

- *Gap Size.* Allows you to adjust the way the Paint Bucket tool handles outlines that are not completely filled.

- *Lock Fill.* Allows you to adjust the way Flash fills areas with gradients. This has the same effect as the Lock Fill option for the previously described Brush tool.

- *Transform Fill.* Allows you to resize, rotate, and skew gradients or bitmaps. (This will be discussed in more detail later.)

Dropper Tool (I)

The Dropper tool lets you *sample,* or pick up, the fill or line style of a simple shape that's already on the stage and apply it to another simple shape on the stage.

Eraser Tool (E)

The Eraser tool does just what its name implies: It erases. You can use it to completely or partially erase lines and fills as well as to erase simple shapes.

The Eraser tool includes the following three options:

- *Eraser Mode.* This mode provides several ways to control how Flash erases areas of your drawing (**Figure 3.15**):

    Erase Normal erases lines and fills.

    Erase Fills erases only fills, leaving lines untouched.

    Erase Lines erases only lines, leaving fills untouched.

    Erase Selected erases only currently selected fills, leaving lines unchanged.

    Erase Inside lets you begin erasing inside a filled area and thereafter erase only within that filled area without affecting any lines.

Figure 3.15
The effect of the different eraser modes.

- *Faucet.* Allows you to erase a line or fill just by clicking somewhere on the line or fill itself. (It acts the same as if you had selected a line or fill and then pressed the Delete key.)

- *Eraser Shape.* Configures the shape of your eraser, allowing you to erase with greater precision.

Drawing Tasks

Now that we've introduced you to the drawing tools, it's time to learn how to put them to work to create graphics and lay out pages. So put on your beret, and get ready to create your first masterpiece!

Simple Shapes vs. Objects

Before we begin to actually draw and create, it's important to note that Flash contains two types of visual movie elements: simple shapes and objects.

Simple shapes consist of the following:

- *Any stroke, fill, or shape created using a Flash drawing tool in its initial state.* An oval, square, line, or brush stroke that you draw on the stage will always begin as a simple shape. You can reshape elements that are in this state, and you can edit their stroke and fill.

- *Any graphic element on the stage whose parts can be edited individually.* This includes objects, such as blocks of text or bitmaps that have been broken apart. For example, a block of text is considered an object because although you can rotate, move, or otherwise edit it as a whole, you can't edit individual characters until the text block has been broken apart, thus turning individual characters into simple shapes (**Figure 3.16**). For more information on breaking text apart, see Chapter 4, "Text" or "Breaking Up is Not Hard to Do" later in this chapter.

Objects consist of the following:

- *Groups.* Groups consist of several simple shapes (or even other objects) that have been *grouped* together to act as a single object. In this state, individual elements within the group cannot be edited. You can, however, convert the elements within a group into simple shapes simply by ungrouping it, or breaking it apart.

Figure 3.16
Normally a text object can only be edited as whole (top). Breaking an object apart lets you edit individual parts of it (bottom).

- *Text.* Similar to groups, text blocks are actually just sections of editable text—and the only element created with Flash's drawing tool that's initially considered an object. Once again, this is because a text block is moved and edited as a whole. Breaking a text block apart turns individual characters into simple shapes so that you can edit them in ways you would not otherwise be able to (for example, reshaping them or adding gradient fills). It's important to note that once you break text apart, you will no longer be able to edit the text (font, font style, tracking, margins, line spacing, and so on) as a whole again.

- *Symbols.* These are special movie elements that can contain all other types of objects as well as sound and animation. For more information, see Chapter 7, "Symbols."

- *Imported graphics.* Flash imports all graphics, including bitmaps, as objects. An imported graphic only becomes a simple shape that you can edit after it has been broken apart.

Simple shapes will always appear below objects if they are all on the same layer.

Breaking Up Is Not Hard to Do

Although it may sound harsh, breaking graphics apart is actually a gentle process. It's what you do to turn objects—including bitmaps, text, and symbols—into simple shapes, thus reducing them to their most basic elements so that you can edit and control them.

To break apart a graphic, select it on the stage and then choose Modify > Break Apart.

Planning Your Project

Metaphors

Have you ever thought about the way you work with your computer? Are you aware of the role metaphors play in making your tasks much easier to execute? Consider a typical graphics program such as Adobe Photoshop or Macromedia Fireworks: If you look at its interface, you'll see that it's made up of a bunch of palettes and brushes, as well as a clean, white canvas—all of which are metaphors for traditional artist tools. In reality, the interface is made up of intangible objects, but disguising them as everyday tools helps us get our jobs done more efficiently. Imagine having to create an image by entering the appropriate computer code!

Interface designers understand the importance of such metaphors: They know it's not enough to just make them easy; they need to make them obvious—which should be your goal in creating Flash content as well. Let's say you're creating the interface for a building-supply Web site. You could design a blueprint for the initial page that shows hammers "nailing" interface elements in the appropriate places. Your navigation buttons could be images of power switches, which users turn off and on to move to various "rooms" on the site.

So as you think about using metaphors for your design, let your imagination run wild. Be forewarned, however, that metaphors are not always necessary or even appropriate. Sometimes it's best to make user interaction as straightforward as possible—that is, to have users enter information via the keyboard without all the allusions to real-life tools. Even graphics programs such as Photoshop or Fireworks sometimes require users to enter information this way.

In addition, when using metaphors, it's best to simulate things that move or change— that is, things that can be clicked, moved, picked up, selected, felt, or heard. You can use buttons and levers (that make clicking sounds when pressed), flashing lights, gauges, doors, animals, staplers, speakers, knobs, and all kinds of other effects. The trick is to make the viewer forget that he or she is actually staring at a computer monitor.

Creating Simple Shapes

As already mentioned, simple shapes are things such as lines, fills, rectangles, ovals, and brush strokes. It's important to note that fills and strokes—which in other vector drawing programs are part of a single vector element—are separate in Flash, which means you can move them independently of one another. For example, after you've created a graphic on the stage that includes both a stroke and a fill, you can select the fill with the Arrow tool and move it to another location— independent of the stroke you also drew (**Figure 3.17**). Although this may seem awkward at first, it actually represents a very efficient way of drawing and is particularly useful for animation (as you'll soon discover).

Figure 3.17
In Flash, strokes and fills are considered separate from each other and can be moved independently.

Creating Lines

Although creating simple lines may not represent the height of your design ambitions, these lines are, nonetheless, an essential part of almost any graphic layout, animated or otherwise.

To create straight lines:

1. From the toolbar select the Line tool, or press the N key.

2. Set attributes for the line by doing one of the following:

- With the Stroke panel open, choose a line color, size, and style.

- Click the Stroke color control on the drawing toolbar to select a line color.

3. Move the cursor to the stage, and you'll notice it changes to a crosshair.

4. Click and drag, and you'll see a basic representation of your line. Release when your line is the desired angle and length (**Figure 3.18**).

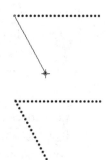

Figure 3.18
A preview of your line appears as you're creating it, which helps set its length and angle.

> **TIPS** *If you've turned on Snapping, the beginning and end points of the line, along with the angle, will "snap" to the grid of the stage.*
>
> *Pressing the Shift key while creating a line will constrain the angle of the line in increments of 45 degrees.*

To create regular lines:

1. From the toolbar select the Pencil tool, or press the N key.

2. From the options that appear, choose a pencil mode.

3. Set attributes for the line by doing one of the following:

- With the Stroke panel open, choose a line color, size, and style.

- Click the Stroke color control on the drawing toolbar to select a line color.

4. Move the cursor to the stage area, and you'll notice it changes to a pencil.

5. Click and drag around the stage to create a line, then release to finish drawing. Depending on which pencil mode you choose, Flash may straighten or smooth the line.

Creating Shapes Using Shape Recognition

Not many of us were born with surgeon's hands. And even if we were, we *still* probably wouldn't be able to draw perfect circles, squares, triangles, and straight lines. However, we know you have the *brains* of a surgeon because you purchased Flash 5—which takes care of drawing for you.

With shape recognition, you draw a rough idea of what you want, and Flash cleans it up, perfecting the shape and smoothing any roughness. Shape recognition does have its limits, however. You must give it a legitimate rough shape to work with—that is, you can't just close your eyes, draw a shape, and expect Flash to turn it into a square. You need to draw something *approximating* a square for shape recognition to work properly.

To use shape recognition to draw shapes:

1. From the toolbar select the Pencil tool, or press the N key.

2. Choose Straighten from the pencil-mode option that appears.

3. Set attributes for the line by doing one of the following:

   • With the Stroke panel open, choose a line color, size, and style.

   • Click the Stroke color control on the drawing toolbar to select a line color.

4. Move the cursor onto the stage and draw a rough shape (for example, a square, triangle, or circle). When you release the mouse, Flash will try to perfect it (**Figure 3.19**).

Figure 3.19
Using Flash's shape recognition capability lets you draw freely while still creating perfect shapes.

TIP *For information on how to adjust the settings that determine how well Flash recognizes shapes, see "Pen and Drawing Preferences" later in this chapter.*

Creating Ovals

You can create ovals in Flash that are either a stroke or a fill. If you're feeling adventurous, you can even create an oval using both strokes and fills in one fell swoop.

To create ovals:

1. From the toolbar select the Oval tool, or press the O key.

2. To set the stroke and fill attibutes, do one of the following:

- With the Stroke panel open, choose a line color, size, and style. With the Fill panel open, choose a fill type.

- Click the stroke and/or fill color control on the drawing toolbar to select a line and/or fill color. If you want your oval to have a fill but not an outline, or vice versa, select the appropriate color control, and then click the No Color button (**Figure 3.20**).

3. Move the cursor to the stage area, where you"ll notice it changes to a crosshair.

4. Click and drag, and you'll see a basic representation of your oval. Release when your oval is the size and shape you desire.

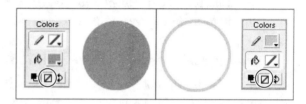

Figure 3.20
Pressing the No Color button when selecting the stroke and fill color of shapes lets you create closed shapes (like ovals or rectangles) without strokes or fills.

TIP *To draw perfect circles, turn on Snapping or hold down the Shift key when dragging.*

Creating Rectangles

Rectangles are probably the most common shape you'll use in your project. Flash allows you to easily create rectangles of all sizes and shapes, even ones with rounded corners.

To create rectangles:

1. From the toolbar select the Rectangle tool, or press the M key.

2. To set the stroke and fill attributes, do one of the following:

- With the Stroke panel open, choose a line color, size, and style. With the Fill panel open, choose a fill type.

- Click the stroke and/or fill color control on the drawing toolbar to select a line and/or fill color. If you want your rectangle to have a fill but not an outline, or vice versa, select the appropriate color control and then click the No Color button.

3. If you want your rectangle to have rounded corners, click the Round Rectangle Radius modifier and set a radius amount.

4. Move the cursor to the stage area, where you'll notice it changes to a crosshair.

5. Click and drag, and you'll see a basic representation of your rectangle. Release when your rectangle is the size and shape you desire.

> **TIPS** *To create perfect squares, turn on Snapping or hold down the Shift key when dragging.*
>
> *An easier way to create a rectangle with rounded corners is to drag while pressing the down-arrow key (for corners with a larger radius) or the up-arrow key (for sharper corners).*

Creating Shapes using the Brush Tool

Using the Brush tool, you can create shapes that look like they've been painted or drawn with a marking pen—great for calligraphy effects or a painterly look.

The Brush tool provides a number of options for configuring your brush strokes. If a drawing tablet is attached to your computer, the Use Pressure option becomes available, allowing you to create pressure-sensitive brush strokes (**Figure 3.21**).

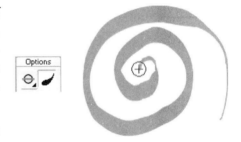

The shapes you create with the Brush tool are really nothing more than brush-shaped fills. Although lines are not added to them initially (even though the stroke color control is available on the drawing toolbar),

Figure 3.21
If you have a drawing tablet, press the Use Pressure option to give your brush strokes a more realistic look.

you can add lines or strokes later using the Ink Bottle tool. For more information on the Ink Bottle tool, see "Working with Strokes" later in this chapter.

To create shapes using the Brush tool:

1. From the toolbar select the Brush tool, or press the B key.

2. To set the fill attributes, do one of the following:

- With the Fill panel open, choose a fill type.

- Click the fill color control on the drawing toolbar to select a fill color.

3. Using the Lock Fill option, specify how you want the Brush to apply strokes and handle gradients.

4. If you use a pressure-sensitive tablet, you can select the Use Pressure option to create brush strokes of varying widths based on the pressure you apply to your tablet. This option is not available if a tablet is not connected to your computer.

5. Move the cursor to the stage, where it will become a representation of what your brush looks like based on the size and shape you selected. If you selected the Use Pressure modifier, the cursor will look like a circle with a crosshair inside.

6. Click and drag, and you'll see a basic representation of your brush stroke. Release when your brush stroke looks the way you desire.

Using the Pen Tool

The Pen tool is one of the most versatile tools in the Flash toolbox; it can also be one of the most difficult to master. Other vector graphics programs such as Adobe Illustrator and Macromedia FreeHand employ a similar tool, as do many drawing programs. Fortunately, Flash's Pen tool works in much the same way as these.

What makes the Pen tool so special? When mastered, it provides the quickest and most precise way to create lines and shapes. To use it effectively, however, you need to know a little bit about its overall operation.

Understanding Paths, Path Segments, Anchor Points, and Tangent Handles

A path that you create with the Pen tool is nothing more than a line or shape made up of three elements: path segments, anchor points, and tangent handles. *Path segments* are small portions of an overall path (line) that have an anchor point at each end. Several path segments make up a path. *Anchor points* connect various path segments and define where the path changes. The length and angle of *tangent handles*—which extend out from an anchor point—determine the shape and size of a curved path segment (**Figure 3.22**). Using these three elements, creating and manipulating shapes is like working with a blob of jelly—but without the mess!

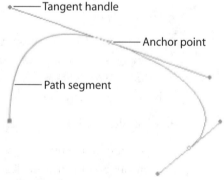

Figure 3.22
The parts of a path.

You can use the Pen tool to create two kinds of paths: open or closed. In an open path, the shape remains partly open (for example, as in the letter *U)*; in a closed path, the shape has no openings (for example, as in the letter *O)* (**Figure 3.23**). Flash will automatically fill a closed path with the current fill displayed on the Fill panel.

Figure 3.23
An open and closed path, respectively.

The best way to understand how the Pen tool works is to use it—which is what we're going to do now.

Creating Paths

Creating straight and curved paths are the main tasks you'll use the Pen tool to perform. The process for creating straight paths is straightforward. However, creating curved lines may take some practice.

To create straight paths with the Pen tool:

1. From the toolbar select the Pen tool, or press the P key.

2. To set attributes for the line, do one of the following:

  • With the Stroke panel open, choose a line color, size, and style.

  • Click the stroke color control on the drawing toolbar to select a line color.

3. Move the cursor to the stage, where you'll see it change to a pen.

4. Click the point on the stage where you want the line to begin.

5. Continue clicking on various spots on the stage. Each time you click, you're creating a new achor point and adding a straight path segment. Pressing the Shift key when clicking from one point to the next will constrain the line's angle by 45-degree increments.

6. To finish drawing, do one of the following:

  • If you want to create a closed path, place your cursor on top of the first anchor point you created. A small circle will appear next to the pen tip indicating that if you click, you'll create a closed path.

  • If you want to create an open path, either double-click the last point you created, select the Pen tool again, or Control-click (Windows) or Command-click (Macintosh) anywhere on the stage **(Figure 3.24)**.

Figure 3.24
The process for creating straight paths.

To create curved paths with the Pen tool:

1. From the toolbar select the Pen tool, or press the P key.

2. To set attributes for the line, do one of the following:

- With the Stroke panel open, choose a line color, size, and style.

- Click the stroke color control on the drawing toolbar to select a line color.

3. Move the cursor to the stage, where you'll notice it changes to a pen.

4. Click and drag on the stage to create an anchor point with tangent handles. Pressing the Shift key while dragging constrains the tangent handle's angle by 45-degree increments.

5. Release the mouse button. The length, direction (dragging it left or right), and angle of the handle determines the shape, size, and direction of the curve.

6. Move the cursor to where you want to place the path's next anchor point.

7. Click and drag to finish creating a curved segment between the two anchor points.

8. Continue to create curved segments by repeating Steps 4 and 5.

9. To finish drawing do one of the folowing:

- For a closed path, place your cursor on top of the first anchor point you created. A small circle will appear next to the pen tip indicating that if you click, you'll create a closed path.

- For an open path, either double-click the last point you created, select the Pen tool again, or Control-click (Windows) or Command-click (Macintosh) anywhere on the stage **(Figure 3.25)**.

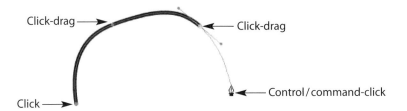

Click-drag

Click-drag

Control/command-click

Click

Figure 3.25
The process for creating curved paths.

Working with Path Segments

By adjusting the length or shape of path segments, you can change the shape of the path they comprise.

To reshape a path segment using the Arrow tool:

1. From the toolbar select the Arrow tool, or press the V key.

2. Click and drag the path segment to reshape it. For addtional information on reshaping path segments, see "Reshaping Simple Shapes" later in this chapter.

To reshape a curved path segment using tangent handles:

1. From the toolbar select the Subselection tool, or press the A key.

2. Click on the path with the segment you wish to reshape to make its anchor points visible.

3. Click on an anchor point that's part of a curved path segment. Tangent handles will appear.

4. Click and drag the end of one of the tangent handles to adjust the curved path segment **(Figure 3.26)**.

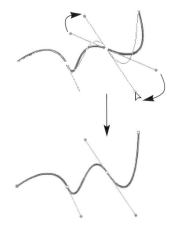

Figure 3.26
Adjust the angle of tangent handles to change the shape of a path segment.

Working with Anchor Points

Every time you use the Pen tool to click or click-drag on the stage, you're laying down anchor points that determine where your path changes. Regardless of how masterful you become with the Pen tool, you'll still need to edit, move, add, or delete anchor points. Fortunately, anchor points are easy to work with once you understand what you can do with them. By manipulating anchor points, you can change the shape and length of path segments and thus the overall path.

You can manipulate anchors in the following ways:

- You can convert a corner point to a curve point and vise versa, changing the way path segments connect.

- Using the Subselect tool, you can move anchor points alone or together, allowing you to change sections of your shape.

- You can add an anchor point to transform a single path segment into two path segments, or you can remove anchor points to make two path segments into one.

- You can stretch and rotate the tangent handle on an anchor point to change the way two path segments connect.

The Subselect tool is the main tool used to edit anchor points and paths created with the Pen tool, which is its sole purpose. Clicking a path with the Subselect tool makes its path segments, anchor points and tangent handles visible. Once visible, you can manipulate and edit them any way you desire.

To convert a corner point to a curve point:

1. From the toolbar select the Subselect tool, or press the A key.

2. Click on the path containing the anchor point you wish to convert. Its anchor points will become visible.

3. Alt-drag on the corner point you wish to convert.

To convert a curve point to a corner point:

1. From the toolbar select the Pen tool, or press the P key.

2. Click on the path containing the anchor point you wish to convert. Its anchor points will become visible.

3. Click once on the curve point you wish to convert.

To move an anchor point:

1. From the toolbar select the Subselect tool, or press the A key.

2. Click on the path containing the anchor point(s) you wish to move. Its anchor points will become visible.

3. To move an anchor point, do one of the following:

   • Click-drag it.

   • Click once to select it (it will be solid in color), and then use the arrow keys on the keyboard to move it in any direction. Holding the Shift key down while pressing an arrow key accelerates the movement of the selected anchor point.

   TIP *You can select and move more than one anchor point at once. Repeat Steps 1 and 2 from above, and then in Step 3 either marquee-select anchor points or hold down the Shift key and click on all anchor points you wish to move. Once anchor points are selected, use the arrow keys to move them (**Figure 3.27**).*

To remove an anchor point from a path:

1. From the toolbar select the Subselect tool, or press the A key.

2. Click on the path containing the anchor point(s) you wish to remove. Its anchor points will become visible.

3. Click once to select the anchor point you wish to remove, then choose Edit > Clear or simply press the Delete key.

   TIP *You can also remove an anchor point by double-clicking on it with the Pen tool.*

To add an anchor point to a path:

1. From the toolbar select the Pen tool, or press the P key.

2. Click on the path where you wish to add the anchor point.

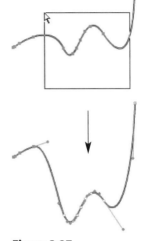

Figure 3.27
Selecting multiple anchor points allows you to move them simultaneously.

Pen and Drawing Preferences

Each of us has our own style when it comes to drawing and creating graphics. Being forced to work in one way could slow down the creative process. Fortunately, Flash allows you to set a number of pen and drawing preferences, giving you the freedom to do what you do best—create stunning Flash movies. To configure these preferences, from the File menu choose Preferences, then select the Editing tab.

Let's take a look at the options (**Figure 3.28**):

- ***Show Pen Preview.*** Determines how the lines you are drawing will appear. Select this option to preview a line as you draw it. You may find that enabling this option allows you to work more accurately with the Pen tool.

- ***Show Solid Points.*** Determines the way a selected path's anchor points will appear on the stage. If you select this option, anchor points will appear hollow when selected but solid when unselected. (Deselecting this option does the reverse.)

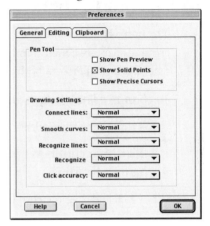

Figure 3.28
Pen and drawing preferences are set on the Editing tab of the Preferences dialog box.

- ***Smooth curves.*** Sets which cursor will appear when you're using the Pen tool. Selecting this option will cause a crosshair pointer to appear when using the Pen tool. Deselecting this option will cause the standard Pen tool icon to appear.

- ***Connect lines.*** Determines how close two end points must be before Flash will connect them.

- ***Smooth curves.*** Sets the degree of smoothing Flash will apply to lines drawn with the Pencil tool when you select the Straighten or Smooth modifiers.

- ***Recognize lines.*** Determines how straight a line drawn with the Pencil tool must be for Flash to recognize and straighten it.

- ***Recognize shapes.*** Sets how close you have to come to a pencil-drawn shape— such as an oval or a square—for Flash to recognize and perfect it.

- ***Click accuracy.*** Determines how close you can click to an element to select it.

Editing Simple Shapes

Occasionally you'll need to tweak a shape to get it to look just right. Thankfully, editing simple shapes is nearly as easy as creating them. When you edit a shape, you change its shape, its smoothness, or the angles of its lines. You can even delete part of it by erasing.

Transforming Lines

The only way you can transform lines is to change their length and angle (essential for creating shape-tweened animation, which you'll learn about later in this book). Fortunately, you can perform both tasks simultaneously.

To change a line's length and angle:

1. From the toolbar select the Arrow tool, or press the V key.

2. Place your cursor over the end of a nonselected line. A small angle will appear next to the arrow.

3. Click and drag the endpoint of the line to change its length and angle.

Straightening and Smoothing Lines and Shapes with Fills

Flash lets you refine a shape or line to your heart's content, so that you can remove bumps and smooth rough edges.

To straighten or smooth a line or shape with a fill:

1. From the toolbar select the Arrow tool, or press the V key.

2. Select the shape or line you want to modify.

3. With your shape selected, press either the Straighten or Smooth button, depending on what you want to accomplish.

> **TIPS** *If one click of the Straighten or Smooth button doesn't perfect your shape, keep pressing it. Eventually you'll have a perfect square or circle or a line that's perfectly straight.*
>
> *You can also do this by selecting the shape or line and then choosing Modify > Smooth/Straighten. However, using the Straighten and Smooth options on the toolbar is much quicker and more efficient.*

Reshaping Lines and Shapes with Fills

Just as a sculptor transforms a lump of clay, digital artists working in Flash can turn lines, squares, circles, and brush strokes into all sorts of things—without even getting their hands dirty.

To reshape a line or shape with a fill:

1. From the toolbar, select the Arrow tool, or press the V key.

Move your cursor over a line or along the edge of a filled shape, and it will change appearance to indicate which type of reshaping you're able to perform at that point (**Figure 3.29**).

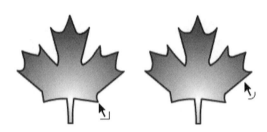

Figure 3.29
When reshaping, an angle appears next to the cursor indicating you can reshape a corner point; a curve appears indicating you can reshape a line.

2. Choose the area you want to reshape: sides of filled shapes and lengths of lines, or corners of shapes.

3. When you've reached the place you wish to reshape, click and drag the cursor until the point is where you want it, then release.

> **TIPS** *If you hold down the Control key (Windows) or Command key (Macintosh) when dragging a side, you can add a new corner point to the shape.*
>
> *If a shape you want to work with has too many corner points, select it and press the Arrow tool's Smooth modifier to eliminate some of them.*
>
> *You can also reshape a line or shape by using the Subselect tool to modify anchor points along the path. For more information, see "Using the Pen Tool," earlier in this chapter.*

Segmenting and Connecting

You don't really segment and connect shapes in Flash; that's what happens automatically when shapes come into contact with one another on the stage—a process that enables you to create fairly complex shapes that would not otherwise be possible using Flash's drawing tools. You can segment and connect any type of shape, including ovals, rectangles, lines, and brush strokes as long as they haven't been grouped or turned into symbols.

To understand how this works, let's first take a look at segmenting. Segmenting allows you cut away and slice shapes in unique ways. It occurs when one shape or line is placed over another line or filled shape on the same layer. Lines and shapes on the stage can be segmented in the following ways (**Figure 3.30**):

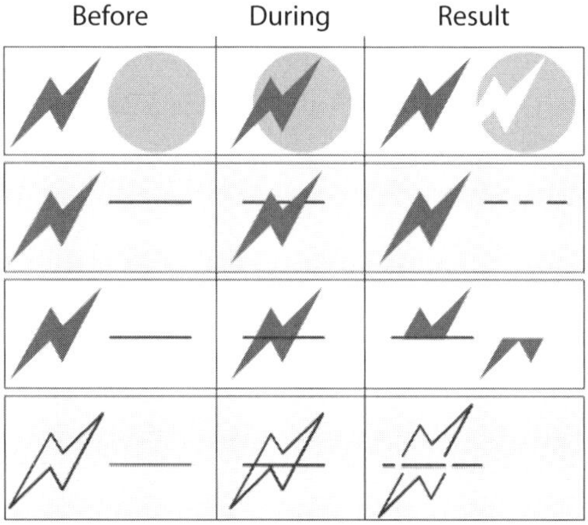

Figure 3.30
The four ways segmenting occurs in Flash.

- Placing one filled shape on top of another of a different color, then deselecting the top shape will cause the bottom shape to be cut out in the same way a cookie-cutter cuts out cookie dough.

- Placing a filled shape on top of a line, then deselecting the filled shape will erase the portion of the line that the shape overlapped.

- Placing a line on top of a filled shape so that it traverses its entire width or height, then deselecting the line will slice in half the filled shape along the path of the line.

- Placing a line on top of another of a different color will cause both lines to become "broken apart" at the point where they intersect.

> **TIPS** *You can segment a bitmap if you first break it apart.*
>
> *Connecting shapes is the opposite of segmenting them: By combining shapes, you can create new ones that would be difficult to make using Flash's drawing tools alone. It's important to note, however, that you can only connect simple shapes of the same color on the same layer (gradient-filled shapes will not work). In addition, shapes that you want to connect cannot be surrounded by an outline.*

To connect two shapes:

1. Select one shape and drag it on top of another.

2. Deselect the shape that you dragged.

   The two shapes automatically connect and become a single shape (**Figure 3.31**).

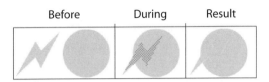

| Before | During | Result |

Figure 3.31
Connecting two (or more) shapes so that they become one.

Erasing

Erasing allows you to remove portions of shapes or lines with precision. You can change the size and shape of the eraser as well as the portions of any shape you want to erase by adjusting the options accordingly.

To erase with the Eraser tool:

1. From the toolbar select the Eraser tool, or press the E key.

2. From the options that appear, select an eraser mode.

3. Choose an eraser size and shape.

   Move the cursor to the stage area, where it will change into a representation of your eraser settings. (Make sure at this point you don't have the Faucet modifier on. If you do, size and shape settings won't work.)

4. Click and drag on a shape or line.

5. Release when you've erased the portions you want to remove.

   TIPS *The Eraser tool normally erases only a portion of a shape at one time. However, by selecting the Faucet option, you can delete entire lines and fills just by clicking them. (This is similar to selecting a line or fill and then pressing the Delete key).*

   To delete everything on the stage, simply double-click the Eraser tool.

Strokes and Fills

Every simple shape you create using Flash's drawing tools is made up of a stroke, a fill, or both, and every stroke or fill has a set of attributes that determines how it looks. For strokes, this includes things such as color, style, and thickness. For fills, this includes fill types such as solid color, gradient, and bitmap.

The Flash drawing toolbar has two color controls that you can use to quickly choose a stroke or fill color to apply to shapes that you're creating or editing **(Figure 3.32)**. However, you'll probably need to adjust more than just these two attributes, and that's where the Stroke and Fill panel can help.

In this section you'll learn how to use various panels to adjust the attributes of a stroke or fill as well as how to customize attributes to fit your needs.

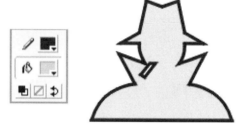

Figure 3.32
The stroke and fill color controls on the Drawing toolbar let you quickly choose colors for the shapes you are creating or editing.

Working with Strokes

Although you may not think you can accomplish much with strokes (also known as lines), they offer a wealth of possibilities once you know how to change their attributes.

In Flash, strokes come in two varieties: regular lines and outlines. A regular line has a beginning and end point. An outline, on the other hand, has no beginning or end (think of a line surrounding an oval or rectangle). The Stroke panel and the Ink Bottle tool are what you employ to add to or alter strokes on existing shapes on the stage.

The Stroke Panel

The Stroke panel is where you configure all of a stroke's attributes, including style, color, and thickness. You work with it in one of two ways: If a stroke is not selected on the stage, any attributes you adjust on the Stroke panel will become the default attributes for all new strokes created. If a stroke *is* selected on the stage, the current attributes for that stroke will appear on the panel, and any adjustments made in the panel will be reflected immediately on the selected stroke. Let's take a look at the attributes that are available from the Stroke panel **(Figure 3.33)**.

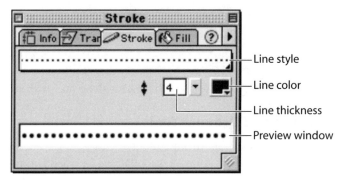

Figure 3.33
The areas of the Stroke menu.

- *Line style.* This drop-down box offers a handful of line styles. If you don't see one you want, you can create a custom style by pressing the Panel Options button (the triangle button at the top-right corner of the panel) and choosing Custom from the menu that appears. A Line Style dialog box appears allowing you to create your own custom styles. For a detailed view of your custom settings' effect, check the Zoom 4x box.

- *Line thickness.* The slider control to the left of the size text box allows you to select a line size of up to 10 points. You can also enter a number directly into the size text box.

- *Line color.* Allows you to select any color from the current palette. If you don't like the colors on the palette, you can always create your own (see the "Color" section later in this chapter). You can also press the No Color button on the drawing toolbar or the Mixer panel when creating ovals and rectangles to create an object without an outline.

- *Preview window.* Displays a preview of the effect your settings will have.

To set the default attributes for new strokes and outlines:

1. Choose Edit > Deselect All to make sure nothing on the stage is selected.

2. With the Stroke panel open, adjust the various stroke attributes.

3. All strokes created from this point on will reflect your adjustments.

> **TIP** *Selecting a pre-existing stroke on the stage will update the default stroke settings to reflect the attributes of the selected stroke.*

To change a stroke's attributes:

1. Select a stroke on the stage.

2. With the stroke panel open, you'll see the selected stroke's current attributes. Adjust them as you see fit, and the selected stroke will be updated automatically.

Using the Ink Bottle and Dropper Tools

The Ink Bottle tool is most useful for quickly adding or changing a stroke on a number of shapes. Using it gives you the Midas Touch: Just clicking on any filled shape will add a stroke where none existed, and using it to click on an existing stroke will change it to reflect the Stroke panel's current settings.

The Dropper tool works in conjunction with the Ink Bottle tool, allowing you to sample, or copy, a line's color, thickness, and style (pulling them into the dropper) and then apply those characteristics to another line (squeezing them out of the dropper).

To add or change a line or outline using the Ink Bottle tool:

1. From the toolbar select the Ink Bottle tool, or press the S key.

2. With the Stroke panel open, adjust the various stroke attributes.

3. Move the cursor to the stage, where it will change to an ink bottle.

4. Use the tip of the bottle (where it looks like ink is pouring out) to click a line to change its attributes. Click the edge of a filled shape with it to add an outline.

To apply one line's attributes to another:

1. From the toolbar select the Dropper tool, or press the I key.

2. Move the cursor over the stage, where it will change to a dropper.

3. When you position the dropper over the line that has the attributes you wish to copy, a Pencil icon appears next to the dropper. Click once. This automatically activates the Ink Bottle tool.

4. Click an existing line to change it, or click the edge of a fill to create a line with the same attributes as those you picked up with the Dropper tool **(Figure 3.34)**.

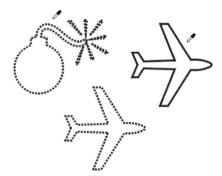

Figure 3.34
It's easy to apply stroke attributes from one image to another. Clicking on the bomb image here using the Dropper tool copies its stroke attributes. Clicking on the plane on the right applies those attributes to the current stroke so that the plane in the center reflects the same stroke as the bomb.

Working with Fills

Although lines and outlines go a long way toward sprucing up designs, to really come up with something special, you need to mix them with something of substance. Adding fills to closed shapes is a great way to start. Combine several filled objects with the right colors and gradients, and you can create some lifelike graphics.

Use the Fill panel and the Paint Bucket tool on the drawing toolbar to add to or alter a fill on an existing shape on the stage.

The Fill Panel

The Fill panel is where you choose and edit fills. You work with it in one of two ways: If no filled shape is selected on the stage, the fill you select on the Fill panel will become the default fill for all newly created filled shapes. If a fill *is* selected on the stage, the current fill for that shape will appear on the panel, and any adjustments made in the panel will be reflected immediately on the selected fill. Let's take a look at the fill types available from the Fill panel **(Figure 3.35)**.

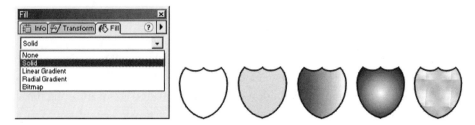

Figure 3.35
The various fills available on the Fill panel.

- **Solid.** Color fills such as red, green, and blue.

- **Linear gradient.** Special fills where one color fades into another from top to bottom or side to side.

- **Radial gradient.** Similar to linear gradients except that they fade from inside to out.

- **Bitmap.** Fills created from an imported bitmap. You can make a bitmap fill look however you want; you can even tile it inside a shape. For more about creating and editing bitmap fills, see Chapter 6, "Bitmaps."

To set the default fill used for newly created shapes:

1. Choose Edit > Deselect All to make sure nothing on the stage is selected.

2. With the Fill panel open, choose a fill type from the drop-down menu. If the Swatches panel is open, you can also choose a gradient from the set of available gradient swatches.

3. All newly created filled shapes will reflect your adjustments.

TIP *Selecting a pre-existing filled shape on the stage will update the default fill settings to reflect the attributes of the selected shape.*

To change a shape's fill:

1. Select a filled shape on the stage.

2. With the fill panel open, choose a fill type from the drop-down menu, edit it if you wish, and the selected filled shape will be updated automatically.

To create or edit a fill:

1. Select a filled shape on the stage, or with the Fill panel open, select either Linear or Gradient from the menu. The Fill panel will change to accomodate the editing of the gradient **(Figure 3.36)**.

2. To change a color in the gradient, click one of the pointers below the gradient definition bar to activate it. Choose a color by clicking the color box that appears next to the gradient definition bar. (For information about adjusting the alpha amount at a particular point in the gradient, see the tip below.)

3. To add a pointer (color) to the gradient, click just below the gradient definition bar then select a color for the pointer as described in the previous step.

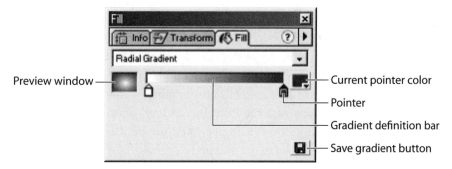

Figure 3.36
The areas of the Fill panel available when creating or editing a fill.

4. To remove a pointer from the gradient, click and drag it away from the gradient definition bar.

5. To add a gradient to the current palette, click the Options button at the top-right corner of the panel, and from the menu that appears, choose Add Gradient. The gradient is now available on the Swatches panel.

> **TIP** *When setting the color for a pointer on a gradient, as described in Step 2 above, you can open and use the Mixer panel to set color values or to adjust the alpha amount of the color (**Figure 3.37**).*

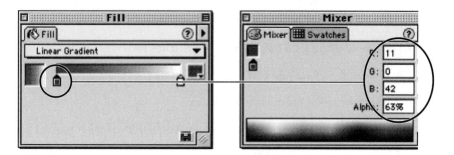

Figure 3.37
Use the Mixer panel in conjunction with the Fill panel when editing colors in the gradient.

Using the Paint Bucket and Dropper Tools

The Paint Bucket tool is used for fills in much the same way the Ink Bottle tool is used for strokes: Clicking on any empty closed shape will add a fill to it, while clicking on an existing fill will make it reflect the Fill panel's current settings. This is a useful tool for quickly adding or changing fills on a number of closed shapes. The Dropper tool works in conjunction with the Paint Bucket tool, allowing you to sample a fill from one shape (pulling it into the dropper) and use the Paint Bucket tool to apply it to another (squeezing it out of the dropper).

When working with the Paint Bucket tool, the following options are available:

- *Gap Size.* Allows you to adjust how the Paint Bucket tool handles unclosed outlines. You can choose from the following four modes: Don't Close Gaps, Close Small Gaps, Close Medium Gaps, and Close Large Gaps

   TIP *Although it can close many gaps, the Close Large Gaps mode only works within reason. If you find that it isn't doing its job, you may need to manually close gaps—or at least make them smaller for this mode to work.*

- *Lock Fill.* Allows you to adjust how Flash fills areas with gradients. When turned on, all fills that use the same gradient will appear to be part of one large gradient stretching across the stage. When turned off, each fill will be distinct and display the entire gradient.

- *Transform Fill.* Allows you to resize, rotate, and skew linear or radial gradients or bitmap fills. See below for more information.

To add or change a fill using the Paint Bucket tool:

1. From the toolbar select the Paint Bucket tool, or press the K key.

2. With the Fill panel open, choose a fill.

3. Move the cursor over the stage, where you'll notice it changes to a paint bucket.

4. Use the tip of the bucket (where it looks like paint is pouring out) to click on a filled shape to change its fill, or to click on an outline to add a fill.

To apply one shape's fill to another:

1. From the toolbar select the Dropper tool, or press the I key.

2. Move the cursor over the stage, and you'll see that it changes to a dropper.

3. When you position the dropper over a fill that you wish to copy, a Paint Brush icon appears next to the dropper. Click once. This automatically activates the Paint Bucket tool.

4. Click a filled shape to change it, or click the outline of a closed shape to add a fill with the same attributes as those you picked up with the Dropper tool.

Transforming a Fill on the Stage

Using the Transform Fill button—an option available from the Paint Bucket tool, you can move, rotate, reshape, or scale a fill within a shape, giving you an almost an inexhaustible number of ways to use fills in your layout.

To transform a linear gradient fill:

1. From the toolbar select the Paint Bucket tool, or press the K key.

2. From the options that appear, press the Transform Fill button. For this demonstration, make sure the Lock Fill button next to it is not pressed.

3. Click anywhere on a linear gradient to make it editable.

Editing handles appear **(Figure 3.38)**, which allow you to move, rotate, and resize a gradient's center point. If you move your cursor over one of the handles, the cursor changes to reflect the handle's function.

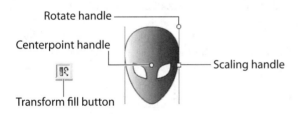

Rotate handle

Centerpoint handle

Scaling handle

Transform fill button

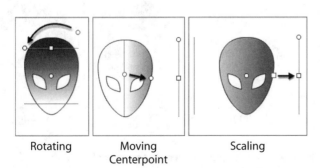

Rotating

Moving Centerpoint

Scaling

Figure 3.38
The handles that let you manipulate a linear gradient fill.

4. Edit the gradient by doing any of the following:

- To move the gradient's center point, click and drag the center handle with the four-headed arrow.

- To rotate the gradient, click and drag the handle with the circling arrow.

- To resize the gradient, click and drag the handle with the two-headed arrow.

To transform a radial gradient fill:

1. From the toolbar select the Paint Bucket tool, or press the K key.

2. From the options that appear, press the Transform Fill button. For this demonstration, make sure the Lock Fill button next to it is not pressed.

3. Click on a radial gradient. The gradient becomes editable, displaying editing handles that allow you to move, rotate, resize, and reshape a gradient. If you move your cursor over one of the handles, it changes to reflect that handle's function.

4. Edit the gradient by doing any of the following **(Figure 3.39)**:

- To move the gradient's center point, click and drag the center handle with the four-headed arrow.

- To rotate the gradient, click and drag the small circle handle with the circling arrow.

- To resize the gradient, click and drag the small circle handle with the circle with an arrow inside.

- To reshape the gradient, click and drag the small square handle with the two-headed arrow.

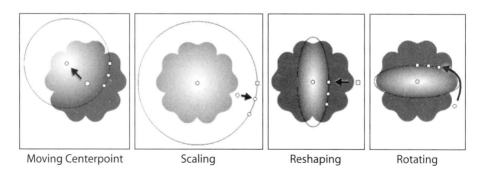

| Moving Centerpoint | Scaling | Reshaping | Rotating |

Figure 3.39
The various handles that allow you to manipulate a radial gradient fill.

TIP *For information about working with and transforming bitmap fills, see Chapter 6, "Bitmaps."*

Line and Fill Effects

Flash provides a few simple but useful effects to aid in the design process **(Figure 3.40)**. For example, although you can't usually fill lines with a gradient, Flash lets you turn a line into a shape that can have a fill of any kind, including a gradient or bitmap. This allows you to spice up those boring one-color lines.

You can also quickly create a larger or smaller version of a shape—a process known as contouring in some illustration programs. Referred to in Flash as *expanding* a shape, this process is a bit different than scaling or resizing. Whereas scaling makes a shape proportionally larger or smaller, expanding a shape makes it appear swollen—that is, it looks bigger and fatter and loses some of its detail and crispness.

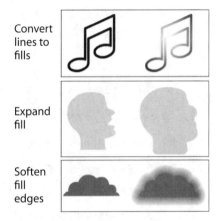

Convert lines to fills

Expand fill

Soften fill edges

Figure 3.40
Line and fill effects give you more freedom when working with vector shapes.

A third Flash effect allows you to give a shape a soft edge. Flash does this by automatically creating a series of incrementally larger versions of the shape, each a little more transparent than the last. This makes the edge of the shape blend more easily with shapes or graphics behind it and makes vector shapes more realistic looking.

To turn a line or outline into a fill:

1. Select one or more lines on the stage that aren't part of a group or symbol.

2. Choose Modify > Shape > Convert Lines to Fills to convert the line into a fillable shape .

To expand a shape:

1. Select one or more shapes on the stage that aren't part of a group or symbol.

2. Choose Modify > Shape > Expand Shape.

3. In the dialog box that appears, choose your settings **(Figure 3.41)**.

Direction. Allows you to choose whether you want the shape to expand outward or inward. (Expand will make the shape appear fatter, and Inset will make it look skinnier.)

4. Click OK.

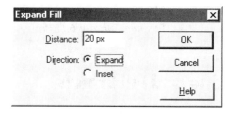

Figure 3.41
The settings on the Expand Fill dialog box.

To soften the edges of a shape:

1. Select one or more shapes on the stage that aren't part of a group or symbol.

2. Choose Modify > Shape > Soften Fill Edges.

3. In the dialog box that appears, choose your settings **(Figure 3.42)**:

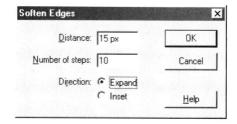

Figure 3.42
Settings on the Soften Edges dialog box.

- **Distance.** Allows you to set the distance, in pixels, from the soft edge to the outside edge of the original shape.

- **Number of steps.** Lets you set the number of steps from the original edge of the shape to the end of the softened edge. You get a smoother edge with a greater number of steps; however, this also results in a larger file size. Using too many steps can adversely affect your movie's playback because Flash has to calculate an individual shape for each step. If you're setting 20 to 30 steps, you're using a lot of processing power.

- **Direction.** Allows you to choose whether you want the soft edge to expand outward or inward. (Expand will soften from the outside edge of the shape outward, and Inset will soften from the outside edge inward.)

4. Click OK.

TIP *Use the Soften Edges option to give your shapes a drop-shadow effect.*

Importing Vector Graphics

Even with all of Flash's powerful capabilities, there are still some tasks that require you look beyond Flash's tool set.

For example, you may be struggling to create polygons, spirals, or 3D objects. Or maybe you've created a bunch of artwork in FreeHand that you wish you could use in a Flash presentation. Or perhaps you just spent some of your hard-earned cash on one of the many wonderful clip-art collections that exist today.

Importing can help in each of these scenarios, allowing you to bring outside graphics into Flash, where you can work with them and animate them just as if you had used Flash to create them.

Most vector graphics programs on the market today—including Macromedia Free-Hand, Adobe Illustrator, CorelDraw, Deneba Canvas, and even Macromedia Flash—can import and export vector graphics, so you can easily create a graphic in one program and use it in another. And when you import and export files, the vector format most accurately reproduces artwork.

SWF—It's Everywhere!

It used to be that the process of creating Flash content in another program resulted in a limited, painful and sometimes frustrating experience. But as Flash has grown more popular, a number of companies are building new software or enhancing existing programs so that they can export their content directly to the SWF file format (Flash's optimized file format), which can easily be imported into Flash and used just as if it had been created in Flash.

A number of third-party developers are creating programs that can quickly create 3D content, cool text effects (that would requires hours of work in Flash to reproduce), and other animations that are exported to the SWF format so they can easily be brought in and used in your Flash project. Even some of the major illustration packages, such as Adobe Illustrator and CorelDraw, let you create content in the SWF format. You can download and install a free plug-in for both of these programs that adds this functionality. And Adobe Illustrator 9 can export to the SWF format right out of the box. For information about either of these plug-ins, visit www.adobe.com or www.corel.com.

For more information about the software available for creating SWF-based content, see Appendix D.

Although Adobe Illustrator may be the most popular format for sharing graphics among programs, it's not the only way. **Table 3.1** *lists the vector graphic formats that Flash can import.*

Table 3.1
Vector Formats Supported by Flash

Type	Windows	Macintosh
Macromedia FreeHand (.ft7, .fh7,.ft8, .fh8, .ft9, .fh9)	X	X
Enhanced Metafile (.emf)	X	
Windows Metafile (.wmf)	X	
Adobe Illustrator (.ai, .eps)	X	X
Flash Player (.swf, .spl)	X	X
AutoCAD DXF (.dxf)	X	X

To import vector graphics into Flash:

1. From the File menu choose Import.

The Import dialog box appears.

2. Locate the file you wish to use, and click Open.

If the imported file's name ends with a number—for example, Ball1.ai—Flash will look for a related sequence of files, such as Ball2.ai and Ball3.ai. If it finds a sequence, it will ask whether you want to import just the file you first specified or the whole sequence of files.

If you use Adobe Dimensions to create animated 3D objects, you can export each animation frame as a separate .ai file of a sequence, and then import the sequence into Flash.

TIP *If you import a .swf file (which is actually a Flash movie), you can't import individual layers, actions, or tweening.*

Importing FreeHand Files

Since FreeHand (the vector illustration tool) comes from the same company that makes Flash (Macromedia), it should come as no surprise that Flash works more harmoniously with it than any other program or file format.

Although Flash can create any number of vector shapes, FreeHand, a professional vector illustration program, provides a number of powerful shape and layout tools that

Flash does not. Using FreeHand, you can easily create storyboards and other graphics that you can import directly into your Flash project, where layers, pages, gradients, blends, and more are preserved.

Flash can import files from FreeHand 7 or later. There are several things to be aware of when importing FreeHand files into Flash:

- Overlapping objects in the Freehand file that are on the same layer are segmented or connected when imported into Flash. If you don't want such objects to be segmented or connected, you need to place them on separate layers within FreeHand and choose Layers on the FreeHand Import dialog box.

- Steps of a blend created in FreeHand are converted to individual shapes when imported into Flash. Thus, a blend with numerous steps can substantially affect your movie's file size.

- FreeHand supports gradients of numerous colors, whereas Flash only supports gradients of a maximum of eight colors. If using FreeHand to create Flash content, be aware of this limitation and don't use more than eight colors in your gradients.

- Flash does not support strokes with square caps. Thus, any strokes in your FreeHand file that contain square caps will be converted to round caps when imported.

To import a FreeHand file into Flash:

1. From the File menu choose Import. The Import dialog box will appear.

2. Locate the file you wish to use and click Open. Flash will display a progress bar for the import process, and the FreeHand Import dialog box will appear.

3. Choose from the following settings on the FreeHand Import dialog box **(Figure 3.43)**:

   - *Mapping Pages.* Determines how FreeHand document pages are imported into Flash: If you choose Scenes, each page is converted into a scene in Flash. If you choose Keyframe, each page is converted into a keyframe.

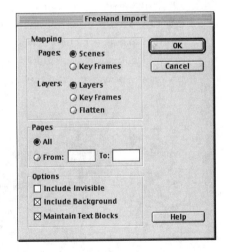

Figure 3.43
The FreeHand Import dialog box.

- *Mapping Layers.* Determines how individual layers within your FreeHand document are imported into Flash: If you choose Layers, the layers in your FreeHand document remain layers in Flash. If you choose Keyframes, they're converted into keyframes. If you choose Flatten, content on an individual layer in your FreeHand document will be placed on a single layer in Flash.

- *Pages.* Lets you determine the page range from your FreeHand Document that you want to import.

- *Options.* Choose from a set of miscellaneous options, including Include Invisible Layers, which determines the fate of layers that were not visible in FreeHand when the file was saved (checking this option includes them in the import process); Include Background Layer, which includes the FreeHand background layer in the import process; and Maintain Text Blocks, which allows editable text blocks in the FreeHand file to remain editable after they're imported into Flash.

Optimizing Graphics

When you create or import an object, you may need to optimize it to remove some of the unnecessary vector curves. Think of this as removing "vector splinters"—things you can't see from a distance but are noticeable up close **(Figure 3.44)**. This is important because fewer curves means smaller files, and small files usually indicate well-done Flash projects. In addition, graphics with lots of vector curves require a lot of processing power and can thus slow down your presentation's animation.

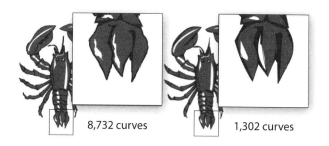

8,732 curves   1,302 curves

Figure 3.44
Before and after results when optimizing graphics.

Imported graphics, such as those from a clip-art gallery, are good candidates for optimization. (We've seen a file reduced by as much as 70 percent after being optimized.) However, imported files aren't the only graphics that can benefit from optimizing. Believe it or not, even shapes you create with Flash's own drawing tools can be optimized.

For example, hand-drawn lines that appear smooth from a distance may look crooked when you zoom in on them; to make them smoother, you can optimize them.

Because optimization actually edits the vectors that make up a shape, it can sometimes change a graphic's appearance, especially with pieces of clip art. Usually, though, such changes aren't very noticeable. And fortunately, Flash lets you control how much optimizing actually occurs, so you can keep distortion to a minimum.

To optimize a graphic:

1. On the stage, select the line or fill you wish to modify.

If you want to optimize an imported graphic, which is normally imported as a group, make sure you ungroup it first.

2. Choose Modify > Optimize. The Optimize Curves dialog box will appear.

3. Select your settings from the following dialog box options:

- *Smoothing.* Use this option to set the degree to which Flash will smooth, or optimize, the item.

- *Use Multiple Passes.* Select this option to have Flash automatically optimize, scan, and then re-optimize a vector graphic until it can't be optimized any further.

- *Show Totals Message.* Employ this option if you want to see just how much optimization Flash applied to your graphic.

4. Click OK.

Flash will optimize the shape based on your settings. If you don't like the results, simply click Undo, and pick new settings.

Using Color

Who can forget the moment in *The Wizard of Oz* when the dull, lifeless, black-and-white world of reality is replaced by the beautiful, full-color world of Oz? Sixty years ago, those filmmakers understood something we still know to be true: Color provokes an emotional response. By using color effectively, you can grab your audience's attention and guide the way they react to your presentation.

Great artists throughout history have used many tools to create and mix the colors in their masterpieces. Digital artists are no different: They need similar tools, and Flash complies by providing eyedroppers, palettes, and Mixer and Swatches panels.

Planning Your Project

Defining Your Audience

When it comes to putting together effective presentations, one of the best things—if not the best thing—you can do is watch TV commercials! One of the first things you'll notice is that certain types of commercials play only at specific times. Watch a male-oriented program (say a football game), and you'll notice that most of the adds involve trucks, scantily clad women, and beer—sometimes all three. Watch a program with a predominantly female audience (say something on the Lifetime Network), and you'll see that most of the commercials deal in some fashion with flowers, families, and love. Watch the Cartoon Network (our favorite), and you'll see commercials touting highly sweetened corn meal, high-octane sodas, and the latest in action figures. Chances are you won't see a commercial about investing on the Cartoon Network. And what good would it do to show a body lotion commercial between timeouts in a basketball game? Few guys are supposed to care about smooth skin; thus, advertising dollars would be wasted.

Another thing to look for in commercials is their use of imagery. You won't find an older gentleman in a three-piece suit promoting the benefits of marshmallow-laced cereal, though you're more than likely to come across a cartoon character doing the same. And when it comes to selling trucks, a mud-soaked pickup making its way across the Grand Canyon conveys just the sort of rugged durability buyers are likely to seek. On the other hand, a scene of a vehicle barreling down the highway at a breakneck speed is probably a more appropriate approach for selling a sports car.

To get the most out of your project, do what TV advertisers do: Define your audience. *Figure out who makes up the target, or majority, you're trying to reach and then define your message. Use adjectives to describe your audience and then ask questions to determine the best approach. To get started, ask yourself some of the following questions:*

- *Do you want to promote, entertain, inform, or convince? Or are you striving for a combination of all four?*
- *What do you want your audience to come away from your presentation thinking?*
- *Is it more important to give a visual presentation or a textual one?*
- *Do you want to build a new image or reuse an existing one?*
- *Do you have overwhelming facts to back up your message?*

These questions are just a starting point. There are many more you could ask, depending on your goals and what you're trying to promote. Once you've gathered this information, you should write a statement that describes your goal in one sentence. Something like, "We want to get kids addicted to our sugar-coated product based on the fact that it's the 'in' thing to do."

Once you've defined your audience and refined your message, you need to establish some project guidelines. Say you've been commissioned to create a Flash-based Web site for a company that wants to promote the benefits of its new vitamin, Perfectium2000. After discussing the project with the folks at the company, you've determined that your audience consists of men and women, ages 20 to 50, who are healthy but concerned about maintaining optimal health. The company wants to get out the message that by taking Perfectium2000 and eating well, you can maintain the high energy levels required for an active lifestyle. It also wants to show that this is easy to do. Your client already has a large base of faithful users, but it wants to attract new customers.

If you're using such adjectives as healthy, active, athletic, *and* informed *to describe your audience, what kind of imagery comes to mind? Sports, healthy-looking people, an organized home life, smiles, facts and figures, the great outdoors, successful people? Any of these images are appropriate for your site because they are all things to which your target audience will relate. Your client also wants new customers to realize that its vitamin regimen is an easy program to start and maintain. Thus, you could contrast a busy lifestyle with a vitamin regimen that takes only minutes a day. Put a small timer on the page with a quickly rotating second hand. To show that the product is safe, present some data along with your images of happy people. To show that it's effective, provide testimonials or show before-and-after pictures. Use morphing to turn fat letters (which may be part of a header) into skinny ones, thereby planting the subliminal message that big turns to small with the help of this product.*

Equally important is the effective use of color in your movie. Because colors evoke moods and promote responses, choose your color scheme wisely. For example, bright, sunny, and earthy colors would be perfect for our vitamin product. Fluorescent colors, on the other hand, may prompt the audience to think the product glows in the dark or is radioactive— obviously, not the result we're after. Get a color wheel at an art store to help select complimentary colors, and be careful not to overuse black, which can send a negative message.

Finally, to make your message more memorable be sure to use humor and movement whenever appropriate. If your presentation can make users at least smile, chances are they'll remember it longer. Movement requires a bit more concentration, but is definitely worth the effort in that it makes your message much more visually interesting.

Selecting Colors Using Color Boxes

Color boxes **(Figure 3.45)** are used throughout Flash to quickly select colors for various tasks. They can be found on the Movie Properties dialog box; the Layer Properties dialog box; the Fill, Stroke, Effect, and Character panels; the drawing toolbar; and the Mixer panel.

Clicking a color box initiates two actions: The current palette of swatches appears, and an Eyedropper tool becomes active. Use the Eyedropper tool to select a color from the swatches shown, or move it around the interface, and the color that's beneath the tip of the eyedropper when you click it will become the color you select. Clicking the top of the swatch palette allows you to close the palette and remove the eyedropper, essentially canceling the color selection process.

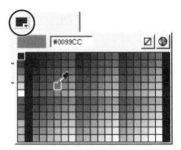

Figure 3.45
When clicked, color boxes display the current palette and an Eyedropper tool for quickly choosing colors.

Using the Mixer Panel

The Mixer panel is where you create, edit, and choose the solid colors used in strokes and filled shapes. Once you've created or edited a color in the Mixer panel, you can add to the list of available color swatches that appear on the Swatches panel.

The Mixer panel is made up of the following areas **(Figure 3.46)**:

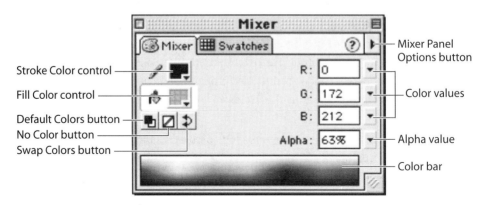

Figure 3.46
Areas of the Mixer panel.

- **Stroke Color control.** Clicking this control will set the stroke color as the focus for any adjustments made in the mixer panel. For example, if both a stroke and a fill are selected on the stage, clicking this control will apply whatever adjustments you've made in the Mixer panel to the stroke. Keep in mind, however, that Flash will not automatically set the focus to the stroke color just because you select a stroke on the stage. You may need to select this option manually. If you select a stroke on the stage, its color will appear in this control's color box.

- **Fill Color control.** Clicking this control will set the fill color as the focus for any adjustments made in the mixer panel. For example, if both a stroke and a fill are selected on the stage, clicking this control will apply whatever adjustments you've made in the Mixer panel to the fill. As with the Stroke Color Control, Flash will not automatically set the focus to the fill color just because you select a fill on the stage. See Stroke Color Control above.

- **Default Color button.** Regardless of the current colors displayed, clicking this button will set the stroke color to black and the fill color to white (the default colors).

- **No Color button.** Clicking this button and then the stroke or fill color control will set the stroke or fill color to no color. This option does not affect selected strokes or fills, only newly created strokes or fills.

- **Swap Color button.** Clicking this button swaps the color in the stroke color control with the color in the fill color control, and vice versa. If the fill color control contains a gradient when swapping occurs, the first color in the gradient (the left-most color of the gradient as shown on the Fill panel) will be used instead since strokes cannot contain gradients.

- **Color bar.** A rectangle strip of various colors that allows you to quickly choose a color by simply clicking an area with the mouse.

- **Color values.** This is the area on the Mixer panel where you create or edit colors by entering values based on the selected color mode (see below). You can enter values by typing them directly into the text boxes or by clicking the arrow button next to the text box and then adjusting the slider that appears. Depending on which color control has focus, these boxes will display the values for the currently active or selected color.

- *Alpha value.* This text box/slider is used to set the alpha (transparency) level for the currently active color in the Mixer panel. This can be either a stroke or fill color, based on which color control is currently selected. You can enter a value by typing it into the text box or by clicking the arrow button next to the text box and then adjusting the slider that appears.

- *Mixer Panel Options button.* Opens a menu that lets you choose a color mode or add a color to the current palette.

To create a new color and add it as a swatch:

1. With the Mixer panel open, do one of the following:

- Type values into the color value boxes.

- Click the color value sliders to enter values using the slider controls.

- Click somewhere on the color bar.

2. Adjust the Alpha value of the color if you want to make it transparent.

3. Click the Mixer panel Options button and choose Add Swatch from the menu that appears. Your color will be added to the bottom of the palette of currently available swatches.

To edit the stroke or fill color of the currently selected shape:

1. On the stage, select a stroke, a fill, or both.

2. With the Mixer panel open, click either the stroke or the fill color control to set the focus of adjustments made on the Mixer panel. If you clicked the stroke color control, any color adjustments you make will be reflected on the selected stroke. If you chose the fill color control, any color adjustments you make will be reflected on the selected fill.

TIP *At this point you can also adjust the selected stroke or fill by using the Stroke or Fill panels.*

Understanding Color Modes

When using the Mixer panel to create or choose colors, you can enter color values in one of three modes: RGB, HSL, or Hex. Each of these modes simply represents a different way of describing colors. The mode you choose is usually a matter of preference, though sometimes your task will determine your mode (as we'll describe shortly). You can create the same basic colors with all three modes.

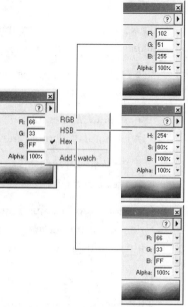

Figure 3.47
The Color Value boxes change depending on the current color mode.

To choose a color mode:

1. Click the Mixer panel Options button. A menu of color modes appears.

2. Select a color mode. The Color Value boxes on the Mixer panel will change accordingly **(Figure 3.47)**.

RGB

RGB stands for *red, green, blue.* Your computer monitor displays every color you see by using a mixture of these three colors. The amount of each color used is based on a value between 0 and 255. Mixing colors on a monitor is different from mixing them on paper with watercolors. Using watercolors, the darker or blacker we want something, the more color we add. The whiter we want something, the less color we use. It works just the opposite way with your monitor and RGB values. If *R, G,* and *B* each have a value of 0 (represented as 0-0-0), your screen will be black. If each have a value of 255 (or 255-255-255), your screen will be white. The value 255-0-0 is pure red because the first number value in the sequence represents red. Likewise, 0-255-0 equals pure green, and 0-0-255 is pure blue.

Although in art class you created orange by mixing the primary colors of red and yellow, with RGB you create orange using the value 255-177-0—the maximum value of red, half the value of green, and no blue. If this seems confusing, experiment a bit, and you'll begin to get the hang of it.

HSB

This mode is probably the most familiar way of describing color. *HSB* stands for *hue, saturation,* and *brightness.*

- **Hue.** Gives colors their names (for example, red, yellow, and blue). Every color falls into a hue category in the *spectrum,* or range, of colors.

- **Saturation.** Describes the intensity of hue. Saturated colors are intense and deep; less saturated colors are washed out or dull.

- **Brightness.** Describes a color's illumination and locates its position in relation to a scale of grays between black and white.

If a color is too dark, just adjust its brightness. If it's too rich or intense, adjust its saturation. Or if the saturation and brightness are fine but you want to a different color entirely, adjust its hue.

Hex

The third way Flash defines color is via hex values. *Hex,* short for *hexadecimal,* is a six-digit value that describes a color. Most HTML documents and Web pages use hexadecimal values to describe colors. Being able to enter the same color value on a Web page as you do in your Flash movie makes it easy to maintain color consistency.

With hex, instead of assigning a value from 0 to 255 to *R, G,* and *B* as described earlier, you assign a value of 00 to ff. Let us explain.

We're used to the base ten system, where the numerals run 0 to 9 and then repeat with a *1* attached to them—10 to 19—and repeat again with a *2* attached —20 to 29—and so on. Hex values are a little different. Instead of going from 0 to 9 and then repeating, hex values run 0 to 9 but continue on with *a* to *f*—...8, 9, A, B, C, D, E, and F—before repeating. The hex system is base 16, so *15* in base 10 is equivalent to F in base 16. When you've run through the first sixteen 0 to F hex values, they repeat with a *1* attached: 10, 11, 12, 13, 14, 15, 16, 17, 18, 19, 1a, 1b, 1c, 1d, 1e, 1f. The value 1f is equal to 31 in our more familiar numbering system, and ff is equal to 255. **Table 3.2** shows the complete hex values for 0 to 255.

Table 3.2
Hex-to-Decimal Conversion Table

	0	1	2	3	4	5	6	7	8	9	a	b	c	d	e	f
0	0	1	2	3	4	5	6	7	8	9	10	11	12	13	14	15
1	16	17	18	19	20	21	22	23	24	25	26	27	28	29	30	31
2	32	33	34	35	36	37	38	39	40	41	42	43	44	45	46	47
3	48	49	50	51	52	53	54	55	56	57	58	59	60	61	62	63
4	64	65	66	67	68	69	70	71	72	73	74	75	76	77	78	79
5	80	81	82	83	84	85	86	87	88	89	90	91	92	93	94	95
6	96	97	98	99	100	101	102	103	104	105	106	107	108	109	110	111
7	112	113	114	115	116	117	118	119	120	121	122	123	124	125	126	127
8	128	129	130	131	132	133	134	135	136	137	138	139	140	141	142	143
9	144	145	146	147	148	149	150	151	152	153	154	155	156	157	158	159
a	160	161	162	163	164	165	166	167	168	169	170	171	172	173	174	175
b	176	177	178	179	180	181	182	183	184	185	186	187	188	189	190	191
c	192	193	194	195	196	197	198	199	200	201	202	203	204	205	206	207
d	208	209	210	211	212	213	214	215	216	217	218	219	220	221	222	223
e	224	225	226	227	228	229	230	231	232	233	234	235	236	237	238	239
f	240	241	242	243	244	245	246	247	248	249	250	251	252	253	254	255

Swatches and Palettes

If you've ever shopped for an item that comes in various colors, you're probably famil-iar with the term *swatches*. These small squares or samples of color allow us to see most, if not all, of our available color choices. A set of swatches is known as a *palette*.

Flash's Swatches panel **(Figure 3.48)** uses the concepts of swatches and palettes to help you work with and organize colors in your movie. The Swatches panel displays all of the available solid colors and gradients for the current palette. Change the current palette (see below), and the colors and gradients on the Swatches panel will change.

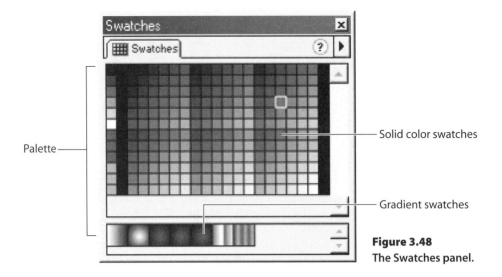

Figure 3.48
The Swatches panel.

Solid color swatches

Gradient swatches

Palette

The Swatches panel is where you select colors and fills for the strokes or shapes that are selected on the stage. For example, choosing a solid color or gradient from the Swatches panel will update the fill of the selected shape on stage. The Swatches panel also allows you to remove or duplicate swatches so that you have a "starting point" for creating a new color or gradient.

To delete a swatch from the current palette:

1. With the Swatch panel open, select the swatch you wish to delete by clicking it. It will appear highlighted.

2. Click the Swatches panel Options button and choose Delete Swatch from the menu that appears.

To duplicate a swatch from the current palette:

1. With the Swatch panel open, select the swatch you wish to duplicate by clicking it. It will appear highlighted.

2. Click the Swatches panel Options button and choose Duplicate Swatch from the menu that appears. A duplicate of the seleted swatch will be added to the bottom of the Swatches panel.

Importing and Exporting Palettes

Flash makes it easy to import color palettes from other Flash projects or different programs such as Macromedia Fireworks. This means you don't need to tediously re-create a custom palette from another project. You can also export your current color palette from Flash for use elsewhere.

Flash can export palettes in two formats: .CLR (or .FCLR for Macintosh) and Adobe color tables, known as .ACT files. CLR files save both solid-color and gradient information, but only Flash can use this type of palette. ACT files cannot store gradient information but can be used in such programs as Flash, Macromedia Fireworks, and Adobe Photoshop. Your needs will determine which format is best.

When importing, you can bring in .CLR or .ACT palettes and import the color palette of a .GIF graphic file. This means all of the colors in a .GIF file will import as a palette.

You use the following options on the Swatches panel **(Figure 3.49)** to import and export palettes:

- **Add Colors.** This allows you to import a palette from a .CLR, ACT, or .GIF file and add it to the current palette. Selecting this option opens the Import Color Swatch dialog box, where you can locate the palette you want.

- **Replace Colors.** This lets you replace the current palette with an imported one. Selecting this option opens the Import Color Swatch dialog box, where you can locate the palette you want.

- **Load Default Colors.** This loads Flash's default color palette or one that you defined with the Save as Default option (see below). Selecting this option automatically updates the current palette with the default one.

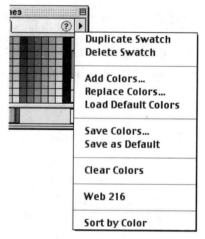

Figure 3.49
The Swatches panel.

- **Save Colors.** This allows you to save the current palette as a .CLR or .ACT file for use either in other Flash projects or in other programs. Selecting this option opens up the Export Color Swatch dialog box, where you can name your palette and choose a format (.CLR or .ACT).

- **Save as Default.** This lets you save the current palette as the one Flash uses automatically when you start a new Flash project. Selecting this option will open an alert box asking you to confirm your decision. Choose Yes or No.

- **Clear Colors.** This clears all colors from the current palette except black and white and one gradient.

- **Web 216.** This option loads the Web-safe palette of 216 colors that Flash shipped with.

- **Sort by Colors.** This sorts the colors on the current palette by their luminosity values.

Interactive Tutorial

 Creating Graphic Elements. This tutorial will review most of the concepts covered in this chapter, including using the tools, working with strokes and fills, using color, and more.

Text

Although graphics are great, by themselves they can't always convey our message—at least not quickly and clearly. Often, we need text to eliminate ambiguity. For example, a picture of the sun can indicate any number of things—heat, nuclear energy, the solar system—but put the word *summer* next to it, and your message is suddenly clear. In Macromedia Flash, your text can slide in, fade in or out, grow or shrink; it can even explode if that's the effect you desire. Although it's not a full-featured word processor by any stretch of the imagination, Flash lets you format text in a number of ways, allowing you to set margins, kerning, line spacing, and many other attributes.

You also can use text elements to display text that never changes, called static text, or to accept user input. You can even display HTML-formatted text that's been loaded from an external file. And if you're really feeling adventurous, you can create animation effects using nothing but text; we'll explain how at the end of the chapter.

What Is Text?

Because Flash more closely resembles a graphics program than a word-processing one, it handles text in a unique way. Any group of characters you type in Flash (such as a paragraph) starts out as a self-contained entity on the stage that you can resize, rotate, and move as a single object **(Figure 4.1)**. As long as they remain in their original state, you can reedit these text elements using any of the available text tools. However, if you break apart a text element, you can no longer edit it as text. Instead, the individual characters are converted into shapes, which you can reshape and dress up in ways you couldn't with normal text. Later in the chapter, we'll discuss the implications of breaking up text objects as well as some of the ways you can improve the look of your text by doing so.

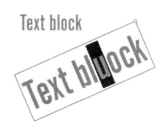

Figure 4.1
Text blocks are groups of characters that you work with as a whole.

Creating Text Elements

Flash creates four types of text elements: static text labels, static text blocks, input text blocks, and dynamic text blocks **(Figure 4.2)**. We'll discuss input and dynamic text blocks later in the chapter. The following describes static text elements and how they work.

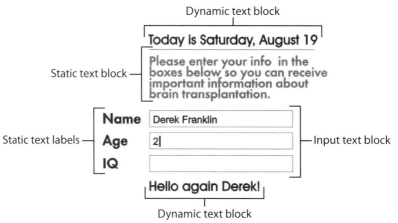

Figure 4.2
The four types of text elements that Flash creates: Static text labels and static text blocks for displaying static information, input text blocks for accepting user input, and dynamic text blocks for displaying up-to-date info that Flash can generate on its own.

Static Text Elements

In contrast to input text blocks and dynamic text blocks, whose contents can change while your movie is playing, the contents of static text elements cannot be changed outside of the authoring environment. Thus, when you create a static text label or static text block, you edit the text so that it appears exactly the way you want in your movie, where it will remain static.

A text label is simply text that continues on a single line until you manually insert a line break by pressing either the Enter key or the Return key. This type of text object does not wrap text automatically, as do most of today's word-processing applications. Instead, text labels allow you to determine what word will appear at the end of each line **(Figure 4.3)**. Text labels are best used for small sections of text that contain one or two words.

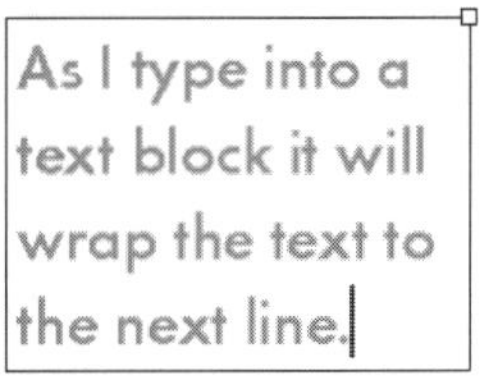

Static text blocks have a fixed width. This means that you assign a width to your text block when you create it, and then any text you type into it will "wrap" to the next line based on the width you defined **(Figure 4.4)**. Text blocks are used for displaying paragraphs of text.

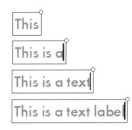

Figure 4.3
Text labels expand as you type text into them and are best suited for short sections of text.

Figure 4.4
Text in a text block automatically wraps to the next line.

To create a static text label:

1. On the toolbar, choose the Text tool, or press the T key.

2. With the Text Options panel open, select Static Text from the menu of choices.

3. With the Character panel open, set the text attributes—font, font size, and color—that you want to use for this label.

   Move the cursor to the stage area, where it will turn into a crosshair with a small *A* in its bottom right corner. The center of the crosshair indicates the bottom left corner of any new text labels created.

4. Click on the stage where you want to place your text label.

   A small box with a circle in its top right corner and a blinking insertion point appears. This is an empty text label.

5. Enter the text you desire, and the text label will automatically expand to accommodate it.

To create a static text block:

1. On the toolbar select the Text tool, or press the T key.

2. With the Text Options panel open, select Static Text from the menu of choices.

3. With the Character and Paragraph panels open, set your text attributes for the block, including font, font size, and color.

   Move the cursor to the stage, where it will turn into a crosshair with a small *A* in its bottom right corner. The center of the crosshair indicates the bottom right corner of any new text blocks you create.

4. Click and drag from left to right to define the width of your text block, then release to complete the action.

   A rectangle with a small square in its top right corner and a blinking insertion point appears.

5. Enter the text you want, and the text block will automatically wrap text to the width you defined.

To change the width of a text block:

1. On the toolbar select the Arrow tool, or press the V key.

2. Click and drag the text block's resize handle. Any text in the block will be automatically reformatted to fit the new size **(Figure 4.5)**.

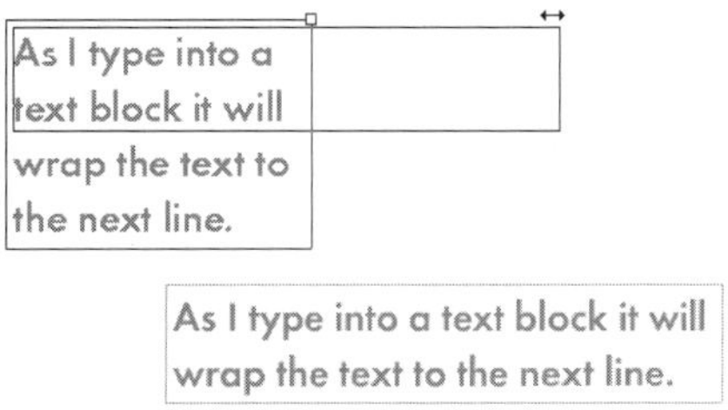

To change a text block to a label, or vice versa:

◆ Double-click the resize handle of the text element.

As I type into a
text block it will
wrap the text to
the next line.

As I type into a text block it will
wrap the text to the next line.

Figure 4.5
Resizing a text block automatically reformats any text within it.

Input and Dynamic Text Elements

Input and dynamic text elements serve a different function than static text elements. Thus, it stands to reason that you create them in a different way as well. Because input and dynamic text fields need to accommodate an unknown amount of text, you are able to drag their size vertically as well as horizontally when creating them. Although you create input and dynamic text elements in the same way, you will need to configure them differently to work in your movie.

To create an input or dynamic text element:

1. On the toolbar select the Text tool, or press the T key.

2. With the Text Options panel open, select either Input or Dynamic Text from the menu of choices.

3. With the Character and Paragraph panels open, set the text attributes you want to use for this element, including font, font size, and color.

Move the cursor to the stage area, where it will turn into a crosshair with a small *A* in its bottom right corner. The center of the crosshair indicates the bottom right corner of any new text blocks you create.

4. Click and drag from left to right and from top to bottom to define the width and height of your text element, then release to complete the action.

A rectangle with a small square in its bottom right corner and a blinking insertion point appears.

5. Enter the text you want, and the text element will automatically wrap to the width you defined.

If these text elements are so dynamic, though, why bother to set text attributes or input text (as described in Step 5 above)? First, by typing in text, you can display what will appear initially (for example, instructions for an input box). That text, then, can subsequently be erased by the user or replaced dynamically **(Figure 4.6)**. Second, by using the Character and Paragraph panels to set text attributes, you can define the default attributes that will be used for user- or dynamically-entered text. For more information, see "Powering Input and Dynamic Text Elements with Rich-Text Formatting" later in this chapter.

Figure 4.6
Any text you type into an input text block—for example, user instructions—will be displayed in that text element until it's replaced by user-entered text.

You can also leave an input or dynamic text element empty and then use ActionScript to dynamically fill it. This is an option when you want to display a dynamic message to your user or accept user input when requesting information (look for more on this later in the chapter and also in Chapter 14, "Building Advanced Interactivity with ActionScript").

To change the width or height of an input or dynamic text element:

1. On the toolbar select the Arrow tool, or press the V key.

2. Click and drag the text elements's resize handle horizontally or vertically to resize its width or height, respectively. Any text will be automatically reformatted to fit the new size.

> **TIP** *You can turn a dynamic text element into a static one by simply selecting it on the stage with the Arrow tool and then changing its definition on the Text Options panel.*

Working with Text Elements

Once you've created a text element, you'll usually want to edit it. You can change character and paragraph attributes such as font, font color, margins, line spacing, and more. You may also want to alter the way a text element is defined (static, input, or dynamic) or change some of its core attributes (which determine how it works within your movie)—especially if you're talking about a dynamic text element. You make all text adjustments via the three text panels: Character, Paragraph, and Text Options. The first thing you need to know, however, is how to link your edits to a particular block or section of text.

Selecting and Editing Text Blocks

You can edit text as blocks, meaning the entire text element, or individual text within the block (for example, correcting spelling or changing words, setting character options for individual characters, and so on). The latter is known as working in text-edit mode.

When you select a text block, you can restyle the text as a block, and you can move, rotate, and scale that text as well. Once it's selected, a colored selection box surrounds the block. Adjustments in the Character panel and alignment adjustments in the Paragraph panel will be reflected in all of the text in the block.

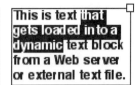

Figure 4.7
When you select a text block, a colored selection box surrounds it (left), whereas individually selected text appears highlighted (right).

When you select text within a block, the color of that text appears highlighted **(Figure 4.7)**. When individual text is selected, adjustments in the Character panel will affect only the selected text and adjustments in the Paragraph panel will affect only the paragraph that the selected text is part of **(Figure 4.8)**.

Figure 4.8
When individual text is selected, any adjustments made on the Character or Paragraph panel will affect only the paragraph the selected text is part of, not the entire text block.

> **TIP** *Character or paragraph edits to individual text will be reflected in the exported movie only if the text is within a static text block. If the text is an input or dynamic text element, the HTML option has to be checked on the text options panel for the edits to be reflected.*

To select and edit a text block:

1. On the toolbar, choose the Arrow tool, or press the V key.

2. Move your cursor onto the stage and click on any text block.

   The text block becomes surrounded by a colored selection box.

3. Resize, move, rotate, or align the text element on the stage, or format text within the text block by making adjustments in the Character and Paragraph panels as described above.

To select and edit individual text inside a text block:

1. Do one of the following:

- On the toolbar, select the Arrow tool, or press the V key.

- Double-click any text to place it in text-edit mode. You can then edit individual letters, words, or paragraphs in the text block.

- On the toolbar, select the Text tool.

When you move the cursor to the stage, it changes into an I-beam when you pass it over a text element.

2. Click between characters to place the insertion point for entering more text.

3. In text-edit mode, do any of the following:

- Select a letter, word, or paragraph for editing by click-dragging from the first letter you wish to edit to the last; then release. This highlights and selects the text, which you can then edit in all sorts of ways (changing font, font size, color, and so on).

- Delete text by click-dragging to select it, and then pressing the Delete or Backspace key.

- Copy text by click-dragging the text you wish to copy and choosing Copy from the Edit menu.

- Paste text by clicking once to place the insertion point where you would like the pasted text to begin. Then from the Edit menu choose Paste.

Character-Level Formatting

Although Flash cannot offer the same type of text control that a dedicated word processor can, it can handle some of the more common formatting tasks, such as setting font size, line spacing, and kerning. You make these kinds of edits—which are known as *character-level formatting* by means of the Character panel.

You work with the Character panel in one of two ways: If no text block or individual text is selected on the stage, any attributes you set on the Character panel will become the default attributes for all new text blocks. If a text block or individual text *is* selected on the stage, the current character attributes will appear on the panel and any adjustments made in the panel will be reflected immediately on the selected text.

> **TIP** *When selecting a text block or individual text that contains more than one set of formatted text (for example, part of the text is green and bold, while the rest is red and italic), the Character panel will display the attributes of the first character of the selected text.*

The Character panel is made up of the usual suspects, including the Font and Font Size, and the Bold and Italic buttons, as well as some others with which you might not be familiar **(Figure 4.9)**:

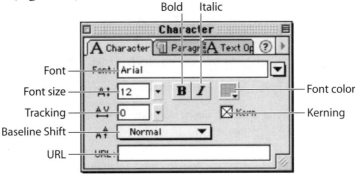

Figure 4.9
The Character panel.

- *Font Color.* Allows you to choose a font color. Clicking this color box will display a list of the available solid colors. You'll notice that gradients are not available for text objects; we discuss a way around this in "Breaking Text Apart" later in the chapter.

- *Tracking.* Defines the amount of even space between characters. You can set a new tracking amount by typing it into the text box or by adjusting the slider next to the text box.

- *Kern.* Most fonts contain information that describes how to handle the space between characters (for example, the letters *AB* require more space (kerning) than the letters *II* or *AV.* Check this box to use the font's built-in kerning information.

- *Baseline Shift.* Controls how text appears in relation to its baseline **(Figure 4.10)**.

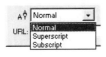

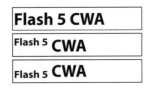

Figure 4.10
Baseline shift is used to set the text's relation to the baseline.

- **URL.** Allows you to associate a URL with currently selected text—similar to creating hyperlinked text in HTML documents. You can associate sections of text within the same text block with different URLs. Text that has a URL associated with it will have a dotted line in the authoring environment. While HTML hyperlinks are normally identified by colored-underlined text, hyperlinks created using this feature will not be visually identified in your exported movie as a hyperlink (other than by a hand cursor) unless you format it differently.

To set default character formatting for new text elements:

- With the Character panel open, adjust the various character attributes the way you want them.

  Afterward, all new text elements will have those attributes.

To change character formatting for selected text:

1. Select a text block or any individual text you wish to edit.

2. With the Character panel open, make any necessary adjustments. The text on the stage will be automatically updated to reflect your edits.

   TIP *Most character formatting options are also available from the Text menu.*

Paragraph-Level Formatting

Paragraphs are sections of text that are separated by a hard return (that is, by pressing Return or Enter on your keyboard). Paragraph-level formatting allows you to set alignment, margin, line spacing, and indentation.

To open the Paragraph panel, do one of the following:

- Choose Window > Panels > Paragraph.

- Press the Show Character button on the Launcher bar, and then click the Paragraph tab.

You work with the Paragraph panel in one of two ways: If no text block or individual text is selected on the stage, any attributes you set on the Paragraph panel will become the default attributes for all new text blocks. If a text block or individual text *is* selected on the stage, the current paragraph attributes will appear on the panel, and any adjustments made in the panel will be reflected immediately on the selected text.

The Paragraph panel includes options for aligning text to the left, right, center, or both right and left; and setting right and left margins, indentation, and line spacing **(Figure 4.11)**.

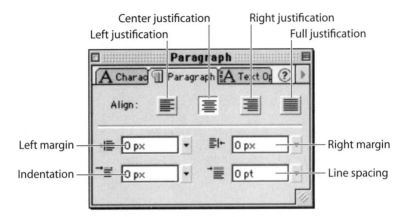

Figure 4.11
The Paragraph panel.

TIPS *With the exception of line spacing (which always defaults to points), the measurement units for paragraph settings default to the measurement units of the rulers.*

You can apply different attributes to individual paragraphs within the same text block.

Alignment options are also available from the Text menu.

To set default paragraph formatting for new text elements:

◆ With the Paragraph panel open, adjust the paragraph attributes. Once you've finished, all new text elements will have those attributes.

To change paragraph formatting for selected text:

1. Select a text block or any individual text you wish to edit.

2. With the Paragraph panel open, make any necessary adjustments. The text on the stage will be automatically updated to reflect your edits.

Text-Block Options

Text block options affect the selected text block as a whole (thus, you cannot apply them to individually selected text). You can apply different options to each text block on the stage. The Text Options panel contains three options—static text, dynamic text, and input text—each of which has its own configurable parameters. You can configure text options for multiple text blocks simultaneously by selecting them all before adjusting the parameters in the Text Options panel.

To open the Text Options panel, do one of the following:

- Choose Window > Panels > Text Options.

- Press the Show Character button on the Launcher bar, then click the Text Options tab.

Static Text

Static text—which will not change while your movie is playing—is best for form element labels, navigation labels, button labels, animated chunks of text, and any sections of text that will not be dynamically loaded from a text file or server. There are two settings available for static text boxes:

- *Use Device Fonts.* Leaving this unchecked will cause Flash to embed font information for any fonts used in the text block so that the font will appear antialiased (smooth) in the exported movie. Checking this option will prevent font information for this text block to be embedded (see "Understanding Device Fonts" for more information).

- *Selectable.* Allows the user to select text within the block to cut or copy into their system's clipboard so that it can be pasted into another program.

Original

After undesirable font mapping

Figure 4.12
Device fonts can sometimes produce unexpected and undesirable results.

Understanding Device Fonts

Most fonts include a built-in description that contains information about how characters look, which character will appear in response to a specific key-press, kerning, and more. This font description also includes info that allows the text you see while working in Flash to appear smooth (antialiased) (if the View > Antialiased Text option is checked)—information that's embedded in your exported Flash movie, too, so that text there will appear smooth as well. Although the results are graphically pleasing, there are drawbacks to embedding this information in your exported movie. For one, smoothing makes small fonts almost impossible to read. In addition, this embedded font information can add to your exported movie's file size. The solution to both of these problems is to use device fonts.

Let's say you create a static text block that uses a font called MyFavoriteFont. You then select the Use Device Font option on the Text Options panel. After you export your movie, everyone who has MyFavoriteFont installed on their machines will see the text exactly as you intended, though it will not appear antialiased. Machines that don't have MyFavoriteFont will use the font that most closely resembles it—a process called font mapping. *This solution is far from perfect, though, because sometimes the font a machine picks looks nothing like the original (**Figure 4.12**).*

Because font mapping can sometimes produce unexpected results, Flash includes the following three built-in device fonts to make font mapping more predictable:

- *_sans*
- *_serif*
- *_typewriter*

The Flash player knows to map these fonts—which can be found at the top of the font list on the Character panel—to specific fonts available on most platforms. For example, the _sans font in Flash looks almost exactly like the Arial font in Windows and Helvetica on a Macintosh. The following describes how Flash's device fonts are mapped.

- *_sans maps to Arial on Windows and Helvetica on a Macintosh*
- *_serif maps to Times New Roman on Windows and Times on a Macintosh*
- *_typewriter maps to Courier New on Windows and Courier on a Macintosh*

Dynamic Text

Dynamic text blocks allow you to display text that's been dynamically generated by ActionScript or a Web server, as well as text that's been loaded from an external text file **(Figure 4.13)**. This means that the text within a dynamic text block can change as your movie is playing, allowing you to display personalized messages, to update information by changing an external file, and even to display HTML-formatted text (see "Powering Input and Dynamic Text Elements with Rich-Text Formatting").

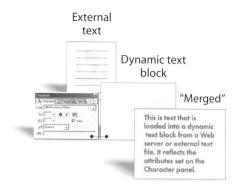

Figure 4.13
Dynamic text blocks can display text that is loaded into it from a source external to your movie, such as a Web server or text file.

When you create a dynamic text block, you assign it a name—or as Flash calls it, a *variable name*. This variable name lets you control the text block any number of ways using ActionScript. For example, if you create a dynamic text block and name it myTextBlock, the following ActionScript code will display the message "Hello, did you know it was the year 2000?" inside the text block:

```
currentDate = new Date();
myTextBlock = "Hello, did you know it was the year " + currentDate.
  getFullYear() + "?";
```

Don't worry about understanding the ActionScript code right now. You just need to understand why you assign variable names to dynamic text blocks and how those variable names are used in ActionScript to evoke interactivity.

The settings for dynamic text boxes include the following **(Figure 4.14)**:

- *Line Display.* This pop-up menu lets you specify how lines of text are displayed. Choose Single Line to allow only a single line of text. Choose Multiline to allow text to wrap to the next line when necessary.

- *Variable.* This is where you assign a variable name to your dynamic text block. It must begin with a letter, not a number or space (though you may use a number after the first character) . By naming your text block, you enable Flash to identify it. We'll discuss this in greater detail in Chapter 14, "Building Advanced Interactivity with ActionScript."

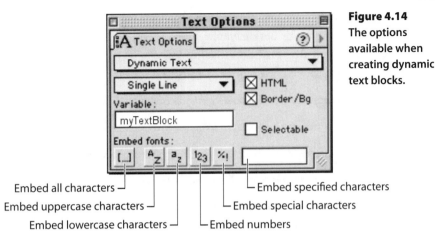

Figure 4.14
The options available when creating dynamic text blocks.

Embed all characters
Embed uppercase characters
Embed lowercase characters
Embed numbers
Embed special characters
Embed specified characters

- **HTML.** Enables the text block to interpret HTML code that's been loaded dynamically. Also, checking this box allows you to use different styles of formatted text within a single input text block. For more information on this feature, see "Powering Input and Dynamic Text Elements with Rich-Text Formatting" later in this chapter.

- **Border/BG.** Allows your text box to be identified (in Flash as well as in your final movie) by a solid thin outline and a background. If you leave this option unchecked, your text field will still be identified within Flash by a dotted outline. However, once you export your movie, the text block will no longer have a border.

- **Selectable.** Allows the user to select text within the text block and cut or copy it to their system's clipboard for pasting in another program.

- **Embed Fonts.** This option determines not only how text appears within the block but also how it affects your movie's overall size. Embedding fonts is primarily a matter of preference. If you don't embed fonts, your text will appear aliased (jaggy). However, text that uses a small font may be easier to read. By embedding fonts, you make your text appear smoother (and thus more graphically pleasing), but your presentation's size increases—and on the Web size is everything. Although there are settings available to minimize font overhead, you need to be aware of how they'll affect your movie's appearance and size. For more information about these settings or fonts see, "Powering Input and Dynamic Text Elements with Rich-Text Formatting" or "Using Font Symbols for Dynamic Type Styling" later in this chapter. Font embedding options include the following:

    Do not embed fonts. Though not a button itself, this is the default setting your machine will revert to if you haven't pressed any of the other Embed Font options.

Embed all characters. Embeds all of a font's characters in your exported movie. If you check this option, your text block will appear smooth, but your file size could increase from 35Kb to 60Kb (on average). Selecting this option grays out the other embed options because it negates their functions.

Embed uppercase characters. Embeds uppercase characters *A* through *Z*.

Embed lowercase characters. Embeds lowercase characters *a* through *z*.

Embed numbers. Embeds numbers zero through nine.

Embed special characters. Embeds special characters such as *?*, *!*, and others.

Embed specified characters. Use this box to type specific characters to embed. For example, if you only want to embed the characters *d, t, f, 3,* and *4,* you would type them into this box (without commas—unless you wanted them included).

Input Text

Input text blocks, such as form elements, password fields, etc., allow users to enter text that your movie can use internally by way of ActionScript or which can be sent to a Web server for processing. With a little creativity, you can produce Flash forms that are as engaging as the rest of your movie.

When you create an input text block, you assign it a variable name which lets you control the text box any number of ways using ActionScript. For example, if you created an input text block and named it myInputBlock, the following ActionScript code would convert any text entered into all lowercase text:

```
myInputBlock = myInputBlock.toLowerCase()
```

In another example, the following code tells your movie to perform an action based on whether the *myInputBlock* input text block contains text. It basically states that if *myInputBlock* is empty (equals ""), go to and stop at Scene 2 frame 1, otherwise go to and stop at Scene 3 frame 1:

```
if (myInputBlock == "") {
  gotoAndStop ("Scene 2", 1);
} else {
  gotoAndStop ("Scene 3", 1);
}
```

The settings for input text boxes include the following:

- *Line Display.* With one exception, this is the same setting as that used with dynamic text: Choose Password to have asterisks (*) replace characters that have been entered into the text field.

- *Variable.* See the Variable setting for dynamic text elements in the previous section.

- *HTML.* See the HTML setting for dynamic text elements in the previous section.

- *Border/BG.* See the Border/BG setting for dynamic text elements in the previous section.

- *Max Chars.* Allows you to set the maximum number of characters that can be entered in the text field. If you enter zero, an unlimited number of characters can be entered.

- *Embed Fonts.* Same as setting for Dynamic Text; allows user-entered text to be antialiased.

  TIPS *Neither input nor dynamic text blocks support kerning or tracking.*

  Neither input nor dynamic text blocks support full justification—just left, right, and center.

  If you wish to perform rotation, alpha-color transformations, or masking (with Mask layers) with dynamic text blocks, you need to embed fonts.

Powering Input and Dynamic Text Elements with Rich-Text Formatting

First, we should probably explain precisely what we mean by *rich-text formatting*. Rich-text formatting allows your input and dynamic text blocks to display text of various font styles, sizes, colors, and even hyperlinks **(Figure 4.15)**. When you select the HTML option for either input or dynamic text blocks, they become HTML-aware—that is, any text displayed in the text block that contains the supported HTML tags (see below) will be displayed in rich-text format based on the tags used. For example, if you

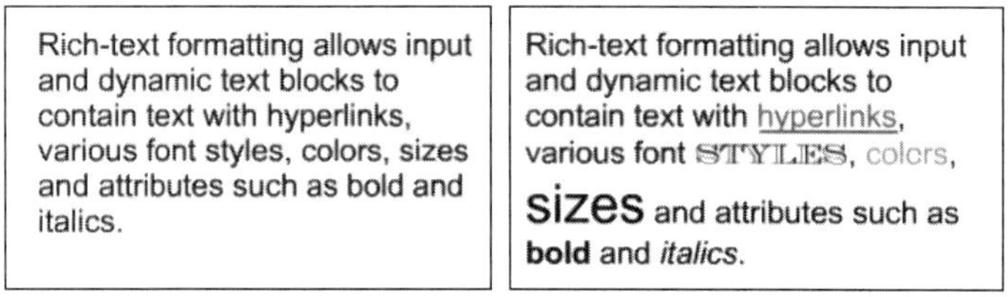

Rich-text formatting allows input and dynamic text blocks to contain text with hyperlinks, various font styles, colors, sizes and attributes such as bold and italics.	Rich-text formatting allows input and dynamic text blocks to contain text with <u>hyperlinks</u>, various font 𝕊𝕋𝕐𝕃𝔼𝕊, colors, sizes and attributes such as **bold** and *italics*.

Figure 4.15
One text block without rich-text formatting (left), one with (right).

create a dynamic text block named myDynamicText and then select the HTML option for the text block, the ActionScript

```
myDynamicText = "Hello there! You are our <b><u>favorite</b></u>reader."
```

will cause the following text to be displayed in the text block:

Hello there! You are our **<u>favorite</u>** reader.

If, however, you had left the HTML option unchecked, the following text would instead be displayed:

Hello there! You are our <b> <u>favorite</b> </u>reader.

(For information on how to do this with a loaded text file, see below.)

Mixing and matching HTML tags allows you to create more sophisticated-looking text in your presentation.

Flash supports the following HTML tags:

```
<A>
<B>
<FONT COLOR>
<FONT FACE>
<FONT SIZE>
<I>
<P>
<U>
```

Combine Flash's support for HTML tags with its capability to load text from an external source such as a text file or Web server, and you have a powerful means of displaying dynamic, rich text in your movie. Updates to text content can easily be accomplished just by updating the external source. Using dynamic text in your movie is a two-step process of setting up your movie to load a file into a dynamic text block, and then actually creating the file that is loaded.

To load an HTML-based text file into a dynamic text block:

1. In Flash, create a dynamic text block, name it `intro`, and then select the HTML option on the Text Options panel.

2. Right-click (Windows) or Control-click (Macintosh) Frame 1 on the timeline and then select Actions from the menu that appears. The Actions panel will appear.

3. In the left pane, click on the Actions group to expand it.

4. Double-click the loadVariables action. to make an unconfigured ActionScript statement appear in the right pane. Parameter settings are at the bottom of the Action panel.

5. In the URL parameter box, type the name and directory path to the text file. (Because our text file will reside in the same directory as our exported .swf file, all we need to enter here is the name of our file, MyMovieText.txt.)

6. Leave the other settings as is, and then export this authoring file to a SWF movie.

To create the HTML-based text file that will be loaded into your movie:

1. Either SimpleText for the Macintosh or Notepad for Windows is more than adequate for this job. Open either one and type the following:

   ```
   &intro=<p align="center"><b><font size="12">Hello!!</font></b></
   p><p>My <fontcolor="#FFCC66">name</font> is <a href="http://
   www.mydomain.com "><u><font color="#0066FF">Gary</font></u></a>.
   What is your <i>name?</i></p>
   ```

2. Name this text file MyMovieText.txt (the same file name we identified in our ActionScript a moment ago) and save it to the same directory as your exported .swf file.

   If you double-click and play the .swf file, this text will load into the `intro` text block and display the text in the external text file with rich-text formatting, based on the HTML tags we used **(Figure 4.16)** .

That's all there is to it. If you re-edit and save this text file, the .swf file will reflect your edits when played again, including any made to formatting tags.

Hello!!
My name is Gary. What is your *name?*

Figure 4.16
This is what would result if we were to enter our text file into the dynamic text block with the variable name of `intro`.

A couple of things to notice about this text file:

- It starts off with the code <u>&intro=</u>. This identifies the text block into which this text will be loaded.

- The standard <HTML> and <BODY> tags are missing: Because they have no effect, they aren't used.

- If this page were wide enough, you'd see that the code resides on a single line. Using returns anywhere in your code will cause Flash to insert a hard return, not always a desirable result.

The Rich-Text Tip Sheet

There are a number of issues you need to be aware of when using rich-text formatting in your movie:

- *Some HTML tags in ActionScript require the use of quotation marks to define certain values (for example, a hyperlink, font face, or font color). However, using quotes in this manner causes conflicts in ActionScript, so you need to employ what's known as an escape character (\")to make everything work properly. Instead of defining a hyperlink this way: <u>\<a href="http://www.mydomain.com"></u>, you would define it as follows: <u>\<a href=\"http://www.mydomain.com\"></u>. (This only pertains to HTML-based text used with ActionScript; it does not apply to quotes used in an externally loaded text file.)*

- *If you define a font style by using the HTML <u>\<font face></u> tag, your user will only see that particular font if it's installed on their machine; otherwise, the closest device font will be used (see 'Understanding Device Fonts" earlier in this chapter). To ensure that the defined font appears as intended, embed that font into your movie.*

- *If you embed a font for use in conjunction with the HTML <u>\<font face></u> tag, be aware that variations of the font face (Bold, Italic) are not embedded. Thus, text using these variations may not appear.*

- *Opening the Character panel and then selecting a text block on the stage will display that text block's default font settings. Any text with characteristics (color, face, size) not defined in the HTML\<font> tag will reflect the text block's default attributes as set in the Character panel.*

- *Using one of Flash's built-in device fonts will give you the most predictable results when displaying rich text.*

- *When defining a font's color using the HTML <font color> tag, use Hex-based values (see the color section in the previous chapter for more information on Hex values).*

- *The font size value defined using the HTML <font size> tag is set in relation to the default size you defined for the text block using the Character panel.*

- *Hyperlinks defined in HTML-based text are not automatically shown in a different color or with an underline as you normally see on an HTML page. If you want to identify a section of text as a hyperlink, you need to set these attributes manually using the <font color> and <u> underline tags.*

- *When the HTML option is selected for an input or dynamic text block, rich-text formatting is only applied to text loaded into the text block. Entering tag-based text directly into a selected text block means that the tags will be included in the text block when your movie is exported **(Figure 4-17)**.*

- *Users cannot input information with rich-text formatting (different fonts, colors, sizes, etc.) into input text blocks: Text entered into input text blocks always reflects the text block's default attributes as defined on the Character panel.*

```
<p><b><font
size="12">Hello!!</font></b></p>
<p>My <font
color="#FFCC66">name</font> is
<a
href="http://www.mydomain.com"
><font
color="#0066FF">Gary</font></u
></a>. What is your
<i>name?</i></p>
```

Selected text block

```
<p><b><font
size="12">Hello!!</font></b></p>
<p>My <font
color="#FFCC66">name</font> is
<a
href="http://www.mydomain.com"
><u><font
color="#0066FF">Gary</font></u
></a>. What is your
<i>name?</i></p>
```

Exported text block

Figure 4.17
Entering tag-based text directly into a selected text block will export tags and text block with your movie.

Using Font Symbols for Dynamic Type Styling

By using font symbols—which allow you to separate characters from their font styles—you can make your Flash movies even more dynamic. Let's say, for example, that your movie uses the text "Hello" throughout. This word contains the characters *H-e-l-l-o* but has no inherent font style—you must give it one. To do so, you create a font symbol based on the Arial font and assign it a name, such as My Favorite Font. In a roundabout way, which you'll learn more about soon, My Favorite Font★ will now appear on the font menu of the Character panel **(Figure 4.18)**. (The asterisk indicates My Favorite Font is a font symbol).

You can now apply My Favorite Font (which is actually the Arial font style) to the text in your movie that reads "Hello." When you export your movie, any text that says "Hello" will appear in the Arial font because that's the style on which it's based. The best thing about all this is that if you ever change the font style associated with My Favorite Font, all the "Hello" text in your exported movie will be converted to the new style (a time-consuming task if performed manually). This is similar to the way HTML uses cascading style sheets to separate content from design.

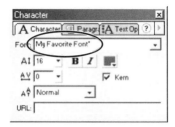

Figure 4.18
Font symbols appear on the font menu of the Character panel with an asterisk next to them.

To create a font symbol:

1. Choose Window > Library to open the library window.

2. Press the Library Options button in the top-right corner of the library window and choose "New Font…" from the menu that appears.

3. In the Font Symbol Properties dialog box that appears, give your font a name such as MyFavoriteFont.

4. From the Font pop-up menu, choose the font that you want to use as a basis for this font symbol (for example, Arial).

5. Check the style options to allow the font to appear in those styles as well.

6. Click OK. The font symbol now appears in the Library window with the name you gave it. It will also appear in the list of available fonts on the Character menu **(Figure 4.19)**.

To use a font symbol for formatting text:

1. Select the text you wish to format.

2. With the Character panel open, the name of your font symbol (My Favorite Font) will appear on the Font menu with an asterisk next to it. Select this font, which applies the Arial font style to the selected text (since it's the style associated with the My Favorite Font font symbol).

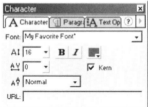

Figure 4.19
When you create a font symbol, it's automatically added to the library and to the font menu of the Character panel.

If you were to export your movie now, all of the text associated with My Favorite Font would appear in the Arial font. However, if you wanted your text to be displayed in Times New Roman instead, all you would need to do is open the library and edit the My Favorite Font symbol to reflect that font style.

To update the style associated with a font symbol:

1. With your authoring file open, choose Window > Library to open the library.

2. Right-click (Windows) or Control-click (Macintosh) the font symbol (My Favorite Font) and choose Properties from the menu that appears. The Font Symbol Properties dialog box will appear.

3. From the Font pop-up menu, choose a different font style (Times New Roman) to associate with this font symbol.

4. Click OK.

Export the movie again and the text formerly associated with My Favorite Font will now appear in Times New Roman **(Figure 4.20)**.

Figure 4.20
Changing the font style associated with a font symbol will update every instance in your movie where the font symbol was applied to text.

Using Font Symbols in Shared Libraries

Once you've created a font symbol, you can make the font symbol into what's known as a *shared library asset*. This entails a few more steps than above, but it opens up a whole new realm of possibilities for using fonts in your movies. By turning a font symbol into a shared library asset, you can use it across multiple SWFs. The benefits of this are two-fold: First, because font information is stored in a central location (the shared library), users only have to download it once rather than embed font information in every movie, thereby minimizing download time. Second, when you update the font style associated with the font symbol in the shared library, all text "linked" to that font symbol will be updated automatically to reflect the updated font style.

For information about shared libraries, see Chapter 9, "Using the Library to Manage Your Assets."

Breaking Text Apart

There are some effects that you cannot apply directly to text objects in their initial state. This includes giving text a gradient or bitmap fill, providing an outline for text, or even reshaping or tweaking individual characters. To perform any of these tasks, you need to convert or break that text apart first. Doing so transforms the text object from a group of editable and configurable characters into its most basic form—a bunch of vector shapes. Only then can you reshape and graphically edit it any way you choose. Notice we said *graphically* edited; this is because once text has been broken apart, you can no longer edit it as text: Font changes, paragraph settings, and other normal text edits are no longer possible. In other words, there's no going back—make sure your text reads and looks just the way you want before you break it apart.

Figure 4.21
Breaking text apart lets you edit it in ways that would not be otherwise possible.

To break text apart:

1. Select any text element on the stage.

A selection box will surround it.

2. From the Modify menu choose Break Apart.

Once broken apart, you can give your text a gradient fill and outline and even perform other graphical edits that were previously impossible **(Figure 4.21)**.

Animation Considerations

Now that you've learned to control your text and its appearance, there's only one thing left to do—animate it! By bringing your text to life, you can create visual effects such as stock tickers, scrolling text, and other animations. However, you still need to achieve a balance between text requirements and processor limitations.

Since each of the 100 or so letters in your text object represents an individual vector shape, animating this text block essentially entails animating 100 shapes simultaneously. Although Flash can handle this type of visual effect, it's extremely processor intensive. Thus, don't be surprised to see your upbeat, fast-moving presentation transformed into a lesson in patience on a slower machine.

Because each project is different, there are no hard and fast rules about when to animate blocks of text; however, the following guidelines should help:

- *Avoid animating large blocks of text.* There are few visual reasons for animating a large block of text. Even if processor speed were not an issue, reading a large block of moving text can be difficult, and you don't want to frustrate your audience.

- *For visual effects, animate only a few words or letters (or even just a single letter) at a time.* This type of text animation can liven up your presentation in ways that no other graphic element can. This also means that if you want to bring a large block of text to life, bring it into the scene a sentence at a time.

- *The smaller the text element, the less processor intensive animation will be.* This means that if you want a full-screen scrolling text effect, you had better provide your audience with plenty of caffeine to keep them awake while they wait for the text to scroll. If you really want to animate blocks of text, make them as small as possible while maintaining their readability.

- *When animating text, avoid animating other elements.* If you choose to animate text, avoid animating other elements at the same time so that you can devote as much processing power as possible to the text animation.

Text Animation to the Max!

Just because you need to be aware of some issues when animating text doesn't mean you can't have fun with it. In fact, quite the opposite is true. There are a number of Flash sites that make use of text in fascinating ways. And they do it not by meticulously animating each letter, as you might expect, but by using one of two animation tools: Swish (www.swishzone.com) or Wildswfx (www.wildswfx.com).

*The sole function of these tools is creating interesting text effects for your Flash movies. Both let you enter a string of text, choose an effect, adjust the setting, and—bam!—instant text utopia. What at one time would have taken hours or even days to construct within Flash can now be accomplished in just minutes (**Figure 4.22**). Both of these tools create SWF animations that you can import into your main Flash movie—forever depriving you of an excuse for using dry, boring, lifeless text. Use these programs to take your text animations to the max!*

Figure 4.22
Sophisticated text effects that would once have required hours of work can now be produced in minutes using available third-party tools.

Interactive Tutorial

 Creating and Working with Text Elements. This tutorial will review most of the concepts we covered in this chapter, including creating text elements, working with text panels, creating and using dynamic text elements, font symbols, and more.

Sound

You may have noticed in recent years that producers are no longer content to simply sit back and watch moviegoers shell out $5 for a 20-cent bag of popcorn to munch on while watching a $7 movie on the silver screen. Instead, the money men are turning their attention to a new type of revenue: *soundtracks*. These days great effort goes into creating soundtracks that not only work well within their movies but also promise commercial appeal as stand-alone products.

In addition to playing on our emotions, music can trigger memories. It's not uncommon to relive the experience of watching a favorite movie when you hear a song from its soundtrack. Whether it excites you, provokes you, or even reduces you to tears, music is certain to elicit some sort of response. There's simply no denying the power of sound: Thus, the more you use of it, the more powerful a message your movie will be able to convey.

Using sound—via HTML—on a regular Web page, however, can be a nightmare for developers and audiences alike. Because sound is even more download-intensive than bitmaps, small sounds (and especially music soundtracks) are rarely used on the Web.

Macromedia Flash, in contrast, provides a bit more latitude. You can add small sound effects for things like button clicks, or you can import a soundtrack to play in the background of your movie. You can even synchronize a sound or vocal track with the visual component of your movie to create a flowing, synchronized presentation.

Before you add any audio masterpieces to your project, however, you should know a few things about the way sound works in the digital world. Even just a basic grasp of these concepts will help you maximize your ability to use sound.

Understanding Sound

Although sound is invisible, tools exist to help us understand its physical representation. They show us that sound is made up of *waves,* which vary in length (to denote time) and size (to denote volume). When these sound waves reach our eardrums, they cause them to vibrate—thus hearing is born. We're able to distinguish among sounds because each one causes our eardrums to vibrate in a different fashion.

Analog sounds, or those we hear naturally, are produced by sound waves that our ears are designed to detect and process. Digital sampling—which transforms analog sound waves into mathematical equations—was invented to record, edit, and play back such sounds in a digital environment. Close examination of a digitally sampled sound reveals a bunch of vertical lines of varying length stacked closely together. Each of these lines represents a *sample*. The quality of a digital sound is determined by the number of samples that exist within each *second* of sound (the *sampling rate*) as well as the number of values each sample can contain (*sample size*) **(Figure 5.1)**. For example, a 16-bit, 44.1-kHz sound contains 44,100 (44.1 kHz) lines, or samples, per second, each of which can have a value between 0 and 65,536 (16 bits). The result? A highly accurate digital sound, but also a large file. On the other hand, an 8-bit, 11.025-kHz sound contains only 11,025 samples per second, each of which can have a value between 0 and 255. The result here is a duller, less clear representation of the original sound— but also a much smaller file.

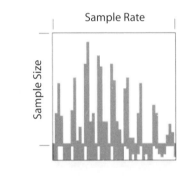

Figure 5.1
The make-up of a digital sound.

To employ sound effects and soundtracks effectively, you need to strike just the right balance between audio quality and file size—a trick that may require some experimentation. Here Flash can provide help, offering tools to maximize audio and the leading technologies for compression.

The first thing you need to do, however, is get sounds *into* Flash—which is what we'll discuss next.

Importing Sounds

You cannot record sounds in Flash; instead, you must import them. This means you need to record your sound files outside of Flash, download them from the Internet, or purchase a sound collection. Flash can import .wav (Windows), .aiff (Macintosh), and MP3 (Windows and Macintosh) sound files. If you have QuickTime 4 (or later), you can import both .wav and .aiff sound files, regardless of which operating system you use. Because any sound you import into Flash becomes part of the authoring file, you can keep your file size reasonable by importing MP3 files.

> **TIP** *You cannot use MIDI files within Flash. The only way to control a MIDI file using Flash is via JavaScript.*

To import a sound file into Flash:

1. From the File menu choose Import to bring up the Import dialog box.

2. Select the sound file you wish to import, and click Open.

   The sound is imported and automatically placed in your authoring file's library **(Figure 5.2)** , although initially it doesn't show up on the timeline.

Figure 5.2
When you import a sound, Flash places it in the library. To use sound in your project, you need to manually add the sound to the timeline.

Once you've imported a sound into your authoring file, you can use the whole thing or just sections of it repeatedly in different places in your movie—without significantly affecting file size. (We'll discuss how to use a single sound for different effects later in this chapter.)

Adding Sounds to the Timeline

A sound that you have imported and placed in the library is considered the *master* version of that sound. Copies of that sound—which you will use at various points in your movie—are considered *instances* of that sound **(Figure 5.3)**. Whenever you update the master version of a sound, all instances of it will reflect that change.

Regardless of what you plan to do with a sound, you work with *instances* of it—rather than the master—which you place on a keyframe within the timeline **(Figure 5.4)**. You can only edit a sound instance *after* you've placed it on the timeline—which you can do in a couple of ways.

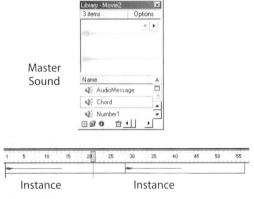

Master Sound

Instance   Instance

Figure 5.3
Copies of a master sound are called instances. A movie can contain many instances of a single sound.

To place an instance of a sound onto a timeline:

1. Create a new layer on the timeline by choosing Insert > Layer or by pressing the Add Layer button.

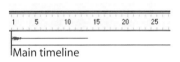

Main timeline

2. Double-click the layer name, and rename it "Sound."

   Although you don't have to create a separate layer for sound, doing so will make your project more manageable.

Button timeline

3. Right-click (Windows) or Control-click (Macintosh) the point on the timeline where you wish your sound to begin playing, then choose Insert Keyframe from the menu that appears.

Figure 5.4
No matter how you use a sound in Flash—whether it's a sound on the main timeline or a button sound—instances of the sound are used and they are always placed on a keyframe of the timeline.

4. With the Sound panel open, choose a sound from the menu of available sounds you've imported.

The timeline will show that you've added a sound, which should begin playing when the timeline reaches that keyframe.

Another way to place an instance of a sound onto a timeline:

1. Create a new layer on the timeline by pressing the Add Layer button or choose Insert > Layer.

2. Double-click the layer name, and rename it "Sound."

3. Right-click (Windows) or Control-click (Macintosh) the point on the timeline where you would like the sound to begin, and then choose Insert Keyframe from the menu that appears.

4. From the Window menu choose Library to open the library window.

5. In the library locate the sound you wish to use.

6. Click the sound's name and drag it onto the stage **(Figure 5.5)**.

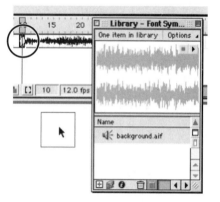

An instance of the sound will be added to the frame you previously selected. Dragging a sound from the library to the stage will cause an outline to appear that makes it look as if you're dragging an object onto it—this is not the case. The outline simply indicates that you're dragging something from the library to the stage or timeline.

Figure 5.5
Dragging a sound from the library places an instance of it at the current keyframe.

Once you've placed an instance of a sound on the timeline, you may need to adjust its location to make it play earlier or later.

To relocate a sound instance on the timeline:

◆ Click and drag the sound instance on the timeline.

> **TIP** *You can have as many layers with sound as you wish. If you use multiple sounds on the timeline, placing them on different layers makes it easier to identify particular sounds for editing purposes. All of the layers will be combined in your final file.*

Configuring/Editing Sound Instances

Once you've added a sound to the timeline, there are several things you need to consider:

- Will the sound instance loop, and if so, how many times?

- Does it need to be synchronized to the animation?

- How loud does the sound need to be?

- Do you want the sound to play through the left speaker, right speaker, or both? Or do you want it to fade from left to right to give the sense of motion?

Because you can configure instances of the same master sound differently, you can set one instance to be fairly quiet and loop 10 times while another instance of the same sound is played loudly and only once.

Once you place an instance of a sound on the timeline, you configure it using the Sound panel.

To open the Sound panel:

- ◆ From the Window menu choose Panels > Sound.

The Sound panel is made up of the following areas **(Figure 5.6)**:

- **Sound.** This is the master sound upon which the instance is based. You can use the pop-up menu to select a different master sound. Any adjustments you make on the Sound panel will only affect that instance of the sound.

- **Sound Info.** Provides information about the instance's master sound, including its sample rate, playing time, and file size.

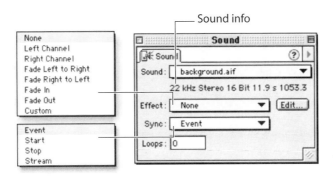

Figure 5.6
The Sound panel.

- *Effect pop-up menu.* Choose from the following effect presets, also called sound-envelope presets, to quickly adjust the volume of your sound's left and right channels (for more information see "Setting the Volume, Panning, and Length of a Sound Instance" later in this chapter).

  None. Use this option if you don't wish to apply a volume, or envelope, effect to your sound, or if you wish to remove a previously configured envelope effect. If you choose this option, the sound will play in its original form.

  Left/Right Channel. Use this option to make your sound play in the left or right channel (left or right speaker).

  Fade Left to Right/Fade Right to Left. Use this option to make your sound fade from one channel to the other.

  Fade In/Out. Use this option to make the sound instance fade in or out.

  Custom. Use this option—which is automatically displayed if you edit the sound envelope in the sound-editing window—to create your own effects.

- *Sync.* This is where you set how Flash synchronizes a sound instance (for more information, see the box "Understanding the Event and Stream Sync Options"). The options are as follows:

  Event. An event-driven sound will play from beginning to end the moment the timeline reaches the keyframe in which it is placed. This option works best for short sounds and background music tracks you wish to loop.

  Start. Normally, multiple instances of the same master sound can play on top of one another. If another instance of the selected master sound is already playing from beginning to end elsewhere on the timeline, this option will halt the first instance and begin a new one.

  Stop. When sound instances based on different master sounds are playing simultaneously, you may want to silence one. This option allows you to do that.

  Stream. This option ensures that animated elements will remain in sync with the sound instance as it plays—even if some animated frames must be skipped to do so. Streamed sound instances stop any time your movie does, and they only play for the duration of the frames they occupy **(Figure 5.7)** .

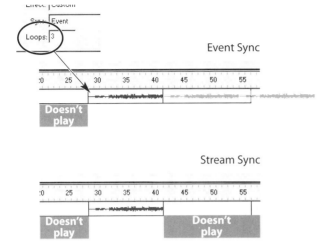

Event Sync

Stream Sync

Figure 5.7
Event-synchronized
sounds can play inde-
pendently of their frames
on the timeline, while
streamed-synchronized
sound instances play only
within the frames they
occupy.

- *Loops.* Use this option to specify how many times you want your sound instance to play. You can loop a sound as many times as you wish, and it will not affect file size. This option is often used to create looping soundtracks for background music.

- *Edit.* Opens the Edit Envelope dialog box to adjust your sound's volume, panning (stereo) effects, and play length (see next section).

> **TIP** *A looped event-driven sound will continue playing for as many times as you've set it to loop, even if the movie comes to a stop.*

Understanding the Event and Stream Sync Options

Once you've placed an instance of a sound on the timeline, you need to figure out exactly how you want to use it in your presentation. Is it a short sound best-suited for an action, like a button-click? Is it a section of music that you want to use in the background? Or is it a soundtrack you need to synchronize with an on-screen animation? Flash deals with each instance of a sound differently, depending on its use. This, as you're about to learn, helps minimize file size and download time.

When you place an instance of a sound on the timeline, you use the Sync options on the Sound panel to configure it. There are two categories of Sync options: event-driven and streamed. Event-driven sound instances are triggered by an action in your movie—the pressing of a button, for example, or the timeline reaching the keyframe where a sound instance is placed. Streamed sound instances, in contrast, are used strictly for synchronizing a soundtrack with animated elements.

Event-driven sound instances

You can use event-driven sounds for button-click sounds and looped music clips as well as anywhere you wish a sound to play from beginning to end without interruption. When working with event-driven sounds, you need to be aware of the following:

- *An event-driven sound instance must be downloaded completely before it can play. Larger sound files may make the download very long.*

- *Once a master sound has been downloaded and used in an event-driven instance, it does not need to be downloaded again. All other event-driven instances based on the sound have immediate access to the sound's information.*

- *Event-driven sounds can play from beginning to end, regardless of what's happening around them—even if your movie's timeline stops.*

- *An event-driven sound only needs to be inserted into a single frame—regardless of the sound's length.*

Streamed sounds

You can use streamed sounds for vocal or soundtracks that need to be synchronized with visual elements of your movie. You can also use them for sounds you only plan to use once. When working with streaming sounds, you need to be aware of the following:

- *You can synchronize streaming sounds with the visual elements of your movie.*

- *Only a small portion of the sound file needs to be downloaded before it begins to play—even with large sound files.*

- *A streaming sound will only play within the frames on the timeline where it is placed.*

Different instances of a single master sound can be event-driven or streamed.

Volume, Panning, and Length of a Sound Instance

A sound, when imported into Flash, contains built-in information that describes its volume, length, and panning, or stereo, settings. When you place a sound on the timeline, you can fine-tune the settings for that particular instance—which means you can use a single master sound any number of ways (see "Getting the Most from a Single Sound," later in this chapter).

You use the Edit Envelope dialog box to fine-tune your sound instances.

To open the Edit Envelope dialog box:

- With the Sound panel open and a sound selected on the timeline, click the Edit button on the Sound panel. The Edit Envelope dialog box will appear.

The Edit Envelope dialog box is made up of the following areas **(Figure 5.8)**:

- *Sound-editing windows.* Displays a digital representation of the master sound on which the current instance is based, plus the controls for editing this instance of it. The top window represents the left channel of the stereo; the bottom window represents the right channel. If you have a mono (nonstereo) sound, each window represents the same mono channel.

  TIP *Each channel in a stereo sound file usually contains unique information: This is what enables our ears to distinguish spatiality in music. In contrast, the channels in a mono sound file contain identical data in both channels. Keep in mind, though, that even if you're not dealing with a stereo sound, you can still create some interesting left-to-right and right-to-left fades as well as a few other effects.*

- *Sound timeline.* Used for sound editing, this timeline initially displays a sound's duration in seconds; however, you can change the unit to frames (see below).

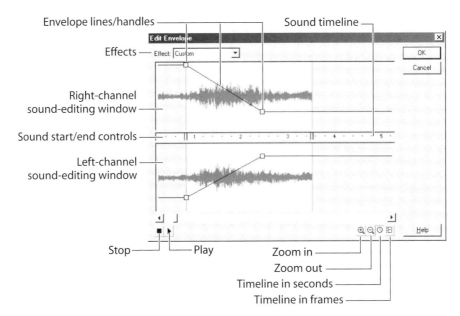

Figure 5.8
The Edit Envelope dialog box.

- **Sound Start/End controls.** Also known as Time In/Time Out controls, these allow you to determine what portion of the master sound you wish to use in a particular instance.

- **Envelope lines and handles.** Use these to adjust a sound's volume at specific points in its playing time. The lines represent the transition from one volume to another in relation to the sound's timeline.

- **Stop/Play buttons.** Use these to test adjustments you made to the sound in the Edit Envelope dialog box.

- **Zoom In/Out buttons.** Use these to fine-tune your sound. You can zoom in to more precisely place Time In/Out controls and Envelope handles so that you can achieve greater accuracy in your sound editing. When zooming in or out, the sound-editing timeline will also reflect a change.

- **Timeline in Seconds/Frames.** These allow you to choose the units used on the sound-editing timeline. Seconds are good for seeing the duration of your sound, whereas frames are useful for synchronizing sound with visual elements because they show the actual frame numbers in which the sound will play in your movie's timeline.

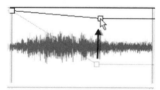

- **Effects pop-up menu.** A set of presets that you can use to quickly adjust the volume of your sound's left and right channels. These are the same as those found on the Sound panel itself.

Figure 5.9
Adjusting a sound's volume by moving envelope handles.

To adjust volume:

- Click and drag an envelope handle. The higher a handle is in a sound-editing window, the louder the sound will be at that point, and vice versa **(Figure 5.9)**.

- You may add as many as eight handles. To add a handle, just click the Envelope line where you would like it to go. To remove a handle, click and drag it out of a sound-editing window.

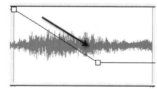

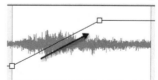

To adjust panning:

- Panning effects are achieved by adjusting the volume in one channel so that it is either louder or quieter than the other channel at the same point **(Figure 5.10)**.

Figure 5.10
Panning occurs when one channel's volume is diminished while the other channel's volume is increased.

To adjust playing time:

♦ Click-dragging the Time In control to the right will cause the sound to start playing at the point to which you dragged it (rather than its original starting point). Likewise, click-dragging the Time Out control to the left will cause the sound to stop playing at the point to which you dragged it (**Figure 5.11**). This is a great way to use different sections of one sound for varying effects—and in so doing dramatically reduce the size of your Flash movie (see next section).

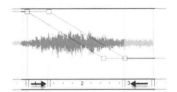

Figure 5.11
You adjust a sound's play length by moving the Time In and Time Out controls.

TIP *Some sounds you import may have stretches of silence at the beginning or end. Use the Sound Start/End controls to get rid of these silences—another way to dramatically reduce the size of your final movie.*

Getting the Most from a Single Sound

Because you can configure each instance of a master sound, it's relatively easy to keep your movie's file size to a minimum—it just takes some resourcefulness and creativity.

For example, you can use the same sound you employed as a music track to provide a plethora of simple effects by simply adjusting controls in the Edit Envelope dialog box (**Figure 5.12**). You can do any of the following:

- Use the whole sound

- Use sections of the sound

- Use sections with volume effects

- Use sections with panning effects

- Use sections with volume and panning effects

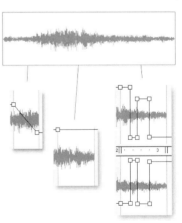

Figure 5.12
You can use a single master sound in many ways by adjusting the volume, panning, and length of various instances of it.

Sound Properties

Each sound you import into Flash has its own properties. While you have learned that individual instances of the same sound can play at different volumes, loop differently, and play at varying lengths, adjustments made to a sound's properties are made to the master sound, which means they affect all instances of that sound. The main adjustments you'll make to a master sound will affect how it's optimized and compressed in the exported .swf file.

You use the Sound Properties dialog box to adjust a sound's properties.

To open the Sound Properties dialog box:

1. From the Window menu choose Library to open the library window.

2. Locate the sound you wish to optimize and double-click the sound icon to the left of its name to open the Sound Properties dialog box.

   TIP *You can also right-click (Windows) or Control-click (Macintosh) the sound's name in the library, and then choose Properties from the menu that appears.*

The Sound Properties dialog box consists of the following areas, settings, and buttons **(Figure 5.13)**:

- *Preview window.* Displays a digital representation of the master sound. If the file is a stereo sound, a representation of the left and right channels will appear in the preview window. If it's a mono (nonstereo) sound, a single representation will appear.

- *File name.* Flash assigns a default name to the master sound based on the name of the original imported file. This is what's used in the library to identify the sound. You can change the name at any time.

- *Directory path.* The directory path from which the sound was imported.

- *File info.* Provides such file data as date last modified, sample rate, sample size, duration (in seconds), and original size.

- *Compression type.* This pop-up menu allows you to determine how you want to compress the sound when you export your project to create a Flash movie. Each master sound can have its own unique settings (which we'll discuss in a moment).

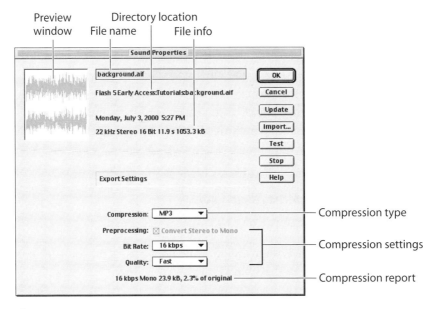

Preview window   Directory location   File info
File name

Compression type
Compression settings
Compression report

Figure 5.13
The Sound Properties dialog box.

- *Update button.* If, within a sound-editing program, you changed or edited the file (the one found at the directory path location) that you imported into Flash, this button allows you to update Flash's sound to reflect your changes. See "Updating Sounds" later in this chapter.

- *Import button.* Use this button to change the sound file referenced by the directory path information. Importing a sound this way changes all references to the current sound to the one you are importing using this button. See "Updating Sounds" later in this chapter.

- *Test button.* Click to see how different compression settings will affect the sound.

- *Stop button.* Use this button in conjunction with the Test button to halt the preview.

- *Compression settings.* See next section.

- *Compression report.* See next section.

Compressing a Sound

Creating a Flash movie is all about getting the most out of the least. Thus, it's important to figure out how to get the best-quality sound while still maintaining a reasonable file size—a process known as compression. To accomplish this, you will need to use the Export settings on the bottom half of the Sound Properties dialog box.

By default, Flash uses general compression settings for all sounds you don't compress individually. To access these settings, go to File > Publish Settings and click on the Flash tab of the Publish Settings dialog box **(Figure 5.14)**. Although you can save time by using these settings (since you don't need to compress each sound individually), we don't recommend this course of action: To produce the best product, you'll want to control every aspect of your movie, including individual sound compression settings. And because you'll use each master sound for a different purpose, you'll probably want to compress each to a different degree. Thus, while you might want to apply very little compression to a musical track so as to maintain its sonic quality, an explosion can be compressed to a large degree. There's no set formula for getting the perfect balance—it varies from project to project.

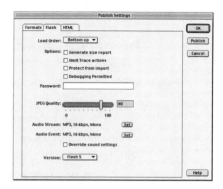

Figure 5.14

Default settings for compressing sounds can be found on the Flash tab of the Publish Settings dialog box.

To make this process easier, Flash provides a Test button that you can use to hear what effect your settings will have. It also offers something called a *Compression report,* which gives you a visual representation of your settings' effect at the bottom of the dialog box.

There are four main compression options available for sound—Default, ADPCM, MP3, and Raw—all of which are available from the Compression pop-up menu. An explanation of each follows.

Default

Choosing this compression option will compress the sound using the default setting on the Flash tab of the Publish Settings dialog box.

ADPCM

This compression type is best for short sounds such as those used for button-clicks and sound effects, or for sounds that you plan to use primarily as event sounds. You'll find this option works well for looped soundtracks because it's quicker to decompress than MP3, which may cause *lags* (unwanted intervals of silence) between loops.

To compress a sound using the ADPCM compression option:

◆ From the Compression pop-up menu choose the ADPCM compression type, and then choose from the following options **(Figure 5.15)**:

> **Preprocessing.** With this option, you can turn a stereo sound into a mono sound, automatically halving the sound's effect on your movie's file size. For example, if a stereo sound file would add 100 KB to your overall file size, checking this option would reduce that amount to 50 KB. The trade-off is that you lose the spatiality of a stereo sound.

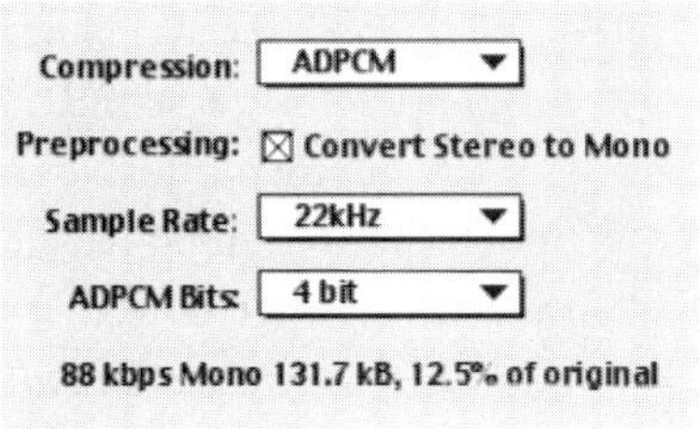

Compression: ADPCM ▼

Preprocessing: ☒ Convert Stereo to Mono

Sample Rate: 22kHz ▼

ADPCM Bits: 4 bit ▼

88 kbps Mono 131.7 kB, 12.5% of original

Figure 5.15
Various settings become available on the Sound Properties dialog box when you select a compression type.

> **TIP** *You can get immediate feedback on how the options you have selected will affect file size by looking at the compression report at the bottom of the Sound Properties box.*

> **Sample Rate.** This option allows you to set the sample rate at which a sound is exported in your final movie. Even if the sound file was originally sampled at 22 kHz, you can have Flash resample it (at export) at 5 kHz. A smaller sample rate reduces the sound's effect on your movie's overall file size; the trade-off is sound quality. Be sure to press the Test button to preview your selection. Usually, you can get away with a lower sample rate if the sound is a vocal track, whereas music tracks typically need to use a higher sample rate to avoid sounding dull.

> **ADPCM Bits.** This allows you to set the sample size at which this sound is exported in your movie. A smaller bit rate will cause the sound to distort but will reduce its effect on overall file size. Again, it's a matter of balance.

MP3

Short for MPEG-1 Layer 3, MP3 is a *lossy* type of audio compression, which means that when sound is compressed in this format, depending on the amount of compression used, nuances in the original file will be sacrificed. Despite this fact, compressing an audio file (WAV) using MP3 can reduce the file to about one-tenth the size of the original without any *significant* loss in quality. This means that a 50 MB WAV file will become a 5 MB MP3 file, with hardly any audible loss in quality. Depending on the bit rate you choose, this number can go much lower—though sound quality will continue to degrade. MP3 is best-suited for long nonlooped soundtracks (see the Looping option under "Configuring Your Sound" in this chapter).

To compress a sound using the MP3 compression option:

◆ Choose the MP3 compression type from the drop-down box, and then choose from the following options:

> *Preprocessing.* This option allows you to turn a stereo sound into a mono sound, automatically halving the sound's effect on your movie's overall file size. Again, the trade-off is that you lose the spatiality of a stereo sound. If the bit rate chosen is too low to support stereo, this option will be grayed out.

> *Bit Rate.* The bit rate of an MP3 file defines the number of bits the encoder can use to describe a second of sound. A high bit rate provides better sound quality; a lower bit rate decreases file size.

> *Quality.* This lets you set the quality of the sound once it's been exported. The setting you choose will depend largely on how you plan to deliver your movie. Use Fast for any movie distributed over the Web and Medium or Best for delivery on a CD.

Raw

Not true compression, this option allows you to resample a sound to a new sample rate at export. For example, you can convert a sound file that was 22 kHz at import to 11 kHz or 5 kHz file on export. This setting does not compress the sound.

Updating Sounds

Consider this scenario: You've completed your movie, and everything looks and acts just the way it should. The soundtrack and all the sound effects are perfect—or so you think. However, after reviewing the movie, your client decides that one sound needs to be changed. You're horrified, knowing you've used more than 50 instances of it in your movie. Opening the authoring file and manually fixing the problem will take all day. Lucky for you, Flash has found a way around this problem. All you need to do is update the master sound, and every instance of it will reflect that change. You can do so in any of the following ways:

• You can use an external sound editor to edit the original sound file (the file used to import a sound on which the master sound is based) and then have Flash "refresh" the master sound in the authoring file.

- You can import a new sound to replace your original master sound.

- You can open the master sound directly in a digital audio program from within Flash. After editing and saving it, the master sound will be automatically updated in Flash.

All three approaches accomplish the same goal. The steps for each are described below.

To update a sound and refresh the authoring file's version automatically:

1. Open the external sound file (the one you originally imported) in your favorite sound editing software and then edit and save the sound.

2. With the library window open in Flash, select the originally imported sound as it appears in the library window.

3. Click the Options button on the top-right corner of the library window and choose Properties from the menu that appears. The Sound Properties dialog box will appear.

4. Press the Update button on the dialog box. The master sound used in Flash and all instances of it will be updated to reflect your edits.

TIP *If you've edited several external sounds and want Flash to update them all in a single shot, shift-select the sounds in the library, then right-click (Windows) or Control-click (Macintosh) on a sound in the library and choose Update from the menu that appears. This opens the Update Media dialog box. Place a check mark next to all files you want to update, then click Update (Figure 5.16).*

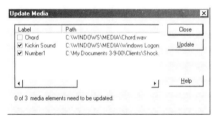

Figure 5.16
The Update Media dialog box lets you update multiple sounds simultaneously.

To import a new sound to replace the master sound:

1. With the Library window open, select the sound you wish to replace.

2. Click the Options button on the top-right corner of the libary window and choose Properties from the menu that appears. The Sound Properties dialog box will appear.

3. Press the Import button on the dialog box to open the Import Sound dialog box.

4. Select a new sound and click Open. The sound that was originally imported is replaced with the sound you just selected.

To open and edit a master sound in a sound editor directly from Flash:

1. With the library window open, select the sound you wish to edit.

2. Click the Options button on the top-right corner of the library window and choose one of the following **(Figure 5.17)**:

- *"Edit with [the name] of a program.* This opens the sound in the default editor used for sounds on your particular system. You can then use that program to edit the sound.

  or

- *"Edit with… ."* This opens a dialog box that allows you to choose the sound-editing program you wish to use. Select a program and press Open. You can then use the program to edit the sound.

3. Edit the sound as you see fit and then save the file.

4. When you return to Flash, the sound will have been automatically updated in the authoring file.

> **TIPS** *When saving the file from your sound editor (as mentioned in Step 3 above), be careful: This action not only updates the file in Flash but also updates the external file as well.*
>
> *Most of the commands available on the Library Options menu can also be accessed by right-clicking (Windows) or Control-clicking on a sound in the Library window.*

Figure 5.17
Commands for editing sounds with an external program can be found on the Library Options menu.

Advanced Sound Capabilities

You can do a number of powerful things with sounds while your movie is playing. You can let users control volume and panning; you can start and stop sounds independently of the timeline; and you can have your movie load sounds dynamically as you need them, keeping file size small. We'll discuss these capabilities and more in Chapter 14, "Building Advanced Interactivity with ActionScript."

Using Sounds in Shared Libraries

Once you've imported a sound into the library, you can turn it into a shared library asset, which allows you to use it across multiple SWF files. The benefits of this are twofold: First, because the sound exists in a central location, you only need to download it once, thereby minimizing download time for your movie. Second, whenever you update the sound in the shared library, any movie to which it's linked will reflect the updated sound.

For information about shared libraries, see chapter 9, "Using the Library to Manage Movie Assets."

Interactive Tutorials

- *Importing and Working with Sound Elements.* This tutorial guides you through most of the concepts you've learned in this chapter, including importing sounds, working with them on the timeline, editing and optimizing them, and more.

- *Adding Sound to a Button.* This tutorial guides you through the steps entailed in adding sound to a button so that it interacts with your audience's cursor in lively ways.

- *Editing a Sound.* This tutorial shows you how to get the most out of a sound using Flash's own sound-editing capabilities.

- *Syncing Sound to Animation.* This tutorial demonstrates how to synchronize a simple vocal track to some animated text.

- *Sound On/Off Button.* This tutorial demonstrates how to create a button that will enable your audience to choose whether to listen to a soundtrack in your movie. In the process, you'll learn how to create and use a variable that tracks whether the music is currently playing or not.

Bitmaps

In designing your presentations, you may find yourself limited in the graphics you can create using Macromedia Flash's drawing tools. If you require more than simple vector shapes, and ovals, rectangles, and lines just won't cut it, you'll need to turn to bitmaps. With these, you can add more complex images to your project such as photos, scanned images, and other natural-looking graphics.

Unlike vector graphics, which are based on mathematical equations, bitmaps comprise a bunch of small dots, or *pixels*, that appear as photographic images when viewed from a distance (see Chapter 1, "Why Flash?").

Although graphically pleasing, bitmaps can dramatically increase your movie's file size, which in turn lengthens download time. There are, however, ways to minimize this problem. In this chapter, we'll look at several Flash options for optimizing bitmaps so that you can keep file size down—though it's still important to use bitmaps sparingly.

You should also know that you can use bitmaps for more than just photographs in your movie. You can also employ them as backgrounds and fills, for special effects, or even as buttons. In addition, you can convert a bitmap into a vector graphic, which can sometimes help minimize the bitmap's effect on your movie's file size. But before you do any of this, you have to get the bitmap into Flash—which is where importing enters the picture. Since this is the first step in using bitmaps in your Flash movie, let's take a look at that process now.

CHAPTER 6

What you'll learn…

Importing bitmaps

Working with bitmaps

Optimizing bitmaps

Using bitmaps in shared libraries

Using animated GIFs

Using PNGs

Importing Bitmaps

It already IS an asterisk in the text font.

Getting bitmaps into Flash is a straightforward process: You simply move the graphic onto your computer's hard drive by scanning it, or by creating it in a photo-editing program or through some other electronic medium. Then you import it into Flash.

Table 6.1 lists the Bitmap file types that can be imported into Flash. An asterisk (*) indicates a file type that is available for import only if QuickTime 4 or later is installed on your machine.

To import a bitmap into Flash:

1. From the File menu choose Import to make the Import dialog box appear.

2. On your hard drive find the bitmap file you wish to import.

3. Select the file you wish to import, and click Open.

   The image will be imported into the current frame and layer, and will appear on the stage.

Bitmaps that you import into Flash such as GIFs or Portable Network Graphics (PNGs) will retain their transparency settings. As you'll learn later, this is a powerful feature **(Figure 6.1)**.

Table 6.1
Bitmap File Types Supported by Flash

	Windows	Macintosh
Bitmap	X	X
PICT	X	X
JPEG Image	X	X
GIF	X	X
PNG	X	X
Photoshop*	X	X
TIF, TIFF*	X	X
QuickTime Image*	X	X
TGA*	X	X
Silicon Graphics*	X	X
MacPaint*	X	X

Figure 6.1
Imported bitmaps are automatically placed in the library, and files with an alpha channel, such as this gecko, retain their transparency.

Any bitmap you import into Flash will be automatically added to the library. As we explain in greater detail in the following chapter, you can reuse a library object (including bitmaps) as many times as you wish (and with varying dimensions) in your movie—without significantly affecting file size.

Importing from Fireworks

Because both Flash and Fireworks (an image-editing program) are made by Macromedia, importing PNG files produced in Fireworks provides you with some options that aren't available with other bitmap file formats.

Fireworks files can contain vector graphics, text blocks, individual bitmap images, and other distinct elements. Normally, when importing a bitmap file these types of elements are "flattened", or become an uneditable part of the overall imported bitmap image. Although such elements can appear flattened in files you import from Fireworks as well, Flash gives you the option to import the file with its elements intact and editable. Thus, once imported, text blocks can be rewritten, vectors can be reshaped, and so on **(Figure 6.2)**.

To import a Fireworks PNG into Flash:

1. From the File menu choose Import to make the Import dialog box appear.

2. On your hard drive find the Fireworks file you wish to import.

3. Select the file you wish to import, and click Open.

   The Fireworks PNG Import Settings dialog box will appear.

4. Select Import Editable Objects or Flatten Image from the options that appear.

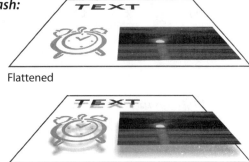

Flattened

Editable

Figure 6.2
A flattened image is imported into Flash as a single element; however, Fireworks images can be imported so that distinct elements in the file remain separate and editable.

Choosing Import Editable Objects lets you select the types of individual objects in the file to include with the import. Choosing Flatten Image combines all objects into a single bitmap graphic.

The image will be imported into the current frame and layer, and appear on the stage.

TIP *For information about updating an imported Fireworks image, see "Updating an Imported Fireworks Image" later in this chapter.*

Adding Bitmaps to Your Movie

When you import a bitmap into Flash, a copy of it is placed on the current layer of the current frame in your movie. If you wish to use the same bitmap elsewhere in your movie, you simply drag a copy from the library onto the stage. You can use a bitmap many times in your movie without increasing its overall file size **(Figure 6.3)**.

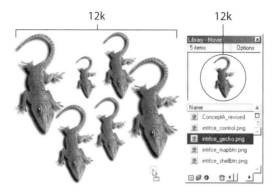

Figure 6.3
You can use an imported bitmap as many times as you want without adding to your movie's file size.

To drag a copy of a bitmap from the library:

1. From the Window menu, choose Library to make the library window appear, or press the Show Library button on the Launcher bar.

2. Locate the bitmap in the Library.

3. Click and drag it from the list or from the preview window onto the stage.

   TIP *Flash does not allow you to paste an image that was cut or copied from an outside source. Use the Import command on the File menu (as described earlier) to initially get bitmaps into Flash.*

Working with Bitmaps

Flash in not an image editor like Fireworks or Adobe PhotoShop; thus, there are limits to what you can do with bitmaps after importing them into the program. With little effort, though, you can perform some simple tasks, such as using a bitmap as a fill, selecting and editing colors in a bitmap, erasing part of bitmap, or even converting a bitmap into a vector graphic.

Using Bitmaps as Fills

You can use any image you import as a fill for a simple shape. This is similar to applying a gradient or solid fill to a filled shape. A bitmapped fill can be scaled, rotated, or skewed inside the shape itself to create some interesting effects **(Figure 6.4)**.

To use a bitmap as a fill:

1. Select a shape on the stage (the shape cannot be grouped or part of a symbol).

2. With the Fill panel open, choose Bitmap from the list of fill types.

    The bottom half of the Fill panel will display thumbnails of all the bitmaps that have been imported and those that currently reside in the library.

3. Click on a thumbnail to apply the bitmap fill to the selected shape **(Figure 6.5)**.

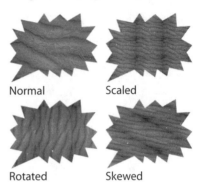

Normal   Scaled

Rotated   Skewed

Figure 6.4
A single bitmap can be used as a fill in a number of ways.

 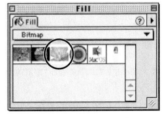

Figure 6.5
Clicking a thumbnail on the Fill panel will apply the bitmap as a fill to the selected shape on the stage.

TIP *You can also use a bitmap fill when creating shapes or painting with the Brush tool by selecting the Bitmap Fill option on the Fill panel, and then clicking on a thumbnail of any of the imported bitmaps prior to actually drawing on the stage.*

Transforming a Bitmap Fill

Although your fill may not look exactly the way you want it right off the bat, Flash allows you to transform it in the following ways **(Figure 6.6)**:

- *Centerpoint.* This handle changes the center point of the bitmap fill.

- *Proportional resize.* This handle resizes the bitmap fill so that it tiles more frequently inside a shape.

- *Vertical resize.* This handle resizes the bitmap fill vertically.

- *Horizontal resize.* This handle resizes the bitmap fill horizontally.

- *Vertical skew.* This handle skews the bitmap fill vertically.

- *Horizontal skew.* This handle skews the bitmap fill horizontally.

- *Rotation.* This handle rotates the bitmap clockwise and counterclockwise.

To transform a bitmap fill:

1. From the toolbar select the Paint Bucket tool.

2. From the options that appear, click the Transform Fill button.

3. Bring the cursor onto the stage and click once on any shape that has a bitmap fill.

The transform handles will appear.

4. Click and drag on a handle to transform the fill in any way you wish.

> **TIP** *Multiple shapes that use the same bitmap fill can each be transformed in a different manner.*

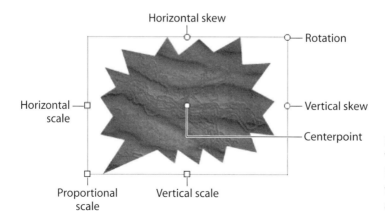

Figure 6.6
The different handles for transforming a bitmap fill.

Breaking Apart a Bitmap

Although you usually work with bitmaps as a whole in Flash, you aren't restricted to working this way. By breaking apart a bitmap, you essentially convert it into a simple shape so that you can work with it and edit it just like you would any other simple shape on the stage (for more information on simple shapes, see Chapter 3, "Graphics"). This means you can use Flash's drawing tools to change individual colors in the bitmap, erase portions of it, or even segment it using lines and shapes **(Figure 6.7)**.

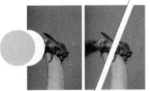

Segment   Erase

Figure 6.7
Some of the edits you can perform on a bitmap once you've broken it apart.

To break apart a bitmap:

1. Select an instance of the bitmap on the stage.

2. Choose Modify > Break Apart.

> **TIPS** *Breaking apart a bitmap will only affect the selected instance on the stage. The bitmap that resides in the library will retain its original form, and you can still use it elsewhere if you desire.*
>
> *Bitmaps used as fills are considered broken apart and can be treated as such.*

Selecting and Modifying Colors in a Bitmap

Once you've broken apart a bitmap, you can move, delete, copy, or swap regions of color **(Figure 6.8)**.

To select colors in a bitmap:

1. First make sure the bitmap has been broken apart.

2. From the toolbar choose the Lasso tool.

3. From the options that appear, press the Magic Wand Properties button.

Figure 6.8
Breaking apart a bitmap lets you select distinct areas of color for editing.

A dialog box will appear allowing you to set two properties for the Magic Wand:

- **Threshold.** Allows you to set a range for how close the color of an adjoining pixel needs to be to the original color you highlighted. A setting of "0" selects only pixels that are the exact color of the one you click; a setting of "100" selects all pixels.

- **Smoothing.** Allows you to set how Flash deals with the edge of the selected color area. The settings for this property range from Pixel, which means that the selected area will have an edge defined perfectly by the selected pixels, to Smooth, which creates a very smooth selection edge.

4. Adjust the properties according to your preferences, and click OK.

5. Select the Magic Wand option from the toolbar.

Move the cursor onto the stage, where it will change into a Magic Wand icon.

6. Place the cursor over the colored area in the bitmap that you want to select, then click and release.

Any pixels that fall within the Threshold range you set earlier will be selected. Once selected, you can move or delete them.

TIP *Once you have selected colors in a bitmap, you can change them in any number of ways using the Fill panel (**Figure 6.9**).*

Figure 6.9
Using the Fill panel you can apply a fill to selected areas of a bitmap.

Tracing Bitmaps

With tracing, Flash offers a powerful way to reduce a bitmap's impact on your project's overall file size. Tracing allows you to easily convert a bitmap graphic into a vector graphic **(Figure 6.10)**. It does this by examining the pixels that make up the bitmap, locating areas with similarly-colored pixels, and then creating vector graphics based on the shapes of those colored areas.

TIPS *Tracing can only be performed on bitmaps that have not been broken apart first.*

Tracing a bitmap only affects the selected instance of the bitmap on the stage. The bitmap in the library is still a bitmap and can be used as such elsewhere in your movie.

You'll get the best results from tracing if you use it on bitmaps with few colors and no gradiated areas—which means steer clear of photographs. Attempting to trace a full-color photo will not only tax your computer's resources, it's likely to result in a vector graphic that's larger than the original bitmap—hardly a desirable outcome!

Original

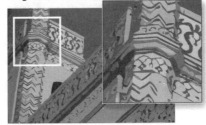
Traced

Figure 6.10
Tracing a bitmap turns it into a number of distinct vector shapes that approximate the look of the actual bitmap.

To trace a bitmap:

1. On the stage, select the bitmap you wish to convert into a vector graphic.

2. From the Modify menu choose Trace Bitmap to bring up the Trace Bitmap dialog box.

   You may adjust the following settings:

   - ***Color Threshold.*** This option lets you set how much the color of each pixel of the bitmap varies from the other pixels it touches before it is considered a different color. The larger the number, the fewer the vector shapes that will be created.

   - ***Minimum Area.*** This option sets the minimum size of any vector shape created by the trace. You can enter a value between 1 and 1,000.

   - ***Curve Fit.*** This option allows you to set how closely the trace-created shapes follow the original bitmap colors.

   - ***Corner Threshold.*** This option lets you set the amount a curve has to bend before it turns into a corner.

3. Once you've adjusted the settings, click OK.

Bitmap Properties

Each bitmap you import into Flash has its own set of properties, which affect how the image appears in the authoring environment, the name it goes by, how it's compressed, and more. Adjustments made to a bitmap's properties are made to the master image, which means they affect every instance of that image. The main adjustments you'll make to a bitmap are how it's optimized and compressed in the exported .swf file.

To open the Bitmap Properties dialog box:

1. From the Window menu choose Library to open the library window.

2. Locate a bitmap in the Library, and click it to select it.

3. From the library Options menu, choose Properties to open the Bitmap Properties dialog box .

The Bitmap Properties box includes the following areas, settings, and buttons **(Figure 6.11)**:

- *Preview window*. This window lets you preview the effect of any changes you've made to the available settings. Clicking the Test button refreshes the image in

File name   File info

Preview   Directory
window   path

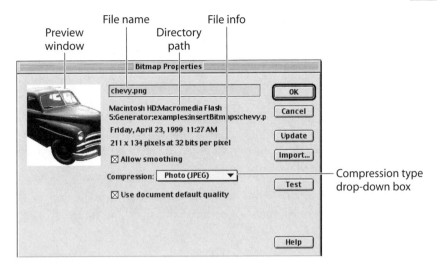

Compression type
drop-down box

Figure 6.11
The Bitmap Properties dialog box.

the Preview window. You can also click and drag the image in the preview
window to change the image area you wish to preview.

- **Name.** Based on the name of the external file that was imported, this is the
  default name given to the bitmap that the library uses to identify the image. You
  can change this name at any time.

- **Directory path.** This is the path from which the image was imported.

- **File info.** This provides file information such as dimensions, color depth, and
  the day it was last modified.

- **Allow Smoothing.** This option affects the way the image appears inside the Flash
  authoring environment. Checking it will cause the image to be antialiased, or
  smoothed **(Figure 6.12).**

- **Compression type drop-down box.**
  This drop-down box allows you to set
  the type of compression you wish to
  use on an image when you export
  your project to create a Flash movie.
  Each bitmap can have its own unique
  settings. (We provide a more in-depth
  discussion of this dialog box later in
  the chapter.)

Figure 6.12
A bitmap with smoothing off (left) and
the same bitmap using smoothing (right).

- *Use document default quality.* See "Compressing Your Images in Flash" below.

- *Update button.* If you've used an image-editing program to edit the file you imported into Flash (the one found at the directory-path location), you can employ this button to update the Flash image to reflect those changes.

- *Import button.* This button allows you to change the bitmap file referenced in the directory-path information (described above). Importing an image in this manner will change all references in the movie from the current graphic to the one you imported with this button.

- *Test button.* You can use this button in conjunction with the Preview window to see how different compression settings will affect your image.

Optimizing Your Images

Although bitmaps can greatly improve your movie's overall look, this benefit comes at a price—the size of your exported movie. Thus, it's important to strike a balance between image quality and file size.

There are several things you can do, both inside and outside of Flash (before the bitmap is actually imported), to ensure you get the most from the bitmaps you use in your project.

Before You Import

The first thing you need to be aware of is resolution, or the amount of pixels (dots) in each inch of a graphic, both horizontally and vertically. For example, a 1-inch-by-1-inch graphic with 10 dots per inch (dpi) would comprise 100 pixels (10 pixels vertically by 10 pixels horizontally). If you bump up the dpi of this graphic to 20, the number of pixels increases to 400 (20 pixels by 20 pixels). A higher dpi gives you clearer, sharper graphics—but at a cost. More dots per inch also means a larger file **(Figure 6.13)**. You shouldn't import bitmaps with resolutions greater than 72 dpi into your Flash project: You will not be able to see the benefits of the higher resolution on your computer monitor, and it will only increase the file size. You can usually set an image's dpi when scanning or exporting it from another program—you cannot do so in Flash.

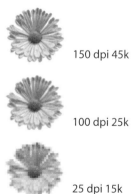

150 dpi 45k

100 dpi 25k

25 dpi 15k

Figure 6.13
Resolution vs. file size.

Before you import a bitmap into Flash you should also make sure it's at least as big (in dimension) as the largest iteration of it you'll need in your movie. If you are using more than one copy—in more than one size—of the imported bitmap, make sure that the size of the image you import is based on the larger of the two bitmaps required by your project. Making a larger graphic smaller has less effect on image quality than vice versa.

Using the fewest number of colors possible in a bitmap is another way to minimize file size. Thus, whenever you're creating graphics such as GIFs, you should export them from your image-editing program with as few colors as you can get away with without sacrificing image integrity.

Compressing Your Images in Flash

As mentioned earlier, you'll need to compress your bitmap image in Flash to minimize its effect on your project's overall size. Compressing, or optimizing, an image gets rid of redundant or unnecessary file information.

By default, Flash uses general compression settings for all bitmaps that you don't optimize individually. These settings can be accessed by going to File > Publish Settings and then clicking the Flash tab of the Publish Settings dialog box **(Figure 6.14)**.

Although you can save time by using these settings (since you don't need to compress each bitmap individually), we don't recommend this course of action: For starters, you'll want to control every aspect of your movie, including individual bitmap compression settings. Second, because each bitmap in the library has a unique look and function, you'll probably want to optimize each to a different degree. Thus, while you may want to apply very little compression to a full-color photograph, you'll probably want to apply a great deal to an image with just a few colors. There's no set formula for getting the perfect balance—it varies from project to project.

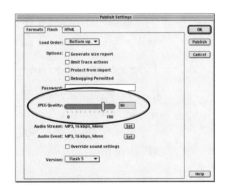

Figure 6.14
Default settings for compressing bitmaps can be found on the Flash tab of the Publish Settings dialog box.

The Bitmap Properties box is where you choose a compression setting for each graphic in your movie. Any optimization you perform here will affect each instance of the bitmap in your movie.

To help you in this process, Flash lets you preview the settings' effect on image quality and movie file size. When you press the Test button, the image in the preview window is updated, as is the Compression report at the bottom of the dialog box.

You can perform two types of compression on bitmap graphics, *photo* and *lossless*—both of which are available from the compression drop-down box. The trick is to find the setting that will allow the image to have the least effect on overall file size while maintaining acceptable quality.

Photo (JPEG)

Photo compression, which is a lossy compression method, is best-suited for photos or for graphics with numerous colors and subtle blends between them. Depending on the settings you choose, the image should closely resemble the original, though it won't be identical.

To compress an image using the Photo Compression option:

1. Choose the photo compression type from the drop-down box.

A checkbox will appear asking if you want to use the document default quality (as described earlier). If you leave this box unchecked, a new option becomes available allowing you to set the compression amount, or quality, for your image. The lower the number you enter into this box, the greater the compression—and also the greater the image degradation.

2. Enter a compression amount in this box, then click Test.

The Preview window will show you how the selected settings will affect your image. In addition, a compression results comparison appears at the bottom of the Bitmap Properties box showing the settings' effect on the bitmap's file size **(Figure 6.15)**.

3. If you're satisfied with your adjustments, click OK.

Lossless (PNG/GIF)

Lossless compression is best suited for images with limited colors such as logos, line art, and nonphotographic images. If you select this option, you are not presented with any additional settings. You may test its effect on the image, however, by clicking the Test button.

> **TIP** *Do not compress a bitmap using a lossy compression method (such as JPEG) prior to importing it. Flash will simply re-optimize it, causing what we call the "copier effect": Quality begins to seriously degrade.*

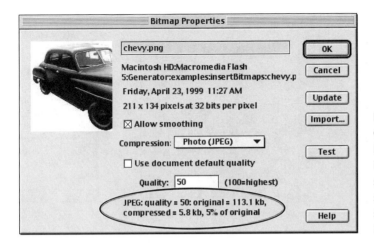

Figure 6.15
Clicking the Test button after adjusting compression settings lets you see how your settings affect the bitmap's file size.

Updating Bitmaps

Updating bitmaps is much like the process for updating sounds that we described in the previous chapter. As a matter of fact, the steps are almost identical but for the use of the term *sound* instead of *bitmap*. To avoid redundancy, review the section on updating sounds with the following guidelines in mind.

Updating an Imported Fireworks Image

When you import a flattened PNG file created in Fireworks 3 (or later), you have some additional options for updating the image in Flash. Because these programs are so tightly integrated, Flash can automatically open the original, editable Fireworks source file, which allows you to edit it with layers, text, and vectors intact. After you've finished editing the source file in Fireworks, you simply click a button to update the image in Flash **(Figure 6.16)**

To edit and update an image created in Fireworks 3 (or later):

1. With the library window open, select an image that was imported from a Fireworks 3 (or later) file.

2. Click the Options button on the top-right corner of the libary window, and choose Edit with Fireworks.

Fireworks will open, and a box will ask whether you want to edit the source file or a copy of it. If you choose to edit the source file, those changes will be

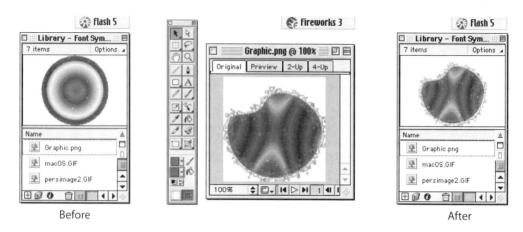

Before   After

Figure 6.16
A bitmap imported from a Fireworks 3 (or later) file can be opened up and edited in Fireworks, and then automatically updated in Flash to reflect the edits.

reflected in the image on your hard drive as well as the one in Flash. If you edit a *copy*, only the image in Flash will be updated.

3. The editable file will appear in the Fireworks document window.

4. Edit the file as you normally would using any of Firework's functionality.

5. When you've finished editing the file, from the Fireworks File menu choose Update. This will update the image in Flash.

Using Bitmaps in Shared Libraries

Once you've imported a bitmap into the library, you can turn it into a shared library asset, which enables you to use it across multiple SWF files. The benefits of this are twofold: First, because bitmaps reside in a central location (the shared library), users only need to download them once (rather than into every movie in which they are used)—which translates to substantially reduced download times. Second, whenever you update an image in the shared library, any movie that's "linked" to it will reflect those changes.

For information about shared libraries, see Chapter 13, "Using the Library to Manage Your Assets."

Using Animated GIFs

When the animated vectors that Flash creates aren't sufficient for your project, animated GIFs can provide a solution. These animated bitmaps abound on pages throughout the Web, and there are tons of cool animated GIF collections available for download and purchase. GIFs facilitate such visual effects as explosions, fires, people in motion, and more. They can have transparent backgrounds (just as they would on a regular Web page), which means you can blend them seamlessly into the rest of your layout.

To use an animated GIF in Flash, you must import it. As you are probably aware, an animated GIF comprises several bitmaps, or *frames,* which when played in succession appear animated. The time between frames determines the speed at which the animated GIF plays. When importing an animated GIF into Flash, each of its frames are placed in individual frames on Flash's timeline. Flash also spaces the animated GIF frames so that the speed at which the GIF plays in Flash is as close to its original speed as possible. For example, if you were to import a four-frame, 1-second animated GIF into a 12-fps Flash movie, Flash would place the individual GIF frames three frames apart on the Flash timeline (4 frames × 3 frames apart = 1 second in a 12-fps movie) **(Figure 6.17)**.

Figure 6.17
When importing an animated GIF, Flash spaces its individual frames so that the GIF will appear and play back at the same speed within Flash.

We recommend using animated GIFs as movie clips inside Flash. Because each movie clip is a self-contained animation (see Chapter 7, "Symbols"), you can reuse a movie clip created from an animated GIF repeatedly throughout your presentation without affecting its overall file size. In addition, you can resize, move, or even rotate the entire animated GIF as a single entity within Flash.

To create a movie clip using an animated GIF:

1. From the Insert menu choose New Symbol to bring up the Symbol Properties dialog box.

2. From the behavior options, choose Movie Clip, and give your movie clip a name.

3. Click OK.

You are automatically taken to the movie-clip editing window. The timeline that appears is your movie clip's timeline, which plays independently of the main timeline. This is where the individual frames of the imported animated GIF will go.

4. From the File menu choose Import to bring up the Import dialog box.

5. Select an animated GIF, and click Open.

Each frame of the animated GIF will be imported and placed in a frame on the movie clip's timeline.

6. Click the Scene List button to return to the scene you were in.

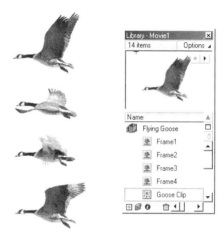

TIPS *When importing an animated GIF to create a movie clip, Flash places the bitmaps that make up its individual frames into the library. Be sure not to delete any of these bitmaps if you want your movie clip to play properly. You may want to place these clips in a folder inside the library (**Figure 6.18**).*

Now that you've created a movie clip from an animated GIF, it's time to use it in your presentation.

Figure 6.18
When importing an animated GIF, Flash places each of the bitmaps that comprise individual GIF frames in the library.

To use an animated GIF/movie clip in your project:

1. From the Window menu choose Library to make the library window appear.

2. Find the movie clip you created.

3. Click and drag it from the list or preview window onto the stage.

TIP *Only the first frame of the imported animated GIF/movie clip will be visible when it is placed on the stage. To see it in action, from the Control menu choose Test Scene. This will allow you to see how your newly created movie clip will appear in your Flash movie. Once you've finished viewing, close the test window.*

Before moving on to the next topic, we should make one thing clear: Flash allows two types of bitmap animations. One, as just discussed, involves importing an animated GIF, which is a sequence of several images that are "flipped" through in order to make it appear to be animated, and then converting it into a movie clip. The other involves actually animating the entire imported bitmap, either static or animated through movement or by means of a transition in size, rotation, or position **(Figure 6.19)**—for example, making a photo slide from one side of the screen to the other, or causing it to grow or shrink. We discuss these effects in greater detail in the chapter on animation. Just be aware of the distinction.

Frame-sequence animation

Transitional animation

Figure 6.19
Bitmaps can be used in Flash for two types of animation.

Using PNGs

PNG, or Portable Network Graphic, is a relatively new graphics standard that offers numerous advantages over GIFs—especially in compression, color capabilities, and transparency.

Like GIFs, PNGs use a lossless compression algorithm. This means that a PNG file is compressed at the time it is created so that when viewed there appears to be no quality degradation from the original. Thus, you can bring or create a 1-MB bitmap in your favorite image-editing program, export it as a PNG, and end up with a file that is every bit as clear and beautiful as the original—but at a fraction of its size. In fact, PNG compression typically surpasses GIF compression by 5 percent to 25 percent (though on tiny images, that number often rises to 40 percent or 50 percent). Many programs on the market today can export to the PNG format, including Adobe Photoshop, Macromedia Fireworks, and Corel Photo-Paint.

Even more impressive than PNG's compression abilities is its support for 24- and 48-bit color (in contrast to GIFs, which only support 8-bit color). This means your images aren't limited to a 256-color palette, as are GIFs; instead, you can use the full range (in the millions, if that's what you wish).

The icing on the cake, however, is these images' support for full alpha transparency, which means each pixel can have a transparency value between 0 and 255. (GIFs, in contrast, only offer on/off transparency, which means that a pixel is either transparent or not.)

PNG's transparency capabilities make it possible to create some impressive effects with bitmaps, including the following:

- Images with gradiated transparencies, which can be used as masks **(Figure 6.20)**.

- Objects with transparent backgrounds **(Figure 6.21)**.

Creating a PNG with a graduated transparency in a bitmap editing program usually only involves masking off image areas that you wish to be transparent, and then, with the mask still active, exporting your image to PNG.

The moral of the story here is, when you import bitmaps into Flash, use PNG graphics wherever possible—for both photographic images and images with few colors. You can do more with graphics in this format than in any other.

Figure 6.20
PNGs exported from a photo-editing program with a gradiated mask can be imported into Flash and still act as gradiated masks.

Figure 6.21
PNG images imported into Flash can have transparent backgrounds, which lets you position and animate them independent of their backgrounds within Flash.

GIFs do, however, offer one advantage over PNGs: You can't import animated PNGs, only animated GIFs. Thus, if you need to use animated bitmaps in your project, don't bother to look for the animated PNG option—it doesn't exist.

Interactive Tutorial

 Importing and Working with Bitmap Elements. This tutorial will demonstrate most of the concepts you learned in this chapter, including importing bitmaps, using bitmaps as fills, tracing, optimizing, and more.

Symbols

A number of today's Web technologies are based on the concept of creating one piece of content for use in any number of applications—not surprising when you consider that no one wants to create the same thing again and again just so that he or she can use it in more than one place. Say, for example, you were creating a logo graphic for a 50-page Web site: It would be ridiculous to painstakingly produce a copy of it for each page when you could instead simply reference the original in each subsequent iteration (making it easier to update your content, too).

This concept of *one object, many uses* is, in fact, the guiding principle behind symbols, one of Macromedia Flash's most important elements for delivering compact multimedia. Designed to help you easily create dynamic yet compact movies, they are a key component of any Flash project. If you're to deliver interactive, compact Flash movies with the smallest file sizes possible, you've got to understand symbols.

Understanding Symbols and Instances

Simply put, a symbol is a *master element*, such as a button, that you create once in Flash. Instances, in contrast, are *copies* of this master element that you use throughout your movie. Symbols can range from a graphic you've drawn to an animation of a bird in flight. Any symbol you create automatically becomes part of the your project's library—which is where your movie's various elements are organized (see Chapter 13, "Using the Library to Manage Your Assets"). To place an instance of a symbol in your project, simply drag the symbol from the library window. If, for example, you wished to create a scene with a flock of birds, you would create a symbol of a flying bird, then drag as many instances of it as you desired from the library onto the stage **(Figure 7.1)**. You'll learn more about this in Chapter 13. You can have as many instances of your flying bird as you want—each of which is only a reference to, rather than a re-creation of, your original, which is stored just once in your final Flash file. Referencing a symbol has very little impact on file size—regardless of the number of instances you use. Therefore, if the element you made into a symbol initially added 25 KB (25,000 bytes) to your movie's overall file size, adding 10, 20, or even more instances of that symbol would add less than 100 bytes to the file's overall size—regardless of symbol size. The real magic of symbols stems from the fact that individual instances don't have to look and act just like the master symbol. Each symbol instance can have its own tint, transparency, rotation, size, or interactive function **(Figure 7.2)**.

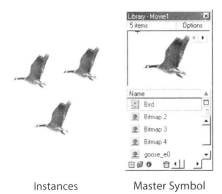

Instances   Master Symbol

Figure 7.1
Instances on the stage are references of the master symbol in the library.

Figure 7.2
Multiple instances of a symbol can look and act quite differently.

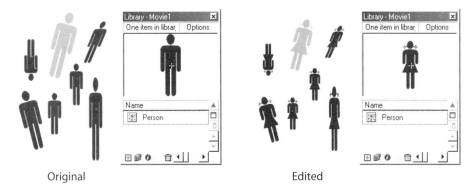

Original   Edited

Figure 7.3
Editing the master symbol in the library updates any instances of it on the stage.

Each symbol has a unique timeline and stage, complete with layers. This means that placing a symbol instance in a scene is a bit like placing a small movie (a symbol instance) inside a bigger movie (your Flash project). In addition, you can animate a symbol instance as a whole. For example, if you had a symbol of a bird flapping its wings, you could animate an instance of that symbol (the whole bird) so that it appeared to be moving across the sky in whatever direction you chose. Another thing to be aware of, at least from a graphical standpoint, is that once you've edited a master symbol's appearance, each instance of that symbol will reflect those changes. However, individual symbol instances can still have their own colors, sizes, and functionality **(Figure 7.3)**.

When creating movies, it's important to understand where and when you can use symbols. First of all, not every graphic in your movie has to be a symbol. Instead, you should create symbols out of any graphic element you plan to use more than once (with the exception of sounds and bitmaps—see the "Special and Pseudo-Symbols" sidebar later in this chapter for more on this topic). If, for example, your movie includes three interface buttons that—apart from their text labels—are identical, separate the labels from the actual button graphic. This way, only the text label on top of the button will change, not the button itself **(Figure 7.4)**. You'll learn more about this when we discuss creating symbols later in the chapter.

Symbol Types

You can create three master symbol types, or *behaviors,* in Flash **(Figure 7.5)**.

Graphics

Graphic symbols are usually made up of static, or non-animated, graphics that are used a number of times in your movie. For example, you could create a field of flowers by placing many instances of one flower symbol in your scene—that single, nonanimated flower represents

Figure 7.4
Since each instance of a button may require a different text label, the master symbol should contain only the button graphic, not the label.

Graphic

Button

Movie clip

Figure 7.5
Use graphic symbols for nonanimated graphics, buttons for interacting with your user, and movie clips for creating complete, independent movies inside your main movie.

a perfect example of a graphic symbol. (This is not to say, however, that graphic symbols cannot be animated. We'll discuss this in more detail in "Working with Symbols" and "Instances" later in this chapter.)

Buttons

Button symbols react to cursor movement; your audience can use them to control and interact with your movie. A button can be set to perform all kinds of actions.

Movie clips

As the most interactive, versatile, and powerful element in Flash, movie-clip symbols are basically small, independent movies that can contain all of the elements of your main movie, including sound, animation, and buttons. These movie clips are able to act independently in Flash because they have their own timelines (which means that even if the main movie's timeline stops, the movie clip's timeline can continue). Think of movie clips, then, as movies within a movie.

You can use movie clips for all sorts of interactive elements, including any of the following (and more):

- Independent animations that can be started and stopped independently of the main timeline

- Custom cursors

- Items you want the user to be able to drag around

- Items that can be duplicated while the movie is playing

- Slider controls

- Items whose visibility, transparency, position, size, and more you want the user to be able to control

- A central location for storing information that your movie may need to track

To make a movie clip interactive, you simply "attach" ActionScript code to instances of it (we'll demonstrate how later in the chapter). For more information on movie clips and ActionScript, see Chapter 12, "Using ActionScript for Advanced Interactivity."

Once you have created a symbol with an associated behavior, you can easily assign different behaviors to various instances of it—for example, making a graphic symbol behave like a button or vice versa (see "Changing a Symbol's Behavior" later in this chapter).

Symbols are made even more powerful by the fact that you can place one within another—for example, putting buttons and graphic symbols inside movie-clip symbols or movie-clip symbols inside button symbols. You can even place movie clips within movie clips. Keep in mind, however, that buttons and frame actions don't work inside graphic symbols.

Special and Pseudo-Symbols

In addition to graphics, buttons, and movie clips, Flash offers a couple special types of symbols:

- ***Smart clips.*** *Think of smart clips as "enhanced" movie clips. Normally, to make a movie clip interactive, you must manually adjust ActionScript code. With smart clips, however, any interactivity associated with the clip is "built in," which means you set attributes and options using the Clip Parameters panel. And that in turn means you don't actually have to view or work with any ActionScript code. This built-in interactive functionality is the only difference between a smart clip and a regular movie clip. (We discuss how to turn a regular movie clip into a smart clip in Chapter 12.)*

- ***Font symbols.*** *This type of symbol pertains to text; thus, you'll find more information on font symbols in Chapter 4, "Text."*

Flash also uses what we call "pseudo-symbols": Though not defined as symbols, bitmaps and sounds are treated similarly to them in Flash. Like symbols, imported bitmaps and sounds are added to the library automatically, becoming elements that don't significantly increase your Flash movie's overall file size when used multiple times in your movie.

Creating Symbols

When you begin to create symbols, it's important to keep in mind that you're essentially producing a movie element with its own timeline. Sometimes that timeline runs in conjunction with the main timeline (that is, it stops when the main timeline stops), and sometimes it runs independently (that is, it continues playing after the main timeline has stopped). You work with a symbol's timeline—which has its own set of layers—in much the same way you would the main timeline. A little later we'll examine each type of symbol's timeline. First, however, we're going to teach you how to create symbols.

General Symbol Creation

Flash offers a couple of ways to create symbols: You can convert stage (or main timeline) content into symbols, or you can create a blank, or empty, symbol, which you later fill with content. Each approach offers advantages.

To create a symbol using content on the stage:

1. Select the element(s) on the stage you wish to convert.

This can include shapes, text, groups, and even other symbols.

2. From the Insert menu choose Convert to Symbol to bring up the Symbol Properties dialog box.

4. In the dialog box, assign a name and behavior (graphic, button, or movie clip) to your new symbol, and then click OK.

5. From the Window menu choose Library to verify that your newly created symbol has been added **(Figure 7.6)**.

Figure 7.6
All newly created symbols are added to the library.

You can now drag instances of this symbol from the library to the stage. For more on this, see "Working with Instances" later in this chapter.

Although the above-described method provides a quick way to create the three symbol types, it's not the most versatile way of doing so. By creating symbols in this manner, you're placing all of the content you selected from the main stage into the first frame of the newly created symbol's timeline, yet no animation has yet taken place **(Figure 7.7)**. To animate your new symbol, you must edit its timeline and stage (see "Editing Symbols" later in this chapter). Sometimes it's better to start from scratch by creating a blank (or empty) symbol, which you can then later add content to or animate.

To create an empty symbol:

1. From the Insert menu choose New Symbol to make the Symbol Properties dialog box appear.

2. Assign a name and behavior (graphic, button, or movie clip) to your new symbol, and then click OK.

You are automatically put into symbol-editing mode, which consists of a blank timeline and stage for your newly created symbol.

3. Use the steps you've already learned to draw or import and add content along your symbol's timeline. (See "Symbol-Specific Creation" for more on this.)

4. When you've finished creating your symbol content, from the Edit menu choose Edit Movie.

This will take you out of symbol-editing mode and return you to the main movie's timeline and stage.

TIPS *When you re-enter your main movie's timeline and stage, your newly created symbol will not initially appear. To place an instance of it, open the library and drag it to the stage.*

Instances of movie clips will not appear animated in the authoring environment. Only the first frame will be visible. Use Control > Test Movie to see your movie clip in all its animated, interactive glory.

Figure 7.7
When using the Convert to Symbol command, all content of the new symbol is initially placed on its timeline's first frame.

Symbol-Specific Creation

When creating a blank symbol as outlined above, the behavior (graphic, button, or movie clip) you assign to it will affect the way you construct or add content to your symbol, how you use your symbol, and the way its timeline works in relation to the main timeline. The following information builds on Step 3 above. For a demonstration of how to create these types of symbols, see "Interactive Tutorials" at the end of this chapter.

Graphic symbols

When creating graphic symbols, you're presented with a stage and timeline that look just like the main stage and timeline. Not surprisingly, then, you create content on them in much the same way you do in your main movie: The drawing tools work the same; layers work the same; and creating animation across a graphic symbol's timeline is also pretty much the same. The only difference is that sounds and interactivity don't function on the graphic symbol's timeline—which means this type of symbol is best suited for movie elements that need to be reused but don't require movement. For elements that require movement, movie-clip symbols are usually a better choice.

This doesn't mean, however, that you can't animate a graphic symbol's timeline. You just need to be aware of a few things. For starters, a graphic symbol's timeline is closely linked to the main timeline. This means that although you can make a graphic symbol's timeline as long (in frames) as you wish, it will only play while the main timeline is playing **(Figure 7.8)**. If you want your symbol's timeline to move independently of the main timeline, use a movie-clip symbol instead.

Button symbols

When creating button symbols, you're presented with a unique timeline, whose four frames—Up, Over, Down, and Hit—represent different button symbol states **(Figure 7.9)**:

- *Up.* This frame, or *state*, represents the button's appearance when the cursor is *not* over it.

- *Over.* This frame represents the button's appearance when the cursor is over it.

- *Down.* This frame represents the button's appearance when clicked by the cursor.

- *Hit.* This frame is where you define the area in which the button will respond to a cursor's movement. A solid object—which can be a different size and shape than the button— usually goes here. Items in the Hit frame will not be visible from your main movie.

A button symbol's timeline doesn't actually play. Instead, it simply reacts to cursor movement and actions by jumping to the appropriate frame based on the position and actions of the cursor.

Each state can have a unique appearance, though it's common to highlight buttons in their Over state and to make them smaller (or appear pressed) in their Down state— these graphic representations simply mimic the way buttons usually work in the real

Main timeline

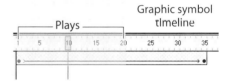
Plays
Graphic symbol timeline

Figure 7.8
If you place an instance of a 35-frame graphic symbol on Frame 1 of the 20-frame main timeline, that instance will only play for 20 frames.

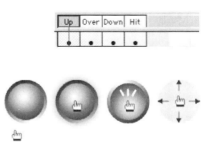

Figure 7.9
The button symbol frames (states).

world. To create dynamic-looking buttons, make full use of your drawing tools as well as the layers on the button's timeline. If you want your button to make a sound when it's in a particular state, place the desired sound on a layer in that state **(Figure 7.10)**. (See "Interactive Tutorials" at the end of this chapter.) You can also place instances of movie-clip symbols into different states of your button symbol to create animated buttons. However, you cannot place buttons inside buttons.

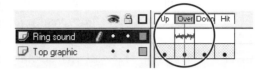

Figure 7.10

If you want a sound to be associated with a button when it's in a certain state—for example, when the cursor passes over it—place the sound at that state on the button's timeline.

To graphically define a button's states:

1. With the button's timeline visible, select the Over, Down, and Hit frames by clicking the Over frame and then dragging to the Hit frame and releasing.

The frames will appear selected.

2. Choose Modify > Frames > Convert to Keyframes.

This converts the selected frames to keyframes. Keyframes on the timeline are necessary for any type of animation since they define where changes (graphical or otherwise) occur in the animation. In the case of buttons, changes occur at each state. There is no need to select the Up state when adding keyframes since it is a keyframe anyway.

3. Click a particular state's name on the timeline and add content to the stage to define how that state of the button will look.

4. When you've defined all four states, click the Scene button above the timeline or choose Edit > Edit Movie.

This returns you to the main timeline.

> **TIPS** *If you leave the Hit state blank, the shape or element in the last defined keyframe will be used instead.*
>
> *For information about adding actions to buttons (so that the button will respond when clicked), see "Adding Actions to Buttons" under "Working with Instances" later in this chapter.*

If you wish to test how your button will look and react to your cursor's movement, once you've returned to the main timeline, from the Control menu choose Enable Simple Buttons. You can now use your cursor to test your button's functionality. You cannot, however, test a button's interactive features; you can only verify its visual response (Up, Down, Over, and Hit states) to cursor movement. After testing your button, turn off the Enable Buttons option so that you can select the button for further editing.

Movie-clip symbols

As mentioned earlier, a movie-clip symbol is really just a small Flash movie—with all of the interactivity, sound, and functionality of your main movie. You can add any type of element to your movie clip's timeline, including buttons, sounds, and even other movie clips.

A movie clip's timeline runs independently of the main timeline, which means that the clip's timeline can continue to play after the main timeline has halted **(Figure 7.11)**.

You create content for your movie clip in the same way you would create content for your main movie. In fact, you can even convert any or all of the content on your main timeline into a movie clip—say, if you wanted to reuse an animation created on the main timeline in various places within your project. For more information on animation, see Chapter 10, "Using Animation to Build Movement."

Figure 7.11
A movie clip can play independently of the main timeline, which means it can exist and play even if it occupies a single frame on the main timeline.

To convert animation on the main timeline to a movie-clip symbol, you must select the frames and layers on the main timeline that make up the section of animation you wish to use.

To create a movie-clip symbol from animation on the main timeline:

1. On the main timeline, while pressing the Control key (Windows) or Command key (Macintosh), click and drag from the first frame of the top layer to the last frame of the bottom layer to select the timeline frames you wish to use in a movie clip.

The frames will appear selected **(Figure 7.12)**.

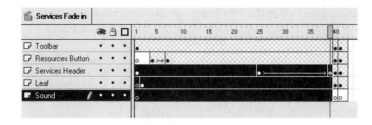

Figure 7.12
The layers and frames of an animation selected in preparation for copying.

2. Right-click (Windows) or Control-click (Macintosh) any one of the selected frames, and from the menu that appears choose Copy Frames.

3. From the Insert menu, choose New Symbol.

The Symbol Properties dialog box will appear.

4. Give your new symbol a name and movie-clip behavior.

5. Click OK.

You will be automatically taken to symbol-editing mode, where the stage is empty and the timeline has just one layer and one frame. This is your newly created symbol's timeline.

6. On the timeline, right-click (Windows) or Control-click (Macintosh) Frame 1 on Layer 1, and from the contextual menu that appears choose Paste Frames.

This pastes the frames that you copied earlier from the main timeline to the timeline of this movie-clip symbol. Any animation, buttons, or interactivity from the frames you copied are now part of an independent animation (a movie-clip symbol) that you can reuse throughout your movie.

Duplicating Symbols

If you've ever spent a great deal of time creating a symbol only to find that you want to create another symbol that's different but very similar, duplicating it may be your answer.

Duplicating a symbol allows you to use an existing symbol as a starting point for a new symbol. Once duplicated, the new symbol is added to the library, and you can change it any way you wish.

To duplicate a symbol:

1. On the stage, select an instance of the symbol you wish to duplicate.

2. Click the Show Instance button on the Launcher bar.

This opens the Instance panel.

3. On the Instance panel, click the Duplicate Symbol button **(Figure 7.13)**.

The Symbol Name dialog box will appear.

4. Give your new symbol a name, and click OK.

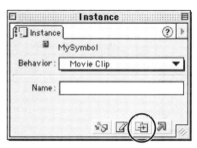

You have now created a new symbol based on an existing symbol. The duplicated symbol will appear in the library.

TIP *When duplicating a symbol, the original instance you select in Step 1 above automatically becomes an instance of your duplicated symbol.*

Figure 7.13
The Duplicate Symbol button on the Instance panel.

Symbols from Other Movies

There's no reason to reinvent the wheel: Flash makes it easy to use symbols from previous projects in your current movie. And once you bring the symbol into your current project, you can work on it in the same way you would any other symbol. There is no link between the symbol in the different files; editing it in one will not affect the other. You can use as many symbols from as many Flash projects as you wish.

To use a symbol from another movie:

1. From the File menu choose "Open as Library."

The "Open as Library" dialog box will appear.

2. Find the Flash authoring file that contains the symbol you wish to use, and click Open.

A library window will appear that contains all of the symbols used in the Flash authoring file that you just opened.

3. Drag the symbol you wish to use from the library onto the stage of your current movie.

The symbol will be automatically added (under its original name) to the library of your current project. An instance of it will also appear on your current project's stage.

4. Drag as many additional symbols as you wish from the open library onto the stage of your current project. When finished, close the library window.

TIPS *If the symbol you wish to drag from a Flash library has the same name as a symbol in your current library, Flash will append a number to the end of the symbol you're dragging.*

*If your current project library is visible, you can move a symbol from another Flash library directly into it by simply dragging between windows (**Figure 7.14**).*

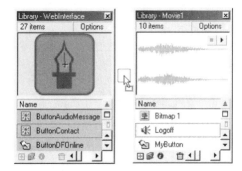

Figure 7.14
Flash lets you drag symbols from one library window directly into another.

Using Symbols in Shared Libraries

Once a symbol exists in the library, you can turn it into a shared library asset, which means you can use it across multiple SWF files. The benefits of this are twofold: First, since the symbol will exist in a central location (the shared library), the user will only need to download it once (rather than each time it's used in a movie), which will minimize download time. Second, whenever you update the symbol in the shared library, any movie that's linked to it will automatically reflect the updated symbol.

For information about shared libraries, see Chapter 13, "Using the Library to Manage Your Assets."

Editing Symbols

Now that you've figured out how to create symbols, it's time to learn how to edit and work with them. Symbol editing involves editing a symbol's content and timeline. When you edit a symbol in this manner, all instances of it—regardless of where they exist in your movie—reflect your changes. Symbol instances *will,* however, retain instance-specific edits—for example, to their size, tint, and any interactivity they're set to perform.

Symbol-Editing Mode

To edit a symbol's content and timeline, you must place it in symbol-editing mode. This changes the context of the Flash authoring environment from one where you're working with and editing your entire movie to one where you're working with and editing the content and timeline of a particular symbol.

To open a symbol so that you can edit it within symbol-editing mode (Figure 7.15):

1. On the stage, select an instance of the symbol you wish to edit.

2. Click the Show Instance button on the Launcher bar.

   This opens the Instance panel.

3. On the Instance panel, click the Edit Symbol button.

   This places you in symbol-editing mode, where you can edit the symbol's timeline and stage.

   or

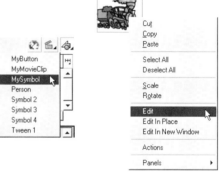

1. Click the Symbol List button.

2. From the list of symbols that appears, choose the one you wish to edit.

   or

Figure 7.15
Three ways you can open a symbol from within symbol-editing mode.

1. Right-click (Windows) or Control-click (Macintosh) on a symbol instance.

2. Choose Edit from the menu that appears.

When you've finished editing your symbol, you can return to edit your entire movie by choosing Edit > Edit Movie.

> **TIP** *While it may seem confusing to select an* instance *to edit the* symbol *on which it's based, that's how it's done.*

Edit in Place and Edit in New Window

There are a couple of additional ways to place a symbol into symbol-editing mode: One is called Edit in Place; the other is Edit in New Window. Edit in Place allows you to edit a symbol in the context of the scene in which it resides. Edit in New Window allows you to enter a symbol's editing mode in a new window: The main timeline and stage will remain visible in the background, but a new window for editing the symbol's timeline and stage will also appear.

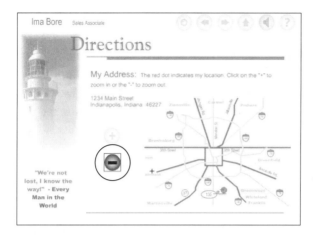

Figure 7.16
When you edit a symbol in place (such as the Zoom out button shown here), you edit it in the context of the other content on the stage.

To edit in place:

1. Double-click an instance of the symbol you'd like to edit.

All of the elements on the stage (except for the symbol itself) will be lightened to indicate they cannot be edited **(Figure 7.16)**. You can, however, edit the elements that make up the symbol and its timeline.

2. Edit the symbol's content or timeline, and then double-click an empty area on the stage to return to the main timeline.

> **TIP** *If you've placed symbols within symbols, you can continue double-clicking on them as described in Step 1 to edit elements in deeper levels. Double-clicking an empty area on the stage always takes you back to the previous or parent level (in relation to the current element)— until finally you're back to editing the main timeline. See "About the Breadcrumb Navigation Bar" below.*

To edit in a new window:

1. On the stage, right-click (Windows) or Control-click (Macintosh) an instance of the symbol you'd like to edit.

2. From the menu that appears choose Edit in New Window.

A new window opens with the symbol in symbol-editing mode.

3. From the Window menu, choose Arrange All to view the main stage and timeline, as well as the symbol's stage and timeline.

4. Edit the symbol's content or timeline, and then click the Scene list button above the Layers interface on the right corner to return to the main stage and timeline.

The Breadcrumb Navigator Bar

Since Flash allows you to place (and edit) elements within elements, it also provides a simple but handy visual indicator to help you navigate this hierarchy when editing. Known as the breadcrumb navigator bar, it's located just above the timeline.

Here's how it works: If you're working on the main timeline, the breadcrumb navigator bar displays the name of the current scene. However, if you're editing an instance of a symbol that resides in Scene 1, the breadcrumb navigator bar displays the name of the scene followed by the name of the symbol (for example, Scene 1 | MySymbol). As you edit elements within elements, this navigation trail continues to grow **(Figure 7.17)**. To return to any level of editing, click that level's name on the breadcrumb bar.

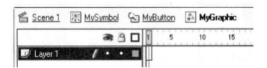

Figure 7.17
The breadcrumb navigator bar sits above the timeline.

Working with Instances

Symbol instances can be configured, transformed, and worked with independently of any other instance on the stage—even those based on the same master symbol. In this section, we'll show you how to maximize the effectiveness of these versatile elements.

Adding Instances to Your Movie

As mentioned earlier, you never use symbols directly in your movie, only instances of them, which you drag from the library to the stage.

To add a symbol instance to the stage:

1. From the Window menu choose Library.

   This opens the library window.

2. From the list that appears, locate the symbol you wish to use.

3. Click the symbol's name and drag it onto the stage. An instance of the symbol will appear on the stage **(Figure 7.18)**.

   TIP *You can quickly create a number of instances of the same symbol: On the stage, simply select the instance you wish to duplicate, and press Control-D (Windows) or Command-D (Macintosh).*

Figure 7.18
Instances of a symbol are added to your movie by dragging them from the library.

Changing an Instance's Tint and Transparency

Changing the tint and/or transparency of an instance allows you to use a single symbol in many ways without graphical redundancy **(Figure 7.19)**.

To change an instance's tint or transparency:

1. Select an instance of a symbol on the stage.

2. Choose Window > Panels > Effects to show the Effects panel, and choose from the following options on the drop-down menu:

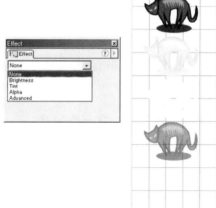

Figure 7.19
By using various tints and transparencies on an instance you can avoid graphical redundancy.

- *None.* Causes the instance to appear as it did originally, without any color or transparency.

- *Brightness.* Allows you to adjust the overall brightness of the instance. A setting of 100 will turn the instance completely white; a setting of –100 will turn the instance completely black.

- *Tint.* Allows you to tint an instance the color of your choosing. The Tint amount allows you to set the tint percentage.

- *Alpha.* Allows you to adjust an instance's transparency. A setting of 0 percent makes the instance completely transparent; a setting of 100 percent makes the instance completely opaque.

- *Special.* Allows you to simultaneously adjust an instance's tint and transparency. The controls on the left are for adjusting values based on a percentage value, while the controls on the right are for adjusting values based on a constant value.

Adjusting any of these parameters on the Effect panel will update the instance immediately.

TIPS *You can only edit color effects on symbol instances. To perform such edits on other movie elements (such as text, groups, or imported bitmaps), you must first turn them into symbols and then drag an instance on stage for editing.*

You can create various tinted and transparent bitmaps by turning a bitmap into a symbol and adjusting the colors and transparency of various instances of it.

Defining an Instance

When you create a symbol and define its behavior—making it, say, a button—any instance of that symbol which you place on the stage will initially share the original's behavior. Defining an instance involves one of two things: fine-tuning its current behavior or changing its behavior altogether (say, from a button to a movie clip). When you define an instance, it does not affect the master symbol or any other instances based on that master symbol.

Figure 7.20
When an instance of a symbol is selected, the Instance panel shows how the current instance is defined. This instance has a Graphic behavior and is set to loop on Frame 1 of its timeline.

To define an instance:

1. On the stage, select an instance of the symbol you wish to define.

2. Click the Show Instance button on the Launcher bar.

This opens the Instance panel, which reflects the current attributes and behavior (graphic, button, or movie clip) of the instance selected on the stage **(Figure 7.20)**. To fine-tune this instance's behavior, adjust any of the available settings (described below). To completely transform this instance's behavior, select a new behavior from the pop-up menu on the Instance panel.

- *Graphic behavior options:*

  Loop. Causes the instance to loop repeatedly. Because you're defining this instance as a graphic, its timeline will be linked directly to the main timeline—that is, the instance will loop as long as the main timeline is playing. When that timeline stops, so will the instance.

  Play Once. Causes the instance to play once and then stop.

  Single Frame. Allows you to show just a single frame of the graphic symbol.

  First Frame. Allows you to choose which frame on the instance's timeline will appear first.

- *Button behavior option:*

  Track as Button or Track as Menu Item. Under normal circumstances—and when the Track as Button option is selected—only one button at a time can react to cursor/mouse movement or actions. However, when Track as Menu Item is selected, multiple instances of buttons can react to the cursor—even when it's pressed down. Basically, this involves stacking buttons and assigning an action to each—used primarily for creating menu bars in Flash (see "Interactive Tutorials" in this chapter).

- *Movie Clip behavior option:*

  Instance Name. You can make any movie-clip instance into what's known as a *target.* By doing so, you can tell it to do all kinds of things within Flash. To make a movie clip a target, you assign a name to it from inside the Instance Name box (for example, MyTarget). Then, using ActionScript you can instruct the target to rotate, move, resize, and so on at the same time the Flash movie is playing. We'll discuss this topic in greater detail in Chapter 12, "Using ActionScript for Advanced Interactivity." For now, just be aware that movie-clip instances become interactive elements once you assign them a name.

  TIP *Names for movie-clip instances cannot contain spaces and it must begin with a character (a-z or A-Z).*

Adding Actions to Buttons

Each button instance on the stage can be set up to perform a different action. This means you can use one button design for many purposes. Remember, though: You don't place actions (telling your button what to do) in the button timeline. Instead, you add them to individual button instances on the stage.

To add an action to a button instance:

1. On the stage, select any instance of a button symbol.

2. On the Launcher bar, click the Show Object Actions button.

   The Actions panel will appear.

3. Click the Add an Action button (+) on the top-left corner of the Actions panel.

4. From the menu that appears, choose an action. For the sake of this demonstration, choose Basic Actions > Get URL.

5. Type the name of the URL in the URL box at the bottom of the panel **(Figure 7.21)**.

6. Close the Action panel.

   You have now assigned an action to your button. If you choose Control > Test Movie, you'll see that when the button is clicked, it opens a browser window and displays the URL you specified. For more details and information on adding an action to a button, see Chapter 11, "Basic Actions for Building Interactivity."

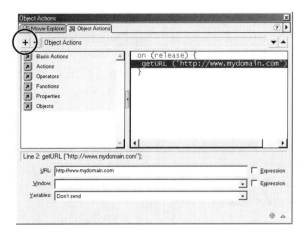

Figure 7.21
By selecting a button instance from the Actions panel, you can add actions and set parameters for your buttons.

Adding Actions to Movie Clips

By adding actions to movie-clip instances you can make the clips perform certain actions—when they appear in a scene, when they are removed from a scene, when the mouse is moved, and more. We'll explore this powerful capability in greater detail in Chapter 12, "Using ActionScript for Advanced Interactivity."

To add an action to a movie-clip instance:

1. On the stage, select any instance of a movie-clip symbol.

2. On the Launcher bar, click the Show Object Actions button.

The Actions panel will appear.

3. Click the Add an Action button on the top-left corner of the Actions panel.

4. From the menu that appears, choose an action. For the sake of this demonstration, choose Actions > setProperty.

Parameters that you set for this action will appear at the bottom of the Actions panel.

5. From the Property drop-down menu, choose _rotation, and in the Value box enter 45. Leave the Target parameter empty.

This action will rotate the movie clip by 45 degrees when it's first loaded into the scene.

6. Close the Action panel.

If you choose Control > Test Movie, you'll see that when the movie clip first appears, it is rotated by 45 degrees. For more details and information on adding an action to a movie clip, see Chapter 11, "Basic Actions for Building Interactivity." For more information about what you can actually do with the actions you attach to movie clips, see Chapter 12, "Using ActionScript for Advanced Interactivity."

TIPS *A movie clip's timeline can also contain frame actions that are performed when it reaches a particular frame. Our discussion, however, only pertained to adding actions to an entire clip **(Figure 7.22)**. For more information about adding frame actions to a timeline, see Chapter 11, "Basic Actions for Building Interactivity."*

Movie clips have a number of properties that you can change dynamically via ActionScript—the only type of symbols to provide such control. You couldn't, for example, rotate a button using ActionScript— unless, of course, that button was part of a movie clip (in which case it would be rotated along with all of the other elements of that clip).

Figure 7.22
Actions can be placed on frames of a movie clip's timeline (left) so that they are triggered when its timeline reaches that frame. Or they can be attached to the movie clip instance as a whole (right) so that they are triggered when different events occur in relation to the instance.

Swapping Symbols

If you've placed a symbol instance just so on the stage and all of its associated actions are working perfectly but you're not completely satisfied with the way it looks, you can simply swap the master symbol on which that instance is based with a different master symbol. Say you have two master symbols in your project: a dog and a cat. You place an instance of the dog on the stage, and spend a great deal of time setting it up but then decide the cat would look better in its place. Instead of redoing all of your hard work, you can simply replace the dog symbol with the cat symbol—the cat will reflect all of the edits, animations, and ActionScripts you applied to the dog.

To swap the symbol an instance is based on:

1. On the stage, select an instance of a symbol.

2. With the Instance panel open, click the Swap Symbols button.

The Swap Symbols dialog box that appears will contain a list of your project's symbols.

3. Select a symbol from the list and click OK.

The instance you selected in Step 1 will immediately reflect the fact that it's now based on the symbol that you selected in Step 3. The instance will retain any edits you made to it before swapping **(Figure 7.23)**.

Figure 7.23
Using the Swap Symbol button on the Instance panel lets you change the master symbol on which a particular instance is based.

Breaking Apart Instances

Breaking up a symbol instance isn't much different from breaking apart text or bitmaps (as we've discussed in earlier chapters). Since a symbol instance is a complete entity with its own timeline and stage, breaking it apart reduces the instance to its most basic graphic elements: text blocks, lines, shapes, and so on. When you break apart a symbol, only the content in its first frame is broken apart; all other frames disappear.

To break apart an instance:

1. On the stage, select an instance of a symbol.

2. Choose Modify > Break Apart.

Interactive Tutorials

- ***Creating a Movie Clip.*** This tutorial walks you through the process of how to create a movie clip symbol and use instances of it in your project. It will also show you how to assign instance names to each instance of your clip.

- ***Creating a Button.*** This tutorial walks you through the process of how to create a button symbol with Up, Over and Down states. It also shows you how to assign actions to button instances.

- ***Creating a Menubar.*** In this tutorial you'll see how a menu bar is created from a movie clip. You'll learn how it "opens" and "closes," as well as how to assign actions to buttons on the menu bar.

- ***Creating an Imagemap.*** In this tutorial you'll see how to create an imagemap using a graphic and a unique feature in Flash, hidden buttons.

Working with Elements on the Stage

Watch almost any kind of artist—from a painter to a sculptor to a musician—and you'll see that regardless of their medium, they have one thing in common: an extraordinary command of their work environment and tools. In fact, an understanding of these tools and mediums is what gives these artists the confidence and proficiency they need to produce works of greatness.

For Flash artists and developers, the stage and its elements represent the digital canvas. The stage is where you make the visual elements of your project come to life; thus, understanding how to work with elements on the stage is an essential part of becoming a proficient animator and interactive designer.

In this chapter we'll show you how to work efficiently within the Macromedia Flash authoring environment as well as how to manipulate the elements you've learned to import and create.

Selecting

Before you move, resize, rotate, or transform an element, you must select it. You'll use the Arrow tool for most of your selecting; however, you can also use the Lasso tool for a few special selection tasks. For now, though, we'll concentrate on the Arrow tool.

Selecting Individual Elements

Before trying any of the following tasks, click the Arrow tool on the toolbar or press V on the keyboard to activate the tool.

- To select a line, fill, or other element such as a group or symbol, click it once.

- To select a simple shape's line and fill simultaneously, double-click the fill.

- To select same-colored lines that touch each other, double-click one of the lines.

When you select an element, several things take place within Flash to help you identify the element, its attributes, and its location on the timeline:

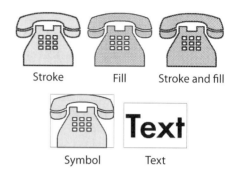

- Selected simple shapes such as lines and fills take on a textured look to indicate their state.

- Selected elements such as text, symbols, and groups, are surrounded by a bounding box—a thin outline of the same color as the layer on which the element resides **(Figure 8.1)**.

Figure 8.1
How different elements appear when they are selected.

TIP *If you want to hide the bounding box while you work with elements on the stage, choose View > Hide Edges. To make the bounding box visible, simply choose this command again.*

- When you select a stroke and/or fill, its current attributes are reflected on the Stroke or Fill panel and its colors appear on the Mixer panel. Any adjustments you make to these panels will be reflected on the selected element.

- The Info panel displays information about the size and position of the currently selected element(s). Any adjustments you make to this panel will be reflected on the selected element.

- If you select a group, symbol, or text element that you previously scaled, skewed, or rotated (which you'll learn to do shortly), the Transform panel will display the amount of these transformations.

- When you select a text element, the various text panels reflect its attributes. Any adjustments made on the panel will be reflected on the selected element.

- When you select an instance of a symbol, the Instance and Effect panels will reflect the current attributes of the instance, which you can then adjust. Any adjustments made to the panel will be reflected on the selected element.

- A selected element's layer and frame span will be reflected on the timeline **(Figure 8.2)**.

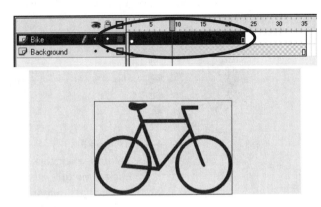

Figure 8.2
When you select an element on the stage, the layer and span of frames it is part of is reflected on the stage.

Selecting Multiple Elements

Selecting multiple elements that all need to be moved, rotated, skewed, or scaled to the same degree can save time over editing them individually. There are several ways you can do this:

Shift-selecting

Shift-selecting involves holding down the Shift key while clicking elements using the Arrow tool. With each click, the selected element is added to the overall selection. Using this method you can add as many elements to a selection as you wish. To remove an element from the overall selection, Shift-click the selected element again.

> **TIP** *If you prefer to add elements to a selection simply by clicking them (as opposed to pressing the Shift key as well), on the Edit menu choose Preferences, and then on the General tab uncheck the Shift select option.*

Marquee selecting

Marquee, or drag, selecting allows you to select entire areas or parts of strokes and fills

To marquee select an area:

1. From the toolbar select the Arrow key, or press the V key.

2. Click and drag in any direction on the stage. As you drag, you will see the outline of the selection box **(Figure 8.3)**.

3. Once you've made your selection, release the mouse button.

You must completely enclose text, groups, and symbols with the selection box to select them. Strokes and fills, however, are a bit different: You select the portion of a stroke or fill that's inside the selection box, not what's outside. This allows you to select parts of a simple shape.

Figure 8.3
Marquee selecting lets you select multiple elements on the stage simultaneously.

TIP *Once you've made a selection using this method, you can add to the selection by holding down the Shift key and marquee selecting another area.*

Selecting Everything

You can select every element on the stage that's not on a locked or hidden layer by choosing Edit >Select All. Using this command in conjunction with the Edit Multiple Frames command (see Chapter 10, "Using Animation to Build Movement") allows you to select and move, or otherwise edit, the entire content of an animated movie, not just a single frame.

Selecting with the Lasso tool

Not every selection task you need to perform can be handled simply by clicking or by dragging a selection box. Using the Lasso tool, you can select nonuniform areas of filled shapes as well as colors in bitmaps. Think of the Lasso as a specialized Arrow tool, since its sole purpose is to select areas that you couldn't using the Arrow tool. (You can only select areas consisting of simple shapes with the Lasso tool.)

To select an area with the Lasso tool's Magic Wand modifier:

1. From the toolbar select the Lasso tool, or press the L key.

2. From the options that appear, select the Magic Wand tool.

Move the cursor to the stage area, where you'll notice it changes to a Lasso icon.

3. Click and drag inside or around a shape (or shapes) on the stage, and you'll see a basic representation of your selection area **(Figure 8.4)**.

Figure 8.4
The Lasso tool lets you select odd-shaped areas inside fills for editing.

4. Release at the same point where you started to drag. The area you have outlined will be selected.

To select a polygon-shaped area with the Polygon modifier:

1. From the toolbar select the Lasso tool, or press the L key.

2. From the options that appear, select the Polygon tool.

3. Click, release, and drag, and you'll see a basic representation of one side of your selection area. To add another side to your selection, click, release, and drag again. You can add as many sides as you wish by continuing to click, release, and drag.

4. Make sure you end up at the point where you started in Step 3. Double-click, and the area you have outlined will be selected.

> **TIP** *For information on how to select colors in a bitmap using the Lasso tool, see Chapter 6, "Bitmaps."*

Selecting Within the Timeline

By clicking on a section of frames on the timeline that begins with a keyframe—that is, a keyframe sequence—you automatically select everything on the stage that's part of that sequence. This is useful for quickly editing all of the elements in a particular sequence **(Figure 8.5)**.

You can select multiple keyframe sequences on different layers by holding down the Shift key and clicking on the additional keyframe sequences. However, you can only select multiple keyframe sequences in this manner if they share a common frame

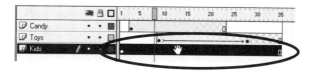

Figure 8.5
Selecting a keyframe sequence on the timeline selects any elements on the stage that are part of that sequence.

number on the timeline, and you must place the playhead on one of these common frames to make the contents of these sequences selected and editable. For example, if you select a keyframe sequence that exists between Frames 15 and 25 on one layer, the second sequence must share a common frame number (15 through 25) on another layer. A second sequence between Frames 1 and 16 would work (frames 15 and 16 would be in common), whereas a second sequence on Frames 30 through 40 wouldn't since there would be no common frame numbers **(Figure 8.6)**.

Deleting

Once you have selected any elements or sections of shapes, you can delete them by pressing the Delete key or by choosing Edit > Clear.

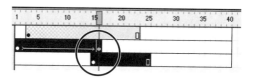

Deselecting

To deselect a selection, click an empty space on the stage or choose Edit > Deselect All. To deselect an individual element, such as a part of a multiple selection, Shift-click on the element.

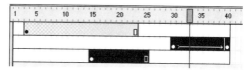

Figure 8.6
To edit elements of multiple keyframe sequences, those elements must share common frame numbers on the timeline.

Locking Elements

Sometimes you'll want to work with elements on the stage without having to worry about selecting the wrong one. You can solve this problem by simply locking elements on the stage. This way, you can't select, move, or edit the locked element until you've unlocked it. You can, however, still see it. You can only lock groups, text elements, bitmaps, and symbols—not simple shapes.

To lock an element:

1. Select the element(s) you wish to lock.

2. Choose Modify > Arrange > Lock.

To unlock all locked elements:

◆ Choose Modify > Arrange > Unlock All.

TIP *You can't unlock individual elements.*

Groups

Creating groups allows you to work on multiple elements as a single unit—for example, applying the same formatting, such as moving or resizing, to several elements at once.

Each element in the group retains its individual properties as well as its relation to the other elements within the group. For example, if you move a group, all of the elements within that group retain their relative positions. Likewise, if you resize or rotate the group, all of its elements will be resized and rotated the same relative amount **(Figure 8.7)**.

To create a group:

1. Select the elements you wish to be part of your group (which can consist of anything on the stage).

2. Choose Modify > Group.

TIPS *Anytime you wish a group to revert to its individual elements, select the group and choose Modify > Ungroup.*

You can only create groups out of elements that reside on the same layer of the timeline.

Figure 8.7
Creating groups lets you work with multiple elements as a single entity when resizing, rotating, or editing them in other ways.

Editing Groups

If you want to edit a group's elements without actually ungrouping them, you can do just that (and not have those changes affect anything else on the stage). This lets you edit a group in the context of other elements on the stage.

To edit a group:

1. Select the group and do one of the following:

   Double-click the group.

   Click the group, and from the Edit menu, choose Edit Selected.

2. Make your changes with the Flash drawing tools.

   Anything on the stage that is not part of the group will be dimmed to indicate you cannot edit it **(Figure 8.8)**.

3. Double-click an empty place on the stage, or from the Edit menu choose Edit All.

Figure 8.8
When you edit a group, like the group of colors on this palette, other parts of the stage—in this case, the palette itself—fade and become uneditable.

Placing Elements on the Stage

Details, details! Just one out-of-place element can disrupt your entire design. In fact, the precise placement of a scene's elements within its frames is what animation is all about—which is why Flash has provided a number of powerful tools to help you in this task.

Moving

Consider yourself lucky when you create an element that is perfectly positioned: It won't happen often. Fortunately, Flash allows you to easily move elements with a great deal of precision.

To move a filled shape, group, text element, symbol, or bitmap, simply click it and drag it to a new location. To move a line, select it, and then click and drag it to a new location.

You can also select an element and press the arrow keys to move it up, down, left, or right a pixel at a time. If you hold down the Shift key while pressing an arrow key, your elements will move 8 pixels at a time **(Figure 8.9)**.

When you need to place an element with more precision than the above methods allow, you can use the Info panel.

To place an element precisely using the Info panel:

1. Select an element on the stage.

2. Choose Window > Panels > Info.

   The Info panel will appear, offering four adjustable properties: *x, y, w,* and *h*. The *x* field sets how many pixels separate the element from the left side of the stage; *y* sets the pixel distance between the element and the top of the stage. The *w* and *h* properties refer to width and height, respectively.

3. In the *x* and *y* fields enter your values, and then press Enter.

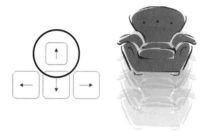

Figure 8.9
By using the arrow keys on the keyboard, you can quickly and precisely move selected elements on the stage.

TIPS *Just to the left of the* x*-value and* y*-value boxes is a graphic of nine small boxes with one box black and another white. This is the Registration Selection tool, which you use to establish the reference points for determining your* x *and* y *values. For example, clicking the small box on the top left of this graphic will make values displayed or entered reflect the distance from the top-left sides of the stage to the top-left sides of the element's bounding box. By clicking the small box in the center of this graphic, you make the reference points the top-left sides of the stage just to the* center *of the element (***Figure 8.10***).*

You can also select multiple elements (see the Selecting section of this chapter) and move them with the Info panel.

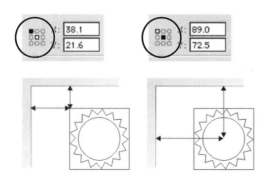

Figure 8.10
The Registration Selection tool is used to select the way *x* and *y* values of elements are measured on the Info panel.

Aligning and Spacing

Most designs require perfectly aligned and spaced graphics—a tedious task if it weren't for the automation Flash provides. With it, you can line up any number of elements in a perfectly straight row or column. You can also align elements to the left, right, top, bottom, or center of each other, as well as create even spacing between your elements.

Flash also allows you to make selected elements match the size—horizontally, vertically, or both—of the largest selected element.

Alignment and spacing tasks are performed using the Align panel.

To open the Align panel:

◆ Choose Window > Panels > Align.

The Align panel **(Figure 8.11)** has four sets of buttons that fall into the following categories: Align, Distribute, Match Size, and Space. There's also a bonus button, labeled To Stage, which we'll discuss in a moment.

The Align panel button icons will help you determine your alignment options. The boxes on the buttons represent elements on the stage, and the lines in the buttons represent the point at which the elements will be aligned, spaced, or distributed. Clicking a button will have an immediate effect on any currently selected elements.

You use one of two reference points to align or space elements: the bounding box of an overall selection or the stage.

Bounding Box Reference

Each selected element has either a visible bounding box (groups, text, symbols, bitmaps) or an invisible bounding box (lines and fills). This bounding box represents the total area (width and height) that an element occupies on the stage. When selecting

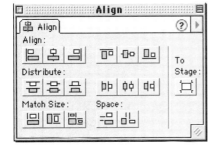

Figure 8.11
The Align panel.

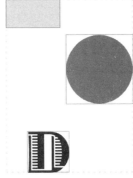

Figure 8.12
When selecting multiple elements on the stage, the overall bounding box, which is actually invisible, represents the outer edges of the overall selection.

multiple elements for alignment purposes, this bounding box (which for multiple selections is invisible) grows to represent the total width and height of the overall selection **(Figure 8.12)**. When the To Stage button on the Align panel is not pressed, this invisible bounding box is used as the reference for tasks performed on the Align panel.

When using the bounding box as a reference, two or more elements on the stage must be selected for any buttons on the Align panel to have an effect.

The following describes the different results that can be produced using the bounding box as a reference **(Figure 8.13)**:

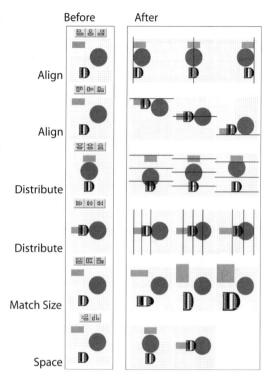

Figure 8.13
The results of using the various commands on the Align panel.

- *Align Left.* Aligns the left edges of selected elements to the left side of the overall bounding box.

- *Align Horizontal Center.* Aligns the horizontal center of selected elements to the horizontal center of the overall bounding box.

- *Align Right.* Aligns the right edges of selected elements to the right side of the overall bounding box.

- *Align Top.* Aligns the top edges of selected elements to the top side of the overall bounding box.

- *Align Vertical Center.* Aligns the vertical center of selected elements to the vertical center of the overall bounding box.

- *Align Bottom.* Aligns the bottom edges of selected elements to the bottom side of the overall bounding box.

- *Distribute Top Edges.* Positions the top edges of selected elements so that they are equally spaced within the overall bounding box. Three or more elements need to be selected for this to have an effect. The top- and bottom-most elements of the overall selection will not change when using this option.

- **Distribute Vertical Centers.** Positions the vertical centers of selected elements so that they are equally spaced within the overall bounding box. Three or more elements need to be selected for this to have an effect. The top- and bottom-most elements of the overall selection will not change when using this option.

- **Distribute Bottom Edges.** Positions the bottom edges of selected elements so that they are equally spaced within the overall bounding box. Three or more elements need to be selected for this to have an effect. The top- and bottom-most elements of the overall selection will not change when using this option.

- **Distribute Left Edges.** Positions the left edges of selected elements so that they are equally spaced within the overall bounding box. Three or more elements need to be selected for this to have an effect. The left- and right-most elements of the overall selection will not change when using this option.

- **Distribute Horizontal Centers.** Positions the horizontal centers of selected elements so that they are equally spaced within the overall bounding box. Three or more elements need to be selected for this to have an effect. The top- and bottom-most elements of the overall selection will not change when using this option.

- **Distribute Right Edges.** Positions the right edges of selected elements so they are equally spaced within the overall bounding box. Three or more elements need to be selected for this to have an effect. The right and left-most elements of the overall selection will not change when using this option.

- **Match Size Width.** Makes all of the selected elements the same width as the widest selected element.

- **Match Size Height.** Makes all of the selected elements the same height as the tallest selected element.

- **Space Vertically.** Positions selected elements so that the spaces between their bottom and top edges are equal within the overall bounding box. Three or more elements need to be selected for this to have an effect. The top- and bottom-most elements of the overall selection will not change when using this option.

- **Space Horizontally.** Positions selected elements so that the spaces between their right and left edges are all equal within the overall bounding box. Three or more elements need to be selected for this to have an effect. The left- and right-most elements of the overall selection will not change when using this option.

Stage Reference

When you press the To Stage button on the Align panel, the top, right, bottom, and left boundaries of the stage (as opposed to the overall bounding box of selected elements) will be used as the reference points for tasks performed on the Align panel. A couple of things to be aware of when using the stage as your reference:

- You can align a single element to the stage by selecting it and pressing one of the alignment options.

- Choosing a Match Size option makes the selected element as wide or as tall as the stage.

> **TIP** *To make alignment tasks easier, you can enable Snapping, Rulers, and the Grid (all of which we'll discuss in a moment) to automate the process.*

Rulers

Rulers provide a visual cue to elements' placement on the stage. When you move, scale, or rotate an element on the stage, lines indicating the width and height of the element appear on the top and left rulers, respectively. You can change these rulers incrementally using any unit you choose.

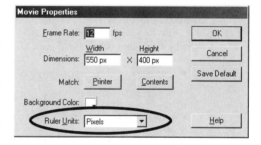

Figure 8.14
Use the Movie Properties dialog box to set ruler units.

To set ruler units:

1. From the Modify menu, choose Movie to make the Movie Properties box appear.

2. From the Ruler Units pop-up box, select the unit you wish to use, and click OK.

   If the rulers are visible, they will reflect your adjustments **(Figure 8.14)**.

   > **TIP** *Whatever unit you choose will be the default unit used throughout Flash in the dialog boxes that reflect size values.*

To view/hide rulers:

- From the View menu choose Rulers.

  This command toggles between showing or hiding the rulers.

Grid

Using a grid in Flash places a set of intersecting horizontal and vertical lines over the stage and work area. The grid is useful for aligning, scaling, and placing elements precisely **(Figure 8.15)**. The grid is never exported in your final movie; it's only visible in the Flash authoring environment.

There are several options you can set for the grid that will affect the way it looks and works.

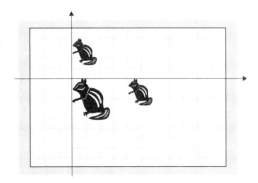

Figure 8.15
The grid lets you easily align elements on the stage by hand or by using the numerous snap points.

To set up and view the grid:

1. From the View menu, choose Grid > Edit Grid.

The Grid dialog box will appear, offering several grid configurations:

- *Color.* Lets you choose the color of the grid by clicking the color box, which brings up a color palette.

- *Show Grid.* Lets you choose whether you want the grid to appear.

- *Snap to Grid.* Lets you choose whether you want elements to snap to the grid (see "Snapping" later in this section).

- *Horizontal spacing.* Sets the amount of space between horizontal lines in the grid.

- *Vertical spacing.* Sets the amount of space between vertical lines in the grid.

- *Snap accuracy.* Lets you choose how close the mouse needs to be to a point on the grid before it snaps to it.

2. When you have completed adjusting your settings, click OK. Your grid adjustments will now be reflected onscreen if the grid is visible.

TIP *Without having to open the Grid dialog box, a couple of these options are available directly from the menu bar by choosing View > Grid > and then the option.*

Guides

Guides are special lines that can run horizontally or vertically across the length of the stage and are used to align elements. As with the grid, guides are only visible within the authoring environment.

To create a guide:

1. With rulers visible and the Arrow tool selected, click on either the horizontal or vertical ruler, and drag toward the stage.

   As you drag the ruler, a guide will appear and move in conjunction with the mouse.

2. When the guide is located correctly, release the mouse.

   TIP *Turning on the Snap to Grid option allows you to place guides accurately in relation to grid points.*

To move a guide:

1. With the Arrow tool selected, place the cursor over a guide. The cursor icon will change to indicate that the guide can be moved.

2. Click and drag on the guide to move it to a new position **(Figure 8.16)**. To delete the guide, drag it off the stage.

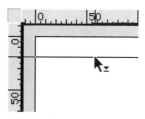

Figure 8.16
To move a guide, click on it and drag it to the desired position.

There are several guide options that affect the way guides look and work.

To set guide options:

1. From the View menu choose Guides > Edit Guides.

   The Guide dialog box will appear, offering the following options:

   - *Color.* Lets you choose the color of your guides (you click the color box to bring up a color palette).

   - *Show Guides.* Lets you choose whether you want the guides to appear.

   - *Snap to Guides.* Lets you choose whether you want elements to snap to guides (see "Snapping" later in this section).

   - *Lock Guides.* Prevents guides from being selected and moved so that you don't accidentally drag a guide that's already perfectly positioned.

- *Snap Accuracy.* Lets you choose how close the mouse needs to be to a guide before it snaps to it.

2. When you've adjusted your settings, click OK. Your guide adjustments will now be reflected on screen (if you've opted to make them visible).

TIP *Without having to open the Grid dialog box, a couple of these options are available directly from the menu bar by choosing View > Grid > and then the option.*

Snapping

When you have snapping enabled, any element that you drag with the mouse to move, create, or scale will "snap" to specific points on the stage or onto other elements, allowing you to quickly align elements in various ways.

You can enable snapping in several ways: On the Standard toolbar (Windows) you can click the button with the magnet on it; you can choose the Arrow tool's Snap option; or from the View menu you can choose Snap to Objects.

Snapping points include the following **(Figure 8.17)**:

- Lines and intersecting points on the grid (the grid must be visible)

- Guides

- Edges and corners of filled lines and filled shapes

- The length and ends of lines

- The center of straight lines and edges

- An invisible line that follows the horizontal and vertical center of a group, text element, symbol, or bitmap

- The center and corner points of a group, text element, symbol, or bitmap's bounding box

- 90-degree angles

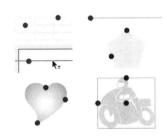

Figure 8.17
Some of the snapping points on various elements.

When you turn on snapping, you will notice a small ring underneath the cursor when you drag to create, edit, or scale an element. When you reach a point where snapping can occur, the ring grows larger.

To snap a point on one element to a snap point:

1. With the Arrow tool, click an element at a point where it is known to snap. For example, click the center of a group or the end of a line.

2. Drag the element on the stage. The small circle underneath the cursor will get bigger as you drag it over another snapping point on the stage.

3. When your cursor is over the snapping point you wish to use, release the mouse.

To snap to a point when scaling an element:

1. With the Arrow tool, select an element on the stage.

2. Press the Scale option button for the Arrow tool.

The scale handles will appear around the element.

3. Click and drag one of the handles to scale your element. The small circle underneath the cursor will get bigger as you drag it over a snapping point on the stage **(Figure 8.18)**.

4. When your cursor is over the snapping point you wish to use, release the mouse.

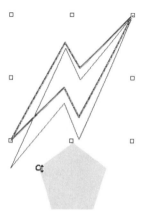

Figure 8.18
A ring appears under the cursor when it is over a snapping point, such as when scaling an element.

Transforming Elements

You movie wouldn't be very interesting if all of its elements were the same size or all of them were perpendicular to the stage. Transforming elements by scaling, rotating, skewing, and flipping them can add variety to your overall design. Such transformations also have a substantial effect on animation (for more information see Chapter 10, "Using Animation to Build Movement").

Scaling

When you resize or scale elements, you make them proportionately or disproportionately bigger or smaller by adjusting their width or height. Scaling changes an element's dimensions without changing its basic graphical structure.

Just as with moving, you can resize or scale an element freehand (basically eyeballing it), or you can resize a shape with more precision by using the Info or Transform panel.

To freely resize or scale an element:

1. Select the element on the stage.

2. Choose Modify > Transform > Scale, or from the toolbar's Arrow tool options, press the Scale button.

   Eight small boxes—known as scaling handles—will surround the element.

3. Place your cursor over one of these handles (it will change into a two-headed arrow), and then click and drag.

   If you drag one of the corner handles, you will scale the element's width and height proportionately. If you drag one of the side handles, you will adjust only the element's width or height, depending on which side handle you choose **(Figure 8.19)**.

To precisely scale or resize an element using the Info panel:

1. Select an element on the stage.

2. Choose Window > Panels > Info.

   The Info panel will appear on the stage with four adjustable properties: *x, y, w,* and *h.* We discussed the *x* and *y* properties in the section on moving elements. The *w* field sets the width of the element; the *h* field sets its height.

3. Enter your new values in the *w* and *h* fields, and then press Enter.

   Depending on what option you selected with the Registration Selection tool, the element will be scaled from its center or from its top-left corner **(Figure 8.20)**.

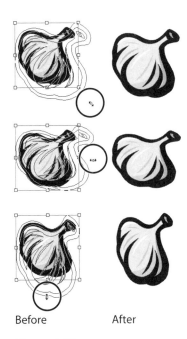

Before   After

Figure 8.19
The different ways a shape can be scaled using the scale handles.

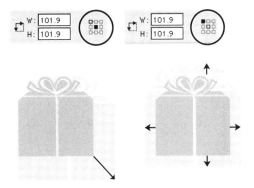

Figure 8.20
The Registration Selection setting determines the point from which elements are scaled.

To precisely scale or resize an element using the Transform panel:

1. Select an element on the stage.

2. Choose Window > Panels > Transform.

The Transform panel will appear on the stage, offering several scale settings (at the top of the panel): two boxes for entering percentage amounts and the Constrain setting. If you enter a percent greater than 100 in this field, your element will become bigger; if you enter a percent less than 100, it will become smaller. Check the Constrain option if you want the amount entered in one of the percentage fields to be the same for the other, thus scaling your element proportionately. If you leave this option unchecked, you can enter separate percentage values in each box.

3. Enter your new values, and then click Enter.

TIPS *Flash offers another way to transform an element using a percentage: Simply select the element, and then choose Modify > Transform > Scale and Rotate. A dialog box will appear. Enter a number in the Scale field, and then click OK.*

By selecting multiple elements, you can resize and scale them simultaneously.

Rotating and Skewing

Rotating, as you may have guessed, allows you to spin an element based on a center point. Skewing, on the other hand, allows you to distort, or bend, an element at a vertical or horizontal angle. Just as with moving and scaling, rotating and skewing can be accomplished in free-form fashion or with greater precision.

Figure 8.21
By moving an element's registration point, you change the point at which it is rotated.

By default, the point that defines each element's center of rotation is the actual center of the element—what's known as the *registration point.* With elements such as groups and symbols, you can move this center point anyplace on the stage **(Figure 8.21)**.

To change an element's registration point:

1. On the stage, select a group, text element, symbol, or bitmap.

2. Choose Modify > Transform > Edit Center.

A small plus (+) sign will appear in the middle of the element. This represents the element's registration point.

3. Click and drag the center point anyplace on the stage, and then release.

Whenever this element is rotated, the center of rotation will be wherever you placed it.

> **TIPS** *Although you can't change a simple shape's registration point, if you really need to rotate a shape from other than its true center, simply turn it into a group, move its registration point, rotate it, and then ungroup it. You've cheated the system; doesn't it feel great?*
>
> *With snapping turned on, you can easily move the registration point on top of a snap point, allowing you to precisely rotate elements in relation to other elements on the stage.*

To freely rotate or skew an element:

1. Select the element on the stage.

2. From the Arrow tool options, press the Rotate button, or choose Modify > Transform > Rotate.

Eight small circles will surround the element.

3. Rotate or skew the element in one of the following ways:

Place your cursor over one of the corner circles (where it will change into a circling arrow), and then click and drag. By clicking and dragging one of the corner circles, or handles, you can rotate the element clockwise or counterclockwise around its registration point.

Figure 8.22
Use the eight handles that appear around an element to rotate.

Place your cursor over one of the side handles (where it will change to a double-sided arrow), and then click and drag. You can skew the element vertically or horizontally, depending on which side handles you move: top and bottom or left and right **(Figure 8.22)**.

TIP *By holding down the Shift key while rotating, you can constrain the rotation to 15-degree increments.*

To precisely rotate and skew an element using the Transform panel:

1. Select an element on the stage.

2. Choose Window > Panels > Transform.

The Transform panel will appear, offering two choices:

- *Rotation.* By entering a non-negative rotation angle (0 to 360), you rotate the element clockwise by that amount. By entering a negative rotation angle (–1 to –360), you rotate the element counterclockwise by that amount.

- *Skew.* When you choose the Skew option, you get two fields in which you can enter a horizontal skewing angle and a vertical skewing angle.

3. Enter your values, and then press Enter.

To quickly rotate an element at a 90-degree angle:

1. Select an element on the stage.

2. Choose Modify > Transform > Rotate Left or Rotate Right.

Rotate Left rotates the selected element 90 degrees clockwise; Rotate Right rotates it 90 degrees counterclockwise. You can choose this option multiple times to quickly rotate the element 180 or 270 degrees.

TIPS *You can also rotate an element in Flash by entering a rotation angle. Select the element, and then choose Modify > Transform > Scale and Rotate. In the dialog box that appears, enter a rotation angle in the Rotate field, and then click OK.*

By selecting multiple elements, you can rotate and skew them simultaneously using the steps above. The registration point of the overall selection will be the center of rotation, and it cannot be moved.

Flipping

Flipping an element creates a reflection effect, similar to holding the element up to a mirror. Flash allows you to easily flip elements both horizontally and vertically.

Normal   Flip vertically   Flip horizontally

Figure 8.23
The effects of flipping an element vertically or horizontally.

To flip an element:

1. Select the element on the stage.

2. Choose Modify > Transform > Flip Vertically or Flip Horizontally **(Figure 8.23)**.

> **TIP** *The way in which an element is flipped is based largely on its registration point. By moving the registration point, you can change the point from which you flip it.*

Removing Transformations

We all know about 20/20 hindsight. If we could just rewrite history, life would be so much better. Well, if you've ever resized, skewed, and rotated an element to death, only to find out it's *still* not what you want, it's time to rejoice because Flash lets you return a group or symbol to its original size and shape so that you can begin the editing process again. Keep in mind, however, that you can only remove transformations from groups, text elements, symbols, and bitmaps—not simple shapes.

To remove transformations from an element:

1. Select the group, text element, symbol, or bitmap on the stage.

2. Choose Modify > Transform > Remove Transform.

   The element will revert to its original state **(Figure 8.24)**.

Figure 8.24
When you remove transformations from an element, it returns to its prior state.

> **TIP** *You can accomplish the same thing from the Transform panel by selecting the element and then clicking the Reset button on the panel.*

Duplicating Elements

If you weren't already aware of Flash's built-in copy machine, you will be now. With Flash, there's no reason to create a graphic more than once. Take, for example, columns on a building or stars in the sky: Since they all look pretty much the same, you can draw just one and then make duplicates. Same thing with symbols: Once you've placed a symbol instance on the stage, you don't need to continue dragging instances from the library window. You can create as many duplicates of an element as you wish; you can even make duplicates of duplicates.

To duplicate elements:

1. Select the element(s) on the stage that you wish to duplicate.

2. Choose Edit > Duplicate, or press Control-D (Windows) or Command-D (Macintosh).

A duplicate of your element will appear on stage, offset slightly from the original.

> **TIP** *A quicker way to duplicate an element is to hold down the Control key (Windows) or Option key (Macintosh), place you cursor over the element, and click and drag a duplicate to any point on the stage.*

Cutting, Copying, Deleting, and Pasting

If you've ever cut, copied, and pasted information from or in another program, you'll find that Flash works in pretty much the same way.

You can employ these functions to do any of the following:

- Move elements on the stage to a different frame, layer, scene, or movie
- Place a copy of an element in a different frame, layer, scene, or movie
- Delete an element
- Import text or graphics from other programs

Cutting, copying, and deleting is pretty straightforward. Pasting, on the other hand, can produce different results, depending on what you're pasting and where you're pasting it. The following should give you an idea of what to expect:

- Anything you cut or copy from Flash will be the same type of element when you paste it back into Flash—regardless of where you're pasting it.

- Text that you copy from an application such as a word processing program will be pasted in Flash as editable text if you place it within an existing text block. Otherwise, it will be pasted as a group, and you will need to ungroup it before you can edit it.

- Vector graphics copied from other vector-based drawing programs (such as Macromedia FreeHand or Adobe Illustrator) are pasted as groups. If you ungroup the graphics, you can edit them just as you would any other shape in Flash. You may need to ungroup imported vectors several times to turn them into editable shapes.

- Bitmaps copied from another program cannot be pasted directly into Flash. They must be imported (see Chapter 6, "Bitmaps.")

To cut or copy an element in Flash:

1. Select it.

2. From the Edit menu, choose Cut or Copy.

To delete an element:

1. Select it.

2. From the Edit menu, choose Clear or press the Delete key on the keyboard.

To paste an element, do one of the following:

- From the Edit menu, choose Paste to paste the element in the center of the stage of the current scene.

- From the Edit menu, choose Paste in Place to paste the element in the same relative position from the top-left corner stage as you cut or copied it from **(Figure 8.25)**.

Cut/Copy

Paste

Paste in Place

Figure 8.25
When you cut or copy an element on the stage, pasting it will place it in the center of the stage, whereas pasting in place will place it in the same relative position that you cut or copied it from.

Interactive Tutorial

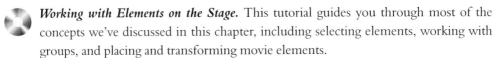

Working with Elements on the Stage. This tutorial guides you through most of the concepts we've discussed in this chapter, including selecting elements, working with groups, and placing and transforming movie elements.

Using Layers to Separate Content and Functionality

If you've ever watched a movie being produced, you know that many people have a hand in the finished product: actors, writers, musicians, camera operators, Foley artists (the people who create sound effects), special-effects teams—the list goes on and on. It's the job of the director and editor, then, to transform the disparate elements created by all these people into a coherent whole—a task made much easier by the fact that each element in the final production (music, sound effects, computer-generated graphics, live action, and so on) can be manipulated separately.

Flash movies are assembled in similar fashion. As a Flash artist, you import sounds and bitmaps, create and animate graphics, and place ActionScripts on layers, or tracks, that you can edit individually. By placing content on individual layers, you can determine its position relative to the other elements in your movie, specifying when it will be seen or heard and how long it will play. Because you can place, edit, and animate elements on their own layers, you can work with them individually—without affecting the other elements that make up your movie. In this chapter we'll show you how to use layers to get the most out of each element.

Understanding Layers

Layers serve as receptacles for symbols, groups, sounds, scripts, and other elements, and they are useful for separating your movie's content and functionality. The following are just some of the effects you can use individual layers for:

- A looping soundtrack

- Navigation buttons

- A background image

- Performing animation tasks on specific elements

- ActionScript

- Timeline comments

- Timeline labels

- Sound effects

Every scene or symbol, such as a graphic, button, or movie clip, contains its own set of layers, which you work with and manage in the same way, regardless of their location.

Although you can place several movie elements—say a soundtrack, some ActionScripts, and a background image—on a single layer, we recommend you use a separate layer for each: Your movie's content will be much easier to work with and edit **(Figure 9.1)**. Now, this doesn't mean you must create a layer for every graphic and sound in your movie. Instead, you will want to split your content into logical "chunks." For example, if your movie's background comprised a bitmap and some text elements, it would make sense to place this *set* of elements on one layer since together they represent a single entity in your movie—the background. If, on the other hand, you had a looping soundtrack *and* a vocal track, it would be more appropriate to place them on separate layers. However, for certain animation tasks, you don't have a choice: Flash requires you place elements on individual layers (you'll learn more about this in the next chapter).

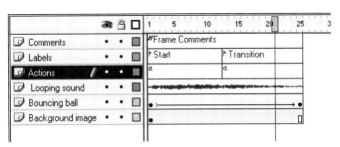

Figure 9.1
You can use layers on the timeline to separate elements and their different functions in your project.

By separating static content (that is, elements that don't change over multiple frames) from content that changes as your movie plays, you can also improve your movie's download time and performance. For example, if you had a scene that included a plane flying across a background, you would want to place the background on its own layer. This is because if you were to place the background and plane on the same layer, Flash would need to redraw the entire scene (background *and* plane) on each frame of the timeline, when the only item that really needs to be redrawn is the plane. In addition, if you were to place the background on the same layer as the plane, you would need a copy of it in each frame in which the plane's movement changed— dramatically increasing file size. The lesson here? In all cases, use layers to separate static elements from animated ones **(Figure 9.2)**.

Figure 9.2
The background is isolated on its own layer so that only the plane is redrawn in each frame of the animation.

Layers and the Stage

The stage is where you display and edit the graphical content of the layers on your timeline. Layers are placed one on top of another on the timeline in what is called the *stacking order* **(Figure 9.3)**. Elements that reside in the top layer will always appear on the stage above elements contained in the layers below. When multiple elements are placed on a single layer, they have their own *internal* stacking order, which determines the depth of elements on that particular layer. What you see on the stage at any moment represents a composite rendering of all the graphical content on all visible layers in their assigned stacking order. For more detail on this, see Chapter 10, "Using Animation to Build Movement."

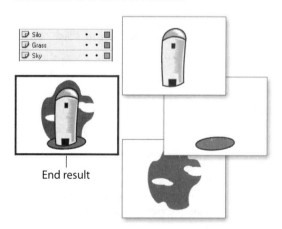

End result

Figure 9.3
The stacking order of this composition is silo, grass, and sky. The silo is the top-most layer; the sky is the lowest layer.

The Relationship between Layers and Frames

Each layer contains a span of frames that determines when and how your movie will use that layer's content. For example, if a graphic of a ball appears in a layer that's made up of 10 frames, once the timeline reaches Frame 11, the ball will no longer appear in your composite movie **(Figure 9.4)**. Although each layer has its own span of frames, the frames correspond directly to frames on other layers. This means that when the timeline reaches Frame 9 in one layer, it reaches Frame 9 in every other layer that makes up that scene as well. For more detail on this, see Chapter 10, "Using Animation to Build Movement."

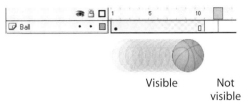

Figure 9.4
The frames of a layer determine how and when content on that layer appears in the composite movie.

Working with Layers

Layers are largely an organizational tool. While you may work with them in any number of ways depending on the needs of your project, using them effectively is the key to creating sophisticated projects with minimal frustration. In general, you'll find that creating and working with layers is pretty straightforward. However, Flash contains some special layers, such as guide, motion guide, and mask layers that require different techniques for creating and managing them. We'll deal with those individually later in the chapter.

Creating Layers

When you create a new scene, graphic, movie clip, or button in Flash, the process always begins with a single layer. Called Layer 1, this layer includes one frame with an empty keyframe **(Figure 9.5)**. From here, you can create a new layer anywhere in the stacking order—and because the number of layers you create and use does not affect the file size, you can use as many layers as you need. If the number of layers exceeds the area of the timeline, a scroll bar will appear to the right of the timeline.

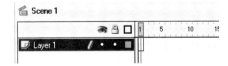

Figure 9.5
By default, the timeline of every new scene or symbol begins with a single layer, initially named Layer 1, which contains a single frame.

To create a layer:

1. Click the layer you wish to place the new layer above; it will become highlighted.

2. On the Layer control panel, click the Insert Layer button **(Figure 9.6)**. Alternatively, you can right-click (Windows) or Control-click (Macintosh) on an existing layer's name bar and then choose Insert from the menu that appears to place a new layer on the timeline.

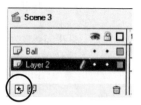

Figure 9.6
The Insert Layer button.

Whenever you add a layer to the timeline, Flash automatically assigns it the same number of frames as the longest sequence on the timeline. This means that if a 20-frame layer is the longest sequence on a particular timeline, Flash will automatically assign 20 frames to any newly created layers **(Figure 9.7)**. This is a convenience feature. You can still add or delete frames from this layer as you see fit.

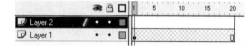

Figure 9.7
When Layer 2 was created, 20 frames were automatically added to it to match the number of frames contained in Layer 1.

Current Layer Mode

Layer mode is an important concept to master as you gain proficiency working with layers. The appearance of the stage and the way in which you edit the authoring file are determined—at least in part—by the layer modes you employ. When a timeline contains two or more layers, one of them is the current layer. Anything drawn, cut from, copied from, pasted to, imported, or dragged onto the stage from the library will affect that layer **(Figure 9.8)**. You can make a layer current in a couple of ways (and only one layer can be current):

- By clicking its name

- By selecting a stage element that resides in a layer (thus making that layer the current one)

Figure 9.8
The current layer appears highlighted; any content drawn, imported, cut, copied, pasted, or dragged from the library is reflected on the current layer.

The current layer is identified in two ways: A pencil icon appears next to its name, and it becomes highlighted in the layer stack.

> **TIP** *You cannot remove or place graphical content on the current layer if that layer is locked or hidden. (If the pencil icon next to the current layer has a red slash through it, it's locked or hidden.)*

Additional Layer Modes

In addition to the current layer mode, layers can be placed in three other modes, or *states*. These modes determine—at least in part—the type of edit you can make to the overall scene as well as what content is visible on the stage. You place a layer in one of the following modes by clicking the appropriate icon on the layer's name bar **(Figure 9.9)**.

- **Hidden mode.** You may occasionally find it useful to hide the contents of one or more layers when you're working on a particular part of your scene. A red *X* on a layer's name bar indicates it is in hidden mode. A dot appears instead when this mode is not active.

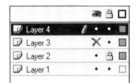

Figure 9.9
Clicking an icon at the right on the layer name bar will place that layer in the mode indicated by that icon.

- **Locked mode.** When a layer is locked, you can see its contents but you can't edit them. Typically you would use this mode when you're satisfied with a layer's contents and don't want to edit or delete them accidentally. A lock on the layer's name bar indicates this mode; a dot appears instead when this mode is not active.

- **Outline mode.** When a layer is in outline mode, its contents appear only as outlines. Outline mode makes the edges of elements easily distinguishable, so they are easier to reshape and edit. A colored outline of a box on the layer's name bar indicates this mode. A solid colored box appears instead when this mode is not active.

Placing Multiple Layers in a Specific Mode

Flash provides several commands that let you place multiple layers in a specific mode: You access these time-saving commands by right-clicking (Windows) or Control-clicking (Macintosh) the layer's name bar and choosing the appropriate command from the menu that appears:

- **Show All.** Use this command to unlock previously locked layers or to make previously hidden layers visible. You would typically employ this command after editing or viewing a single layer using one of the other commands listed here.

- **Lock Others.** Use this command to lock all but the layer whose contextual menu you are using to initiate this command. That layer becomes the current layer (if it wasn't already), so you cannot edit any of the other layers.

- **Hide Others.** Use this command to hide all but the layer whose contextual menu you are using to initiate this command. That layer becomes the current layer (if it wasn't already), so you cannot see or edit any of the other layers.

Figure 9.10

Clicking one of the mode icons at the top of the layer name bar will place all layers in that mode.

> **TIP** *By clicking one of the three icons located above the layer stack—the Show All, Lock Others, and Hide Others commands—you place all layers in the scene in that mode (**Figure 9.10**).*

Deleting Layers

If you decide you no longer need a layer's contents, it's easy to delete that layer and all of its associated frames.

To delete a layer:

1. Select the layer you want to delete by clicking its name.

2. From the Layer control panel click the Delete Layer button **(Figure 9.11)**. You can also right-click (Windows) or Control-click (Macintosh) on the layer's name, and then from the contextual pop-up menu choose Delete.

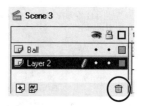

Figure 9.11
The Delete Layer button.

> **TIP** *If you delete the wrong layer, you can always choose Edit > Undo to undo the deletion.*

Renaming Layers

Flash assigns a default name (Layer 1, Layer 2, and so on) to each layer you create. Although you don't have to assign new names to your layers, their usefulness is diminished if their names don't in some way describe their contents. For example, if you were to place a background image on a layer, it might be wise to make it the only element on that layer and to give that layer a descriptive name (of not more than 65 characters) such as Background.

To rename a layer:

1. Right-click (Windows) or Control-click (Macintosh) the layer you would like to rename.

2. From the pop-up menu that appears, choose Properties.

3. Type in the name for this layer, and then click OK.

The layer name will be displayed.

> **TIP** *A faster way to complete the same task would be to double-click the layer's name to select it, and then type in a new name. Once you've given the layer a new name, click elsewhere on the screen to set it.*

Reordering Layers

When you change your layers' stacking order, you also change the sequence in which their contents appear on the stage.

To reorder a layer:

1. Click and hold the name of the layer you wish to reorder.

A dark-gray line will appear along the bottom indicating that layer's position relative to the other layers in the stack.

2. Drag the layer up or down (depending on where you want to reposition it), and then release the mouse **(Figure 9.12)**.

The layer and all its contents will appear in its new position in the stacking order.

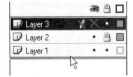

Figure 9.12
Click and drag a layer's name to reposition it in the layer stack. As you do so, a gray line will appear indicating the layer's position.

Copying Layers

You may sometimes wish to copy a layer's contents and frame sequences to create a new layer—useful for transferring layers between scenes or movies. You can even simultaneously select all of a scene's layers and paste them elsewhere to duplicate an entire scene. Alternatively, you can copy sections of a layer's frames to create a new layer.

To copy a section of a layer:

1. If you have not already done so, create an empty layer that can receive the copied layer's contents.

2. On the layer that contains the content you wish to copy, hold down the Control key (Windows) or Command key (Macintosh), click and drag from the first frame through the final frame you wish to copy, and then release. To select all of the frames in a layer, click the layer's name.

The contents should appear highlighted to show that they've been selected.

3. Right-click (Windows) or Control-click (Macintosh) one of the selected frames, and from the Frame pop-up menu choose Copy Frames.

4. In the empty layer you created earlier, right-click (Windows) or Control-click (Macintosh) Frame 1, and from the Frame pop-up menu choose Paste Frames **(Figure 9.13)**.

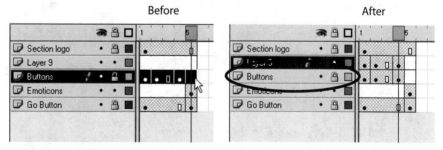

Figure 9.13
To reuse the elements of the Buttons layer, the layer is copied and pasted into Layer 9.

To copy multiple layers:

1. Create at least one empty layer, which can receive the copied layers' contents.

Even if you're pasting multiple layers, you only need one empty layer, which occupies the top-most position of the multiple layers that will be pasted in.

2. From the layers whose contents you wish to copy, hold down the Control key (Windows) or Command key (Macintosh), click and drag from Frame 1 in the top-most layer to the last frame on the bottom-most layer, and then release.

The contents should appear highlighted to show they have been selected. You cannot perform this type of edit unless all layers are contiguous in the stacking order.

3. Right-click (Windows) or Control-click (Macintosh) one of the selected frames, and from the Frame pop-up menu choose Copy Frames.

4. In the empty layer you created, right-click (Windows) or Control-click (Macintosh) Frame 1, and then from the Frame pop-up menu choose Paste Frames.

You now have duplicate copies of the layers. Note that the pasted layers retain their relative positions.

Identifying Graphical Elements on Different Layers

In complex scenes it can be difficult to keep track of which layers contain what elements. Don't despair: Flash offers some features that make this task easier.

When you select an element on the stage, two visual cues appear: The name of the layer that contains it is highlighted; and the bounding box of the selected element is the same color as the layer on which it resides, as long as you're using the proper preference setting **(Figure 9.14)**.

TIP *This preference setting can be found by choosing Edit > Preferences, then the General tab. On the Highlight color option, select the "Use Layer Color" setting.*

You can also keep track of elements and their corresponding layers by turning on layer outlines, which displays all elements as color-coded outlines that correspond to the layer on which they reside. This is a bit less dynamic way of keeping everything straight, but is still quite effective.

Figure 9.14
When you select an element on the stage, its layer becomes highlighted and its bounding box takes on the color of the layer.

To identify elements on layers using colored outlines:

1. Select the layer whose contents you want to view as outlines; it will be highlighted.

2. From the Modify menu choose Layer, or right-click (Windows) or Control-click (Macintosh) and choose Properties from the contextual pop-up menu.

   The Layer Properties box will appear.

3. Under Outline options, select the color you wish to use for outlines and check the "View layer as outlines" option.

4. Click OK.

   The layer will now display its objects as outlines.

   TIPS *You can also accomplish this task by simply clicking the Outline On/Off toggle on the right side of the layer's name bar (**Figure 9.15**).*

   When using outline colors to identify movie elements on a layer, the elements lose their fill temporarily. However, you can still edit them just as you normally would; the only thing that's different is that fills and fill changes will not appear until you turn the Outline feature off.

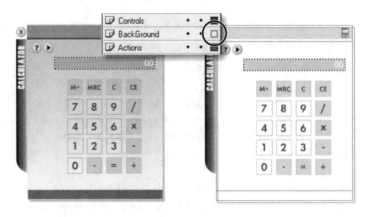

Figure 9.15
Displaying a layer's contents as outlines makes them easier to identify.

Using Guide Layers

Guide layers can make laying out your Flash movie a breeze: Say you've used Flash (or your favorite graphics program) to create a killer layout—with menu bars and graphics placed just so—and you want to use it as the basis for your Flash movie. If you place your layout on a guide layer in Flash, you can use it as a backdrop for your movie's layout **(Figure 9.16)**. Although you could accomplish the same thing by placing the graphic as a background on a normal layer, its contents would be included in the exported movie. Guide layers, in contrast, are not exported, which means their contents will not appear in the final product. You can use multiple guide layers in a scene and as many guide layers in your movie as you see fit.

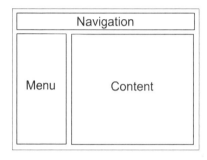

Figure 9.16
A guide layer comprising a basic layout you want to emulate provides the basis for how your Flash project will look.

To create a guide layer:

1. Once you've placed the graphics on a layer, right-click (Windows) or Control-click (Macintosh) that layer's name bar.

2. From the contextual menu that appears, choose Guide.

   A new icon will appear next to the layer's name, indicating that the layer is a guide **(Figure 9.17)**.

Figure 9.17
Two intersecting lines on a layer's name bar indicate that it is a guide layer.

TIPS *Although guide layers are used primarily for layout, you can turn any layer into a guide if you want to see how a movie will look without that layer's contents. If you don't like the results, just go back to the layer and uncheck the Guide option on the Layer pop-up menu so that you can once again see that layer's contents when the movie is exported.*

A guide layer can take on any mode a normal layer can, which means you can hide or lock a guide layer when you want to check your layout.

Special-Purpose Layers

Most layers you'll create can be used for nearly any content or purpose, as mentioned at the beginning of the chapter. These are known as normal layers. But there are other layers, specifically mask layers and motion guide layers, that are reserved for specific uses. These layer types are different from normal layers in that they don't contain just any kind of content like normal layers do, and they always work in conjunction with at least one normal layer to which they are linked. In other words, by themselves these special layers do nothing. Once linked to at least one normal layer, they affect the content of that linked-normal layer in a unique way, as you'll soon learn.

Mask Layers

Mask layers add a wealth of possibilities to the seemingly endless array of effects that can be achieved with this wonderful animation tool. You can think of a mask layer as a stencil. When you place a stencil over a surface and spray paint over that stencil, paint is applied only to those areas not covered by the stencil; the rest of the surface is blocked off, or *masked*, from the paint.

In a similar way, mask layers are used to hide content on linked layers. For example, if you were to draw a solid circle on a mask layer and link a normal layer to it, you would be able to view only the normal-layer content within that circular area **(Figure 9.18)**.

In other words, the circle on the mask layer behaves like a window to the content on the normal layer. You can use any solid shape—groups, text, and even symbols— as a mask. However, keep in mind that if you use a symbol, it can only contain a single shape or text element. Lines cannot be used as masks. You can achieve some very interesting effects by animating the element used as a mask on the mask layer (see "Creative Uses for Masks" later in this section).

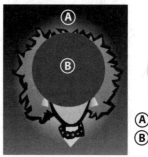

Ⓐ Normal layer
Ⓑ Solid shape on mask layer

Figure 9.18
The effect of linking a normal layer to a mask layer.

When a normal layer is linked to a mask layer, it becomes a masked layer. So although it retains all of the functionality of a normal layer, its content can be animated and contain many graphical elements. In addition, more than one normal layer can be linked to a single mask layer. In doing so, the content of each of the normal layers would only be visible through a single mask. The content of any layer(s) below the mask layer and any normal layer(s) linked to it will show through **(Figure 9.19)**.

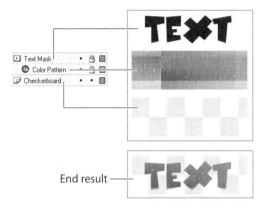

End result

Figure 9.19
Unlinked layers located below the mask and any linked layers are unaffected. In this example, the Checkerboard layer is not linked to the layer stack, so although it falls below the mask layer, it is not affected by it.

To create a mask layer:

1. Once you've decided which layer's content you want to mask, place a solid shape, text element, or symbol on the layer above it.

This object will act as the mask.

2. Right-click (Windows) or Control-click (Macintosh) the name bar of the layer on which you placed the solid object.

3. From the Layer pop-up menu that appears, choose Mask.

The content in the bottom layer will be masked. An icon will appear next to the mask layer's name and the layer directly below it indicating they are linked by a mask **(Figure 9.20)**. By default, these layers are automatically locked.

Figure 9.20
A mask layer and the layers linked to it are identified by arrow icons.

> **TIP** *You can also convert a normal layer to a mask layer by changing its type through the Layer Properties box, which you access by double-clicking the Layer icon or by selecting the layer and then choosing Modify > Layer.*

As already mentioned, only the layer directly below the mask layer is linked to it initially. However, you can link as many additional layers to a single mask layer as you want.

To link additional layers to a mask layer:

1. Select the normal layer's name bar to link it to the mask layer.

A dark-gray line will appear along the bottom indicating that layer's position relative to the other layers in the stack.

2. Drag the layer until the gray line denoting the dragged layer's position appears just below the name bar of the mask layer itself; then release.

The layer is now linked to the mask layer **(Figure 9.21)**.

End result

Figure 9.21
The content on the Phone text, Numbers and Gradient layers are all linked to the Phone mask layer, thus they all share the same mask.

To unlink a layer from a mask layer:

1. Select the linked layer's name bar.

A dark-gray line will appear along the bottom indicating that layer's position relative to the other layers in the stack.

2. Drag the layer until the gray line denoting its position appears either above the name bar of the mask layer itself or below any other normal layer; then release.

The layer is now unlinked from the mask layer.

Figure 9.22
When you reorder layers linked to a mask layer, the content within the masked area will appear in a different stacking order.

> **TIPS** *You can also unlink a normal layer from a mask layer by changing it from a masked layer back to a normal layer using the Layer Properties box. You can access this by double-clicking the masked layer icon or by choosing Modify > Layer.*
>
> *Once you've linked several layers to a mask layer, you can reorder them within the linked stack just as you would normal layers **(Figure 9.22)**.*

Because both the layers associated with a mask are initially locked, you must unlock them before you can edit their contents. Once you've completed your edits, you can re-establish the mask by locking the layers again.

To edit content on masked layers:

1. Click the masked layer you wish to edit; it will appear highlighted.

2. Click the Lock/Unlock toggle button.

You can now edit the layer's contents.

3. When you've completed your edits, right-click (Windows) or Control-click (Macintosh) the layer's name bar, and from the menu that appears choose Show Masking to re-establish the mask effect.

TIP *When editing the contents of masked layers, the mask itself can sometimes get in your way. To get around this problem, hide the mask layer using the hidden mode on the layer's name bar. To re-establish the mask effect after you've completed your edits, right-click (Windows) or Control-click (Macintosh) the name bar of one the mask's associated layers, and choose Show Masking from the contextual pop-up menu that appears.*

Creative Uses for Masks

You can achieve some interesting effects by using multiple masks, tweening or animating the element on the mask layer, or tweening or animating elements on any of the masked layers. This allows you to create real-world visual effects, such as kaleidoscopes, spotlights, and movement inside a window.

To add some visual finesse to a mask, you can create a layer directly *above* it and add a transparent shape or gradient **(Figure 9.23)**.

 Another way to enhance the look of a mask, especially when animating the mask object is to create a layer *above* the mask layer and put a symbol, group, or other element there to mimic the movement of the object on the mask layer. The following are some additional effects you can achieve via masks (look on the accompanying CD-ROM for examples of these):

Figure 9.23
You can use layers above a mask layer to add gradients or other graphical elements, making masked areas visually more interesting.

Figure 9.24
Masks let you create "magnifying" effects.

- *Magnifying glass and focus.* You can use a magnifying-glass effect to bring something into focus, make it larger, or both. By adding animation, you can make it appear that the magnifying glass is moving across the page **(Figure 9.24)**.

- *X-rays.* In this interesting effect, a "beam" passes over a normal object to reveal an X-ray version of it **(Figure 9.25)**.

- *Spotlight.* You can see this effect in Flash's own help files. We take it a step further by adding a gradient transparency to make it more lifelike **(Figure 9.26)**.

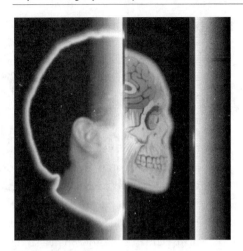

Figure 9.25
Masks can give the illusion that one is peering into hidden places.

- *Holes and windows.* This effect is best suited for creating animation or movement inside a window **(Figure 9.27)**.

- *Multiple masks.* By placing multiple masks in a scene, you can have one mask effect on top of another mask. This effect is demonstrated in the holes and windows sample.

Figure 9.26
By placing a circle with a gradiated transparency above the masked area, you can provide the illusion of diffused lighting.

Figure 9.27
Animating masked content creates a feeling of depth.

Motion Guide Layers

Motion guide layers serve a simple but important function in the animation process: They contain the lines or paths that animations on linked (normal) layers must follow. For example, if you were to place a curved line on a motion guide layer and then linked a normal layer to it, the animation on that normal layer will follow the curved line **(Figure 9.28)**. Thus, the sole purpose of the motion guide layer is to provide you with the means to animate elements in other than a straight line.

Since you need to know something about the way Flash's animation features work to understand motion guide layers, we discuss them in greater detail in Chapter 10, "Using Animation to Build Movement."

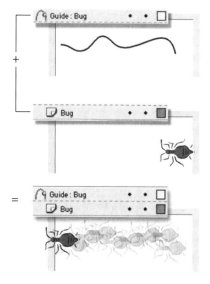

Figure 9.28
Linking a normal layer to a motion-guide layer causes the animation on the normal layer to follow a line drawn on the motion-guide layer.

Layer Properties

Now that you've learned how layers can be used in your project, it's time to look at the Layer Properties box, which allows you to configure layers in a number of ways, changing their names, behavior, and appearance in one centralized location. Each layer has a unique set of properties, which can include the following **(Figure 9.29)**:

- *Name.* Use this text box to assign a name to a layer. (See "Renaming Layers" earlier in the chapter.)

- *Show.* Sets whether a layer's graphical contents will be visible on the stage.

- *Lock.* Sets whether the layer's graphical contents can be edited on the stage.

- *Normal.* Lets you set the layer type to "normal."

- *Guide.* Allows you to set your layer as a motion guide (for creating animations that follow a path).

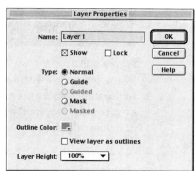

Figure 9.29
The Layer Properties dialog box.

- **Guided.** Sets your layer type as Guided, which means it will be linked to a motion-guide layer. This option is only available if the layer whose properties you're adjusting is directly below a motion-guide layer or another linked, guided layer.

- **Mask.** Allows you to set your layer as a mask (see "Mask Layers" earlier in this chapter). This type of layer masks the content of any layers linked to it.

- **Masked.** Lets you set your layer as masked, which means it's linked to a mask layer. This option is only available if the layer whose properties you're adjusting is directly below a mask layer or another linked, masked layer.

- **Outline Color.** Sets the color used for outlining graphical elements on this layer as they appear on the stage (see "Identifying Graphical Elements on Different Layers" earlier in this chapter).

- **View Layer as Outlines.** Allows you to determine whether the graphical contents of the layer will be visible as outlines on the stage.

- **Layer Height.** Allows you to set your layer's height—100 percent, 200 percent, or 300 percent. This setting is helpful if you're working with waveforms (sounds) in the layer, because the graphical representation of the waveform changes in relation to the layer's height, which helps detect specific spots in the waveform that need to be synchronized with an animation **(Figure 9.30)**.

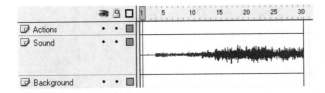

Figure 9.30
By adjusting a layer's height, sounds placed on the timeline appear larger, making them easier to work with.

To change layer properties:

1. Select the layer whose properties you wish to change.

2. From the Modify menu choose Layer, or right-click (Windows) or Control-click (Macintosh) and choose Properties from the pop-up menu.

   The Layer Properties box will appear.

3. Make your setting adjustments, then click OK.

   The layer will reflect your changes.

   TIP *The quickest way to access a layer's Property box is to double-click the Layer icon just to the left of the layer's name.*

Interactive Tutorials

- ***Working with Layers.*** This tutorial demonstrates how layers work as well as how to use them effectively.

- ***X-Ray Mask.*** This tutorial shows you how to create an X-ray effect using mask layers.

Using Animation to Build Movement

If all you wanted to do was create Web sites with cool graphics and a few text descriptions, you could easily stick with plain old HTML. However, even though HTML is effective for presenting a message, it does so in a manner that's about as exciting as watching the hair grow on your arms. If you have even an ounce of visual savvy, you'll to want to move beyond HTML and its limitations. In fact, your interest in Macromedia Flash likely stems from your desire to not only bring your message to the world but to *bring it to life* as well. That, after all, is what animation is all about.

From the early days of Disney to the current crop of movies with their unbelievable computer-generated graphics, we've long been fascinated by combining beautiful artwork with movement. Although in life much movement is left to chance, as an animator you determine not only what happens in a scene but when it happens as well. Talk about control. You can make birds fly and cartoon characters talk. You can even determine what they say and whether they get their lights punched out for saying it.

All that you've learned about Flash so far means nothing without this chapter's ingredients. This is where the real excitement begins. By animating your message, you make it much more powerful. And if you do it right, you'll find that you can control your audience's emotions in ways they'll not soon forget. Sound appealing? Read on.

How Animation Works

At one time or another you've probably seen the physical film that makes up a movie. Basically, it looks like a bunch of pictures strung together on what appears to be a strip of plastic. A Flash animation is no different. Just like a motion picture, it comprises individual frames, each slightly different than the preceding one. Special frames known as *keyframes* define where changes in your animation occur—for example, when movie elements are moved, rotated, resized, added or removed, and so on. Each frame can contain any number of symbols or graphics placed on different layers.

Equivalent to the strip of plastic film that makes up a real movie, Flash's timeline includes all of your animation's layers and frames. When the playhead on the timeline is moved manually or your movie is played, the graphic content of each frame is reflected in what you see on stage. When played back at a fast enough speed, the illusion of movement occurs. And just as in a real movie, the timeline in Flash uses scenes to shift from one area of the story to another, allowing you to break your movie's overall timeline into main sections.

The timeline can be as long as you wish and play at whatever speed (frames per second) you designate—within reason. The speed at which any movie, including your Flash movie, plays back is known as frames per second, or fps.

Flash differs from regular movies in two important ways: Frame actions can be placed at particular frames on the timeline to perform specific interactive tasks (for example, jumping to other frames in your movie or opening URLs in a browser). And Flash movies can contain mini-movies (movie clips) or buttons.

Animation Methods

Flash actually has two methods of animating: *Frame-by-frame animation,* which provides greater control over the way graphical content is animated but is more time-consuming to create, and *tweened animation,* which provides less control but is much faster to implement. Let's take a look at both.

Frame-by-frame animation

As the most recognizable and widely used form of animation, the frame-by-frame method is employed for everything from creating animated cartoons to bringing clay figures to life. This type of animation involves taking a snapshot of a frame's content, changing it slightly, taking another snapshot, changing the content again, and so on. When these snapshots are played in quick succession, movement appears and animation

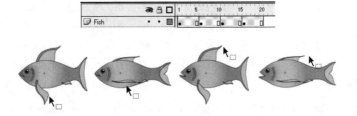

Figure 10.1
In a frame-by-frame animation, every movement made is edited manually.

is accomplished. In Flash, creating this type of animation involves moving the timeline to a frame, adjusting the content on the stage, moving the timeline to the next frame, adjusting the content on the stage, and so on.

With frame-by-frame animation, you manually edit an element's every movement on the stage (**Figure 10.1**). In addition to being time-consuming, this kind of animation can increase your movie's overall file size. Thus, you should only use frame-by-frame animation when absolutely necessary—for quick or refined movements, such as a mouth moving or hands playing a piano.

We provide a more in-depth discussion of frame-by-frame animation later in this chapter in "Creating Animation."

Tweened animation

Since we use computers to make our lives easier, there's no reason to manually create an animation that requires smooth transitions in movement, size, rotation, shape, or color when Flash can do so automatically.

With a tweened animation, you use keyframes to define two points in a movie element's movement: its appearance at the beginning of the animation and at the end. You determine how long it should take (based on frames) for the animation to get from its starting point to its ending point, and then Flash calculates what the animated graphic should look like in all of the frames in between (**Figure 10.2**).

Figure 10.2
In a tweened animation, you define the look of the graphic at the beginning and ending keyframes, and Flash calculates how it should look in the intermediate frames.

As you can see, it's much faster to produce animations using tweening than via the frame-by-frame method. Tweened animations are also much easier to edit because there are only two editable frames—the beginning and ending keyframes. Changing either one of these will cause Flash to recalculate the look of all of the frames in between. In contrast, you must manually edit each frame of a frame-by-frame animation.

As you begin to animate, you'll find that tweening works for most animation tasks that involve fluid and smooth movements as well as transitions, *or morphing,* of shapes. Frame-by-frame animation works best for delicate, complex, and quick movements. Layers make it possible for you to use both types of animation simultaneously on different graphic elements that appear at the same time in a scene.

Understanding the Timeline

The timeline is where the bulk of the animation process takes place. This is where you control how fast a movie element moves, when it enters and exits the scene, and its depth in relation to other elements in the scene (**Figure 10.3**). Most of what you'll learn in this chapter will also apply to animating symbols' timelines (especially graphic and movie-clip symbols).

Layers

Although we provided a detailed discussion of layers in Chapter 9, we think you'll find it helpful to review a couple of points here—especially those that have to do with the relationship between layers, frames, and the stage.

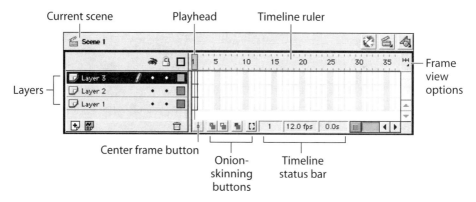

Figure 10.3
The various parts of the timeline.

A single frame on the timeline can have multiple layers, the content of which you can view on the stage (**Figure 10.4**). (For more information about how content on various layers represents the composite animation on the stage, see "Putting It All Together" later in this chapter.) This means you can split the various animated elements of each frame's content into individual layers. Just remember that a single frame can comprise hundreds of layers. Layers are useful for creating complex animations in which a number of movie elements are used simultaneously but in different ways.

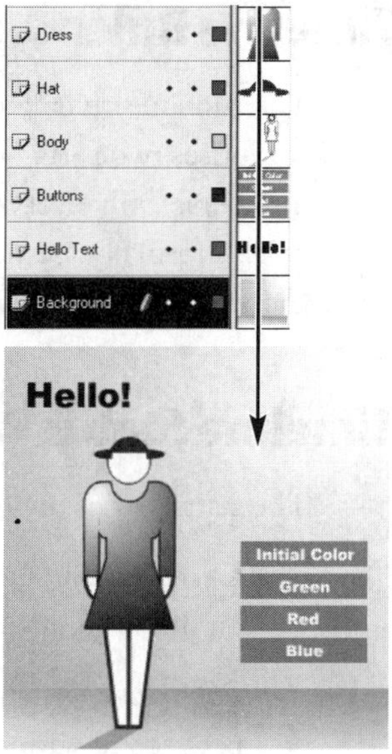

Figure 10.4
The stage reflects the graphical content of all visible layers.

Playhead

The playhead is to the timeline what the Arrow tool is to the stage. It allows you to identify the frame being edited, select a frame to work on, and *scrub* the movie—that is, watch it play by dragging the playhead. The red vertical line of the playhead stretches across multiple layers to help you identify all of a frame's content.

To move the playhead to a particular frame:

- ◆ Click a frame on any available layer, or select a frame on the timeline ruler.

  The playhead will jump to the frame you selected.

To scrub the playhead:

- ◆ Click and drag the playhead left or right.

  As you move the playhead, your movie will play forward or backward, depending on the direction you're dragging the playhead.

  > **TIP** To perform either one of these actions, your timeline must include at least one blank frame. The white and gray rectangular boxes that appear initially on the timeline are placeholder frames. With the exception of the first frame, you must add frames manually to the timeline. For more on this, see "Inserting Frames" later in this chapter.

Timeline Ruler

The timeline ruler provides an incremented display of frames along the timeline. It comprises two parts—frame *ticks,* which are small vertical lines on the ruler, and frame numbers. Only every fifth frame is indicated by a number; the rest are indicated by ticks. Normally, frame numbers are centered between the two ticks that define the frame. Three-digit frame numbers are left aligned to the frame they represent.

Timeline Status Bar

The status bar of the timeline provides the following information (**Figure 10.5**):

- *Current frame.* Indicates the frame number whose contents are currently visible on the stage. Also indicates the current position of the playhead.

- *Frame rate.* When your movie is not playing, this box displays the current frames-per-second setting for your movie. When your movie is playing in the authoring environment, this box (which is dynamically updated) reflects the *actual* playback speed. Actual playback speed can differ from the frames-per-second setting you selected in the Movie Properties dialog box—often as the result of processor-intensive animation, which can cause your movie to slow in places.

  TIP *Double-clicking the frame-rate area of the timeline status bar will open the Movie Properties dialog box.*

- *Elapsed time.* Indicates the amount of time (in seconds) between the first frame of your movie and the current frame. The number is dynamically updated as you play your movie in the authoring environment.

Current frame   Frame rate   Elapsed time

Figure 10.5
The various elements of the timeline status bar.

Planning Your Project

Choosing the Proper Frame Rate

In one of the old I Love Lucy episodes, Lucy and Ethel get jobs packing chocolates into boxes as they come off an assembly line. In this classic TV moment, the humor stems from a malfunctioning conveyor belt that begins spitting out chocolates faster then Lucy and Ethel can process them—in the end, the gals resort to stuffing candies in their mouths to keep pace. A huge mess—and much hilarity—ensue.

The lesson here is that faster is not always better. Although it would be nice to think that by upping your movie's frame rate, you could create video-like transitions that never skipped, jumped, or appeared choppy, Flash's reliance on processor speed means this is not always possible. In fact, a higher frame rate can sometimes even harm your presentation.

No matter what frame rate you choose, each processor can handle information only so quickly—and because there are so many factors involved, you can't possibly know just how fast that is. If a particular computer can render your movie at a maximum rate of 20 fps, setting Flash's fps to 100 won't improve matters. That computer will still show your movie at 20 fps—max. Now, a faster computer may be able to play the same movie at 100 fps, but few of us own the supermachines capable of this.

So upping a movie's speed doesn't help; in fact, it could even slow things down. Here's how: Let's say your presentation is 10 seconds long. At 12 fps, there are 120 frames (10 seconds x 12 frames per second) that need to be played through from beginning to end. If you increase your fps rate to 20, you will have 200 frames from start to finish—or an additional 80 frames to draw over the course of your presentation. While slower computers can handle 120 frames over 10 seconds fairly easily, those additional 80 frames could slow your movie to a crawl because they make more than 50 percent more work for the computer to accomplish in the same 10 seconds (or over the course of your presentation). Now can you see how you could end up with precisely the opposite effect you were trying to achieve?

So, what's a reasonable frame rate? The default setting of 12 is usually a good rate to try, with 20 fps at the high end and 24 fps the absolute maximum you should consider. (Of course, this is just our humble opinion.) The only exception to this rule would be if you were to export your Flash presentation as a video file such as QuickTime or Windows AVI. Because these formats are not as processor intensive, you can pump up the frame rate without too many problems.

We don't want you to think you can't produce impressive results within these parameters. In fact, quite the opposite is true: There are many examples of beautiful and exciting Flash content out there that have been created using these exact guidelines. All it takes is some planning.

Center Frame Button

If you click the Center Frame button in the lower left of the timeline, Flash centers the playhead's current frame position on the timeline. This means that if you scroll to Frame 900 of a 1,000-frame movie while the playhead remains on Frame 200, clicking this button will cause the timeline to quickly scroll back to Frame 200, with the playhead centered on the timeline (**Figure 10.6**).

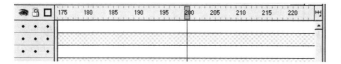

Figure 10.6
Clicking the Center Frame button positions the playhead on the center of the timeline.

Frame View Options

The Frame View button, which is located in the upper right of the timeline window, allows you to view frames on the timeline in a number of ways. By clicking this button, you are presented with the following options:

- *Frame Width.* Options include Tiny, Small, Normal, Medium, and Large (**Figure 10.7**).

- *Frame Height.* This option shrinks the height of frames on the timeline by 20 percent. If your movie contains a number of layers, choosing this option shrinks the entire stack of layers in a scene, which may help you to avoid having to constantly scroll the timeline to access frames on a particular layer.

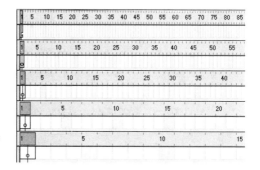

Figure 10.7
The effect of the Frame Width setting on the timeline.

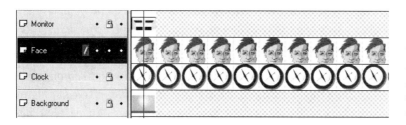

Figure 10.8
The graphics of each frame are scaled to fill boxes that represent frames.

- **Tinted Frames.** By default, sections of frames are tinted different colors to help you distinguish them. You can turn this option on or off (see the next section for more details).

- **Preview.** This option causes the graphics on each frame in every layer to be displayed within the boxes on the timeline that represent frames. Flash scales the graphics to fit within the frame boxes (**Figure 10.8**).

- **Preview in Context.** With one exception, this option is similar to the previous one: The graphics are scaled to show their size relative to the overall movie (**Figure 10.9**).

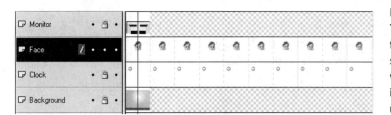

Figure 10.9
The graphics of each frame, shown in their size relative to the whole movie, appear in boxes that represent frames.

Timeline Menu

The context-sensitive Timeline menu provides quick access to several timeline-related commands, including adding and deleting frames, defining frame properties, creating motion tweens, and more (**Figure 10.10**).

To display the Timeline menu:

- Right-click (Windows) or Control-click (Macintosh) any frame on the timeline to make the Timeline pop-up menu appear.

The contextual menu contains the following options:

- **Create Motion Tween.** Uses the current frame's content to automatically create a motion tween. To do so, it converts all content into graphic symbols. We discuss this option in more detail later in the chapter.

- **Insert Frame.** Adds a regular frame after the currently selected one. If you select a range of regular frames, Flash will add that number of

Figure 10.10
The Timeline menu.

frames to the timeline. If you select a placeholder frame, Flash will add regular frames up to the point of the selected placeholder frame.

- **Remove Frame.** Deletes the currently selected frame. If you select a range of frames, this command deletes all of them.

- **Insert Keyframe.** Inserts a keyframe on the timeline at the point where the cursor was located when you activated the menu. If a regular frame was at this position, the keyframe replaces it; if a placeholder frame was at this position, a keyframe is inserted and regular frames are added so that there are no placeholder frames prior to the newly inserted keyframe. A newly inserted keyframe starts out with the same content as the previous keyframe.

- **Insert Blank Keyframe.** Inserts a blank keyframe on the timeline at the position where the cursor was located when the menu was activated. This command executes in the same fashion as the Insert Keyframe command above.

- **Clear Keyframe.** Converts the selected keyframe to a regular frame. If a range of keyframes is selected, this command converts all of them.

- **Select All.** Selects all frames on all unlocked and visible layers of the current scene. This is useful for duplicating entire scenes.

- **Cut Frames.** Cuts a frame or range of frames for pasting elsewhere.

- **Copy Frames.** Copies a frame or range of frames for pasting elsewhere.

- **Paste Frames.** Pastes any frames on the clipboard onto the timeline after the currently selected frame. If the clipboard contains a range of frames across multiple layers, these frames and layers will be pasted onto the timeline in their same relative positions.

- **Reverse Frames.** Flips, or reverses, the positions of the currently selected range of frames. The result is reversed playback.

- **Synchronize Symbols.** Displays looped graphic symbols properly even if the loop occupies an odd number of frames on the main timeline. For example, if you placed an instance of a graphic symbol with a timeline that looped every 10 frames on the main timeline to play over a stretch of 20 frames, it would loop twice without a hitch. If, however, you placed an instance of this same symbol on the main timeline to play over a stretch of 17 frames, it would loop once and then be abruptly cut off at Frame 17 during the second loop. By synchronizing symbols, you ensure that the graphic symbol will loop properly within the allotted frames on the main timeline.

- *Actions.* Opens the Actions panel so that you can add frame actions.

- *Panels.* Opens a submenu that allows you to open the Frame or Sound panels, both of which are used when working with frames.

> **TIP** *All of these commands are also available on the Insert and Modify > Frames menus on the menu bar. When selected, they affect the currently selected frame or range of frames.*

Working with Scenes

Scenes provide an easy way to break your movie's timeline into sections of frames. You can also think of scenes as animated "pages," each of which can be unique, though they all belong to the same timeline (**Figure 10.11**). A single movie can comprise any number of scenes played in the order you place them. And each movie automatically starts with one scene; you manually add (or delete) the rest.

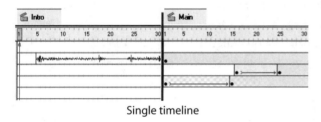

Single timeline

Figure 10.11
Scenes allow you to break up a single timeline into manageable sections.

Let's say you have a movie that consists of three scenes: Intro, Body, and Conclusion.

Your movie will first play the Intro from beginning to end, then the Body, and finally the Conclusion (at which point the movie will stop). Keep in mind, however, that you can also easily reorder these scenes to change their flow.

Scenes serve no function other than to help you organize content. A timeline that spans multiple scenes is still considered a single timeline—important to remember, especially if you're working with and updating variables in a timeline (for more on this, see Chapter 12, "Using ActionScript for Advanced Interactivity"). Scenes are not available for symbols.

Scene Management

Scene management can encompass (among other things) adding and deleting frames, renaming scenes, and changing the order in which scenes appear in the movie—most of which you can accomplish via the Scene panel.

To display the Scene panel:

◆ From the Window menu choose Panels > Scene.

The Scene panel will appear (**Figure 10.12**), and the movie's scenes will be listed.

To add a scene, do one of the following:

● On the Scene panel click the Add Scene button.

● From the Insert menu choose Scene.

Either one of these actions creates a new scene with the default name Scene appended by a number. The timeline also automatically jumps to your newly created scene.

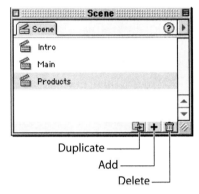

Duplicate ——
Add ——
Delete ——

Figure 10.12
The Scene panel.

To delete a scene:

1. On the Scene panel, select the scene you wish to delete from the scene list.

2. Click the Delete Scene button on the Scene panel.

An alert box will ask you to confirm the deletion.

3. Click OK.

or

1. Go to the scene you wish to delete.

2. From the Insert menu choose Remove Scene.

An alert box will ask you to confirm the deletion.

3. Click OK.

To rename a scene:

1. From the scene list in the Scene panel, double-click the scene whose name you wish to change.

2. Enter a new name for the scene, then press Return/Enter.

To reorder scenes:

1. From the scene list in the Scene panel, click and hold the name of the scene you'd like to reorder.

2. Drag the scene to a new position in the list and release (**Figure 10.13**).

The scenes will now play sequentially in the order they appear.

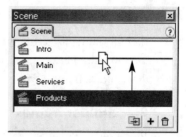

Figure 10.13
Repositioning a scene in the Scene panel determines when it plays in relation to other scenes in the movie.

To navigate between scenes, do one of the following:

- From the scene list in the Scene panel, click the name of the scene you wish to navigate to.

  The timeline will automatically jump to that scene.

- From the View menu choose Go To and then one of the available scenes from the list.

Duplicating scenes

Duplicating a scene allows you to make an exact replica of it—including all frames, layers, animations, and sounds—to form a new scene. This enables you to use one scene as a starting point for a new one.

To duplicate a scene:

1. From the scene list in the Scene panel, click the name of the scene you wish to duplicate.

2. Press the Duplicate Scene button on the Scene panel.

The new scene is given a default name and appears on the scene list.

Frames

Dictating each segment of time and movement, frames are at the core of any animation. The number of frames in your movie and the speed at which they're played back will determine your movie's overall length.

Frame Types

Not all frames are created equal. Different frames types are designed for certain animation tasks. However, by quickly glancing at the timeline, you should be able to easily determine a frame's type, which can help you diagnose animation problems.

Placeholder frames

Placeholder frames are not really frames but rather rectangular boxes where frames can be placed. They are indicated by the grid on the timeline. Devoid of content, these frames make up the majority of the timeline when you begin your Flash project. Although you cannot manually create placeholder frames, they will remain present until you convert them to actual frames. Because your movie needs real frames on at least one layer of the timeline in order to play, it will cease playing once it reaches a point where all layers contain only placeholder frames (**Figure 10.14**).

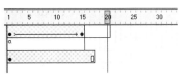

Figure 10.14
This scene will not play past Frame 20 because Frame 21 and beyond contain only placeholder frames.

Keyframes

Any time you wish your animation to undergo a visual change or you want an action to occur, you must use a keyframe at that point on the timeline (**Figure 10.15**). Obviously, frame-by-frame animations require numerous keyframes because you must edit each frame individually. A tweened animation, on the other hand, requires only two keyframes—one that begins the tween and one that ends the tween. Changes that occur between the beginning and ending keyframes are calculated by Flash and thus do not require additional keyframes.

Although most keyframes contain content that is visible on the stage, they can also be blank—usually the result of removing a movie element from the animation. Every new project you begin in Flash starts with a blank keyframe on Frame 1 of Layer 1. A regular keyframe is identified by a solid black dot; a blank keyframe is identified by a small, black vertical line; and a keyframe with an attached action is identified with a small *a*.

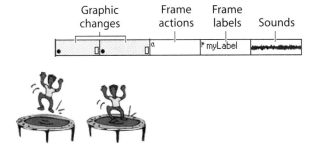

Figure 10.15
Keyframes, identified by vertical lines to the left of each frame, define where changes occur on the timeline.

Regular frames

Regular frames always follow keyframes and contain the same content as the last keyframe on the same layer. Confused? Let us explain.

A keyframe on the timeline denotes a change; regular frames proceeding a keyframe denote the duration of that change. Let's say you have a movie element that you want to appear in the middle of the stage at the beginning of your movie: You would need to place that element on a keyframe at Frame 1. If you wanted it to remain in the middle of the stage until it jumped to the top-left corner at Frame 11, you would need to make Frames 2 through 10 regular frames (since the element will not move or change), and then add a keyframe at Frame 11 to denote a change in the element's on-stage position (**Figure 10.16**).

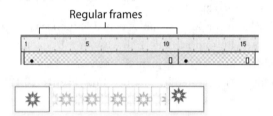

Figure 10.16
Regular frames always follow keyframes and contain the same content as the last keyframe on the same layer.

A keyframe and the span of regular frames that follow it are known as a *keyframe sequence.* The timeline can contain any number of keyframe sequences. If the keyframe in a sequence contains content that is visible on the stage, the regular frames that follow it will appear gray. If the keyframe in a sequence contains no content visible on the stage, the regular frames that follow it appear white (**Figure 10.17**).

Tweened frames

Tweened frames are always part of a tween sequence consisting of two keyframes and any number of frames in between. The frames between the two keyframes represent computer-calculated graphics.

You can perform two types of tweening with Flash: *motion tweening* and *shape tweening.* You use motion tweening to tween the size, position, rotation, and so on of symbols, groups, or text blocks in your animation. You use shape tweening to morph one simple shape into another—for example, smoothly transforming a red circle into a blue square

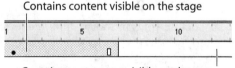

Contains content visible on the stage

Contains content not visible on the stage

Figure 10.17
If the keyframe in a sequence contains content visible on the stage, the regular frames that follow are gray. If the keyframe in a sequence contains no content on the stage, the regular frames that follow are white.

or the letter *T* into the letter *I* (**Figure 10.18**). Shape tweening only works with simple shapes such as lines and vector shapes, not symbols or groups. If text is to be used in a shape tween, you must first break it apart, then place each letter you plan to tween on a separate layer (see below).

If you plan to simultaneously tween multiple elements in a scene, each tween requires its own layer. Translation? You can't tween separate movie elements on the same layer at the same time.

A motion-tweened sequence is identified by at least two keyframes separated by intermediate frames with a black arrow and light-blue background. A shape-tweened sequence is identified by at least two keyframes separated by intermediate frames with a black arrow and light-green background. A problem in a tween sequence—for example, a tween that lacks a starting or ending keyframe—is indicated by a dashed line (**Figure 10.19**).

Motion tween

Shape tween

Figure 10.18
Motion tweening tweens the size, position, rotation, and so on. Shape tweening morphs one simple shape into another.

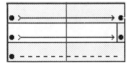

Figure 10.19
A motion tween (top), a shape tween (middle), and a problem tween (bottom).

Working with Frames

Now that you're familiar with the frame types and how to use them to create animations, let's look at the ways you can work with them on the timeline. For more information about using frames, see "Creating and Editing Animations" later in this chapter.

Selecting frames

Before you can move, duplicate, or change a frame, you must first select it. When a frame is selected, the playhead automatically moves to that frame and the contents of its layers appear on the stage.

To select an individual frame:

◆ Press and hold the Control key (Windows) or Command key (Macintosh), then click a frame once to select it.

The frame will appear highlighted. The selected frame becomes the current frame, and any commands pertaining to frames will affect it.

TIP *You can select the beginning and end frames of a keyframe or tweened sequence by simply clicking them.*

To select a range of frames:

◆ Press and hold the Control key (Windows) or the Command key (Macintosh), then click the first frame you want to be part of the range and drag to the last frame you want to be included, and then release.

All selected frames will appear highlighted. You can now move, delete, and duplicate them as a whole.

To select a keyframe or tweened sequence:

◆ Click once on any frame that is part of the sequence.

The sequence will appear highlighted (**Figure 10.20**). You can now move, delete, and duplicate the sequence.

TIP *Pressing the Shift key allows you to select multiple sequences on the timeline.*

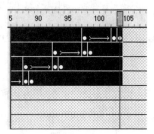

Figure 10.20
A range of selected frames is highlighted to show that they have been selected.

Moving and duplicating frames

By moving frames, you can edit the points where actions occur along the timeline, such as the starting and ending points of frame sequences or when frame actions occur.

By duplicating frames, you can use their content elsewhere along the timeline without reconstructing that content.

To move or duplicate frames:

1. Select a frame, range of frames, or frame sequence.

2. Click and drag the selected frames to a new location on the timeline, then release (**Figure 10.21**).

3. To duplicate the frame or range of frames at a new location, hold down the Alt key (Windows) or the Option key (Macintosh) while you drag.

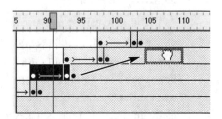

Figure 10.21
Drag selected frames to their new location and release.

Extending or shortening the length of a frame sequence

Selecting, then moving the beginning or end frame of a keyframe sequence determines its length on the timeline and thus the duration of its content in the overall animation.

Selecting, then moving the beginning or end frame of a tweened sequence determines not only its length on the timeline and its duration in the overall animation, but also how quickly the tween occurs between the beginning and ending frames.

Adding and inserting regular frames

Adding or inserting frames at any point along a layer changes the timeline position of all frames on that layer that exist to the right of the added or inserted frame(s).

To add regular frames to the timeline:

1. Select a placeholder frame on the timeline.

2. Choose Insert > Frame.

Regular frames are added until the selected placeholder frame is reached.

To insert regular frames in the middle of an existing range of frames:

1. Select a single frame, range of frames, or frame sequence within the middle of an existing range of frames.

2. Choose Insert > Frame.

The same number of frames you selected will be inserted onto the timeline, and the previously selected frames will be moved to the right of the newly inserted ones.

Adding keyframes

As mentioned earlier, you use keyframes on the timeline to define when changes occur in your animation. Thus, your animation is likely to contain numerous keyframes. When you add a keyframe to a layer, you have the choice of adding a normal or blank keyframe. When adding a normal keyframe, any graphical content (instances of symbols, text elements, and so on) that is part of the last keyframe on the same layer is automatically duplicated in the new keyframe. Adding a blank keyframe to a layer places a point on the timeline where that layer's contents are no longer visible (**Figure 10.22**).

Blank keyframe

| 45 | 50 | 55 | 60 | 65 | 70 | 75 | 80 |

Figure 10.22
The difference between adding a normal or blank keyframe.

To add a keyframe to the timeline:

1. Select a placeholder or regular frame on the timeline.

2. Choose Insert > Keyframe/Blank Keyframe to add a keyframe.

If the originally selected frame was a placeholder frame, regular frames are added up to the point of the newly created keyframe. If the originally selected frame was a regular frame, it is simply converted to a keyframe/blank keyframe.

To add a range of keyframes to the timeline:

1. Select a range of frames or a frame sequence.

2. Choose Modify > Frames > Convert to Keyframes or Convert to Blank Keyframes.

A range of keyframes will be added.

Removing frames

Removing frames at any point along a layer changes the timeline position of all frames on that layer to the right of the removed frame(s).

To remove frames:

1. Select a single frame, range of frames, or frame sequence.

2. Choose Insert > Remove Frame.

Reversing frames

Reversing frames will cause the graphical content of the selected frames to play in reverse.

To reverse frames:

1. Select a sequence of at least two frames.

2. Choose Modify > Frames > Reverse.

Adding a frame action

Frame actions allow your movie to perform an action when the timeline reaches a particular frame during playback. For more information, see Chapter 11, "Basic Actions for Building Interactivity."

To add a frame action:

1. Right-click (Windows) or Control-click (Macintosh) on the the keyframe where you would like to add an action, and select Actions from the menu that appears.

   The Actions panel will appear.

2. Click the Add Action button to add any actions to this frame, then close the Action panel.

   The keyframe now includes a small *a* to indicate an action has been assigned to it.

Labels and comments

Just as a name is used to identify a face in a crowd, a frame label in Flash is used to identify a keyframe in your movie. This is especially useful when assigning frame or button actions to certain frames in your movie (see Chapter 11, "Basic Actions for Building Interactivity").

Imagine setting up your movie so that several buttons, when clicked, begin playing your movie at Frame 35. You decide later, however, that you want to delete five frames from the beginning of your movie. This means that the content which once began at Frame 35 will now begin at Frame 30; however, the buttons you set up earlier will still go to Frame 35 when clicked—not the result you were looking for. By using a label, you can alleviate this problem.

Assigning a label—for example, MyLabel—to Frame 35 and setting all of those button-clicks to begin playing your movie from that label would allow you to add and delete frames as needed; button clicks would always point to MyLabel.

Frame comments allow you to write notes, or comments, in frames of your movie. In this way you can remind yourself of the thought process that informed some portion of your movie's timeline.

Because frame labels are exported with your final movie, they can affect its overall file size. For this reason, you should use short, descriptive labels. Frame comments, in contrast, are not exported and can therefore contain as much information as you want.

Where room on the timeline permits, frame labels are identified by a small red flag followed by the label name, and frame comments are identified by two green forward slashes followed by the comment text (**Figure 10.23**). Where room on the timeline does not permit, only icons appear with no accompanying text.

To add a label or comment to a keyframe:

1. Click the keyframe once to select it.

2. Choose Window > Panels > Frame.

The Frame panel will appear.

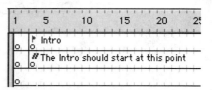

Figure 10.23
A frame label and a frame comment.

3. In the Label box, enter the text you would like to use as a label for this keyframe. Entering two forward slashes (//) prior to any text creates a frame comment.

4. Press Return/Enter.

The label or comment will appear on the timeline.

TIP *If you pause your cursor over a frame on the timeline, a "tooltip" appears with a description of the frame type. If the frame your cursor is paused over contains a label or comment, the label name or comment text appears.*

Onion-Skinning

If you've ever watched a pencil-and-paper animator, you've probably noticed that he or she customarily works with a pencil in one hand and a couple of pages, or eventual frames, of the animation in the other. While drawing on the current frame, the animator will flip among frames that precede and follow it to get an idea how the drawing sequence will emulate movement when it's eventually played. Flash provides similar functionality in the form of *onion-skinning,* which allows you to view and edit multiple frames simultaneously.

To view multiple frames using onion-skinning:

◆ Click the Onion Skin button (**Figure 10.24**).

This brings up a set of onion-skinning markers, which appear next to the playhead on the timeline. The content of the frames between these two markers now appears on the stage, some before the current frame and some after (**Figure 10.25**). The current frame is the one over which the playhead is

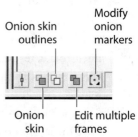

Figure 10.24
The Onion Skin buttons.

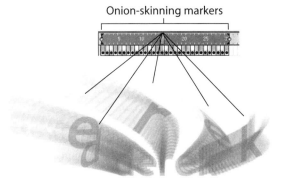

Onion-skinning markers

Figure 10.25
When onion-skinning is turned on, the stage reflects the content of multiple frames, with the current frame's content the most visible.

positioned. In this mode, it is the only one whose contents are editable. Content on uneditable frames appears dimmed in color. Dragging the playhead allows you to see onion-skinning on other frames.

TIP *You will not be able to see content on locked or hidden layers when using onion-skinning. Thus, you can lock or hide layers to specify which content is visible and editable when onion-skinning.*

To view onion-skinned frames as outlines:

◆ Click the Onion Skin Outlines button.

This option works in much the same fashion as the Onion Skin button, with the exception that content on all but the current frame appears as outlines. You can assign a different outline color to each frame to help identify which layer's content needs to be edited.

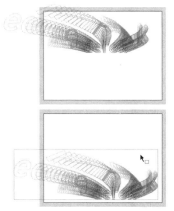

Figure 10.26
The Edit Multiple Frames feature lets you edit the content of multiple frames at the same time.

Editing multiple frames

Normally, you can only edit content on the current frame when using onion-skinning; however, by making multiple frames editable during onion-skinning, you can select, move, rotate, resize, and otherwise alter the content of multiple frames simultaneously. This is a great feature for moving entire sections of the timeline **(Figure 10.26)**. For example, if you wanted to move a layer's content by 50 pixels, you could manually place the playhead at a frame, move the layer's contents, move the playhead forward, move the layer's contents, and so forth; however, this is a tedious process, not to mention a waste of time. By editing multiple frames simultaneously, you can move everything on the layer across multiple frames simultaneously.

To make multiple frames editable:

1. Unlock and make visible all layers whose content you wish to move.

2. Click the Edit Multiple Frames button.

All content on unlocked and visible frames between the onion-skinning markers becomes editable, meaning you can move, rotate, and otherwise edit it as a whole.

Onion-skinning markers

You use the onion-skinning markers to determine the range of frames that are onion-skinned. Usually, the markers maintain their same positions relative to the playhead; however, you can also anchor them while the playhead moves. You can adjust onion-skinning markers manually or via the Modify Onion Markers pop-up menu.

To move the onion-skinning markers manually:

◆ Click a marker and drag it to its new position, then release.

You can't move either marker beyond the playhead.

To modify the onion-skinning markers:

◆ Click the Modify Onion Markers button.

This brings up the Modify Onion Markers pop-up menu, which includes the following options:

Always Show Markers. Normally, onion-skinning markers only appear when onion-skinning is turned on. This option causes them to be displayed even when it's not.

Anchor Onion. This option anchors, or locks, the onion-skinning markers to their current position—that is, they remain stationary rather than retain their positions relative to the playhead.

Onion 2. This option lets you quickly set onion-skinning markers two frames before and two frames after the current frame (playhead position).

Onion 5. This option lets you quickly set onion-skinning markers five frames before and five frames after the current frame.

Onion All. Onion-skins all the frames in the current scene. Obviously, this is best suited for viewing a limited number of layers; lock or hide certain layers to make them invisible.

Creating Animation

In this section, we'll take you through the process of creating three simple types of animations: frame by frame, motion tweened, and shape tweened. The techniques you'll learn here can be used to create animations on a graphic or movie-clip symbol's timeline as well as your movie's main timeline.

Planning Your Project

Processor Considerations

Hollywood has a way of distorting reality. Just as teenage girls drooled at the thought of being trapped on a sinking Titanic with Leonardo DiCaprio, anyone who regularly uses a computer has surely salivated over the speed at which they run in the movies. In Hollywood's vision of the world, every home computer is connected to the Net; you never have to boot your machine; and that desktop box contains enough power to coordinate a shuttle mission, find a cure for cancer, and crunch out the graphics for Jurassic Park—all at the same time!

*Well, here's the cruel reality: Processor speed—which today can range from 200 MHz to faster than 1 GHz—is a major determinant of computer power. And this means that what takes 1 second to show up on the 1-GHz machine could take 10 seconds or longer on a slower machine (**Figure 10.27**). As you can imagine, this is a major factor in animation. On slow computers, your animated movie will probably end up playing fairly choppy. And you can forget about those cool motion effects. All is not lost, however: Even though you can't anticipate every possibility in creating your movie, you can take some steps to minimize the effect slower machines will have on your movie's playback. For starters, you can pay attention to the following guidelines:*

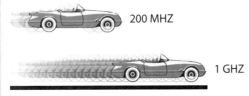
200 MHZ

1 GHZ

Figure 10.27
The speed at which your presentation will play varies depending on the processor speed of a viewer's machine.

- ***Avoid animating too many things at once.*** *By too many, we mean primarily large objects that require a lot of screen space to move. Although it's tempting to animate everything at once, all you need to do is play your movie on a slow computer to realize that a little self-control is in order—that is, if you can stay awake long enough to watch your movie play!*

- **Animate in the smallest area possible.** *Not surprisingly, it takes less process-ing power to animate something small than it does to animate something large. You can usually animate several small things simultaneously without too much trouble. So, instead of making that monster movie element rotate, make it smaller and do something else creative with it. And if you do decide to animate a large movie element, avoid animating anything else on the screen at the same time. This way, you free up additional resources to handle the large object.*

- **Avoid tweening too many objects at once.** *Although tweening can be a real time-saver in developing your Flash project, it eats up a lot of resources. Use tweening all you can; just be sure not to use a bunch of it at once.*

By following these guidelines, you can avoid overstressing a slow processor.

Creating a Frame-by-Frame Animation

Creating frame-by-frame animations usually entails numerous keyframes, each with different content. You can use frame-by-frame animation in conjunction with other forms of animation; you just need to place each type on a separate layer.

To create a simple frame-by-frame animation:

1. Create a new Flash document by choosing File > New.

Your new Flash document will initially include a single layer with one keyframe.

2. Click the Text tool on the Drawing toolbar.

3. With the Character panel open, select any available font, choose 48 as the size, and specify whatever color you wish.

4. Click the stage to start a text label, and type a capital *H* in the lower left corner of the stage.

5. Select the next placeholder frame on the timeline (it will appear highlighted), then choose Insert > Keyframe.

A keyframe will be inserted on Frame 2 that initially contains the same content as Frame 1 (our capital *H).*

6. Click the Arrow tool on the Drawing toolbar, then select the text label (if it's not already selected).

7. With the *H* selected, hold down the Shift key and press the up-arrow key three times to move the text element upward.

8. Select the Text tool again, place its insertion point just after the *H* you just moved, and type a capital *E*.

9. Repeat Steps 5 through 8 until you have completed the word *HELLO* (**Figure 10.28**).

Figure 10.28
The entire sequence of our frame-by-frame animation.

If you move the playhead on the timeline, you can see your animation spring to life.

Obviously, this is a simplified animation used to demonstrate the process. Some frame-by-frame animations consist of many layers with numerous elements requiring movement at each keyframe. The frame-by-frame interactive tutorial on the CD covers this same animation with a few additional techniques thrown in.

> **TIP** *If you want your animation to loop, place a Go To action at the end of the animation that tells it to Go To and Play Frame 1 of the same scene. For more on this action, see Chapter 11 "Basic Actions for Building Interactivity."*

Creating a Shape-Tweened Animation

Shape tweening, or *morphing,* describes the process of transforming one simple shape into another over a period of time. In Flash, you can tween the shape, color, transparency, size, and location of a vector graphic element.

Although Flash will normally attempt to tween two shapes in the most logical manner without any additional input from you, this will not always produce the results you were looking for since each shape has unique curves and corners. When you need complete control over a shape tween, you can use *shape hints* to select common points on the beginning and ending shapes that correspond to each other in the shape tween.

You cannot shape-tween symbols, groups, or bitmaps—only simple shapes and text (and the latter only if you've broken it apart first; see Chapter 4, "Text"). You can, however, *motion*-tween symbols, groups, and text. Although more than one shape can be tweened on a layer at a time, you'll get better results from using separate layers.

In the following, we'll show you how to create a simple animation of a box tweening into the letter *V.* You'll learn how to tween not only shapes but color and location as well. A little later, we'll show you how to use shape hints to gain more control over the actual tween. An interactive tutorial on the CD demonstrates the way we put this animation together.

2Advanced

http://www.2advanced.com

2Advanced is an excellent example of the work of Eric Jordan, a well-respected motion graphics designer in the Flash community. Jordan's unique style is evident in the incredible detail he used to create this site. Numerous, well-planned transitions have been incorporated using tweening, and the interactive interface—featuring menus, draggable windows, sound controls, and more—highlights Flash's interactive capabilities.

Banja

http://www.banja.com

Following its numerous successes in online entertainment, the French company cHmAn created Banja, an entertainment server where players navigate through an interactive environment in 3D animation. To play, users click on various spots in a scene, which transports them to new areas in the game. This site is an excellent example of how a Flash movie can flow in a nonlinear manner, since various choices made by the user result in a different outcome each time the game is played.

Blair Witch Store

http://store.artisanent.com/cgi-bin/storeartisan/bwstore/flash/index.html

The Flash version of the Blair Witch store, designed by Click Active Media *(http://www. clickmedia.com)*, is one of the most interactive shopping carts you'll find on the Web. To purchase items, users drag them from the main window into their shopping carts, which evokes a series of opening and closing doors and associated sounds. When they're finished, Flash programming enables the shopping cart data to be sent to a server to complete the transaction.

Cyberteks Design

http://www.cyberteks.net

Cyberteks Design has all the recognition you might expect of a world-class design firm—it has won national awards from highly coveted competitions and it's showcased on Macromedia's Web site. The sophisticated motion graphics employed throughout the site display an obvious mastery of Flash. But what really makes this site exemplary is the fact that it was designed by 12-year-old Keith Peiris, president of Cyberteks Design. It is an inspiration to all of us who work in the world of Flash to know that despite the tool's complexity, with a little effort and practice even very young Flash developers can redefine the face of design.

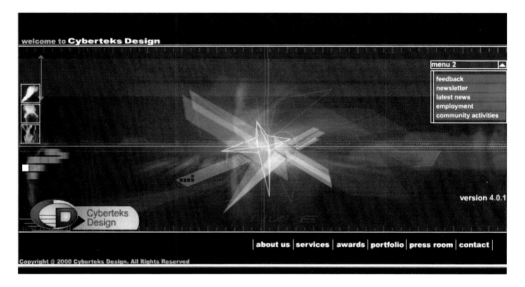

Derbauer

http://www.derbauer.de

There are so many brilliant and unique uses of Flash on the Web that it becomes difficult to choose between them. Debauer, however, is in a class all its own. It is not so much a site as an experience that is both cool and creepy. The developers have combined the extensive use of mask layers, unique bitmap effects, and a synced soundtrack to deliver a simple, but remarkable user interface that can send chills down your spine. Don't miss it!

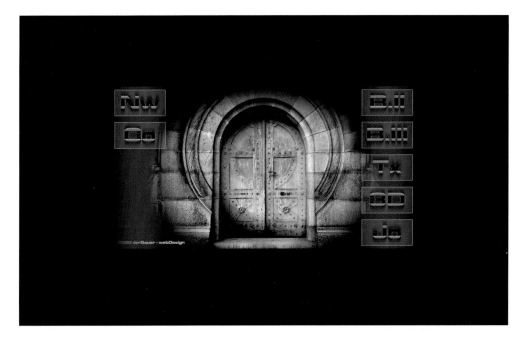

The Flash Challenge
http://www.flashchallenge.com

The Flash Challenge, an ongoing Flash competition site, is both an impressive example of Flash technology at work and a great resource for Flash developers. The sophisticated fusion of back-end database content and Flash design has produced a highly interactive, 3D interface that lets users view content from a variety of databases and perform advanced searches, not only on this site but on competing sites as well.

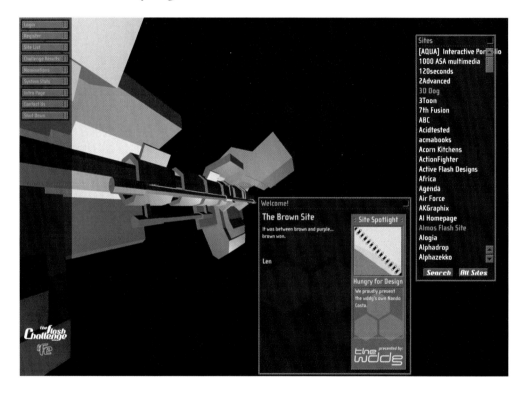

Joe Hargrave

http://www.joehargrave.com

The Flash site designed for magician Joe Hargrave by Crazy Raven Productions, Inc. *(http://www.crazyraven.com)* is a good example of how Flash helps create engaging navigational controls that go well beyond the simple rollover buttons found on most HTML sites. While the Flash Player cannot play back video, the multimedia section of this site demonstrates a workable solution to this dilemma through Flash's ability to open custom browser windows via JavaScript.

Harman Kardon
http://www.harman-multimedia.com

Harman Kardon's Flash site not only is a work of art, it is also very functional and easy to use, with awesome 3D spinnable views of its products. Not ironically, audio is a large part of this site's content (audio products are the mainstay of Harman Kardon's business). Placing all the audio content in a single Flash movie would have meant unacceptably slow downloads, so site developers incorporated Flash's ability to load and unload individual Flash movies into the movie window, so that content downloads only on an as-needed basis.

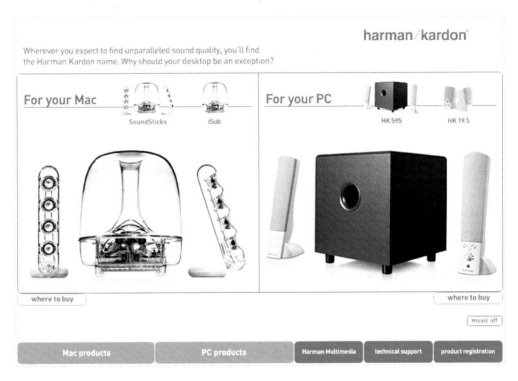

Lee Fit

http://www.leefit.com

The Lee Fit site designed by Look and Feel New Media *(http://www.lookandfeel.com)* is another great example of how you can use Flash to inform and educate your audience in an interactive manner. Lee Fit features a dressing room that helps users find the right size and style of Lee jeans. Its Flash-based menus have adjustable settings that create a custom product display based on the user's choices. Because graphics for every conceivable style, color, and fit would be impractical if they were placed in a single Flash movie, the site utilizes Flash's ability to load and unload individual movies so that custom content is delivered on an as-needed basis.

lucidCircus

http://www.lucidcircus.com

lucidCircus is an excellent example of how to incorporate 3D graphics into a Flash movie to provide a stimulating, yet smooth transition from one section of the site to another. The effect is lively, and the pages load incredibly fast as well. The opening page for this site features a great example of how motion graphics can be used to build the initial interface.

Mandalay

http://www.mandalay.com

Mandalay's Web site, designed by Fusion Media Group *(http://www.fusionmediagroup.com)*, is a great study in clean, effective design. The opening page utilizes video footage that was traced in Flash to recreate the introduction to Mandalay's film and TV productions. The site's interface includes toolbars that are dockable and scrollable and a full-screen background image that sets the mood for the entire site.

Matinee Sound & Vision

http://www.matinee.co.uk

Matinee Sound & Vision has long been considered a leader in multimedia development and design, and its Web site is a great reflection of this talent. The site's sophisticated use of motion blurs, shock waves, and reflections is an excellent example of what can be accomplished using Flash's built-in vector capabilities to create graphical content that downloads quickly. Its catchy soundtrack and unique navigational style make it a "must-see."

m-axis

http://www.m-axis.com

This design of m-axis' Web site is generally regarded as groundbreaking. Its fascinating text and navigational transitions utilize both frame-by-frame and tweened animation, and the guest book is an excellent example of how Flash can communicate with a database to display information in a lively manner. But what is perhaps most interesting about this site is that a newcomer to the design world, Mike Luis, created it as a means of landing himself a job after college. Instead, it helped him land a position with a design house half a year before he graduated.

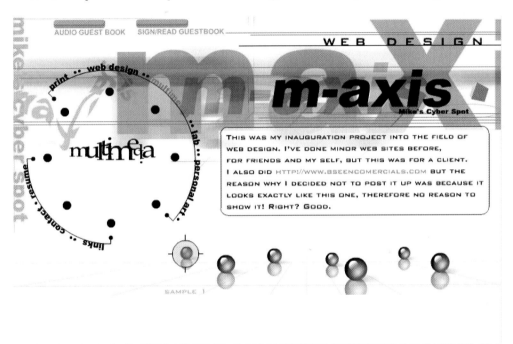

n.fusegfx

http://www.nfusegfx.com

n.fusegfx is an award-winning site on the cutting edge of cool. One of the best things about it is a 3D head that introduces users to the site and then welcomes them along the way as they navigate from section to section. The head was created in another program and then imported into Flash, and its mouth movements were synced to various sounds clips, all of which results in a very high-tech, sci-fi feel that makes visiting the site a fun experience.

Oringe Interactive

http://www.oringe.com

Oringe Interactive's motto is "Throw away your mouse." The company uses Flash to create sites that are navigated using a keyboard instead of a mouse, with pleasant voices that guide users along the way. The site is a great example of how to provide an easy navigational structure for the visually impaired.

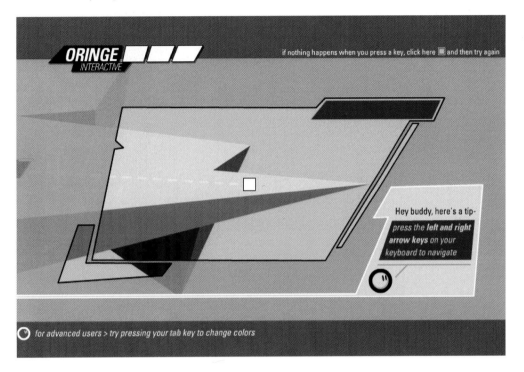

Ultimate Arcade Inc.

http://www.ultimatearcade.com

Ultimate Arcade, a Flash game-development company and online resource for Flash game designers, uses Flash to develop online games with the end goal of enhancing its clients' businesses and increasing their customer retention. Using ActionScript, one of the founders of this site applied his knowledge of physics and how objects react in the real world to create some of the most amazing games you'll find on the Web. The graphics are equally impressive. It's a great place to learn what is possible with Flash and have a great time doing it.

To create a shape-tweened animation:

1. Create a new Flash document by choosing File > New.

   Your new Flash document initially includes a single layer with one keyframe.

2. Click the Rectangle tool on the Drawing toolbar.

3. Draw a square with no outline and a red fill color in the middle of the stage.

4. Select the placeholder frame on Frame 25 on the same layer of the timeline (it appears highlighted), and then choose Insert > Blank Keyframe.

   A blank keyframe is inserted at Frame 25.

5. With the playhead on Frame 25, select the Text tool on the Drawing toolbar.

6. With the Character panel open, choose a bold font (we chose Arial Black), enter *150* as the size, and choose "blue" as the color.

7. Click somewhere on the upper right corner of the stage to create a text label, and type a capital *V.*

8. Select the Arrow tool; the text you just typed will be automatically selected.

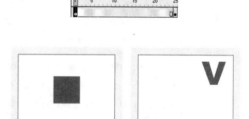

Figure 10.29
The beginning and ending keyframes of what will be our shape-tween sequence.

9. Choose Modify > Break Apart to turn the text into a shape (**Figure 10.29**).

10. Click on Frame 1 to automatically move the playhead back to that frame.

11. With the timeline at Frame 1, open the Frame panel by choosing Window >Panels > Frame.

12. Choose Shape from the Tweening drop-down menu on the Frame panel, and then choose from two additional options:

    - *Blend Type.* This lets you set the way the shapes' curves and corners are blended: Distributive works best for blending smooth and curvy shapes; angular works best for shapes with sharp corners and straight sides.

    - *Easing.* Easing is all about acceleration and deceleration. In real life, few objects move at a constant speed. Thus, easing makes a tweened animation move faster or slower at its beginning than at its end. Easing In causes the animation to move slower at the beginning of the tween, and Easing Out causes it to move faster at the beginning of the tween. If you place the Easing slider in the middle, motion speed will be constant for the duration of the tween (**Figure 10.30**).

13. Set the Blend Type to Angular, and leave the Easing slider at its initial setting.

The timeline will now reflect your shape tween. If you move the playhead back and forth, you can see the tweened animation you just created. Notice that the actual shape is tweened, as are color and position.

TIPS *After creating a tweened animation sequence, you can move the beginning or ending keyframe to lengthen or shorten the sequence, and Flash will automatically recalculate the tween.*

*If you add a keyframe to the middle of the current tweened sequence, you can add a shape on the newly created keyframe. The result: two distinct tweened sequences (**Figure 10.31**).*

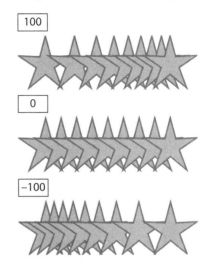

Figure 10.30
The effect that different Easing settings have on a tweened animation.

Shape hints

Although our shape tween appears to work decently, you can achieve greater control over the way your shapes blend by using shape hints to tell Flash how the shape tween should occur.

You can add as many as 26 shape hints, labeled *a–z*, per tween. Although not absolutely necessary, it's best to position them counter-clockwise from the upper left corner of the shapes. Flash is designed to understand this order with greater accuracy.

Inserted keyframe

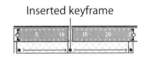

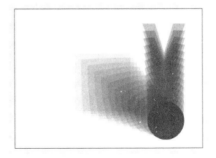

Figure 10.31
Adding a keyframe in the middle of an existing tweened sequence creates two distinct tweens.

To add shape hints to a shape tween:

1. Place the playhead on Frame 1.

This is where the first keyframe of our tween is located; shape hints are always added on the first keyframe of a tween.

2. Choose Modify > Transform > Add Shape Hint.

This places a shape hint labeled *a* on your initial shape (our red square).

3. Click and drag the shape hint to the side or corner of the shape you wish to use as a reference.

For our demonstration, move the shape hint to the upper left corner of the square.

4. Place the playhead on Frame 25.

This is where the last keyframe of our tween is located. The shape hint labeled *a* appears on the shape.

5. Click and drag the shape hint to the side or corner of the shape you wish to correspond with the point you marked on the first shape.

For our demonstration, move the shape hint to the upper left corner of the *V*.

You can move the playhead any time you wish to test a shape hint's effect on a tween.

6. Repeat Steps 1 through 5 until shape hints appear on the beginning and ending shapes, as shown in **Figure 10.32**.

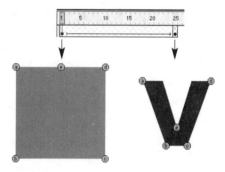

Figure 10.32
This graphic shows the location of shape hints on the beginning and ending keyframes of the tween sequence.

TIPS *Even though it may seem like more work, you should add a shape hint to the beginning shape, set its corresponding point on the end shape, go back to the beginning shape and add another shape hint, set its corresponding point on the end shape, and so on. You'll get unpredictable results if you add several hints to the beginning shape before setting corresponding points on the ending shape.*

Place your shape hints in a logical order. Illogical placement will produce unpredictable results (defeating their purpose).

To remove a shape hint:

♦ Click and drag it off the stage.

The labels of any other shape hints used for this tween will be updated to reflect the deletion.

To remove all shape hints:

♦ Place the playhead at the beginning keyframe of a tweened sequence, and choose Modify > Transform > Remove All Hints.

Only the shape hints used for that tween will be removed.

To display or hide shape hints:

♦ Place the playhead at the beginning or ending keyframe of a tweened sequence, and choose View > Show Shape Hints.

This option toggles the visibility of shape hints in a tween.

Creating a Motion-Tweened Animation

Whereas shape tweening allows you to morph simple shapes, motion tweening lets you tween symbols, groups, and text blocks. With the exception of morphing, you can accomplish pretty much the same things with motion tweening as you can with shape tweening. With motion tweening, you can tween size, skew, location, rotation, color, and transparency of symbols and groups—all of which allow you to create many of the great Flash transitions you see on the Web these days. You can also use a motion tween in conjunction with a path (line) to create an object that is not only tweened but follows the shape of the line as well (see Motion Tweening Along a Path for more information).

In the following demonstration, we'll create a simple animation of a ball whose size, location, rotation, and transparency all change. A bit little later you'll learn how to add a motion path so that the ball can appear to bounce down a street in a nonlinear fashion. The CD includes an interactive tutorial that demonstrates how this animation was put together.

To create a motion-tween animation:

1. Create a new Flash document by choosing File > New.

   Your new Flash document will initially include a single layer with one keyframe.

2. Click the Oval tool on the Drawing toolbar.

3. Draw a medium-size red circle, with no outline, in the lower left corner of the stage.

4. Click the Rectangle tool on the Drawing toolbar.

5. Within the red circle you just drew, draw a wide white rectangle with no outline (**Figure 10.33**).

This will help you to later see how rotation works within a motion tween.

6. Select the placeholder frame on Frame 25 of the timeline, and choose Insert > Frame.

This inserts 24 regular frames after the keyframe on Frame 1, all of which initially have the same content as that keyframe.

Figure 10.33
Draw a wide white rectangle within the circle.

7. Right-click (Windows) or Control-click (Macintosh) the keyframe on Frame 1 to bring up the Timeline menu.

8. From the menu that appears, choose Create Motion Tween.

Because a motion tween only works with symbol instances, groups, and text blocks, this command automatically converts content of any other type (such as simple shapes) into a symbol instance and adds a new master symbol to the library with the name Tween appended by a number. Because our red ball and white rectangle were simple shapes, Flash converted them to a symbol called Tween 1, and then placed that symbol in the library. Flash then converted what was on the stage into an instance of that symbol. The timeline now shows that a motion-tween sequence exists, but the dotted line indicates that there's a problem with the tween: The reason for this is that so far, we've only defined the *beginning* of the tween. Let's now define the end of it.

9. Move the playhead to Frame 25, which is where we want the tween to end.

10. With the playhead at Frame 25, click the Arrow tool on the Drawing toolbar, then select the red circle on the stage and drag it to the middle right portion of the stage.

This action automatically adds a keyframe to Frame 25, which completes the motion tween.

11. Move the playhead back and forth to view your animation.

Since we want our animation to spin, shrink, disappear, and speed up as it moves from left to right, we'll take care of the visual edits first (size and transparency) and then edit the movement of the tween (rotation and easing).

To customize a motion tween:

1. Place the playhead at Frame 25.

Because we want our red ball to be smaller in size and completely transparent at this point in the tweened sequence, let's edit it accordingly.

2. Click the Arrow tool on the Drawing toolbar, and select the red ball on the stage.

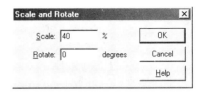

Figure 10.34
Enter 40 as the percentage to scale our red ball (to make it 40 percent of its original size).

3. Choose Modify > Transform > Scale and Rotate to bring up the Scale and Rotate dialog box (**Figure 10.34**).

4. Enter *40* in the Scale box, then click OK.

The red ball on Frame 25 reflects the fact that it has been scaled to 40 percent of its original size. If we had wanted to make it bigger, we could have entered an amount greater than 100 percent. If you move the playhead back and forth, you can see the effect of this edit. Let's now make our ball transparent on this keyframe.

5. With the Arrow tool still selected, choose Window > Panels > Effect.

The Effects panel will appear.

6. Choose Alpha from the drop-down menu that appears.

7. Enter *0* in the percentage box and press Enter/Return on the keyboard, or move the slider control all the way to the bottom.

Even though the ball seems to have disappeared from the stage, it's actually still there—it's simply transparent. If you move the playhead back and forth, you can see the effect of this edit.

8. Click the first keyframe of the tweened sequence (which in our case is on Frame 1) and open the Frame panel, which will let us edit the tween's movement.

9. On the Frame panel, enter the following settings:

- *Scale.* Checked

- *Rotate.* CW (Clockwise)

- *Times.* 2

- *Orient to path.* Unchecked

- *Easing.* Push slider all the way to the bottom or enter *-100* in the amount box next to the slider control

- *Synchronize.* Unchecked

- *Snap.* Checked

Because all of these edits are to the tween's movement, you will only be able to see them when moving the playhead back and forth. Two things to notice about the red ball in the tween: It rotates clockwise twice between the beginning and ending keyframe, and it moves more slowly at the beginning of the tween than it does at its end. This is the result of the Rotation and Easing settings we selected.

Motion-tweening properties

Motion tweens have several adjustable properties, which you can access from the Frame panel (**Figure 10.35**):

- *Tweening.* Allows you to choose the type of tweening used.

- *Scale.* If the symbols or groups at the beginning and ending keyframes differ in size, checking this option will tween that size difference. Leaving this option unchecked will cause the group or symbol to remain the same size throughout the tween.

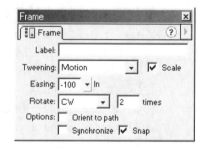

Figure 10.35
The Frame panel, where you can set motion-tween properties.

- *Rotate.* The options on this drop-down menu let you tween a rotation of the group or symbol between the beginning and ending keyframes:

    None. The group or symbol will not rotate.

    Auto. If you manually rotated the group or symbol in one of the keyframes, this option would tween that rotation in the direction that requires the least amount of motion.

    CW/CCW (Clockwise/Counterclockwise). This option will rotate the group or symbol instance in a clockwise or counterclockwise direction. The adjacent box indicates the number of full rotations that will be completed over the duration of the tween.

- *Orient to Path.* This is only useful if you are performing a motion tween along a path (see "Motion Tweening Along a Path" later in this section). It allows you to determine whether the baseline of a motion-tweened group or symbol instance remains at the same angle relative to the path throughout the tween (**Figure 10.36**).

- *Easing.* See the "Creating a Shape-Tweened Animation" section above for an explanation of easing.

- *Synchronize.* See the "Timeline Menu" section earlier for an explanation of this option.

- *Snap.* When using a motion guide with a tween, objects on the keyframes of the tween snap to the path, or line, on the motion-guide layer (see "Motion Tweening Along a Path" for more information).

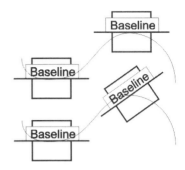

Figure 10.36
The top portion of this graphic illustrates how a motion tween follows a path with the "Orient to path" option turned off; the bottom illustrates how it works with it on.

Motion tweening along a path

Chances are, you won't want to move every motion-tweened animation in a straight line from Point A to Point B. Not to worry: Using motion-guide layers, Flash can move a motion-tweened animation along any line you draw or import. You simply link the layer with the motion-tweened animation to the motion-guide layer—which can contain a line of any length, shape, or twist you desire—and the motion-tweened animation will follow the line you drew.

Using the motion-tweened ball animation we already created, we'll now add a motion path to it to make it appear as if it's bouncing.

To motion tween along a path:

1. Select the layer that contains our motion-tweened animation, and press the Add Guide Layer button.

   This adds a motion-guide layer above the tweened animation layer (**Figure 10.37**). Whenever you create a motion-guide layer, Flash places it above the current layer. The name of the layer that includes our tweened animation is indented under the name of the motion-guide layer above it to signify that it is linked to the motion-guide layer. You can link any number of layers to a motion-guide layer.

Figure 10.37
Pressing the Add Guide layer adds a motion-guide layer directly above the current layer, which becomes linked to the motion-guide layer.

2. Click the name of the motion-guide layer to make it the current layer (if it isn't already).

3. On the toolbar click the Pencil tool.

4. From the Pencil tool options, choose Smooth as the pencil mode.

5. Draw a curvy line on the stage similar to the one shown in **Figure 10.38**.

Figure 10.38
Draw a curvy line similar to the one shown here; this is the motion path the tween will follow.

If the "Snap to guide" option is checked for the tween (which it should be by default), the symbol instances on the beginning and ending keyframes will snap to the closest point along the path you just drew.

6. Move the playhead back and forth to see the effect of adding a motion guide.

> **TIPS** *The line drawn on the motion-guide layer can be edited and reshaped like any other line on the stage. Flash will simply recalculate the tween to follow the edited path.*
>
> *You can create paths in an external vector program and then import them onto the motion-guide layer. Because many vector drawing programs allow you to create spirals, stars, and other sophisticated shapes, this can result in some great motion-tween effects.*
>
> *You can reposition the tweened object on the path at both its beginning and ending points so that it only travels along a portion of the path.*

To move the beginning and ending points of a motion tween along a path:

1. Click the Lock column to lock the motion-guide layer.

   This makes it uneditable.

2. Place the playhead at Frame 1, which contains the beginning keyframe of our tweened sequence.

3. Click the Arrow tool on the toolbar, and select the center of the instance of the red ball on the stage and drag it to the end of the path.

   The ball instance will snap into place as you drag (**Figure 10.39**). You can place the symbol instance anywhere along the path—if you drag away from the path, the group or symbol will still snap back onto the path.

4. Move the playhead to the end keyframe of our tween, then perform the same actions that you did in Step 3.

A motion path is never visible when the movie is exported.

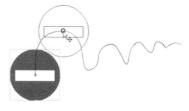

Figure 10.39
The symbol instance will snap to the path as you drag along it.

To make a motion path invisible in the authoring environment:

◆ On the motion-guide layer, click the Eye column.

Although the motion path is no longer visible, the linked animations will still follow it.

You can link any number of normal layers containing motion tweens to a single motion-guide layer if you want all of the motion-tweened elements on the linked layers to share a common path.

To link additional layers to a motion-guide layer:

1. Click and drag the name bar of the layer you wish to link to the motion-guide layer.

A dark-gray line will appear along the bottom indicating that layer's position relative to the other layers in the stack.

2. Drag the name bar until the gray line denoting its position appears just below the name bar of the motion-guide layer itself, then release (**Figure 10.40**).

The layer is now linked to the motion guide.

To unlink a layer from a motion-guide layer:

1. Click and drag the linked layer's name bar to unlink it from the motion-guide layer.

A dark-gray line will appear along the bottom indicating that layer's position relative to the other layers in the stack.

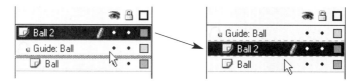

Figure 10.40
Dragging a layer underneath a motion-guide layer links it to the motion-guide layer. Thus, if the layer named Ball 2 has a motion tween on it, it will follow the same path as the layer named Ball.

2. Drag the name bar until the gray line denoting its position appears either above the name bar of the motion-guide layer itself or below any other normal layer, then release.

The layer is now unlinked from the motion-guide layer.

Putting It All Together

Imagine trying to figure out what a 5,000-piece puzzle is supposed to look like without any kind of visual reference. Chances are, that puzzle will soon find its way into the nearest fireplace. Like that pesky puzzle, Flash animations comprise many pieces, and you're likely to get confused unless you have some reference for how it's supposed to come together.

To that end, we've constructed a fictional scene to demonstrate most of the items and principles we've discussed here, as well as to give you a better idea of how to construct your own animation (**Figure 10.41**).

We've included the source files on the accompanying CD-ROM so that you can follow along. Here's what you need to know about our scene:

- This scene is made up of eight layers and 60 frames. The four composite pictures represent the way the animation appears on that frame of the timeline. Each layer has a name that corresponds with its content.

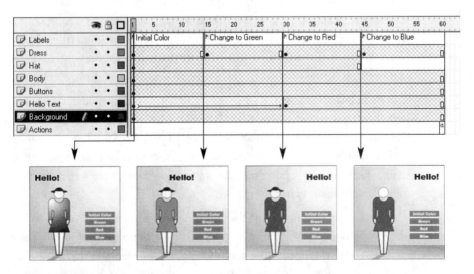

Figure 10.41
Composite animation.

- The stacking order of the layers determines which elements appear above others. For example, the Background layer is meant to appear behind everything else, so it's beneath the other layers (with the exception of the Action layer, which contains no content).

- The Label layer contains four labels, indicated by flags, which highlight portions of the timeline we wished to emphasize. We have assigned Go To actions to the Initial Color, Green, Red, and Blue buttons in the lower right corner of the scene so that the timeline will jump to the appropriate label when a button is clicked.

- Labels can only be assigned to keyframes. Because the labeled keyframes have no graphic content that appears on the stage, they are represented simply by small red flags on the timeline. Likewise, the regular frames that follow the keyframes on this layer have no content and thus appear white.

- The Dress layer includes four keyframes, each of which represents a place along the timeline where the color of the dress changes. Because these keyframes contain content that appears on the stage (the dress with different colors), they are represented by solid black dots on the timeline. Likewise, the regular frames that follow these keyframes appear light gray to indicate that their content is the same as that contained in the last keyframe on the layer. Thus, regular Frames 2 through 14 of this layer contain the same content as the keyframe on Frame 1; regular Frames 16 to 29 contain the same content as the keyframe on Frame 15; and so on.

- The Hat layer holds the hat graphic. Frame 1 of this layer is where the hat graphic was initially placed. The light-gray regular frames that follow this keyframe indicate that the hat does not change in appearance on the stage until Frame 45, which is a keyframe indicating where the hat graphic is removed from the scene. Since this keyframe, on Frame 45, no longer holds any graphic content, the regular frames that follow it on this layer also have no content, and thus appear white.

- The Body layer contains the legs, head, and hands of our model, which are initially placed on the keyframe on Frame 1. This keyframe appears as a solid black dot indicating that it contains content. These graphic elements remain static throughout the sequence, hence the lack of additional keyframes on this layer. The light-gray regular frames on this layer contain the same content as the initial keyframe on Frame 1.

- The Buttons layer contains the four buttons used in the scene (which we initially placed on Frame 1's keyframe). A solid black dot denotes that this keyframe contains content (our four buttons). These graphic elements do not change during the sequence; thus, no additional keyframes are needed on this layer. The light-gray regular frames on this layer contain the same content as the initial keyframe on Frame 1.

- The Hello Text layer contains the text *Hello,* which is motion tweened between Frames 1 and 30 to move from the left to the right. On the keyframe on Frame 1, the text is positioned where it should be at the beginning of the tween, while the keyframe on Frame 30 is where the text will be at the end of the tween. Because the text does not move or change from that point forward, no additional keyframes are needed on this layer. The light-gray regular frames that appear after the last keyframe on this layer indicate that the content remains the same from Frame 30 (the position of the last keyframe) to Frame 60.

- The Background layer contains our background, which was initially placed on the keyframe on Frame 1. This keyframe has a solid black dot in it denoting that it contains content (our background). The background remains unchanged throughout the sequence; thus, no additional keyframes are needed on this layer. The light-gray regular frames on this layer contain the same content as the initial keyframe on Frame 1.

- The Action Layer contains two blank keyframes, one at Frame 1, the other at Frame 60. The keyframe on Frame 1 is there because every layer initially starts with a keyframe that can't be deleted. The keyframe on Frame 60 has a frame action that causes the timeline to go back to the first frame of the animation and begin playing it again. Because the keyframes themselves on the Action layer contain no graphic content that is visible on the stage, the regular frames that follow them have no content and thus appear white.

Planning Your Project

Transitions and More

Generally, people don't do well with instantaneous or immediate change—we usually like to ease our way into situations. For most of us, just getting out of bed is a major transition that requires time and determination to pull off—and still we sometimes fail. The point is, we use transitions constantly to deal with change. Your Flash project should be no different.

Using transitions to transform objects, or even whole scenes, in your movie creates a smooth-flowing presentation. While you may sometimes want to create a shock effect or give the feeling of "popping" into the scene, you don't want your presentation to turn into a simple slide show—especially when you can do so much more.

Using the many tools and techniques we've discussed thus far, you can create any of the following as transitions in Flash:

- ***Fade in/fade out.*** *You achieve this transition by making the beginning or ending element in a tween more transparent than its counterpart.*

- **Enlarge/shrink.** You achieve this transition by making the beginning or ending element in a tween larger or smaller than its counterpart.
- **Slide in/slide out.** You achieve this transition by making the beginning or ending element in a tween appear or disappear from the stage.
- **Rotate/spin.** You achieve this transition by adding a rotation to your tween from the Frame panel.
- **Flip.** You achieve this transition by selecting the beginning or ending element in a tween and flipping it horizontally or vertically using the Modify > Transform > Flip Horizontally or Flip Vertically command.
- **Skew.** You achieve this transition by selecting the beginning or ending element in a tween and skewing it horizontally or vertically.
- **Blink.** You achieve this transition by placing a graphic element on the stage, then creating a number of successive keyframes that contain the same element. You then remove the element from every other one of those keyframes.
- **Bounce.** You achieve this transition by placing a graphic element on the stage, then creating a number of successive keyframes that contain the same element. Once you have done this, you reposition the element slightly (up, down, left, right, or a combination of all four) in each successive keyframe.
- **Morph.** You achieve this transition by creating shape tweens on mask layers.
- **Color change.** You achieve this transition by making the beginning or ending element in a tween a different color than its counterpart.
- **Add.** You achieve this transition by adding elements quickly, as if they are "popping" into a scene.
- **Subtract.** You achieve this transition by removing elements quickly from a scene.
- **Gradient blind.** You achieve this transition by using an alpha-gradiated element to slowly reveal another element underneath it.
- **Focus.** In this transition, several copies of the same element—each of which starts out transparent and offset from the other copies—are tweened on different layers so that at the end of the tween they are all opaque and at the same position on the stage.

You can combine any number of these transitions to create even more sophisticated effects.

Using QuickTime Video

Sometimes nothing can get the point across as effectively as video. To this end, you can mix Flash content with QuickTime video to create fully interactive videos. You can even use Flash actions to control the QuickTime video timeline (if you want to make it go to specific frames or play certain sections), just as you would with regular Flash content. You can also place Flash content, such as buttons and movie clips, on top of a QuickTime video to act as an interface or a way of annotating the QuickTime movie.

There are, however, a few limitations: QuickTime 4 is the only format that can play back content that combines Flash and QuickTime video; The Flash 5 Player does not support this functionality. When creating a Flash project that uses QuickTime video, you *must* export it to QuickTime format, not Flash, and your audience *must* have the QuickTime plug-in or player installed on their computers to view it. For more information, see Chapter 16, "Publishing."

The QuickTime 4 plug-in or player currently only supports Flash 3, which means that features specific to Flash 5 will not work when exported to the QuickTime format.

Although visible in the authoring environment, QuickTime video will not appear in your movie when you use the Test Movie feature. To test a Flash project that includes QuickTime content, you must first export it directly to the QuickTime 4 format.

Working with QuickTime Content

To import a QuickTime video:

1. From the File menu choose Import.

2. In the Import dialog box, select the video and click Open.

   The video will be imported into Flash and added to the library (see Chapter 13, "Using the Library to Manage Your Assets").

   TIP *For organizational purposes, it's usually best to place a QuickTime video on its own layer.*

Even though you can import QuickTime video into Flash, you cannot directly edit the video itself; you can only manipulate the movie's timeline. When using button and frame actions to jump to certain frames in your movie, the QuickTime video frame number will correspond with the Flash frame number. For example, if you were to start a QuickTime video on Frame 30 of the Flash timeline, Frame 1 of the QuickTime video would be referenced as Frame 30 within Flash.

Because the Flash and QuickTime timelines are so closely linked, the QuickTime time-line will not move unless the Flash timeline also moves. If you import a 50-frame Quick-Time video into Flash, you must provide at least 50 frames on the Flash timeline so that all of the video's frames can play. By using buttons and frame actions, you can jump to various frames of a QuickTime movie much like you can in a regular Flash movie.

Transparent Flash content used on top of a QuickTime video will remain transparent at export (**Figure 10.42**).

Because you can see frames of a QuickTime movie within the Flash authoring environment, you can synchronize Flash content and sound with the QuickTime video. Simply scrub the playhead on the Flash timeline to see various frames of your QuickTime movie (see "The Playhead" section earlier in this chapter).

Figure 10.42
You can create semi-transparent naviga-tional controls for QuickTime movies.

Interactive Tutorials

- *Creating a Frame-by-Frame Animation.* This tutorial demonstrates the principles behind frame-by-frame animation.

- *Creating a Shape-Tweened Animation.* Learn how to easily morph one shape into another with this simple tutorial, which also demonstrates how to use shape hints to specify how a morphed transition should look.

- *Creating a Motion-Tweened Animation.* In this tutorial, we create a motion-tweened animation similar to the sample in this chapter so that you can see how size and transparency arc tweened. We also place this tween along a path to help you better understand the concept of motion guides.

- *Creating a Preloader.* This tutorial shows you how to create a simple animation that can play as your main movie downloads in the background.

Basic Actions for Building Interactivity

Humans thrive on interaction. We're more than willing to make fools of ourselves just to bring a smile to a baby's face. And we love to push buttons to make things work. But a mute audience, a battery-dead remote control, a frozen computer—these are the things that drive us nuts. If we can't provoke a response, we move on to something else.

Which is precisely what you *don't* want your audience to do. The surest way to hold your audience is to interact with it. While sound and animation may capture your viewers' attention, interactivity will captivate them. As the lifeline between your movie and the audience, interactivity can be used in all kinds of ways. You can use it to let viewers control playback and appearance. And with it, you can create games, customizable interfaces, forms, and more. To do so successfully, however, you need to understand some of the logic *behind* interactivity. But don't panic: You don't need to be a computer programmer to add simple interactivity to your presentation.

In this chapter we'll look at some of the basic building blocks that will help you bring your creations to life almost immediately. For a more advanced, in-depth look at what Macromedia Flash can do with interactivity, see Chapter 12, "Using ActionScript for Advanced Interactivity."

Interactivity in Flash

Flash requires three things for interactivity: an event that triggers an action, the action triggered by that event, and the target (or object) that performs the action or is affected by it.

Think about your alarm clock: When you set it at night, you're programming it to perform an interactive function—the underlying logic of which might look something like this:

Event: The clock reaches the time you set the alarm to go off (which sets the action into motion).

Action: The alarm sounds (the action performed by the object).

Target: The alarm clock (the object affected by the event).

If you can successfully set your alarm, you're well on your way to becoming an interactive guru.

You use Flash's internal scripting language, *ActionScript,* to create interactivity. ActionScript itself is simply a set of instructions that defines an event, a target, and an action—all of which we'll explain in the following sections.

> **TIP** *In ActionScript, a target is sometimes referred to as an* object *and an action is often referred to as a* method. *You'll learn more about these programming terms in the next chapter; for now, just be aware of the distinction.*

Events

The first thing you need to define to add interactivity to your movie is the event. Events are categorized as follows:

- Mouse events

- Keyboard events

- Frame events

- Movie-clip events

Mouse events (button actions)

Mouse events occur when your audience interacts with a button instance in your movie. Such events are also known as *button actions* because they are always attached to buttons and they always trigger an action. A user can employ the pointer in any of the following ways to trigger a mouse event (**Figure 11.1**):

- on(press)

  The Press event occurs when the user moves the pointer over a movie button and presses the mouse button.

- on(release)

  The Release event occurs when the user moves the pointer over a movie button and then clicks and releases the mouse button. (This is the default event for most actions.)

- on(releaseOutside)

  The Release Outside event occurs when the user presses a movie button but releases away from the button.

- on(rollOver)

  The Roll Over event occurs when the user moves the pointer over a movie button.

- on(rollOut)

  The Roll Out event occurs when the user moves the pointer away from a button.

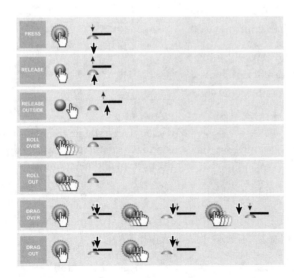

Figure 11.1
The down arrow represents the mouse button being pressed down; the up arrow represents it being released. No arrow represents a mouse event that doesn't require the mouse button to be pressed or released.

- on(dragOver)

The Drag Over event occurs when the user places the pointer over a movie button while pressing the mouse button, then drags the pointer away from the movie button (while still pressing the mouse button), and moves it back over the movie button.

- on(dragOut)

The Drag Out event occurs when the user places the pointer over a movie button, presses the mouse button, and drags it away from the movie button (while still pressing the mouse button).

These events, which are known as *handlers* (because they *handle*, or manage, an event), can only be attached to button instances.

To define a mouse event that triggers an action:

1. Click a button instance on the stage to select it.

2. On the Launcher bar, press the Show Actions button.

   The Actions panel will appear.

3. Click the plus sign (+) to assign an action or actions that you want triggered by the mouse event.

4. For our demonstration, choose Basic Actions > Stop to halt your movie.

   The Actions List window will show your completed ActionScript, indicating that the action will occur when the button is released. This is the default mouse event that Flash assigns to an action. Now, let's configure the mouse event more to our liking.

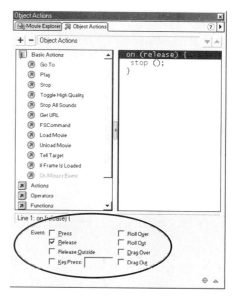

Figure 11.2

If you select a statement in the Actions List window, its parameters will be displayed at the bottom of the Actions panel.

5. In the Actions List window, select the on (release) statement.

   The statement will be highlighted and mouse event parameters will become available on the bottom of the Actions panel (**Figure 11.2**).

6. Check any and all mouse events you want to trigger this action.

As you check various events, the on() statement is updated in the Parameter pane. When the movie is played, the action you assigned this button will be performed when any of the mouse events you checked are triggered.

TIPS *Mouse events assigned to one instance of a button have no effect on other instances of the button—even if they're both on the stage simultaneously. Each can be assigned different events and actions.*

To assign the mouse event before assigning an action to it, perform Steps 1 and 2 above, but in Step 3, select Basic Actions > On Mouse Event to define the mouse event. Then from the same menu, select an action.

Many button actions cannot be tested in the authoring environment. To test buttons completely, choose Control > Test Movie.

Keyboard events

A keyboard event occurs when the user presses a letter, number, punctuation mark, symbol, arrow, or the Backspace, Insert, Home, End, Page Up, or Page Down key. Keyboard events are case sensitive, which means that *A* is not the same as *a*. (If you assign *A* to trigger an action, *a* will not trigger it.)

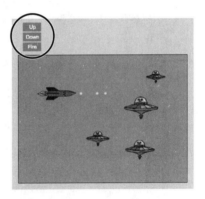

Figure 11.3
Hide buttons that contain keyboard events in areas that will not be seen when the final movie is exported—for example, outside the stage area.

Keyboard events are attached to button instances. Although you don't need to interact with the button instance, it must be present in a scene for the keyboard event to work (though it doesn't need it to be visible or even present on the stage). It can even reside in the work area of the frame so that it is not visible when the movie is exported (**Figure 11.3**).

To define a keyboard event that triggers an action:

1. Perform Steps 1 through 5 above (for adding a mouse event).

2. On the Parameter pane of the Actions panel, check the Key Press event.

3. In the small text box next to the Key Press option, type the key that will be used to trigger the action (**Figure 11.4**).

   When the movie is played, the actions you assigned this button instance will be performed when the user types the key you assigned.

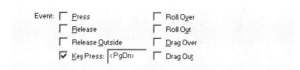

Figure 11.4
To assign a keypress to the event triggering an action on a button, from Event options, select Key Press, and then type the key on the keyboard.

Frame events

Whereas user interaction triggers mouse and keyboard events, the timeline triggers frame events (which are also known as *frame actions* because they are attached to frames and always trigger an action).

Frame events—which are always placed at keyframes—are useful for actions that you want to occur at certain points in time (**Figure 11.5**). For example, a Stop action will cause your movie to halt playing, and a Go To action will cause your movie to jump to another frame or scene on the timeline.

To create a frame event that triggers an action:

1. Click the keyframe on the timeline where you would like the frame event to occur.

2. On the Launcher bar press the Show Actions button.

 The Actions panel will appear.

3. Click the plus sign (+) to assign an action or actions that you want triggered when the timeline reaches this keyframe.

4. For our demonstration, choose Basic Actions > Stop, which will cause your movie to cease playing.

 The Actions List window will display your completed ActionScript. You will notice that even though this is the same action that was assigned to the mouse event we configured earlier, the script is different: It lacks the on (release) statement, which is only required to define mouse or keyboard events (because both can take so many forms). A frame event can only be triggered one way—by the timeline reaching that frame.

 When the movie is played, it will perform the action you assigned when the timeline reaches this keyframe.

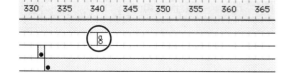

Figure 11.5
Frame actions are placed on the timeline and occur when the playhead reaches the keyframe where they reside.

Movie-clip events

The following movie-clip events are attached to movieclip instances and are triggered when certain things occur in relation to the movie clip (**Figure 11.6**):

- onClipEvent(load)

  The Load event is triggered by the first appearance of the movie-clip instance in your movie. You can use this action to initiate the movie clip's variables or properties when it first appears.

- onClipEvent(enterFrame)

  An EnterFrame event is triggered each time the movie clip's timeline enters a new frame. Thus, if your movie plays at 12 frames per second, this event is triggered 12 times a second. If the movie clip is only one frame long, the event will continue to occur—useful for constantly updating your movie's data. If you attach this event to a movie clip instance, the only way to stop it is to remove the instance from your movie.

- onClipEvent(unload)

  The Unload action is triggered when the timeline reaches the first frame in which the movie-clip instance is no longer used.

- onClipEvent(mouseDown)

  The Mouse Down event occurs when the user presses down the left mouse button anywhere in the Flash movie window while the movie clip to which this event is attached is also present in the movie window. Thus, this event is a catch-all for any mouse downs that occur.

- onClipEvent(mouseUp)

  The Mouse Up event occurs when the user releases the mouse button anywhere in the Flash movie window while the movie clip to

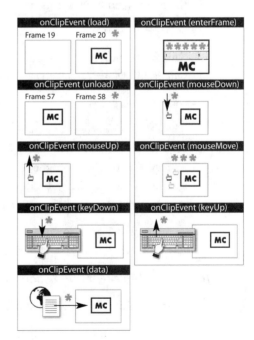

Figure 11.6

The down arrow represents the mouse button being pressed down; the up arrow represents it being released. The asterisk represents an occurrence of the event.

which this event is attached is also in the movie window. This event is a catch-all for any mouse ups that occur.

- onClipEvent(mouseMove)

The Mouse Move event occurs once for each pixel that the mouse is moved anywhere in the movie window while the movie clip to which this event is attached is in the movie window,. For example, if the user moves his mouse five pixels, this event is triggered five times. This can be used in conjunction with the _xmouse and _ymouse properties to constantly track the position of the mouse so your movie can take a specific action based on that position.

- onClipEvent(keyDown)

The Key Down event is triggered when the user presses any key while the movie clip to which the event is attached is in the movie window. You can use additional ActionScript to determine precisely which key was pressed and then base an action in your movie on that particular key—a way to let users control the movie (and its elements) via their keyboards.

- onClipEvent(keyUp)

This Key Up event occurs when the user releases a key while the movie clip to which this event is attached is in the movie window.

- onClipEvent(data)

The Data event occurs when the movie clip receives data via the loadVariables() and loadMovie() actions. When used in conjunction with a loadVariables() action, the data event occurs only once (when the last variable is loaded). When used in conjunction with a loadMovie() action, the onClipEvent(data) event occurs repeatedly, as each section of data is retrieved.

These events, which are known as handlers (because they *handle*, or manage, an event), can only be attached to movie-clip instances.

To define a Clip event that triggers an action:

1. Click a movie clip instance on the stage to select it.

2. On the Launcher bar, press the Show Actions button.

    The Actions panel will appear.

3. Click the plus sign (+) to assign an action or actions you want triggered on the Clip event.

4. For our demonstration, choose Basic Actions > Stop to halt your movie.

The Actions List window will show your completed ActionScript, which indicates that the action will occur when the movie-clip instance is loaded for the first time. This is the default Clip event Flash assigns to an action. Let's configure it more to our liking.

5. In the Actions List window, select the `onClipEvent(load)` statement.

The statement will become highlighted and the Clip event parameters will become available on the bottom of the Actions panel.

6. Choose the Clip event you want to trigger this action.

When the movie is played, the action you assigned to this movie clip will be performed when your chosen Clip event is triggered.

TIP *Unless you specify a target (see below), actions attached to a movie-clip instance affect the movie-clip instance itself. For example, the Stop action we added in Step 4 causes the movie-clip instance to immediately stop upon being loaded.*

Targets

Now that you know how to use events to trigger actions, you need to learn how to specify which object, or target, will be affected by the event that occurs. Events control three primary targets: the current movie and its timeline, other movies and their timelines (such as movie-clip instances), and external applications (such as browsers). The following sample ActionScripts show how each of these targets can be used to create interactivity. More in-depth explanations follow.

In the following script, a Roll Over (event) on a button in the current movie (target) causes the movie's timeline to stop playing (action).

```
on (rollOver) {
   stop ();
}
```

In the following example, a Roll Over (event) on a button in the current movie causes a different movie's timeline—the movie-clip instance myMovieClip (target)—to stop playing (action).

```
on (rollOver) {

  tellTarget ("myMovieClip") {

    stop();

  }

}
```

The following ActionScript opens the user's default browser (target)—if it's not already open—and loads the specified URL (action) when the Roll Over (event) is triggered.

```
on (rollOver) {

  getURL ("http://www.derekfranklin.com");

}
```

For more information on ActionScripting syntax, see Chapter 12, "Using ActionScript for Advanced Interactivity."

Current movie

When defining a target in an ActionScript, the current movie is defined as the movie that both *contains* the button, movie clip or frame that triggers an action and is *affected* by the action. Thus, if you assign a mouse event to a button, and that event triggers an action which affects the movie or timeline containing the button, the target of the action is considered to be the current movie (**Figure 11.7**). If, however, you assign a mouse event to a button that affects a movie other than the one it's part of, your target becomes another movie. The same principle applies to frame actions. Unless you define another movie as your target, ActionScripts will target your current movie by default for most events. For an example, take a look at the following ActionScript:

```
on (rollOver) {

  stop();

}
```

This ActionScript indicates that a mouse event triggers the action. When the button in your movie is rolled over (event), the current movie's timeline (target) stops playing (action).

With ActionScript, the current movie is a relative target based on the timeline on which the script is placed. For example, if you attached the above ActionScript to a button in the main movie, the main movie would

Figure 11.7
When an event, such as a mouse event, causes its own timeline to do something (for example, stop), the target for the event is considered the current movie.

be considered the current movie, or target, of the script. If, however, you attached the same ActionScript to a button inside a movie-clip instance, that movie clip's timeline would be the current movie, or target, of the action (**Figure 11.8**).

Other movies

If you wish to target another movie with an action, you must define that target in your ActionScript. Thus, if you assign an action to a button on the main timeline that targets a movie-clip instance named `myMovieClip`, you would use a script similar to the one shown below. Compare the following ActionScript for controlling another movie with the ActionScript used to control the current movie in the previous example:

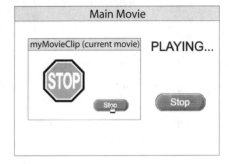

```
on (rollOver) {
    tellTarget ("myMovieClip") {
        stop();
    }
}
```

Figure 11.8
A script's placement determines the current movie.

This ActionScript indicates that a mouse event triggers the action. When the button in your movie is rolled over (event), the movie clip instance named myMovieClip (target) will stop playing (action) (**Figure 11.9**).

In ActionScript, the previous script could be rewritten in various ways to achieve the same result:

```
on (rollOver) {
    with (myMovieClip) {
        stop();
    }
}
```

or

```
on (rollOver) {
    myMovieClip.stop();
}
```

Figure 11.9
Specifically targeting another movie in the current movie window using script allows you to control one movie from another.

If you find the concept of controlling one movie via another confusing, hang in there—we'll continue exploring these concepts throughout this chapter. For more information, see "Working with Multiple Timelines" in the next chapter or review some of the interactive tutorials available on the CD.

> **TIP** *Our discussion of controlling one movie from another involves multiple movies within a single movie window. To facilitate communication between movies on an HTML page with separate <object> or <embed> tags, you must use JavaScript.*

External targets

An *external* target exists outside the realm of your movie. With the Get URL action, for example, you need a Web browser to open the specified URL. Several Flash actions can target external sources, including Get URL, FS Command, Load Movie, Load Variables, Print, and some XML actions. The bottom line here is that all of these actions require the help of an outside application. Targets for these actions can be Web browsers, Flash projectors, Web servers, or other applications. The following Action-Script targets a Web browser to open the specified URL:

```
on (rollOver) {
    getURL ("http://www.flash.com");
}
```

This ActionScript indicates that a mouse event triggers the action. When the button in your movie is rolled over (event), a browser (target) opens the specified URL (action).

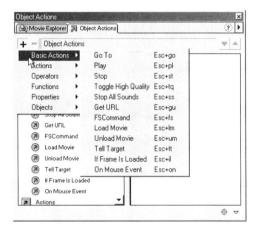

Figure 11.10
Clicking the Add button on the Actions panel reveals a list of available basic actions.

Actions

Actions are the final pieces of the interactivity puzzle. They allow you to instruct your movies (or external applications) to perform specific tasks. A single event can trigger multiple actions, which can be executed simultaneously on a single target or on different targets.

Flash can perform many actions; this chapter deals with the basic ones available in Flash. These actions are described briefly in the following table and more in depth below. You can access them by clicking the Add (+) button on the Actions panel and selecting Basic Actions from the menu that appears (**Figure 11.10**):

Table 11.1
Basic Actions

Action	Description
Go To	Causes a movie to jump to the specified frame or scene on the timeline and stop or begin playing from that point forward.
Play	Causes a movie to begin playing from its current position on the timeline.
Stop	Causes a movie to stop playing.
Toggle High Quality	Turns antialiasing off and on.
Stop All Sounds	Stops all currently playing audio tracks.
Get URL	Opens a browser window with the specified URL loaded, or sends variables to the specified URL.
FS Command	Sends data to the application hosting your Flash movie (such as a browser, projector, Director movie).
Load Movie	Loads a Flash movie, at the specified URL, within another Flash movie.
Unload Movie	Unloads a previously loaded movie.
Tell Target	Identifies a movie so that you can get it to perform an action.
If Frame Is Loaded	Determines whether a particular frame on a timeline has been loaded and, if it has, performs an action.
On Mouse Event	Mouse events are actually triggers rather than actions. For more information, see Events earlier in this chapter.

Actions Panel

The Actions panel is where interactivity is born in Flash. You use it to add or edit actions attached to objects, including button and movie-clip instances as well as frames (keyframes).

There are a number of ways to open the Actions panel (**Figure 11.11**).

To open the Actions panel do one of the following:

- Press the Show Actions button on the Launcher bar.

- Press the Edit Actions button on the Instance panel.

- Choose Window > Actions.

- Right-click (Windows) or Control-click (Macintosh) a button or movie-clip instance, or a frame on the timeline; then choose Actions from the menu that appears.

- Double-click a frame on the timeline.

For more information about the Actions panel, see Chapter 12, "Using ActionScript for Advanced Interactivity."

Figure 11.11
The Actions panel can be quickly opened by pressing the Edit Actions button on the Instance panel (top) or the Show Actions button on the Launcher bar (bottom).

Normal/Expert Modes

So you're not an ActionScript expert? Need help configuring actions and setting up your scripts? No problem. You can work with the Actions panel in one of two modes, depending on your scripting expertise and desire for control.

Normal mode

In Normal mode, you use the Toolbox list and the Add button to add actions, the Delete button to remove actions, the Up/Down buttons to change the sequence of actions, and the Parameters pane to configure actions' parameters.

In Normal mode, the interface is made up of the following areas (**Figure 11.12**):

- *Toolbox List window.* Contains a hierarchical list of ActionScript actions, operators, functions, properties, and objects. Double-clicking an icon (a book with an arrow) opens or closes a category in the Toolbox List window.

- *Actions List window.* Contains the code of the ActionScript attached to the currently selected button, movie clip, or frame. Each line represents a *statement/action* in the overall ActionScript code. Selecting a statement by clicking it causes the Parameter pane (see below) to change, so that relevant parameters can be entered or edited.

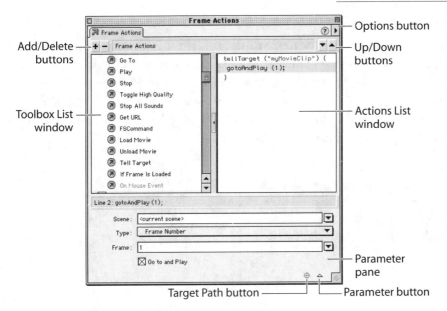

Figure 11.12
Parts of the Actions panel.

- *Parameter pane.* This is where you can enter or edit information pertaining to the currently selected statement. The pane is context sensitive and changes according to the type of statement selected in the Actions List window.

- *Parameter button.* You use this button to display or hide the Parameter pane.

- *Target Path button.* Pressing this button opens the Insert Target Path dialog box, which lets you quickly choose a target for an action. This button is only activated if the parameter you are setting requires a target path. For more information on this feature, see "Working with Multiple Timelines" in the next chapter.

- *Add/Delete buttons.* Use these buttons to add or delete actions from the Actions List window.

- *Up/Down buttons.* Use these buttons to move a selected statement/action up or down in the overall ActionScript. This changes the sequence of actions in the ActionScript, which in turn can change the way it works.

- *Options button.* Press this button to display a menu that contains commands pertaining to the Actions panel.

Unless otherwise stated, the instructions in this book relate to using the Actions panel in Normal mode.

Expert mode

In Expert mode, the Actions list acts like a text editor. You can type and edit the script directly inside of this window. You can still add actions using the Toolbox list or the Add button, but you cannot delete actions, change their sequence, or configure their parameters as you would in Normal mode. The areas for performing these edits are either grayed out or invisible (**Figure 11.13**). These edits must be performed by directly editing the text in the Actions List window.

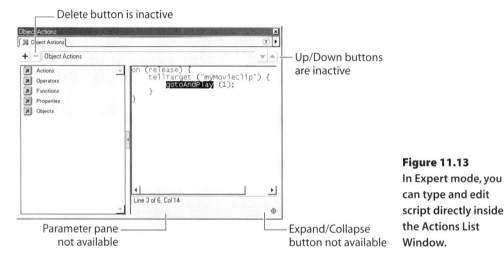

Delete button is inactive

Up/Down buttons are inactive

Parameter pane not available

Expand/Collapse button not available

Figure 11.13
In Expert mode, you can type and edit script directly inside the Actions List Window.

Choosing a mode

By default, the Actions panel opens in Normal mode. If you would prefer that it open to Expert mode instead, you can set this preference.

To set the default Actions panel mode:

1. Choose Edit > Preferences.

This opens the Preferences dialog box.

2. Select the General tab, and choose a mode from the drop-down box at the bottom of the tab.

3. Click OK.

By default, the Actions panel will now open in the mode you chose.

Flash also lets you choose a mode on a script-by-script basis. For example, you can create a script attached to a button instance in Normal mode and another script on a frame in Expert mode. What's more, Flash remembers the mode in which each script was created and will open the Actions panel in that mode when editing that script.

To choose a mode for a particular script:

1. With an object selected and the Actions panel open, press the Options button.

2. Choose either Normal or Expert mode from the menu that appears.

You can now configure this script in the selected mode. If you return to this script, it will still be editable in the mode you selected.

Attaching Actions

Attaching actions to a button or movie-clip instance or to a frame is as simple as selecting it, and then opening the Actions panel. Because the Actions panel is context sensitive, it always displays the actions of the currently selected object (**Figure 11.14**).

This means if you select a keyframe with an attached ActionScript, that script will appear. If the keyframe doesn't already have an ActionScript attached to it, any actions entered in the Actions panel will be attached to that keyframe. The Actions panel is deactivated when the selected object can't have an attached action, such as a simple shape, bitmap, or graphic symbol instance.

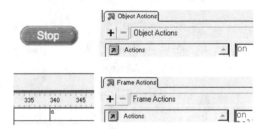

Figure 11.14
The Actions panel is context sensitive. Selecting an object automatically puts the Actions panel in the context of that object.

Working with Actions in the Actions Panel

Actions can perform many powerful tasks in your movie. Understanding some of the basic principles of how to work with them in the Actions panel can go a long way toward making your own ActionScripts more powerful.

Adding actions

You build ActionScripts (which you attach to objects) by adding actions, one at a time, from the Toolbox List window to the Actions List window.

To add actions from the Toolbox List window to the Actions List window:

● Click the Add action button.

● Double-click an action in the Toolbox List window.

Adding Multiple Actions

Flash can perform multiple actions for any event in your movie. For example, if you want a single mouse event to send the current timeline to Frame 15 while also setting the transparency property of the myMovieClip instance to 50 percent, you would follow the steps outlined below.

The following example is based on the assumptions that the main timeline is at least 15 frames long, and that it contains a button instance and a movie-clip instance (named myMovieClip).

To add multiple actions to a single event:

1. Select the button instance on the stage.

2. Open the Actions panel.

3. Click the Add (+) button to display the action menu.

4. Because we want a Roll Over mouse event to trigger our action, choose Basic Actions > Mouse Events.

   The mouse event will be added to the ActionScript, and parameters for this will appear on the bottom of the Actions panel.

5. Uncheck the Release checkbox and check the Roll Over checkbox.

   Our mouse event is now set. The Actions List window will display our mouse event, which appears highlighted.

6. Click the Add (+) button again, and select the Basic Actions > Go To action.

   The action will be placed below the mouse event in the Actions List window, and parameters for it will appear on the bottom of the Actions panel.

7. Select Frame Number as the type and enter *15* in Frame box.

8. Click the Add (+) button to display the list of actions, and select Actions > Set Property.

   The action will be placed below the Go To action in the Actions List window, and parameters for it will appear on the bottom of the Action dialog box.

9. From the Property list at the top of the Parameters pane, choose _alpha.

10. In the Target box below, enter the target whose property you want to change.

    For our demonstration, enter myMovieClip, which is our target's name and path. (For more information about target names and paths, see "Working with Multiple Timelines" in Chapter 12.)

11. In the Value box enter the number *50*.

12. Click OK.

The button instance is now configured to perform multiple actions simultaneously when it is rolled over.

You could also set it up so that on a single instance of a button, one mouse event did one thing and another mouse event did something else. The following script borrows from the example we just demonstrated; however, instead of using a Roll Over event to trigger both actions, in this script a Roll Over event triggers one action, while a Roll Out event triggers another.

```
on (rollOver) {
    gotoAndStop (15);
}
on (rollOut) {
    setProperty ("myMovieClip", _alpha, 40);
}
```

A word about nested actions

Nesting is not a difficult concept to grasp; however, it is an important one. By themselves, some Flash actions don't do much. A Tell Target action, for example, allows you to set a target to perform an action; however, a secondary action must tell the target what to do. Using one action within another in this way is known as *nesting*. Nested actions are indented in the Actions List window so that you can easily identify them (**Figure 11.15**).

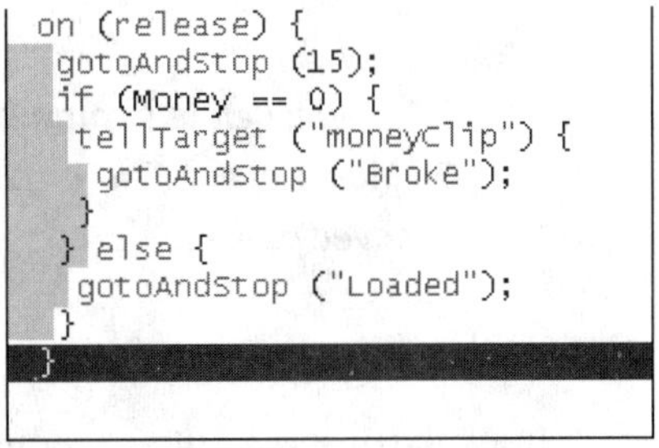

The way in which actions are nested can affect the way your ActionScript performs. Take a look at the following script:

```
on (release) {
    tellTarget ("myMovieClip") {
    gotoAndPlay (20);
    }
}
```

```
on (release) {
    gotoAndStop (15);
    if (Money == 0) {
        tellTarget ("moneyClip") {
            gotoAndStop ("Broke");
        }
    } else {
        gotoAndStop ("Loaded");
    }
}
```

Figure 11.15
Nested actions are indented in the Actions List window so that they are easier to locate.

In the preceding script, the `gotoAndPlay()` action is nested in the `tellTarget()` action, which is nested in the on (release) mouse event. This script causes the movie-clip instance named `myMovieClip` to go to and play Frame 20 when the on (release) mouse event occurs. Compare that with the following script:

```
on (release) {
  gotoAndPlay (20);
  tellTarget ("myMovieClip") {
  }
}
```

Although this script contains the same ingredients as the previous one, it works differently because the `gotoAndPlay()` action is not nested within the `tellTarget()` command. This script causes the *current* timeline (not the `myMovieClip` timeline) to go to and play Frame 20. The `tellTarget()` action in this script is useless because no action is nested inside.

See "Sequence of Actions" in this section for information about moving actions up or down in the script for nesting purposes.

Deleting actions

If you've put an action somewhere that it doesn't belong, you can easily remove it from the Actions list.

To delete an action:

♦ Select the action in the Actions list, and click the minus (–) button at the top of it.

> **TIP** *If you delete a command that includes nested actions (such as an On Mouse event, Tell Target, or If statement, all nested actions are removed as well.*

Sequence of actions

In Flash—just as in life—actions need to be performed in a certain order for things to take place in a logical and coherent manner. Flash executes actions, from top to bottom, in the order they appear in the Actions list. If the sequence of actions isn't quite right, your script may not perform the way you intended.

Take, for example, the following scripts; the first shows the proper order:

```
on (release) {
  dynamicFrame = 20;
  gotoAndStop (dynamicFrame);
}
```

This script shows a mouse event that creates a variable named `dynamicFrame` with a value of 20. Once that variable is created, a `gotoAndStop()` action is set up to go to a frame number based on the value of dynamicFrame. Because dynamicFrame has been assigned a value of 20, the `gotoAndStop()` action will go to Frame 20. This is the proper sequence. In comparison, look at the following script, which switches things around a bit:

```
on (release) {
  gotoAndStop(dynamicFrame);
  dynamicFrame = 20;
}
```

The preceding script shows a mouse event that triggers a `gotoAndStop()` action that is set to go to a frame number based on the value of `dynamicFrame`. Problem is, according to the sequence of actions, `dynamicFrame` has not yet been created. In fact, it will not be created until *after* the action; thus, the `gotoAndStop()` action does nothing.

The moral here is to be aware of the order in which actions are performed. That order could make or break your script.

> **TIP** *If the user triggers the mouse again with a second click of the mouse button, the* **gotoAndStop()** *action will go to Frame 20. This is because the first click created the dynamicFrame variable and set it to a value of 20. Thus, dynamicFrame is available through any subsequent button clicks.*

Figure 11.16
Press the arrow keys above the Actions List window to reorder actions.

To reorder actions:

1. In the Actions List window, click once to select the action you want to reorder.

2. Click the arrow buttons at the top of the Actions panel to move the action up or down in the overall sequence (**Figure 11.16**).

Cutting, copying, and pasting actions

If you've created the perfect sequence of actions on a keyframe or button and you wish to use it elsewhere, you don't need to repeat your efforts. Instead, you can simply copy and paste.

To cut (or copy) and paste actions:

1. In the Actions List window, select the actions you wish to cut or copy:

   To select a single action, click it once.

   To select multiple actions, hold down the Control key (Windows) or Option key (Macintosh) while clicking multiple actions.

   To select a range of actions, click the first action in the range once, then hold down the Shift key and click the last action in the range.

2. Right-click (Windows) or Control-click (Macintosh) a selected action, and from the menu that appears, choose Cut or Copy to place the selected action or actions on the system clipboard.

3. Select the button instance, movie-clip instance, or keyframe where you would like to paste these actions.

4. In the Actions List window, right-click (Windows) or Control-click (Macintosh), and from the menu that appears, choose Paste.

   The actions you placed on the clipboard now appear in the Actions List window.

Basic Actions in Depth

In Flash, basic actions actually take you far beyond the basics, allowing you to create powerful interactivity with little effort. In this section, we'll show you how to use Flash's Basic Action set to turn your movies into multimedia extravaganzas.

In the following section on actions and their values, we use the terms *expression* and *evaluate* frequently. These require a brief explanation. You must set parameters for most of the actions in Flash to make them function the way you want. For example, the Go To action, which you'll learn about shortly, requires that you identify a frame to *go to* by frame number or label. You can enter an exact value, such as *25*, or you can set the value of the parameter based on *the value an expression evaluates to*. Let's say you needed to specify the frame number to go to. Instead of simply entering a value of *25*, you entered something like *18 + 7:* The latter is an *expression*—in other words, an equation or phrase that *evaluates* to, or equals, a specific value (in this case 25). Using this expression for the parameter's value would cause the Go To action to go to frame 25 just as if you had directly entered *25*. Expressions can take many forms and can evaluate to many types of values, including numbers and text. There are many reasons why you might want to enter an expression rather than an exact value, but let's just say for now that by using them, your movies can take on a life of their own. For more detailed information about expressions, see Chapter 12, "Using ActionScript for Advanced Interactivity."

> **TIPS** *You cannot see or test the effect of most actions within the Flash authoring environment. To test interactivity, choose Control > Test Movie from the menu bar.*
>
> Timeline, target, movie, *and* movie clip *are used interchangeably in the sections that follow.*

Go To

You use the Go To action to make a movie's timeline jump to a specific frame number, frame label, or scene, where it can stop or play from that point forward (depending on how you set it up).

Parameters

The following parameters are available for this action (**Figure 11.17**):

- *Scene.* Allows you to choose a scene as a starting point for the Go To action. Once you've defined a scene, you can then define a frame number or label within that scene. When using this action within symbols, the scene parameter is not available. The available options include:

    <current scene>. Allows you to choose a frame number or label (see "Frame" below) from the current scene as the point on the timeline to go to.

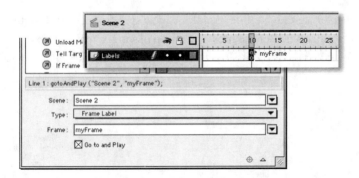

Figure 11.17
Use the Go To action to send a movie to a specific point.

<next scene>. Causes the action to go to Frame 1 of the next scene. You cannot use this option to go to a specific frame number or label in the scene; for this, you would use Scene_Name.

<previous scene>. Causes the action to go to Frame 1 of the previous scene. You cannot use this option go to a specific frame number or label in the scene; for this, you would use Scene_Name.

Scene_Name. Select a scene name from the list that appears.

- ***Type.*** Based on the scene option you selected, this allows you to choose a specific frame in the scene to go to. The available options include the following:

  Frame Number. Select a frame number to go to (which is entered in the Frame box).

  Frame Label. Select a frame label to go to (which is entered in the Frame box).

  Expression. Allows you to dynamically set the destination frame based on the value an expression evaluates to (which is entered in the Frame box). For more information on expressions, see the next chapter.

  Next Frame. Causes the timeline to jump to the frame following the frame in which the action was triggered. This is only available when selecting <current scene> for the scene parameter.

  Previous Frame. Causes the timeline to jump to the frame that preceded the frame in which the action was triggered. This option is only available when selecting <current scene> for the scene parameter.

- ***Frame.*** If you chose Frame Number from the Type drop-down box, you would enter the frame number here. If you chose Frame Label, you would enter the name of the label here (applicable frame labels are displayed in this drop-down menu). If you chose Expression, you would enter the expression here.

- ***Go To and Play.*** Once the timeline has jumped to a specific frame, this option allows you to specify whether the movie will stop playing at that frame or continue playing from that frame. If you leave this box unchecked, the movie will halt.

Sample script

The following script shows a mouse event that causes the current movie to go to Frame 10 of the Intro scene and then begin playing:

```
on (release) {
  gotoAndPlay ("Intro", 10);
}
```

The following script shows a mouse event in the current movie that causes another movie, a movie-clip instance named Baby, to go to a frame labeled Sleep and then stop (**Figure 11.18**):

```
on (release) {
  tellTarget ("Baby") {
  gotoAndStop ("Sleep");
  }
}
```

Figure 11.18
You can control another movie's timeline using the Go To action.

Real-world use

The Go To action is Flash's way of creating hyperlinks within a Flash movie.

Play

The Play action causes a movie to begin playing from its current position. If your movie stops (due to a Stop action or a Go To and Stop action), it cannot begin playing again until you use the Play action to start it.

Parameters

Play has no parameters.

Sample script

The following script shows a mouse event that causes the current movie to begin playing from its current position:

```
on (press) {
  play ();
}
```

The following script shows a frame event on the current movie's timeline that causes another movie—the movie-clip instance named `Guitar`—to start playing (if it's not already):

```
tellTarget ("Guitar") {
  play ();
}
```

Real-world use

Use the Play action to create Start/Stop buttons for various timelines.

Stop

The Stop action will cause a movie to cease playing. You can use it during any points in the movie that you wish to remain visible for an extended period of time.

Parameters

Stop has no parameters.

Sample script

The following script shows a mouse event that causes the current movie to stop playing:

```
on (press) {
  stop ();
}
```

The following script shows a frame event on the current movie's timeline that causes another movie, a movie-clip instance named `Guitar`, to stop (if it's playing):

```
tellTarget ("Guitar") {
  stop ();
}
```

Real-world use

Use the Stop action to create Start /Stop buttons, or place this action on any keyframes where the movie should be stopped.

Toggle High Quality

The Toggle High Quality action turns antialiasing off and on (**Figure 11.19**), which affects the visual quality and playback speed of your movie. With antialiasing on, visual quality improves but playback slows on older computers. With it off, just the opposite occurs. This action cannot affect a single target: When toggled, it affects all presently playing movies and movie-clip instances within Flash Player.

Parameters

This action has no parameters.

Sample script

The following script shows a mouse event that causes the high-quality setting of all movies currently playing in Flash Player to be toggled on or off, depending on its current setting:

Figure 11.19
Toggling the High Quality action affects how smooth your graphics appear while the movie is playing.

```
on (release) {
    toggleHighQuality ();
}
```

Real-world use

Use this action to determine view quality and to turn off antialiasing for intensely animated portions of a movie.

Stop All Sounds

The Stop All Sounds action halts all currently playing audio tracks in all movies and movie-clip instances within Flash Player. This action does not affect the visual aspects of your movie.

Parameters

This action has no parameters.

Sample script

The following script shows a mouse event that stops the audio tracks in all movies and movie-clip instances currently playing in Flash Player:

```
on (release) {
    stopAllSounds();
}
```

Real-world use

Use this action to turn off sounds (sound On/Off buttons), and to silence sound tracks.

Get URL

The Get URL action does two things: It either loads a specified URL into a browser window (in the same way an HTML hyperlink does), or it sends variable data in the movie to the specified URL. For example, variable data (such as that entered into a Flash form) can be sent to a CGI script for processing in the same way an HTML form can. When using this action to send variables, only variables for the movie specified in the action are sent. The specified movie can be the main movie, a movie clip, or a .swf file loaded using the Load Movie action. (For more information, see "Working with Multiple Timelines" in Chapter 12.)

Although you will use the Get URL action primarily when your Flash movie exists on a Web page, you can also use it in a Flash projector to automatically open a browser window and display a specified URL.

Parameters

Get URL has the following parameters:

- **URL.** This is where you define the URL for the Get URL action. It can be a relative path, such as *mypage.html*, or an absolute path, such as *http://www.mydomain.com/mypage.html*.

  If you are using this action to send movie variables to a CGI script or a Cold Fusion template, the URL entered into this box could look like *http://www.mydomain.com/cgi-bin/myscript.cgi* or *http://www.mydomain.com/mycftemplate.cfm*, respectively.

  If your Flash movie is on an HTML page, you can use this area to define a JavaScript function to call—such as *javascript:newWindow()*—when an event is triggered.

  You can dynamically set the URL to retrieve based on what value an expression evaluates to by selecting the Expression option to the right of the URL text box. For more information on expressions, see the next chapter.

- **Window.** Specifies the browser window or HTML frame in which to load and display the specified URL. If you have defined an HTML window or frames with a name and you want the specified URL to load into that window, simply type its name into this box. Otherwise, you can choose among the following options:

  _self. Loads the specified URL into the window or frame now occupied by the Flash movie.

  _blank. Opens a new browser window and loads the specified URL into it.

_parent. Opens the URL in the parent window of the current window.

_top. If the Flash movie is in an HTML frame, this removes the frame set and loads the URL into the browser window.

You can dynamically set the window or frame into which a URL is loaded based on what value an expression evaluates to. Select the Expression option to the right of the Window text box.

- *Variables.* Variable values in a movie can be sent to a server for processing. This option lets you choose how variables are dealt with when using the Get URL action. The following options are available:

  Don't send. Doesn't send variables. This option is best suited for simply opening a URL.

  Send using GET. Sends variable values that are appended to the specified URL for processing by the server. For example, passing two variables—name and age—using the GET method will result in something resembling the following URL:
  http://www.mydomain.com/mypage.html?name=Derek+Franklin&age= unknown.

  Send using POST. Sends variables separate from the URL, which makes it possible for you to send more variables. On regular HTML pages, this method is most frequently used to post information collected from a form to a CGI script on the server. In the same way, it can send variable values in your Flash movie to a CGI script for processing.

  TIP *When sending variables, only those from the specified movie get sent (rather than the variables from all of the movies in the Flash movie window).*

For more information about variables, see Chapter 12.

Sample script

The following script shows a mouse event that opens the specified URL in a new browser window:

```
on (release) {
    getURL ("http://www.mydomain.com/mypage.html", "_blank");
}
```

The following script shows a mouse event that posts the variables in the current time-line to a CGI script on the server.

```
on (release) {
  getURL ("http://www.mydomain.com/cgi-bin/myscript.cgi", "", "POST");
}
```

The following script shows a mouse event that posts the variables in the movie clip instance named flashForm to a CGI script on the server (**Figure 11.20**).

```
on (release) {
  tellTarget ("flashForm") {
  getURL ("http://www.mydomain.com/cgi-bin/myscript.cgi", "", "POST");
  }
}
```

Real-world use

Use this action to open URLs in a browser or to send variable data in a movie to a CGI script for processing.

FS Command

FS Command allows your Flash movie to communicate with other programs—say a Web browser or any program that can host your Flash movie (that is, one in which you can embed your Flash movie). Most people use this command to make their Flash movies interact with JavaScript on HTML pages.

Figure 11.20
Using the tellTarget() command in conjunction with a Get URL action allows you to post the variables in a specific movie to a Web server for processing.

To use FS Command to open custom alert boxes:

1. Create a Flash movie with a button that includes a mouse event that triggers an FS Command action.

2. When setting up the FS Command, type *Infobox* in the Command box and *We're Doing OK* in the Arguments box.

   You make up the command name, which can be anything from *turtle* to *hairspray*. It's just a unique identifier.

3. For the purposes of our example, if you wish to create a second button with an FS Command action on it, simply type *Infobox* in the Command box but *We're not so good* in the Argument box. You now have two buttons that use the same command but different arguments.

You now place your movie on the HTML page containing a JavaScript function that can detect when an FS Command has been activated in your movie. In our example, we set up this JavaScript function to evaluate the FS Command in a way that says, "If the command equals InfoBox, create an alert box that reads whatever the arguments of the FS Command were." Thus, depending on which button you click, an alert box opens that reads either "We're doing OK" or "We're not so good."

Obviously, there are all sorts of things you can accomplish via the FS Command, but they usually require a lot more JavaScripting. For most users, Flash's internal scripting (ActionScripting) engine should be more than sufficient for most jobs.

Parameters

This action has the following parameters:

- *Command.* This is a unique name you assign to an FS Command; it can be anything from *sausage* to *escalator.*

  You can dynamically set the command to perform based on what value an expression evaluates to by selecting the Expression option to the right of the Command text box.

- *Arguments.* If the command requires that any information be passed—for example, to a JavaScript function—you must enter it here. That information can take the form of a text string, such as "Hey Bob," or a numeric value, such as 35.

  You can dynamically set the arguments to be used based on what value an expression evaluates to by selecting the Expression option to the right of the Arguments text box.

- *Commands for stand-alone player.* You can use the following settings to control a Flash projector when distributing your movie as a stand-alone application:

  Fullscreen. To display a projector so that it can be seen at full screen, choose true. False displays it at the size set in the Movie Properties dialog box (**Figure 11.21**).

  Allowscale. Choose true to allow your user to resize the Projector window. False prevents the window from being resized.

Figure 11.21
A projector at full screen (left) and one the size of the move as set in the Movie Properties dialog box.

Showmenu. Choose true to make the Projector menu available when the user right-clicks (Windows) or Control-clicks (Macintosh) the projector window. False prevents the menu from being displayed.

Quit. Quits the projector and closes its window.

Exec. Use this command to start an external application from Flash. Enter the directory path to the application in the Argument box.

Sample script

The following script shows a frame event that opens a Projector window to full screen:

```
fscommand ("fullscreen", "true");
```

Real-world use

Use this action to control a Flash projector (stand-alone Flash application), as well as to interact with JavaScript.

For more information about parameters, see Chapter 12.

Load Movie

The Load Movie action allows you to do any of the following:

* Load a new movie into the Flash movie window to replace an existing one (which means you can display a new movie without loading a different HTML page).

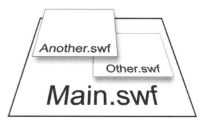

Figure 11.22
Loading movies using the Load Movie action lets you have multiple .swf files in the Flash Player window at once.

- Load an additional movie into the Flash movie window (**Figure 11.22**).

- Load a movie into a movie-clip target (thereby replacing the movie clip instance with an entire movie).

Parameters

This action has the following parameters (**Figure 11.23**):

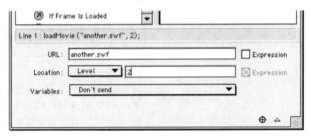

Figure 11.23
Available parameters for the Load Movie action.

- ***URL.*** This is the directory path to the .swf file you want to load. It can be a relative path, such as *mymovie.swf*, or an absolute path, such as *http://www.mydomain.com/mymovie.swf*.

    You can dynamically set the URL based on the value an expression evaluates to by selecting the Expression option to the right of the URL text box.

- ***Location.*** This parameter defines the level or target that will be affected by the specified action.

    Level. Levels can be thought of as layers of separate .swf files stacked on top of each other in the Flash Player window (**Figure 11.24**). The number assigned to a level determines its position relative to the other levels. As the bottom .swf file in the stack, Level 0 usually represents your original movie. The movie in Level 0 sets the frame rate, background color, and frame size for all other loaded movies. Movies can be loaded into levels that already contain another movie. Doing so simply replaces the existing .swf file on that level. For more information see "Working with Multiple Timelines" in Chapter 12.

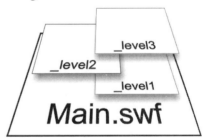

Figure 11.24
Loading a movie into a level places all of its content above any levels below it.

    You can dynamically set the level in which to load a movie based on what value an expression evaluates to by entering the expression directly into the Location text box.

Target. Allows you to load an entire .swf into a space currently occupied by a movie-clip instance. Doing so causes the loaded .swf to inherit all of the movie clip's current properties, including its name, target path, size, and position (**Figure 11.25**). In addition, if the target movie-clip instance is used in a motion tween or frame-by-frame animation, the loaded .swf will be used in its place.

You can dynamically set the target name in which to load a movie based on the value an expression evaluates to by selecting the Expression option to the right of the Target text box.

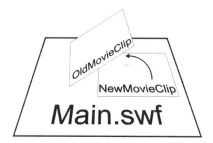

Figure 11.25
Loading a movie into a target allows a .swf file to replace a space originally occupied by a movie-clip instance.

- ***Variables.*** If you want to pass the current movie's variables into the one that's being loaded, you use this parameter to determine how those variables are sent. This means that a movie can receive variable data before it's loaded so that it can react to that data immediately. The following options are available:

    Don't send. Doesn't send variables from the current movie to the one being loaded.

    Send using GET. Sends variables appended to the specified URL.

    Send using POST. Sends variables separate from the URL (which allows you to send more variables).

To load a new movie into the Flash movie window to replace the existing one:

1. Select a frame, button, or movie-clip instance (depending on how you want the action triggered).

2. Choose Window > Panels > Actions to open the Actions panel.

3. In the Toolbox List window, double-click the Load Movie action.

    This adds the action to the current ActionScript as shown in the Actions List window.

4. For the URL parameter, enter the directory path to the .swf file you want loaded.

5. For the Location parameter, enter a level number that is currently occupied by another movie, or choose a movie-clip target to replace.

6. In the Variables parameter choose an option.

To load an additional movie into the Flash movie window:

1. Select a frame, button, or movie-clip instance (depending on how you want the action triggered).

2. Choose Window > Panels > Actions to open the Actions panel.

3. In the Toolbax list window, double-click the Load Movie action.

This adds the action to the current ActionScript as shown in the Actions List window.

4. For the URL parameter, enter the directory path to the .swf file you want loaded.

5. For the Location parameter, enter a level number that is not occupied by another movie.

When loading movies into levels, you are not required to choose sequential level numbers. You can load one movie into Level 6 and the next into Level 87.

6. In the Variables parameter choose an option.

TIP *Once loaded, various .swf files in the movie window can communicate with and control each other. For more information, see "Working with Multiple Timelines" in the next chapter.*

Real-world use

This action allows users to view various Flash movies without loading additional HTML pages. You can also use this action to replace a movie-clip instance with an entire .swf movie (which makes for more dynamic movies).

Unload Movie

The Unload Movie action allows you to unload a movie that had been loaded into the movie window using the Load Movie action.

Parameters

This action includes the following parameter:

- *Location.* This parameter defines the level or target containing the movie that will be unloaded.

  Level. Unloads the movie at the level specified.

  You can dynamically set the level from which to unload a movie based on the value an expression evaluates to by entering the expression directly into the Location text box.

Target. Unloads the movie at the specified target.

You can dynamically set the target name from which to unload a movie based on the value an expression evaluates to by selecting the Expression option to the right of the Target text box.

To unload a movie that was previously loaded into the movie window with the Load Movie action:

1. Select a frame, button, or movie-clip instance (depending on how you want the action triggered).

2. Choose Window > Panels > Actions to open the Actions panel.

3. In the Toolbax list window, double-click the Unload Movie action.

   This adds the action to the current ActionScript as shown in the Actions List window.

4. For the Location parameter, enter the level number or target path of the movie you want to unload.

Real-world use

This action is used to remove loaded movies from the movie window.

Tell Target

The Flash movie window can contain any number of timelines (the main movie, movie clips, and loaded movies). You use the Tell Target action—which is always employed in conjunction with an action—to control one timeline from within another. A target is identified by either its level (if it was loaded into the movie window) or its instance name (if it is a movie clip). The main movie is identified as _level0 or as _root (**Figure 11.26**). For more information, see "Working with Multiple Timelines" in the next chapter.

Figure 11.26
This graphic demonstrates some of the various ways a target is identified.

You can use the Tell Target action to start, stop, drag, hide, rotate, scale, and otherwise control any movie in the movie window.

Parameters

This command has only one parameter—target. This is where you define the movie that will be targeted for any actions. Pressing the Insert Target Path button (which resembles a crosshair) opens the Insert Target Path dialog box, where you can choose a target for an action. For more information on this feature, see "Working with Multiple Timelines" in Chapter 12.

You can dynamically choose the target based on what value an expression evaluates to by selecting the Expression option to the right of the Target text box. For more information on expressions, see Chapter 12.

> **TIP** *If you've used the Load Movie action to load another .swf into the movie window, you can target that movie by entering the level number in which it was loaded into the Target box above. Thus, if the movie was loaded into Level 5, you would enter _level5 in the Target box.*

Sample script

The following script shows a mouse event that causes the timeline of a movie-clip instance (myMovieClip) to jump to the frame label "myFrameLabel" (which is on the movie clip's timeline) and then stop:

```
on (release) {
  tellTarget ("myMovieClip") {
  gotoAndStop ("myFrameLabel");
  }
}
```

The Tell Target command isn't the only way to address a specific timeline. The following scripts demonstrate three ways a target can be addressed to perform an action. In the top script the target is defined using the tellTarget() command; in the middle script it's defined via the setProperty() command; and in the bottom script it's defined using a with statement. All three scripts perform the same action, which is to make myMovieClip 40 percent transparent:

```
on (release) {
  tellTarget ("myMovieClip") {
  setProperty ("", _alpha, 40);
  }
}
```

The second script:

```
on (release) {
    setProperty ("myMovieClip", _alpha, 40);
}
```

The third script:

```
on (release) {
    with (myMovieClip) {
    _alpha = 40;
    }
}
```

Real-world use

The Tell Target action is used to control one movie from another.

If Frame Is Loaded

If Frame Is Loaded is another command used to preface an action (and it's always used in conjunction with an action). The underlying logic goes something like this: If frame *x* is loaded, do these actions. If frame *x* is not loaded, ignore the "If Frame Is Loaded" command. This is known as a conditional statement: The action is only performed if the condition is met.

This command is commonly used to create a loop that constantly checks to see if the back end of a movie has been completely downloaded. This is also known as a *preloader* (see the sample script below).

Parameters

This action has the following parameters:

- *Scene.* Allows you to choose a scene as a starting point for the If Frame Is Loaded command. Once a scene has been defined, a frame number or label within that scene can be defined (below). The scene parameter is not available for symbols. The available options include the following:

  <current scene>. Allows you to choose a frame number or label from the current scene as the frame to check (see the Frame parameter below).

  Scene_Name. Select a scene name from the list that appears.

- **Type.** Based on the scene option you selected, this allows you to choose a specific frame in the scene as the frame to check for this action. The available options include the following:

    Frame Number. Select a frame number (which is entered in the Frame box below).

    Frame Label. Select a frame label (which is entered in the Frame box below).

    Expression. Allows you to dynamically set the frame to check for this action based on what value an expression evaluates to (which is entered in the Frame box below). For more information on expression, see Chapter 12.

- **Frame.** If you chose Frame Number from the Type drop-down box, you would enter the frame number here. If you chose Frame Label, you would enter the name of the label here (applicable frame labels are available from this drop-down menu). If you chose Expression, you would enter the expression here.

Sample script

The following scripts show how a basic preloader is put together. A frame event on Frame 1 of our movie triggers the `ifFrameLoaded()` action, which verifies that the frame labeled "`Start`" on a scene named "`MainScene`" (this is the scene that contains our main animation) has been loaded. If it has, the `gotoAndPlay()` action is carried out, causing the timeline to start playing your movie from that label forward. If the label has not been loaded, the command is ignored and the timeline continues on to Frame 2 (see below for the script that goes on Frame 2):

```
ifFrameLoaded ("MainScene", "Start") {
    gotoAndPlay ("MainScene", "Start");
}
```

The following script shows a frame event on Frame 2 that simply sends the timeline back to Frame 1 of our movie:

```
gotoAndPlay (1)
```

This triggers the `ifFrameLoaded()` command from the first script. Once again, if the "`Start`" frame still hasn't been loaded, the command is ignored, the timeline continues, and the `gotoAndPlay()` action on Frame 2 is triggered again, which starts the process all over again. This is known as a loop. This loop will continue until the "`Start`" label has been loaded, at which point the `gotoAndPlay()` action on Frame 1 as shown in the first script will be triggered.

Real-world use

This command is used to create a preloader or to prevent certain actions from being triggered before the necessary content has been downloaded by the viewer.

On Mouse Event

See "Mouse Events" earlier in this chapter.

Interactive Tutorials

- *Working with the Actions panel.* This tutorial will demonstrate how to add and delete actions and change their sequence as well as help you understand the overall workflow in the Actions panel.

- *Understanding Targets.* Flash novices often find targets mysterious. This tutorial removes the mystery by showing you how to target different timelines in the movie window.

- *Creating Interactivity.* This tutorial shows you how to use Flash's basic actions in your own presentations.

Building Advanced Interactivity Using ActionScript

CHAPTER 12

What you'll learn…

ActionScript basics

Working with multiple timelines

Working with objects

Using Smart Clips

Using the Actions panel for ActionScript

Printing from Flash

For many Flash users, creating sophisticated animations and interactive buttons is enjoyable, but the thought of actual programming makes their toes curl. There are all kinds of reasons users might shy away from the type of programming entailed in ActionScripts; however, the bottom line is this: To take your Flash movies to the next level, you need to understand ActionScripting. Armed with even the most basic knowledge of it, you'll be able to create games, interactive forms, highly-interactive interfaces, and much more.

Although you may find some of the concepts of ActionScripting new—and you may find it tough going at first—eventually things will fall into place. In this chapter we've tried to make the learning process as simple as possible by including plenty of scripts and real-world examples to demonstrate ActionScript's logic and flow. Be patient if you have to review the information more than once— few people are able to pick up scripting languages the first time around. And be sure to look at the interactive tutorials on the CD for examples of how to use ActionScripts to make your projects more exciting.

Keep in mind this chapter is not intended as an exhaustive examination of all that ActionScript can do. Instead, it should provide a solid basis for continuing to explore Action Scripting on your own.

What Is ActionScript?

Think of ActionScript as a basic programming language that gives you the ability to control timelines, sounds, colors, cursors, graphics, and data. However, although ActionScript is a programming language, it often reads much like a regular sentence. Take a look at the following script:

```
if (savings == 50000) {
  vehicleToBuy = "Porsche";
}else if (savings == 200) {
  vehicleToBuy = "Bicycle";
}
```

Even if you aren't familiar with ActionScript, you could probably make sense of the above script, which basically states, "If I have $50,000 in savings, I'm going to buy a Porsche; if I have $200 in savings, I'll have to settle for a bicycle."

A movie can contain a number of ActionScripts attached to frames, button instances, and movie clip instances. Each ActionScript is triggered to execute based on what it is attached to. For example, an ActionScript attached to a keyframe will execute when the playhead reaches that point in your movie. The art of using ActionScript comes in coordinating them to create interactivity.

ActionScript is based on the same standards as JavaScript, so if you're familiar with that scripting language, learning ActionScript should be a breeze.

ActionScript uses events, variables, operators, expressions, statements, functions, and objects to do what you ask of it. We'll explain all of these terms as we progress through the chapter.

Deconstructing a Script

To give you a taste of ActionScript's power and simplicity, we're going to explain how a sample script works and what it accomplishes. While not all of the syntax will make sense, we'll explain enough at this point for you to follow along.

Here's the set-up: On the stage is an input text element with a variable name of savings and a dynamic text element with a variable name of myGreeting. In addition to these two text elements, there are two movie clips on the stage as well as a button. One of the movie clips is of a Porsche with an instance name of myPorscheMovie; the other is a bicycle with an instance name of myBicycleMovie. The button labeled Enter is used to trigger the script below (**Figure 12.1**).

We ask the user if the amount in his or her savings account is closer to $50,000 or $200 and to enter that number into the input text element with the name `savings` and to then press the Enter button, which executes this script:

```
on (release) {
    if (savings == 50000) {
        vehicleToBuy = "Porsche";
    } else if (savings == 200) {
        vehicleToBuy = "bicycle";
    }
    if (vehicleToBuy == "Porsche") {
        myBicycleMovie._visible = false;
        myPorscheMovie.play();
        myGreeting = "Hope you enjoy your new " + vehicleToBuy + ".";
    } else if (vehicleToBuy == "bicycle") {
        myPorscheMovie._visible = false;
        myBicycleMovie.play();
        myGreeting = "Hope you enjoy your new " + vehicleToBuy + ".";
    }
}
```

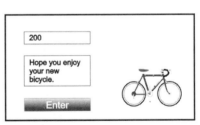

Figure 12.1
A graphical view of our fictitious project.

The first part of this script checks the number that the user entered. It states that if `savings` equals 50,000, set the value of `vehicleToBuy` to "Porsche"; if `savings` equals 200, set the value of `vehicleToBuy` to "Bicycle". The next part of the script performs several actions simultaneously, depending on the value of `vehicleToBuy`. If `vehicleToBuy` has a value of "Porsche" the script does three things: It makes the `myBicycleMovie` movie clip instance invisible; it starts playing the `myPorscheMovie` movie clip instance;

Figure 12.2
The result of entering a value of 200 in the "savings" text element and pressing the Enter button.

and it displays the message "Hope you enjoy your new Porsche" in the dynamic text element named `myGreeting`. If `vehicleToBuy` has a value of "bicycle" the script makes the `myPorscheMovie` movie clip instance invisible; it starts playing the `myBicycleMovie` movie clip instance; and it displays the message "Hope you enjoy your new bicycle" in the dynamic text element named `myGreeting` (**Figure 12.2**).

Thinking Like a Programmer

If you've looked at many Flash sites lately, you know that there are some amazing graphic artists and animators who are pushing Flash to its visual limits. What we see less of are sites that truly make use of Flash's interactive power. This is because for most designers, animation represents a natural evolution of their skills and interests; programming, on the other hand, is best left to others—or so they think. As a result, these artists miss an opportunity to express their talents in even more exciting ways.

Programming is an art in itself, and one that can easily elicit the type of response usually reserved for visual masterpieces. In the following, we'll briefly explain the process many programmers employ to get to the heart of their work—that is, solving problems.

Problem Solving

Consider yourself a Flash designer/engineer. Most engineers have one all-encompassing responsibility: to solve the problems with which they're presented. However, before an engineer can solve a problem, he or she must define it. Likewise, in Flash, you need to define what you want your project to accomplish before you even open the program. To do so, ask questions like the following:

- Do you want the user to enter information? If so, what kinds of information: name, address, phone numbers? Do you want to validate the information they enter?

- What navigational sections do you want your project to include? Is it important that the movie track what the current section is, and—if so—why?

- What types of interactivity do you want to include? Will there be custom cursors and/or draggable objects? If so, when will they appear and for what purpose?

- What sorts of things do you want to keep track of while your visitor is at your site—the amount of time they spend at a certain section, their names, how many times they click a certain button?

Such questions are extremely important in developing a Flash project. If you jump in without thinking about the many issues that may arise in the development process, you may find it nearly impossible to accomplish what you set out to do. However, if you ask these types of questions and develop your project on paper first, you can save a lot of time and frustration in the long run.

Breaking It Down

Goals worth pursuing often appear overwhelming at first, requiring time, money, and resources that far exceed our current means. Once we break these goals into manageable chunks, however, they begin to look doable. The same holds true for Flash programming. Take, for example, a Flash form that the user fills out: To validate, or verify the information entered into the entire form, you need to perform a number of separate validation tasks, including the following:

- Checking to make sure there is text in each input box.

- If a phone number is required, checking to make sure it contains no letters and that the characters at Positions 4 and 8 are dashes (–), as they are when phone numbers are written out.

- If you ask for a state, checking that a valid state name is entered.

You can use ActionScripts for each of these tasks—it's just a matter of determining which elements need to be checked to verify the whole. Once you have done this, Flash makes it easy to break your project into manageable chunks. Because Flash can load various .swf's into a single movie window, you can create content in different .swf's that can be loaded and unloaded when needed, easing the development of complex projects.

It's About Style

As you work with ActionScript, you'll discover that there are multiple ways of accomplishing a single objective. The following examples each accomplish the same thing: changing the visibility of the movie clip instance named `invisibleMan`:

Example 1

```
invisibleMan._visible = false;
```

Example 2

```
setProperty ("invisibleMan", visible, false);
```

Example 3

```
with (invisibleMan) {
  _visible == false;
}
```

None of these examples is right or wrong; the one you use is a matter of preference and style. In fact, just as a graphic artist can be known for his or her style, so, too, can a programming artist. No two programmers tackle a problem exactly the same way, nor does Flash require them to do so. Work the way that's most comfortable to you.

Coding Like a Pro

Although all programmers have their own styles, when it comes to constructing scripts, it's smart to follow some simple practices that will make your code easier to understand.

The first thing you should get into the habit of doing is using descriptive names for things you assign names to in your code, such as variables. No one says you have to use one-word names; in fact, short phrases can be extremely helpful. For example, the following variable names easily indicate the values they contain:

```
totalNumberCorrect
```

```
totalNumberWrong
```

You'll notice that the first word of all of our scripts begins with a lowercase letter, and that all following words begin with a capital letter:

```
thisIsAnExample
```

```
thisIsAnotherExample
```

This naming convention helps you distinguish programming code, such as variable names and ActionScript, from actual sentences in your scripts.

One way to construct scripts so that they will always make sense is to use comments as much as you can. Although many beginning programmers shun this step for the sake of speed, changing just one aspect of a complex script that *does not* have well-placed comments can cost you an entire day. Comments provide a way for developers to make sense of their code when they need to come back to it.

To create comments in ActionScript, you type two forward slashes (//) followed by the text of your comment:

```
//This is a comment
```

When this script is run, Flash ignores any input that follows those two forward slashes.

To add a comment to your script:

Click the Add (+) button on the Actions panel, and choose Actions > Comment from the menu.

You can use single lines of comments:

```
//Create a variable and give it a value of Joe
myVariable = "Joe"
```

If the Actions panel is in Expert mode, you can even add in-line comments:

```
if (myVariable < 5) { //check the value of myVariable
  myMessage = "You Lose"; //if less than 5, display "You Lose"
  in the input text element named myMessage
}
```

We use comments in some of the scripts in this chapter to help you understand not only how and when they can be used, but also what's going on in the script—which brings us to a point about using comments: Don't use them to explain every line in your code; that just adds to the confusion. Only use them in places where you think a brief description will help you decipher your code later in case you ever need to return to it.

Variables

Variables are an important part of just about any programming script, and ActionScript is no exception. As you can see from the following examples, a variable is basically a container that holds a value:

```
X = 25
Name = Derek
Age = 29
Income = 500
Best Band = The Beatles
IQ = 47
```

X, Name, Age, Income, BestBand, and *IQ* are all variable names, and the information that follows the equal sign is the value of that variable. In ActionScripting the same principles apply. Using ActionScript, you might create several variables, as the following script indicates:

```
//Create three variables
name = "Derek";
age = 29;
income = 500;
```

In Flash, variables can store any of the following (and more):

- A user's name
- Text greetings
- The number of times a button has been clicked
- A URL
- The value of a movie property (for example, width, height, location)
- The number of times an event has occurred
- The current frame number

In addition, variables can also be used for all sorts of dynamic functionality, including the following (and more):

- To display text in a dynamic text element *(see Script 1 below)*
- To dynamically set various parameter values in other actions *(see Script 2 below)*
- To send the timeline to a specific frame *(see Script 3 below)*

Script 1

The following script assumes there is a dynamic text element on the stage with a variable name of myGreeting. This script will cause the dynamic text element named myGreeting to display the message "Boy, aren't you glad today is Saturday?"

```
//create a variable and assign it a value of Saturday
myFavoriteDay = "Saturday";
myGreeting = "Boy, aren't you glad today is " + myFavoriteDay + "?";
```

Script 2

This script shows a mouse event that sets the value of seeThrough to 45. As soon as it is set, this variable's value is used to set the transparency value of the movie clip instance myMovieClip:

```
on(release){
  //create a variable and assign it a value of 45
  seeThrough = 45;
  myMovieClip._alpha = seeThrough;
}
```

Script 3

This script shows a mouse event that sets the value of `favoriteFrame` to 34. As soon as it is set, this variable's value is used in a `gotoAndPlay` action that sends the timeline to Frame 34:

```
on(release){
    //create a variable and assign it a value of 34
    favoriteFrame = 34;
    gotoAndPlay (favoriteFrame);
}
```

Types of Variables

In Flash, variable values can take the following basic forms:

- **Numbers.** A number value refers to anything from 0 to 999,999+. An `age` variable might have a value of 20, which in ActionScript would look like this:

  ```
  age = 20
  ```

- **Strings.** The term *string* is commonly used in programming languages to denote text values. Typical string values can include anything from "a" to "Hello, what's your name? Does your dog bite or is it a nice dog?" A string value can contain almost any number of letters (within reason) and can include text, spaces, punctuation, and even numbers. The value "345" can be thought of as a string value even though it involves numbers. String values that contain numbers are distinguished from actual number values through the use of quotation marks (that is, ActionScripting uses quotation marks to denote strings). Thus, while 1966 is considered a number value, "1966" is considered a string value. Variables that contain string values might look like the following:

  ```
  phraseThatPays = "Flash 5 Rocks!";
  favoriteWife = "Kathy";
  favoriteWifesAge = "Amazingly, the same as in Flash 4 book, 29.";
  ```

- **Boolean.** This type of value refers to whether a condition exists. The possible Boolean values are `true` and `false`. In Flash, `false` has the numerical equivalent of 0, and `true` can be any nonzero number. Boolean values are used for creating scripts that can analyze data and then take action accordingly (for more information see "Statements" later in this chapter). Assigning a Boolean value to a variable in Flash would look something like this:

```
macromediaRocks = true;

macromediaRocks = 1;
```

There are a couple of other supervariable types in ActionScript: Objects and Arrays. We will discuss these in more detail later in the chapter.

Creating Variables

You create variables by simply entering a variable name (that you come up with) followed by an equal sign (=) followed by a value you determine. This is known as assigning a variable to a value. Each timeline has its own unique set of variables, including the main movie, each movie clip instance, and any loaded movies. Unless you specify a timeline in which to create a variable, it becomes a variable in the current movie. For more information, see "Working with Multiple Timelines" later in this chapter.

To create a variable and assign it a value:

1. Select a button or movie clip instance on the stage or a keyframe on the timeline.

2. Open the Actions panel.

3. Click the Add (+) button, and choose Actions > set variable from the menu that appears.

    The Set Variable parameters appear on the bottom of the Actions panel.

4. In the Variable box enter a name to describe the variable.

5. In the Value box, you need to make a choice (**Figure 12.3**):

    If the value of this variable will contain a text string (such as, "Hi, how are you?"), just enter it (without quotes) into the box. Because the Expression option to the right of the Value box is unchecked by default, Flash treats whatever you enter as a string value (even if you enter something like *465*).

    If you wish this value to be treated as a number, Boolean value, or even an expression, check the Expression option. If you look at the script in the Action list window while you're doing this, you'll see that the quotation marks are removed from the value portion of the assignment (which is necessary when assigning a number, Boolean, or expression as a value).

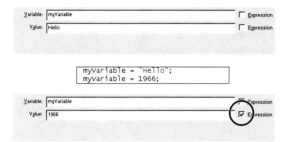

Figure 12.3
Leaving the Expression box unchecked (top) assigns a string value to the variable. Checking the Expression option (bottom) means the value will be treated as a number, Boolean, or expression.

6. Close the Actions panel.

- A variable is not created and its value cannot be used until the event that triggers the set-variable action, which creates the variable, occurs.

- Once a variable is created, it doesn't exist in any special place; it's simply a value that becomes available to scripts when you want to use it. Consider a variable like a radio wave and a script that uses the variable like a receiver. The variable, once created, simply floats around until it is needed or updated.

- Each movie or movie clip instance has a unique set of variables (**Figure 12.4**). Under most circumstances, a variable exists in the timeline in which it was created. Thus, if a frame action on the main timeline is used to create a variable, it exists as part of the main timeline. If, however, a frame action in a movie clip instance is used to create the variable, the variable is part of that movie clip instance's timeline. This concept is important to understand when you want to use the value of a variable. The name of the timeline that it's part of acts as the variable's address (as shown below).

```
on(release){
    //use the value of the variable named myVariable, which exists
    in the movie clip instance named myMovieClip, to set the
    transparency of the movie clip instance named myWindow
        myWindow._alpha = myMovieClip.myVariable;
}
```

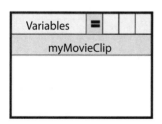
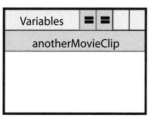

Figure 12.4
The movie clip instance on the left contains a different set of variables than the movie clip instance on the right.

- The variables in a timeline continue to exist, and their values can be set or retrieved as long as the timeline is present, whether it is moving or not. Thus, if a movie clip contains a variable that you've used in your scripts, and that movie clip is removed from the movie window, its variables are removed as well and are no longer available. For more information, see "Working with Multiple Time-lines" later in this chapter.

Variable names

When naming variables in Flash, be aware of the following:

- *All variable names must begin with a character.* The characters that follow can be letters, digits, or underscores. In addition, names are not case-sensitive, so MyVariable is the same as myvariable. Names cannot contain spaces.

```
//Examples of valid variable names
myVariable
my_variable
my_variable_2

//Examples of invalid variable names
27myVariable
my variable
my@variable
```

- *Variable names should make sense.* If a variable holds a value for the number of times the user has clicked a mouse button, you could name that variable mouseClicks or something similar.

- *A dynamic or input text element is assigned a variable name in a different manner.* Whereas you use the set-variable action to assign most variable names, dynamic and input text elements are assigned names as one of their properties on the Text Options panel (**Figure 12.5**). The value of an input or dynamic text element (the text it displays) is determined by text the user enters while the movie is playing, or it can be dynamically generated using the

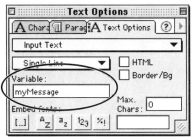

Figure 12.5
Variable names for dynamic and input text elements are set using the Text Options panel.

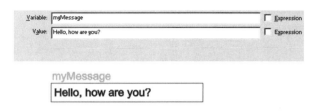

Figure 12.6
If a user types new text into an input or dynamic text element, the typed text automatically becomes that element's new value.

set-variable action (**Figure 12.6**). For more information, see "Working with Input and Dynamic Text Elements" later in this section.

- *Even though a variable's value may change, its name will remain the same.* For example, at one point in your movie, the value of x might be 25, while later in your movie it might be 720.

Assigning values

You can assign either a *literal* or an *expression* value to a variable. A *literal* is a value explicitly and definitively assigned to a variable, whereas an *expression* is a value based on a phrase that is evaluated (see "Expressions" later in this chapter). Take a look at the following *literal* assignments:

```
cost = 25.00;
```

Or this one:

```
name = "John Doe";
```

Notice that the values assigned to the variables are not really dynamic. For example, if you wanted to use the value of cost elsewhere in your ActionScript, it would always have a value of 25.00. Likewise, the value of name would always be "John Doe." Not very exciting. To create more dynamically assigned values, you could use an expression instead. For example:

```
product = 20.00;
tax = 5.00;
cost = product + tax;
```

In the preceding script, the value of the cost variable is product + tax, which are themselves variables. To break cost into its most basic parts, it could be read as "cost = 20.00 + 5.00," which would total 25.00. However, if the value of product changed to 22.00 and the value of tax became 6.00, the value of cost would automatically become 28.00

because cost is based on the value of `product + tax`. Here's another example where the value of the variable `name` is based on an expression:

```
firstName = "John ";

lastName = "Doe";

name = firstName + lastName;

//name has a value of "John Doe'
```

You can assign values to variables in several other ways. For more information, see "Operators" later in this chapter.

Updating variable values

At times, you'll want to update a variable's value—for example, changing its value from `Joe` to `Fred`.

Updating a variable is as simple as assigning a new value to an existing variable name:

```
//Create a variable and give it a value of Joe

myVariable = "Joe";

//Update the value of myVariable to Fred

myVariable = "Fred";

//myVariable no longer has a value of Joe but now has a value of Fred
```

Or using numbers:

```
//Create a variable and give it a value of 10

myVariable = 10;

//Update the value of myVariable to 20

myVariable = 20;

//myVariable no longer has a value of 10 but now has a value of 20
```

You can even change the value of a variable from a string to a number or Boolean as the following script shows:

```
//Create a variable and give it a value of 10

myVariable = 10;

//Update the value of myVariable to true

myVariable = true;

//myVariable no longer has a value of 10 but now has a value of true
```

Whichever manner you decide to do it, updating variables is an important aspect of a dynamic movie. If a number of ActionScripts rely on the value of the variable, changing it will change how those scripts work.

Any number of mouse, frame, or clip events can be used in updating variables. For example, if you wanted to track what button a user has clicked, you would attach the following scripts on each button, respectively:

```
//Button 1
on(release) {
  whatButton = 1;
}
//Button 2
on(release) {
  whatButton = 2;
}
//Button 3
on(release) {
  whatButton = 3;
}
```

Depending on what button the user presses, the value of whatButton would change and that value could be used in various ActionScripts to perform certain actions based on the current value of whatButton.

The string value of an input or dynamic text element (which is considered a variable; see "Working with Input and Dynamic Text Elements" in this section) is always displayed in the element and updated constantly. Thus, if a text element displays the word *Mushroom,* this is its value; however, if your user types *tomato* into that element, that becomes the new value automatically.

Using Variables

Once a variable has been created, anytime you wish to use its value in your scripts, you simply refer to the variable's name as shown in the following script.

```
on(release){
  //create a variable and assign it a value of 27
  favoriteNumber = 27;
  //send the timeline to the frame on the value of favoriteNumber
  gotoAndPlay (favoriteNumber);
  //set the transparency and width of myMovieClip based on
  the value of favoriteNumber
  myMovieClip._alpha = favoriteNumber;
  myMovieClip._width = favoriteNumber;
  //output a greeting to the dynamic text element named myGreeting
  based on the value of favoriteNumber
  myGreeting = "The greatest number in the world is " + favoriteNumber
+ ".";
}
```

This script demonstrates the power of variables in the sheer number of elements that are affected by the value of favoriteNumber: If its value changes, so will the results these actions produce.

Input Text Elements and Dynamic Text Elements

As you learned in Chapter 4, input and dynamic text elements are dynamic blocks of text identified by a variable name. You can use this variable name (and hence its value) in ActionScripts as you would any other variable.

For example, imagine an input text element on the stage with a variable name of frameNumber. Someone has entered 27 in it. A button is pushed, and the script below is executed:

```
on (release) {
  gotoAndPlay (frameNumber);
}
```

This script would send the timeline to Frame 27.

If you wanted to dynamically generate a message that is displayed in a dynamic text element with a variable name of `message`, you could use the following ActionScript (which is triggered by a mouse event). This ActionScript would generate a message based on the text that was entered into an input text element with a variable name of `name`. For our demonstration, we enter *Ashlie* in this field:

```
on (release) {
    message = "Hello," + name + ", is your homework finished?";
}
```

This script would generate the following message in the dynamic text element with a variable name of `message` when the mouse event occurred:

"Hello, Ashlie, is your homework finished?"

Inserting Line Breaks in Dynamically Generated Text

Using the newline *function (found on the Actions panel by choosing Functions > newline), you can insert line breaks in dynamically generated text.*

Imagine a text field on the stage with a variable name of name; *a user has entered the word* Jim *in the field. The user clicks a button, and the script below is executed:*

```
on (release) {
    greeting = "Hello there, ";
    phrase = greeting + name + "." + newline + "How are you today?";
}
```

When this script has executed, based on the information entered into the name text element, *another text element with a variable name of* phrase *will display a string that looks like this:*

"Hello there, Jim.

How are you today?"

Operators

Variables and their values are only part of the ActionScript picture. Variables simply contain data; to create truly dynamic movies, you need a way to manipulate that data to produce new data. This is where operators come into play. The most common operators are arithmetic operators such as plus (+) or minus (-) signs. Take a look at the following script:

```
10 + 5
```

In this script the plus sign is the operator and the numbers *10* and *5* are known as *operands* (since they are the values being used by the operator to calculate a new value). You can also use variable names in conjunction with an operator to produce a similar result:

```
number1 = 10;
number2 = 5;
total = number1 + number2;
```

Flash uses many types of operators for all sorts of data manipulation. In the following section, we'll look at the most common.

Arithmetic Operators

Arithmetic operators are commonly used for manipulating numbers by adding, subtracting, multiplying, dividing, and returning the value of a remainder (as you get when one number cannot be divided evenly by another number). **Table 12.1** provides a list of arithmetic operators and a brief description of their functions.

Table 12.1
Arithmetic Operators

Operator	Function
+	Adds one value to another value
-	Subtracts one numeric value from another
*	Multiplies one numeric value by another
/	Divides one numeric value by another
%	Divides one number from another and returns the value of the remainder
++	Increments a number
--	Decrements a number

Let's look at some sample scripts to explain how these operators work.

Sample script

In the following script, `total` has a value of 11 because it simply adds the values of `price` and `tax` together.

```
on (release) {
    price = 10;
    tax = 1;
    total = price + tax;
}
```

Sample script

In the following script, `total` still has a value of 11, but notice how the value of `tax` is determined: The value of `price` is multiplied by .10—essentially the same as saying 10 * .10, which equals 1. Thus, `tax` is assigned a value of 1. Then, the value of `price` + `tax`, or 10 + 1), is assigned to `total`.

```
on (release) {
    price = 10;
    tax = price * .10;
    total = price + tax;
}
```

Sample script

The addition operator (+) can also be used with strings of text to concatenate (connect) them. It is the only arithmetic operator that can be used with text. In the following script, `myLocation` has a value of "Bloomington, Indiana."

```
on (release) {
    city = "Bloomington, ";
    state = "Indiana";
    myLocation = city + state;
}
```

> **TIP** *If you attempt to add a string of characters and a number, Flash will convert the number to a text string and treat it as such. Thus, 1812 becomes "1812" in such cases.*

Sample script

The modulo operator (%) is used to automatically divide the first number by the second and then return the value of the remainder. In the following script, finalNumber has a value of 1. This is because 10 divided by 3 equals 3 with a remainder of 1.

```
finalNumber = 10 % 3;
```

This operator is great for determining whether a number is odd or even, as the following script demonstrates:

```
if (inputNumber % 2 == 0) {
  gotoAndStop ("Even");
} else {
  gotoAndStop ("Odd");
}
```

In English this script reads, "If the current value of inputNumber divided by two has no remainder, go to the frame labeled Even; otherwise, go to the frame labeled Odd. The name inputNumber could apply to a variable or a dynamic text element where the user entered a number.

Sample script

The increment (++) and decrement (--) operators will increase or decrease by 1 the value of the variable supplied to it. Thus, homeRuns++ increases the value of homeRuns by 1. Take a look at the following script:

```
homeRuns = 15
score = homeRuns++;
```

In this script, the variable score is assigned the current value of homeRuns (which, for our demonstration, is 15). Afterwards, homeRuns is then incremented by 1 to have a new value of 16. Notice the position of the increment operator in relation to the variable it's incrementing—it's to the right. If we moved the increment operator to the left of the homeRuns variable (++homeRuns), the variable would be increased by 1, and the result would be assigned to score, meaning score would be assigned a value of 16.

The decrement operator works the same as the increment operator, but in the opposite direction—that is, it decreases the value of the specified variable by 1.

Using these operators to increment and decrement values is an important aspect of creating scripts that can handle numerous tasks at once, as you'll learn in the section on "Statements" later in this chapter.

Assignment Operators

Assignment operators are used to assign values to variables. The only one we've used thus far is the equal sign. **Table 12.2** provides a list of assignment operators and a brief description of their functions.

Table 12.2
Assigment Operators

Assignment	Function
x = y	The value x is assigned the value of y
x += y	The value x is assigned the value of x + y or x = x + y
x -= y	The value x is assigned the value of x - y or x = x - y
x *= y	The value x is assigned the value of x * y or x = x * y
x /= y	The value x is assigned the value of x / y or x = x / y
x %= y	The value x is assigned the value of x % y or x = x % y

By now, you're familiar with the first operator in the table: It assigns the variable on the left side of the equal sign the value of whatever exists on the right side of the equal sign. The rest of these table entries are known as *compound assignment operators,* and they represent shortcuts for writing code, as shown in the description in the right column of the table.

Sample script

```
on (release) {
    x = 50; //x is assigned a value of 50
    y = 200; //y is assigned a value of 200
    x += y; // x is assigned a new value of 250, or the value of x + y
}
```

The = and =+ assignment operators are also used for text, as the following script demonstrates:

Sample script

```
on (release) {
    x = "Bryan "; // x is assigned a value of "Bryan "
    y = "Modders"; // y is assigned a value of "Modders"
    x += y; // x is assigned a new value of Bryan Modders, or the value
of x + y
}
```

Comparison Operators

Adding and subtracting values is just one way you can manipulate values. Using comparison operators, you can also *compare* the values of variables that contain numbers or strings.

Table 12.3 provides a list of comparison operators and a brief description of their functions.

Table 12.3
Comparison Operators

Operator	Function
==	Equal to
!=	Not equal to
<	Less than
>	Greater than
<=	Less than or equal to
>=	Greater than or equal to

Comparison operators are used to return a value of true or false.

Sample script

The following variables have a value of true:

```
myVariable1 = 10 == 10;
myVariable2 = 50 > 20;
```

Now let's put these examples in terms you can understand: For example, 10 == 10 in English would be "Does 10 equal 10?" The answer is *yes,* or in ActionScript, true. In the next example, "Is 50 a greater value than 20?" the answer is *yes,* or true.

Sample script

Comparison operators can also be used on string values as well to determine the value of strings based on their first character. *A* has a lower value than *Z*. Small characters (*a* to *z*) hold greater value than capital letters (*A* to *Z*). Values of strings are case sensitive, which means that "kathy" does not equal "Kathy." The following variables have a value of true:

```
myStringValue1 = "Jack" == "Jack";
myStringValue2 = "bcdef"> "abcde";
myStringValue3 = "Eddie"< "eddie";
```

TIP *It's easy to confuse the assignment operator (=) with the comparison operator (==). Just remember, = is used to assign values, whereas == is used to test equality between two values.*

Sample script

The following variables have a value of `false`:

```
myVariable1 = 10 == 9;
myVariable2 = "Camille"> "camille";
```

Sample script

You can also compare variables using any of the comparison operators:

```
myValue = myVariable1 == myVariable2;
```

Sample script

The not equal (!=) operator needs a bit of explanation. Take a look at the following scripts, which assign a value of `true` to each variable:

```
myVariable1 = 10 != 20;
myVariable2 = "Dog"!= "Cat";
```

In these scripts, we're checking for *inequality,* and saying that if it exists, then the value of the variable is `true`.

Sample script

Let's take a look at a couple more scripts to see how a comparison operator could be used:

```
on (release) {
  paycheck = 200;
  bills = 500;
  if (paycheck >= bills) {
    gotoAndStop ("Happiness");
  } else {
    gotoAndStop ("NotSoHappy");
  }
}
```

This script created two variables, `paycheck` and `bills`, and assigned them numeric values. The `if` statement (which you'll learn about shortly) checks whether the value of paycheck is greater than or equal to the value of bills. If it is, the timeline jumps to a frame labeled Happiness; if not, it jumps to a frame labeled NotSoHappy.

> **TIP** *You can only compare numbers to numbers or strings of text to other strings.*

Sample script

Imagine an input text element on the stage with a variable name of password. Someone has entered the text *Boom Bam* into the field. The user pushes a button, and the script below is executed:

```
on (release) {
  if (password == "Boom Bam") {
  gotoAndStop ("Accepted");
  } else {
  gotoAndStop ("AccessDenied");
  }
}
```

When this script has executed (based on information entered into the password text field), the timeline will go to and stop on the frame labeled Accepted.

Logical Operators

Logical operators are used to compare Boolean values of true and false. They can also be some of the trickiest operators to understand, so feel free to review this section several times.

Table 12.4 provides a list of logical operators and a brief description of their functions.

Table 12.4
Logical Operators

Operator	Function
&&	Logical AND
||	Logical OR
!	Logical NOT

The AND operator (&&) compares two Boolean values to see if they're both true. The OR operator (||) compares two Boolean values to see if at least one is true. The NOT (!) operator checks whether a Boolean value is not true.

Like comparison operators, logical operators return a value of true or false.

Sample script

```
myValue1 = (10 == 10) && (a < b);
```

In this script, myValue1 is assigned a value of true because (10 == 10) is true and so is the code (a < b). The AND operator in this equation is used to ask "is the first comparison AND the second comparison true?" Compare this with the following:

```
myValue1 = (10 == 5) && (a < b);
```

In this script, myValue1 is assigned a value of false because (10 == 5) is false, even though (a < b) is true. They must both be true in order for the AND operator to return a value of true.

Logical operators can also be used with variables, as the next example demonstrates:

```
question1 = true;
question2 = false;
hundredPercentCorrect = question1 && question2;
```

In this script, hundredPercentCorrect is assigned a value of false because only one variable contains a value of true. The AND operator in this equation is used to ask "Do question1 *and* question2 both have a value of true?"

Sample script

```
myValue2 = (10 == 5) || (a < b);
```

In this script, myValue2 is assigned a value of true because while (10 == 5) is false, (a < b) is true. The OR operator only requires that one *or* the other be true. If neither one is true, the OR operator returns a value of false.

Sample script

The NOT operator (!) can be a bit confusing. To help you understand it, let's take a look at the following example:

```
myValue3 = !(10 == 5);
```

In this script, myValue3 is assigned a value of true. The NOT operator in this equation is used to ask, "Is the equation in parentheses—10 equals 5?—untrue?" Since the operator is trying to determine whether the equation is untrue, it returns a value of true if the numbers aren't the same. If the operator doesn't find what it's looking for, it returns a value of false—a concept you may need to review several times to grasp.

Sample script

```
on (release) {
  paycheck = 1000;
  decision = "Buy";
  if (paycheck >= 1000 && decision == "Buy") {
  gotoAndStop ("New Computer");
  } else {
  gotoAndStop ("Cry");
  }
}
```

This script checks to determine whether the numeric value of paycheck is greater than or equal to 1000 *and* whether the string value of decision equals "Buy". If they do, go get a new computer; if not, cry your brains out!

Whew! That's enough about operators for now. Although there are still more operators that can be used in ActionScripts, they go well beyond the scope of this book. The ones we've discussed here are the ones that begnning or intermediate Flash users are most likely to use.

Expressions

Expressions represent the heart of any truly dynamic and interactive Flash movie, making each user's experience unique. Although many of the scripts you've seen up to this point contain expressions, it's time to describe and explain their function in your ActionScripts.

Basically, an expression is a phrase—or collection of variables, numbers, text, and operators—that represents one evaluation, result, or assignment. Expressions are evaluated to carry out a number of tasks, including setting a variable's value, defining which targets it will affect, determining which frames to go to, and more. Take a look at the following script, which uses an expression to evaluate which frame number to go to:

```
on (release){
  gotoAndPlay (24 + 26);
}
```

The expression in the preceding script—what 24 + 26 evaluates to—would cause the timeline to jump to Frame 50. Pretty simple, don't you think? You could go even further and create a script that used variable values to accomplish the same thing in a different way:

```
on (release){
    favoriteNumber = 24;
    secondFavNumber = 26;
    gotoAndPlay (favoriteNumber + secondFavNumber);
}
```

Using expressions in your scripts is easy. Many parameters that you'll set for actions in the Actions panel have an Expression option. Use expressions to set dynamic values in your scripts. A single script can contain many expressions.

To use an expression in a script:

1. Select a button instance or a movie clip instance on the stage or a keyframe on the timeline.

2. Open the Actions panel.

3. Click the Add (+) button, and choose Basic Actions > Get URL from the menu that appears.

   The Get URL action parameters will appear on the bottom of the Actions panel.

4. Check the Expression option next to the URL box, and enter an expression in the URL paremeter box, such as the following:

   ```
   "http://www." + currentDomain + ".com";
   ```

5. Close the Actions panel.

   Depending on the value of `currentDomain`, this action will open the appropriate URL. For example, if `currentDomain` had a value of `"Macromedia"` this action would open Macromedia's site; however, if `currentDomain` had a value of `"CNN"` this action would open CNN's site.

Parentheses and Precedence

The evaluation of an expression follows what's known as *an order of precedence.* This term refers to the order in which parts of an expression are evaluated. Anything in parenthesis is evaluated first, followed by anything multiplied or divided and then by anything added or subtracted. Be keenly aware of this rule: The order can affect the end value of an expression. Use parentheses to clarify how the expression should be evaluated.

```
10 + 25 * 3 - 1
```

This expression evaluates to a value of 84. This is because 25 is multiplied by 3 first (since multiplication has precedence in an expression), which equals 75. Then, the 10 on the left is added to the 75, which makes it 85. Finally, 1 is subtracted from 85, which results in a value of 84. Compare this to the following expression, which uses the same numbers and operators but uses parentheses to clarify how the expression should be evaluated.

```
(10 + 25) * (3 - 1)
```

This expression results in a value of 70. This is because 10 is added to 25, which results in a value of 35. Then, 1 is subtracted from 3, which results in a value of 2. Finally, 35 is multiplied by 2, which results in a value of 70.

Statements

A statement in ActionScript can be likened to a sentence describing a set of instructions to be performed (including how and in what order). Like a sentence, a statement contains words (usually variable names, operators, and expressions) to provide meaning, and punctuation to denote structure. We'll explain this structure as we go along.

Controlling the Flow

Statements control the way actions are executed in a script. Normally, lines in an ActionScript are executed one after another from top to bottom. However, statements can alter this flow so that actions are executed based on varying conditions. Think of a flowchart as a visual representation of an ActionScript statement. The following examines some of the types of statements ActionScript allows you to use.

If/Then Statement

An If/Then statement is also known as a *conditional* statement: If a condition is met, certain actions are performed. Take a look at the following conditional statement:

```
if (outside == "rain") {
  gotoAndStop ("Bed");
}
//next line of code
```

In this script, if outside has a value of "rain," the action gotoAndStop ("Bed"); is executed; if not, the action is ignored and the script moves to the next line of code.

If/Else Statement

An If/Else statement is also a conditional statement that builds on the last one: This one says that if a condition is met, certain actions are performed; if the condition is not met, a different set of actions is performed. Take a look at the following conditional statement:

```
if (outside == "rain") {
  gotoAndStop ("Bed");
} else {
  gotoAndPlay ("Park");
}
```

The above conditional statement shows that if outside has a value of "rain," go to bed; however, if outside has a value of anything else, go to the park.

If/Else-If Statement

An If/Else-If statement lets you check for multiple conditions. Take a look at the following example:

```
if (outside == "rain") {
  gotoAndStop ("Bed");
} else if (outside == "sun") {
  gotoAndPlay ("Park");
} else if (outside == "snow") {
  gotoAndPlay ("SkiResort");
} else if (outside == "tornado") {
  gotoAndStop ("Basement");
} else {
  gotoAndPlay ("TV");
  lifeIsGood = true;
}
```

This conditional statement also checks the value of outside; however, it does so with a twist. In our new conditional statement, different actions are possible depending on the condition that's met. This is due to the addition of *else if* to our conditional statement. For example, if `outside` has a value of "`rain`" it's time to go back to bed. If it has a value of "`sun`" it's time to go to the park and have fun. If it has a value of "`snow`" it's off to the ski resort. If it has a value of "`tornado`" head for the basement. And if it doesn't match any of our conditions, go watch TV and update the value of `lifeIsGood` to `true`.

The Anatomy of a Statement

Many beginners have a hard time understanding the way a statement's syntax works. How to make sense of the curly brackets, parentheses, quotes, and semicolons that are used sometimes but not others? Just remember that ActionScripts are similar to sentences, and that all of these different characters simply denote punctuation. And keep in mind these few simple rules:

- *Most statements begin with what is known as a keyword such as if or while. A keyword sets the context of the script. In the case of the if keyword, the script checks to see whether a certain condition exists and then performs various actions based on what it discovers.*

- *Data in parentheses makes a script function in a unique way. In the case of an if statement, parentheses contain a condition to look for.*

- *Data between curly brackets ({}) usually denotes actions that need to be carried out, such as sending a timeline to a particular frame label, setting the value of a variable, and so on.*

- *Semicolons separate each action.*

- *Quotation marks are used only to denote string values used in scripts.*

While Statements

You use a While statement to perform a series of actions while a condition is true—what's known as a *looping statement*. The logic used in a While statement might look something like this: While *x* equals 10, perform these actions repeatedly (loop); however, as soon as *x* no longer equals 10, stop performing these actions and begin performing whatever action follows the While statement. If you don't provide a means for the condition to eventually become false, you'll be create an endless loop that prevents your movie from functioning properly.

Sample script

A While statement provides for some sophisticated scripting within Flash. The following script shows the concept behind the way it works:

```
count = 1;
myPhrase = "";
while (count <= 10) {
  myPhrase += "Echo ";
  count++ ;
}
//next line of code
```

Let's look at each section of this script. The first thing that happens in this script is that two variables are created: The variable count is assigned an initial value of 1, and myPhrase is assigned a string value of "" (meaning nothing).

```
count = 1;
myPhrase = "";
```

Next, the While statement is set up, which basically says that while count has a value less than or equal to 10, repeat or loop through the actions defined between the curly brackets ({}).

```
while (count <= 10) {
```

The first action sets the value of the variable myPhrase to be updated on each loop.

```
myPhrase += "Echo ";
```

Going into the first loop, myPhrase only has a value of "" (as we initially set it to have), so when the action that says myPhrase += "Echo "; is executed, myPhrase is updated to its current value plus "Echo". Since myPhrase was empty to begin with, this results in myPhrase containing an updated value of "Echo ". On the second loop, myPhrase is updated to its current value, which is now "Echo ", plus "Echo ". This results in myPhrase having a new value of "Echo Echo ". In this script, each loop simply adds "Echo" the value of myPhrase, so at the end of the loop, myPhrase has a value of "Echo Echo Echo Echo Echo Echo Echo Echo Echo Echo ".

The second action that is repeated is the updating of the value of count by 1 using the increment operator (++) that you learned about earlier.

```
count++ ;
```

Thus, after 10 loops, count will have a value of 11 and the loop will stop. This is an important action because without it, your While statement would be an endless loop, resulting in errors.

Looping through actions using a statement such as the previous one happens in a split-second. Unless you have a superslow computer, you won't see the result of each loop iteration individually, only the result of the entire looping statement.

When Would I Use a Looping Statement?

After looking at our example looping statement, you may be thinking, "OK, so I can repeat words—big deal." What you really want to know is how to use a looping statement in the real world. Here's a hint: They're great for repeating a set of actions; take a look at the following ActionScript:

```
on (release) {
    count = 1;
    while (count <= 3) {
        duplicateMovieClip ("myMovieClip", "newClip" + count, count);
        count++;
    }
}
```

The While statement in this script has one purpose: to create three duplicate movie clips when a button is clicked. It does so in very simple fashion: The duplicateMovieClip() action has three parameters, as indicated in the parentheses next to it. A comma separates the parameters. The first parameter indicates the instance name of the movie clip to duplicate. The second parameter indicates the instance name to assign to the duplicate. The third parameter indicates what level number to place the duplicate on. You'll notice the values of the second and third parameters are dependent on the current value of count. Since this statement is set up to loop three times and the value of count gets updated by 1 with each loop, this looping statement would create the following results:

- A duplicate movie clip instance named "newClip1" on Level 1
- A duplicate movie clip instance named "newClip2" on Level 2
- A duplicate movie clip instance named "newClip3" on Level 3

One button-click creates, names, and places three move-clip instances on different levels in the movie window. Very powerful!

The real power, though, comes from being able to dynamically set the number of loops. You accomplish this by using a variable. Look at the next script, which is the same as the last except that a variable name is used to determine the number of times the statement is looped through:

```
on (release) {
    count = 1;
    while (count <= myVariable) {
        duplicateMovieClip ("myMovieClip", "newClip" + count, count);
        count++;
    }
}
```

You'll notice that 3 has been replaced by a variable named myVariable. If this were the variable name of an input text element, a number the user entered into it would affect the number of times the While statement looped and thus the number of duplicate movies created. In many looping statements, the number of loops is dynamically set in a similar manner.

For Statements

The For statement also creates a loop, but it does so a bit differently than the While statement. In most cases, either type of statement will work for the same task. If you understand the While statement, the For statement should be a breeze to learn. Look at the following script, which performs the same actions as the While statement example (shown earlier) but uses the For statement's syntax:

```
myPhrase = "";
for (count = 1; count <= 10; count++) {
  myPhrase += "Echo ";
  }
//next line of code
```

Here's how the For statement works. The first thing that happens in this script is that the variable myPhrase is created and given an initial value of "" (nothing).

```
myPhrase = "";
```

Next, the For statement is set up.

```
for (count = 1; count <= 10; count++) {
```

The variable count is created and given an initial value of 1. The condition count <= 10; is set up, basically stating that as long as count has a value of less than or equal to 10, it should loop through the actions that follow between the curly brackets ({}). And finally, count++ is used to increment the value of count with each iteration of the loop. As you can see, the For statement has all the same ingredients as the While statement, only in a single, convenient place.

Next, the action:

```
myPhrase += "Echo ";
```

is repeated with each loop so that at the end of the loop, myPhrase will have a value of "Echo Echo Echo Echo Echo Echo Echo Echo Echo Echo ".

Continue and Break Statements

Both Continue statements and Break statements are used in conjunction with loops to change the way they behave.

Normally, with each loop, a set of actions (as defined by the curly brackets {}) is executed. With a Continue statement, however, you define an exception in the loop where you don't want the actions to be executed. When this exception is encountered, the loop will skip executing any actions but will continue to loop. Take a look at the following example:

```
myPhrase = "";
for (count = 1; count <= 30; count++) {
  if (count % 3 == 0)
  continue;
  myPhrase += count;
}
```

Here's how the Continue statement works. The first thing that happens in this script is that the variable myPhrase is created and given an initial value of "" (nothing).

```
myPhrase = "";
```

Next, the For statement is set up.

```
for (count = 1; count <= 30; count++) {
```

The variable count is created and given an initial value of 1. The condition count <= 30; is set up, basically stating that as long as count has a value of less than or equal to 30, it should repeat through the actions that follow between the curly brackets ({}). And finally, count++ is used to increment the value of count with each iteration of the loop.

Next, the Continue statement is set up. Once again, this statement defines an exception in the loop where it should do nothing but continue on to the next iteration of the loop. In this case, we state that if the current value of count is divisible by 3 (see modulo operator discussed earlier in this chapter), don't do anything but continue on with the loop:

```
if (count % 3 == 0)
    continue;
```

Next, the action that should be performed with each iteration of the loop is defined, which basically states that the value of myPhrase is to be updated with each iteration to include the current value of count.

```
myPhrase += count;
```

At the end of the loop, myPhrase will have a value of "1 2 4 5 7 8 10 11 13 14 16 17 19 20 22 23 25 26 28 29" (notice any number divisible by *3* was not added to the value).

Break statements work in much the same way as Continue statements—with one exception: Instead of skipping an iteration of a loop, a Break statement will abort the looping sequence (even if the loop isn't complete) and move on to the statement that follows. Take a look at the following example:

```
myPhrase = ""
for (count = 1; count <= 30; count++) {
    if (count == 12)
    break;
    myPhrase += count;
}

    //Next Statement
```

This Break statement in this looping statement will cause it to abort after only 12 loops even though it is set up to loop 30 times. This results in myPhrase having a value of "1 2 3 4 5 6 7 8 9 10 11 12".

There's no room here to list all of the ways Break and Continue statements can be used; just remember that they're both employed to deal with exceptions in looping statements.

Functions

Functions are a powerful aspect of ActionScript programming, allowing you to assign a name to a section of code that has a specific purpose, or *functionality*. Once you have defined and named a function, you can use it in other scripts simply by referencing its name. This is known as *calling* the function. Functions save coding time by eliminating the need to create redundant code to perform the same actions or sets of actions across your various scripts. With functions, you script once and use many times, similar to what symbols allow you to do graphically.

Defining and Calling a Function

Functions are simply statements similar to those discussed in the previous section. To define a function, you use the `function` keyword (accessible via the Actions panel by choosing Actions > Function), followed by the name you assigned to the function, followed by a closed set of parentheses. Then, the actions this function will perform are defined. Function names have the same requirements and restrictions as variable names.

For example, look at the following code, which defines a function:

```
function doStuffFunction () {
  gotoAndPlay ("myFrameLabel");
  stopAllSounds ();
  getURL ("http://www.mydomain.com");
}
```

Our function is now defined. This function, named doStuffFunction(), does three things: It sends the timeline to the frame labeled myFrameLabel; it halts any playing sounds; and it opens a URL in a browser window. Simple enough, right? Now for the even easier part of using functions—calling them. Take a look at the following script, which calls the function we just defined:

```
on (release) {
  doStuffFunction();
}
```

As you can see, this function is called when a button is released. Thus, when the button is released, the following happens: The timeline is sent to the frame labeled myFrame-Label; all sounds stop playing; and the URL opens in a browser window—everything the function was designed to do. This same function can be called using any event, as the next script shows with a clip event:

```
onClipEvent (keyDown) {
  doStuffFunction();
}
```

The function will always execute as designed—regardless of where it's called from.

TIPS *The actions that make up a function are executed only when the function is called from another script, not when it is defined.*

A function cannot be called unless it has been defined first. It's a good idea to define a function in one of the first few frames of your movie (using a frame event/action) so that you can call it at any time.

You can use multiple function calls on a single event, as the following script shows:

```
on (release) {
  doStuffFunction();
  doMoreStuffFunction();
}
```

You can even use function calls mixed with other ActionScript, as the next script shows:

```
on (release) {
  doStuffFunction();
  doMoreStuffFunction();
  play();
  flash = "fun, fun, fun!"
}
```

By now you should understand how functions can speed project development: Define once, and use often. Anywhere you wish to use the function, you simply call it by its name, followed by parentheses. But what in the world are those parentheses for? That's what we'll look at next.

For information on how to define a function in Flash using the Actions panel, see the interactive tutorials at the end of this chapter.

Passing Values to a Function

Although the doStuffFunction() that we created is a fine piece of code, it has one draw-back: It always does the same thing. Let's look at the function again. In its current form, it does three things: It sends a timeline to a frame label; it stops all sounds; and it opens a URL in a browser. The frame it sends the timeline to will always be the one labeled myFrameLabel, and the URL that is opened will always be www.mydomain.com. However, by changing the way our function is defined, we can make it considerably more versatile. Take a look at the following example:

```
function doStuffFunction (whatFrame, whatURL) {
    gotoAndPlay (whatFrame);
    stopAllSounds ();
    getURL (whatURL);
}
```

In between the parentheses in our updated function are now two *arguments*, or para-meters—separated by a comma—that represent placeholders for values that can be sent to the function when it is called. To understand how this all works, take a look at the following function call:

```
on (release) {
    doStuffFunction("intro", "http://www.yahoo.com");
}
```

Here you can see that we added two values (separated by a comma) to our function call. These values are sent to our function (known as passing arguments) so that it can use them to perform its duties based on those values. In our example, the values "intro" and "http://www.yahoo.com" in our function call replace the whatFrame and whatURL placeholders, respectively, in our function definition. The result looks some-thing like this:

```
function doStuffFunction ("intro", "http://www.yahoo.com") {
    gotoAndPlay ("intro");
    stopAllSounds ();
    getURL ("http://www.yahoo.com");
}
```

As you can see, the placeholders are replaced with the values that are sent to the function when it is called. The great thing about this is that whenever we call our function again, we can send it different values. Take a look at the following function calls:

```
on (release) {
  doStuffFunction("start", "http://www.cnn.com");
}
on (release) {
  doStuffFunction("end", "http://www.excite.com");
}
on (release) {
  doStuffFunction("learn", "http://www.derekfranklin.com");
}
```

Each of these function calls is to our single function, but because different values are sent to the function in each function call, it performs the same actions using the different values.

When sending values to a function, you can also use variables in your function call.

```
on (release) {
  doStuffFunction(myVariable1, myVariable2);
}
```

In doing so, the current value of the variable is passed to the function. Here are some important things to remember when defining and calling functions in your scripts:

- You can create a function that accepts many parameters, but it's best to limit how many you use.

- When defining parameters in a function, remember the order in which they exist in the parentheses. Respective values that are sent to the function should be listed in the same order in the function call.

- Parameters that are defined are only used within the realm of the function. In our example, whatFrame and whatURL have no meaning or use outside of the function itself.

Returning a Result

Functions are not only great for executing sets of actions, they can also be used like miniprograms within your movie, processing information sent to them and then returning values. As always, an example is in order. Take a look at the following function definition:

```
function buyCD (availableFunds, currentDay) {
    if (currentDay != "Sunday" && availableFunds >= 20.00) {
    myVariable = true;
    } else {
    myVariable = false;
    }
    return myVariable;
}
```

In this function definition, two parameters' values—availableFunds and currentDay—are sent to the function when it is called. The function then processes those values using an If/Else statement. At the end of this function, myVariable will contain a value of true or false. Using the Return statement (as shown at the bottom of the function definition), the value of myVariable is returned to where the function was called. To understand this, take a look at how this function is called in the following script:

```
on (release) {
    idealCircumstances = buyCD(19.00, "Friday");
    if (idealCircumstances == true) {
    gotoAndPlay ("Happiness");
    } else {
    gotoAndPlay ("StayHome");
    }
}
```

Pay particular attention to the line that reads:

```
idealCircumstances = buyCD(19.00, "Friday");
```

To the right of the equal sign is our actual function call, which sends the values of 19.00 and "Friday" to the buyCD() function for processing. If you look back at how our function was defined, these values are used to determine a true or false value for myVariable.

Sending these particular values (19.00, "Friday") to the function causes `myVariable` to evaluate to a value of `false`. Since the last line of code in our function says,

```
return myVariable;
```

the value of `myVariable` is *returned* to the script where the function was called. Thus,

```
idealCircumstances = false;
```

Essentially, we've used a function call to assign a value to the variable `idealCircumstances`. This all happens in a split second. After the assignment has been made, the value of `idealCircumstances` can be used in the rest of the script, as our example demonstrated.

Using Local Variables in a Function

Local variables are variables that exist only within a function definition. Take a look at the following example:

```
function buyStuff(productCost) {
  //Create a local variable with a value of 200
  var myLocalVariable = 200;
  if (productCost < myLocalVariable) {
  gotoAndPlay ("Purchase");
  }
}
```

In this function definition, the variable `myLocalVariable` only exists within the scope of this function. It cannot be referred to or manipulated outside this function. Once this function has been executed, the local variable disappears until the next time the function is called. All of the variables that we've created thus far in the chapter are known as *global* variables, which means their values can be used or changed from any script.

To define a variable as a local variable, you simply put the keyword `var` before the variable's name when you assign a value to it. The reason you would use a local variable is to distinguish data manipulated solely within the function from data manipulated by all ActionScripts. Thus, if you have a global variable named `myVariable`, manipulating a local variable with the same name does not affect the global variable.

Working with Multiple Timelines

A single Flash player movie window can contain many movies, including the main movie, movie clip instances, and movies loaded into that window via the loadMovie() action. Each of these movies is a separate entity with its own timeline, scripts, variables, functions, and properties (**Figure 12.7**). One of Flash's most powerful features is its ability to have a set of actions that are attached to a mouse, clip, or frame event in one movie affect the movement, properties, and variables of any other present timeline in another movie. A timeline is considered present as long as it exists in the Player movie window. For example, if a particular movie clip instance only appears in your movie for 40 frames, it can be considered present (and thus targeted) only during those 40 frames.

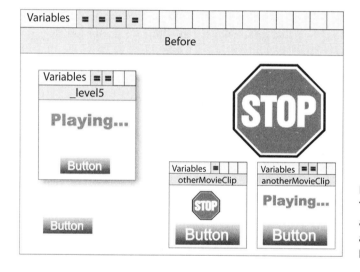

Figure 12.7
The main movie can act independently of any movie clips or levels, and vice-versa.

Each timeline present in the Player window has an address that is used to target it to perform an action. In this section, we'll show you how to target specific movies to perform different tasks and what this functionality allows you to do.

Addressing Targets in ActionScripts

To target a specific movie or timeline in a script, you need to address it in a unique way. This address is known as that movie's *target path*. Any of the following can be targeted: the current movie, the main movie, a movie clip instance, a parent movie, or a movie that has been loaded into a level. Let's take a look at each of these in more detail.

Current movie

When a target name or level number does not preface an action, the target is understood to be the current movie or timeline. For more information on the current movie, see "Targets" in Chapter 11, "Basic Actions for Building Interactivity."

Targeting the current movie looks something like this:

```
on (release) {
  age = 32;
}
```

This script creates the variable age in the timeline where the button action originated. Thus, if the button is on the main timeline, the variable will exist on the main timeline as well. If the button is in a movie clip instance, the variable will exist there instead.

Another way of addressing the current movie is by using the *this* keyword. Look at the following example:

```
on (release) {
  this.age = 32;
}
```

Main movie

The main movie represents the main timeline of a .swf file. This timeline is what you see when you start a new Flash authoring file.

Targeting the main movie from any movie clip instance within it looks something like this:

```
on (release) {
  _root.alpha = 45;
}
```

This script, if placed on a button in a movie clip instance, will make the main movie 45 percent transparent.

No matter where a script exists, _root always signifies that you are targeting the main movie.

When addressing movie clip instances, you may find it useful to preface their target path with _root, indicating their relation to the main timeline. To help you better visualize this concept, most of the remaining scripts in this chapter will use this notation.

Movie-clip instance

You assign names to instances of movie clips to identify them in ActionScripts (see "Defining an Instance" in Chapter 7). By so doing, you make it possible to control them via ActionScripts. You can give different instances of the same movie clip unique names so that they can be targeted separately (**Figure 12.8**).

Figure 12.8
Separate instances of the same movie clip symbol can be targeted and act independently of one another if given different instance names.

When targeting a movie clip instance in an ActionScript, you must spell its name correctly, but it does not have to be case sensitive (that is, *MyMovieClip* is the same as *mymovieclip*).

Targeting a movie clip instance can look like this:

```
on (press) {
  _root.myMovieClip.gotoAndPlay(20);
}
```

Targeting a movie clip instance inside another movie clip instance would look something like this:

```
on (press) {
  _root.myMovieClip.anotherMovieClip._width = 20;
}
```

Parent movie

Just as a real family is built on a hierarchy of parents, children, and even children's children, a Flash movie can contain several movies, any of which can contain several more movies, and so on. The relationship between these movies is considered a parent-child relationship. A *parent* movie is any movie (including movie clips) that contains other movies, or *children*. For example, the main timeline is considered the parent movie to movie clip instances within that timeline. Thus, targeting the main timeline (parent) from a movie clip instance (child) would look something like this:

```
on (press) {
  _parent._width = 200;
}
```

Movies on levels

Whenever you use the Load Movie action, you are essentially loading another .swf file into an existing one. This action gives you the option of loading the file onto a specific level: By identifying the level on which you want your movie to reside, you make its timeline (and the timelines of any of the movie clip instances it contains) available for targeting. If, for example, you were to load a movie into Level 5, its content would appear above content in Levels 0 through 4 (0 being the original, or main, movie).

Targeting a level's main timeline can look like this:

```
on (release) (
  _level5.gotoAndStop (25);
}
```

Targeting a movie clip instance on a particular level would look something like this (**Figure 12.9**):

```
on (release) {
  level5.myMovieClip._rotation = 30;
}
```

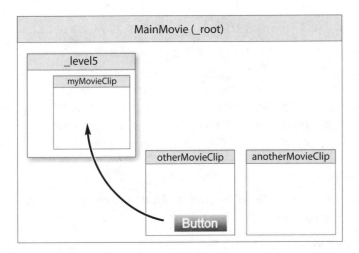

Figure 12.9
Movie clip instances on any level can be targeted from any other timeline. For example, the button in otherMovieClip can contain an ActionScript that affects myMovieClip on Level 5.

Using a With statement

A With statement is used in Flash as a special way of addressing a movie in order to perform a number of actions on it. Take a look at the following example:

```
on (release) {
  with (_root.myMovieClip) {
    _rotation = 30;
    _alpha = 25;
    play()
  }
}
```

In this script, using a With statement, we've addressed a movie once in order to rotate it, make it transparent, and start it playing. We could easily use the With statement to affect any target. Take, for example, the following:

```
on (release) {
  with (_level5) {
    _rotation = 30;
  }
}
```

or

```
on (release) {
  with (_parent) {
    _rotation = 30;
  }
}
```

Dot Syntax

As you may have noticed, dots, or periods, play a major role in ActionScript syntax. This is because ActionScript is based on what is known as dot *syntax. In ActionScripts, dots can be used for any of the following:*

- *To address movies*

  The following addresses myMovieClip2, *which is inside* myMovieClip1 *(which resides on the main timeline):*

  ```
  _root.myMovieClip1.myMovieClip2
  ```

- *To address variables in a specific movie*

  The following sets the value of the variable myVariable, *which is inside* myMovieClip, *to 27:*

  ```
  _root.myMovieClip.myVariable = 27;
  ```

- *To address properties of a specific movie*

  The following rotates the movie clip myMovieClip *by a value of 45 degrees:*

  ```
  _root.myMovieClip._rotation = 45
  ```

- *Flash 4 users will see that in Flash 5, dots have replaced slashes (/) and colons (:) in ActionScript syntax.*

Putting it all together

To help you understand how to target various movies, try thinking of your Flash project in the form of a family structure, with your main movie being the *mother* movie. Now, mom has some kids—Joe, Lucy, and Bob—who in Flash represent movie clip instances within the main movie. These movie clip instances are referred to as *child* movies.

The following shows how our family structure would look within Flash (**Figure 12.10**):

Mother (_level0)

Joe

Lucy

Bob

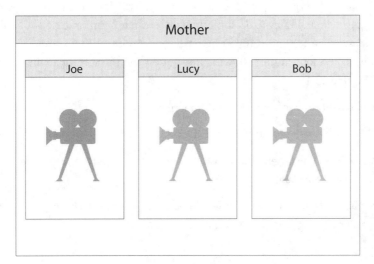

Figure 12.10
The various timelines present within the Flash Player window at any given time can be thought of as a family structure with parent movies containing other movies, or children.

If you clicked a button in the Mother movie to make Lucy invisible, the target path in the script might look like the following:

```
on (release) {
    _root.Lucy._visible = 0:
}
```

Now, let's say that Joe has a couple of kids himself: Junior and Youngster. If Joe represents a movie clip instance, his "kids" represent movie clip instances within a movie clip instance.

The overall family structure now looks like this:

```
Mother (_level0)
Joe
    Junior
    Youngster
Lucy
Bob
```

With this in mind, if you were to click a button in the Mother movie that made Joe's child Junior invisible, the target path in the script would look like the following:

```
on (release) {
    _root.Joe.Junior._visible = 0
}
```

Now let's initiate some power struggles within the family: Mother isn't the only one in control here. Joe can tell Lucy to do something; Bob can tell Junior to do something; and even Youngster can tell mom (or in his case, grandmother) to do something. To understand this, take a look at the following illustration and the accompanying sample target paths (**Figure 12.11**).

For a mouse, clip, or frame event in Mother to target:

- *Mother.* The target path would be blank or this.

- *Joe, Lucy, or Bob.* The target path would be Joe, Lucy, or Bob or _root.Joe, _root.Lucy, or _root.Bob.

- *Junior or Youngster.* The target path would be Joe.Junior or Joe.Youngster or _root.Joe.Junior or _root.Joe.Youngster.

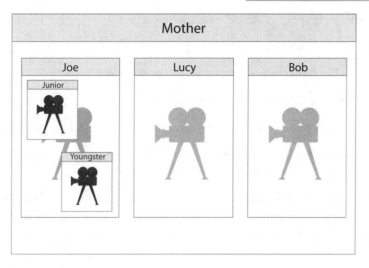

Figure 12.11
It's important
to grasp the
hierarchical
structure when
you're targeting
various movies.

For a mouse, clip, or frame event in Bob to target:

- ***Mother***. The target would be _root or _parent.

- ***Lucy or Joe.*** The target path would be _root.Lucy or _root.Joe.

- ***Junior or Youngster***. The target path would be _root.Joe.Junior or
  _root.Joe.Youngster.

For a mouse, clip, or frame event in Lucy to target:

- ***Mother***. The target would be _root or _parent.

- ***Bob or Joe***. The target path would be _root.Bob or _root.Joe.

- ***Junior or Youngster***. The target path would be _root.Joe.Junior or
  _root.Joe.Youngster.

For a mouse, clip, or frame event in Joe to target:

- ***Mother***. The target would be _root or _parent.

- ***Lucy or Bob***. The target path would be _root.Lucy or _root.Bob.

- ***Junior or Youngster***. The target path would be Junior or Youngster or
  _root.Joe.Junior or _root.Joe.Youngster.

For a mouse, clip, or frame event in Junior to target:

- ***Mother***. The target would be _root.

- ***Lucy or Bob***. The target path would be _root.Lucy or _root.Bob.

- ***Joe***. The target path would be _root.Joe or _parent.

- ***Youngster***. The target path would be _root.Joe.Youngster or _parent.Youngster.

For a mouse, clip, or frame event in Youngster to target:

- *Mother*. The target would be _root.

- *Lucy or Bob*. The target path would be _root.Lucy or _root.Bob.

- *Joe*. The target path would be _root.Joe or _parent.

- *Junior*. The target path would be _root.Joe.Junior or _parent.Junior.

The last target paths we're going to look at are those created whenever a new .swf file is loaded into the Flash movie window using the loadMovie() action.

Whenever a movie in addition to the main movie is loaded into the Flash movie window, it is given a level number. The original movie is automatically assigned Level 0. Any new movie loaded into a level can be thought of as another parent movie containing child movies.

For our analogy, the structure of a loaded movie placed on Level 5 would look like this:

```
Mother (_level5)
  Kathy
  Ashlie
    Carla
  Jack
  Liz
```

As you can see, in addition to our original family on Level 0, a new family exists on Level 5 (**Figure 12.12**).

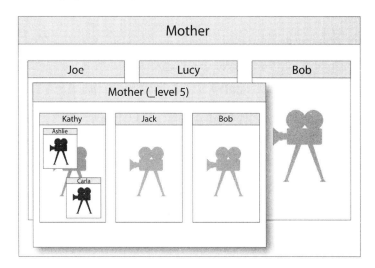

Figure 12.12
Loading another movie into the Flash Player (i.e., Level 5) introduces a new hierarchy.

To target the main timeline of the movie on Level 5 from any other movies loaded into the Flash Player window, your script might look like this:

```
on (release) {
  _level5.gotoAndStop (10);
}
```

To target the movie clip instance named `Ashlie` (which is contained in the movie on Level 5) from any other movie within the Flash Player window, your script might look like this:

```
on (release) {
  _level5.Kathy.Ashlie.gotoAndStop ("Bed");
}
```

> **TIP** *If your script's syntax looks correct but it's still not working, chances are a target isn't being addressed properly.*

Inserting a target's path

Flash includes a useful utility called the Target Editor to help you define target paths in your ActionScripts. The Insert Target Path dialog box shows a movie's hierarchy, or *display list*. From this display list, you can select a target whose path is subsequently inserted into your script.

To use the Insert Target Path dialog box:

1. Select an action where a target must be defined. For our demonstration choose Actions > With.

2. Click inside the "Object parameter" text box to make the "Insert a Target Path" button active (this step is necessary to activate the button).

3. Click the "Insert a Target Path" button at the bottom of the Actions panel.

   The Insert Target Path dialog box will appear with the following areas (**Figure 12.13**):

   Display list. This window displays a directory of available movie clip targets. If a plus sign (Windows) or a twirly (">"Macintosh) appears next to a movie clip instance's name, that movie clip has an associated child movie clip. Clicking a name in the list displays its target path in the Target window (see below).

   Target. This window displays the target path that will be inserted when the OK button on this dialog box is pressed.

Display list

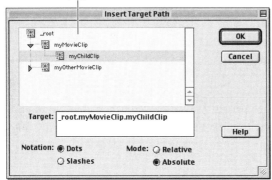

Figure 12.13
The Insert Target Path dialog box helps you define specific movies as targets for actions.

Notation. This option lets you choose what syntax you want to use to define the target's path. Dots are the preferred notation; however, slashes can also be used.

Mode. This option lets you choose how much of the target path to include. *Absolute* inserts the complete target path from the _root of the movie. *Relative* displays only instances of movie clips that exist in the current frame of the current Timeline, and their children instances.

4. Once you have selected a target in this box, click OK to insert its target path in the script.

TIP *The path of a level or a movie clip on a level must be inserted manually into your scripts. The Insert Target Path dialog box does not provide the functionality for doing so.*

A Special Note About onClipEvent

By default, unless a target is specified, any action associated with an onClipEvent event pertains to the movie clip instance that the action is attached to. For example, take a look at the following script:

```
onClipEvent (load) {
   _rotation = 60;
   play();
}
```

In this example, as soon as the movie clip instance to which this script is attached loads, the instance itself is rotated 60 degrees and begins to play.

Using and Changing Individual Timeline Properties

Each movie/timeline has its own group of properties that can be changed dynamically while the movie is playing and whose current values can be evaluated and used in conditional or looping statements as well as in other areas of your scripts. As you'll learn in the sample scripts provided, to access a specific movie's properties, you simply use its target path. In this section we'll show you what a movie's properties relate to and how you can use and manipulate them to create interactive movies.

One important thing to keep in mind when changing a parent's properties is that its children inherit those same properties. For example, if you make a parent movie transparent, its children will become transparent as well. However, the reverse is not true: Changing the properties of a child will not affect its parent.

_alpha

The Alpha property represents a movie or movie clip's transparency (expressed as a percent).

The following script evaluates the transparency of the movie clip instance dress. If the clip is more than 50 percent transparent, the variable wearSlip is set to true before going to "DanceParty." Otherwise, you go straight to "DanceParty."

```
if (_root.dress._alpha > 50) {
  wearSlip = true;
  gotoAndPlay ("DanceParty");
} else {
  gotoAndPlay ("DanceParty");
}
```

_currentframe

The Currentframe property provides the current frame-number position of a timeline for a movie or movie clip.

In this script, when the on (release) mouse event occurs, the following script will send the main movie's timeline forward 20 frames from its current position:

```
on (release) {
  _root.gotoAndStop (_root._currentframe + 20)
}
```

_droptarget

The Droptarget property represents the target path that a dragged movie is currently on top of (**Figure 12.14**), allowing you to emulate drag-and-drop behavior.

The following script lets you emulate drag-and-drop behavior. When the clip event `onClipEvent (mouseDown)` occurs, `_root.myMovieClip` is dragged while remaining centered underneath the moving mouse. When the `onClipevent (mouseUp)` event occurs, dragging halts and an expression is used to evaluate the movie clip's position. The movie clip directly beneath the one being dragged is always considered the droptarget. In this script, when the drag operation stops, the droptarget is identified. If it equals `_root.myTarget`, `_root.myMovieClip` becomes invisible; otherwise, nothing happens.

Figure 12.14
In this illustration, the droptarget for OldPC is Trash. This property is constantly updated.

```
onClipEvent (mouseDown) {
    startDrag (_root.myMovieClip, true);
}

onClipEvent (mouseUp) {
    stopDrag ();
    if (eval(_root.myMovieClip._dropTarget) == _root.myTarget) {
        _root.myMovieClip._alpha = 25;
    }
}
```

_focusrect

The Focusrect property returns a Boolean value of `true` or `false`, depending on whether the focus rectangle property is on or off. A focus rectangle is a yellow box that appears around buttons and text elements in your exported movie after the user has clicked them (**Figure 12.15**). As a global property, it pertains to all movies currently playing in the Flash Player window. The following script turns off this functionality.

```
_focusrect == false
```

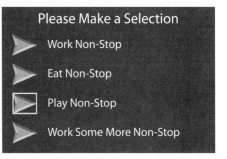

Figure 12.15
The focus rectangle surrounds buttons and text elements when the Tab key is used to navigate between them.

_framesloaded

The Framesloaded property represents the number of frames of a movie that have loaded. This property is similar to the If Frame Is Loaded command; however, it allows the number returned to be evaluated in an expression.

The following script is placed on Frame 2 of the timeline. If the number of frames loaded were to exceed 200, the timeline would jump to and begin playing Scene 2, Frame 1. Otherwise, the timeline would go to and begin playing from Frame 1 of the current scene. This causes a loop that is not broken until more than 200 frames have been loaded.

```
if (_framesloaded > 200) {
  gotoAndPlay ("Scene 2", 1);
} else {
  gotoAndPlay (1);
}
```

_height

The Height property provides and sets the current height of a movie; its value is based in pixels. For an example of this type of script, see the sample script for the Width property.

_highquality

The Highquality property represents a numeric value of 0, 1, or 2 based on the current playback-quality setting. As a global property, it pertains to all movies currently playing in the Flash Player window.

```
if (_highquality == 2)
  Actions...;
} else {
  Actions...;
}
```

> **TIP** *The _quality setting (see below) provides Flash users more options and is the recommended property for setting playback quality.*

_name

The Name property denotes the name of a movie clip instance in the form of a string value such as `"myMovieClip"` .This is similar to the Target property (see below), though without the full path being included.

The following script gets the name of the current movie clip when the `onClipEvent` (`mouseDown`) event occurs and then outputs it to a dynamic text element on the main timeline named `movieName`:

```
onClipEvent (mouseDown) {
  _root.movieName = this._name;
}
```

The result is that the text element displays the movie's name (for example, "myMovieClip").

_quality

The Quality property is a string value of `LOW`, `MEDIUM`, `HIGH`, or `BEST`, which specifies the playback quality of your movie. As a global property, it pertains to all movies currently playing in the Flash Player window. The following script sets the value of the movie's quality to `MEDIUM`:

```
_quality = "MEDIUM";
```

_rotation

The Rotation property represents a movie's rotation, in degrees, relative to the movie's parent (**Figure 12.16**).

The following script is triggered by the on (`release`) mouse event. When triggered, a random numeric value between 0 and 359 is generated and assigned to the variable `spin`. This value is used to set the rotation value for the movie clip named `myMovieClip`. In addition, the value of `spin` is evaluated: If it is between 0 and 45 degrees, "You spun a 1, you win!" is displayed in a dynamic text element with the variable name of `message`. Otherwise, "Try again" is displayed.

```
on (release) {
  spin = random (360);
  _root.myMovieClip._rotation = spin;
  if (spin >= 0 && spin < 45) {
    message = "You spun a 1, you win!";
  } else {
    message = "Try again.";
  }
)
```

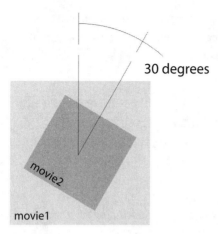

30 degrees

Figure 12.16
In this graphic, movie2 is rotated 30 degrees relative to its parent (movie1); thus, the value of its rotation property is 30. If movie1 were rotated by 60 degrees, movie2 would rotate that much additionally (for a total of a 90-degree rotation) but its rotation value would still be 30 since this value is based on its rotation relative to its parent, not its rotation overall.

_soundbuftime

The Soundbuftime property is a numeric value that denotes the number of seconds of streaming sound that need to be downloaded by the user before your movie can begin to play. The default setting is 5 (for 5 seconds). Because this is a global property, it pertains to all movies currently playing in the Flash Player window. This would normally be set on the first frame of your movie. The following script sets this property so that streamed audio will not begin playing until the user has downloaded 15 seconds of it.

```
_soundbuftime = 15;
```

_target

The Target property provides the target name and full path (in slash syntax) of a movie clip instance in the form of a string value such as /myMovieClip.

The following script gets the target path and name of the current movie clip when the on (release) event occurs. The script then outputs it to a dynamic text element on the main timeline named currentMovie:

```
on (release) {
  _root.currentMovie = this._target;
}
```

_totalframes

The Totalframes property represents the number of frames in a movie or movie clip.

In the following script, when the on (release) mouse event occurs, the following script will create the variable timeToPlay. This variable's value is based on the number of frames in the main movie divided by the frame-per-second rate. `Math.round()` is used to remove any decimal places in the calculation. The next variable, `_root.message`, is a dynamic text element on the main timeline that will display a message based on the value of `timeToPlay`:

```
on (release) {
  timeToPlay = Math.round(_root._totalframes / 12);
  _root.message = "This movie will take " + timeToPlay +
  " seconds to play.";
}
```

If the movie has 240 frames, a text element with a variable name of `_root.message` will display the following:

```
"This movie will take 20 seconds to play."
```

_url

This property represents the complete URL for a .swf or any of its child movie clips. You are most likely to use this property in conjunction with a .swf that has been loaded into the Flash Player window via the `loadMovie()` action. For example, if a .swf were loaded into the Flash Player window from the URL http://www.mydomain.com/secondmovie.swf, checking this property of the movie would return a string value of `"http://www.mydomain.com/secondmovie.swf"`

Using this property ensures that others don't "borrow" your work. You can place a script on Frame 1 of a movie that checks its URL property and instructs it to take one action if it was loaded from the "correct" URL and another if it was loaded from the "wrong" URL. In this way, you can prevent others from stealing a .swf file from their cache and using it as their own.

The following script   which is placed on Frame 1 of your movie   evaluates the URL property of the main movie. It will continue to play if the URL is what it should be; however, it will cease playing and jump to (and stop at) the frame labeled Denied if the URL is not what it should be:

```
if (_root._url == "http://www.properdomain.com") {
  play();
} else {
  gotoAndStop ("Denied");
}
```

_visible

The Visible property is a Boolean value of true or false: true if visible, and false if not. It denotes a movie's visiblity.

The following script checks the visibility of the movie clip teacher. If it's not visible, the movie clip kids is sent to a frame labeled Recess; if it is visible, kids is sent to Desk:

```
if (_root.teacher._visible == false) {
  _root.kids.gotoAndPlay ("Recess");
} else {
  _root.kids.gotoAndStop ("Desk");
}
```

_width

The Width property represents the current width of a movie; its value is based in pixels. The following script evaluates the width of the current movie and acts accordingly:

```
on (release) {
  nextMeal = 50;
  if (_width + nextMeal >= 400) {
  message = "I'm too fat.";
  } else if (_width + nextMeal <= 100) {
  message = "I'm too skinny.";
  } else {
  message = "I'm just right.";
  }
}
```

When executed, this script creates a variable named nextMeal and gives it a value of 50. Using an If statement, the width of the current movie is determined, and the value of nextMeal is added to it. The combined total is then evaluated to determine whether it's greater than or equal to 400, less than or equal to 100, or somewhere in between. For our demonstration, the width of the movie was determined to be 230, which when combined with 50 equals 280. Thus, a dynamic text element with a variable name of message will display the string "I'm just right."

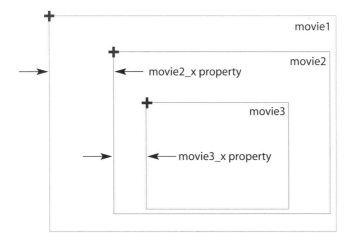

Figure 12.17
The X property is a relative value based on the horizontal distance of its registration point (marked by a + in this graphic) in relation to the registration point of its parent.

_X

The X property of a movie represents the horizontal distance between its registration point in relation to the registration point of its parent (**Figure 12.17**).

The following script evaluates the horizontal position of the current movie and acts accordingly:

```
on (release) {
  if (_x < 200) {
  message = "I'm on the left.";
  } else if (_x > 200) {
  message = "I'm on the right.";
  } else {
  message = "I'm stuck in the middle somewhere.";
  }
}
```

For our demonstration, when this script has executed, the horizontal position of the current movie is evaluated to be exactly 200; thus, a dynamic text element with a variable name of message will display the string "I'm stuck in the middle somewhere."

_xmouse

The Xmouse property represents the current horizontal position of the mouse in relation to the registration point of a particular movie (**Figure 12.18**).

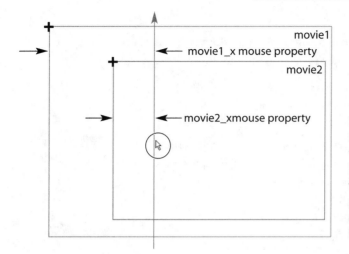

Figure 12.18
Each movie's Xmouse value is based on the horizontal distance of the mouse from that movie's registration point (indicated by a + in this graphic).

The following script evaluates the current horizontal position of the mouse in relation to the registration point of the movie clip myMovieClip each time the mouse is moved. It then displays that value in a dynamic text element on the main timeline with a variable name of message:

```
onClipEvent (mouseMove) {
  _root.message = _root.myMovieClip._xmouse;
}
```

_xscale

This property represents how much of a movie or movie clip (in a percentage) has been scaled horizontally from its original size as the result of previous actions where its Xscale property was changed. Thus, if a movie has been scaled to 50 percent of its original size, the value of its Xscale property is 50.

When the on(release) mouse event occurs, the following script evaluates the amount that the movie clip myMovieClip has been scaled from its original size. If it is more than 100 percent, it gets reset to 100 percent; otherwise, it remains its current size:

```
on(release) {
  if (_root.myMovieClip._xscale > 100) {
    _root.myMovieClip._xscale = _100;
  }
}
```

_y

The Y property of a movie represents the vertical distance between its registration point in relation to the registration point of its parent.

See the X property script for an example of how this property works.

_ymouse

The Ymouse property represents the current vertical position of the mouse in relation to the registration point of a particular movie.

See the X property script for an example of how this property works.

_yscale

This property represents the percentage a movie or movie clip has been scaled vertically from its original size as the result of previous actions in which its Yscale property was changed (**Figure 12.19**).

For an example of this type of script, see the Xscale script sample above.

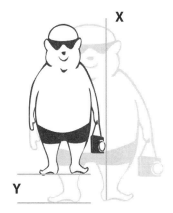

Figure 12.19
The X and Y scale properties let you scale a movie's size based on a percentage amount.

Special Text Properties

Because input and dynamic text elements contain lines of text, you can use two unique properties to create scrolling functionality for them.

Scroll Property
- *Syntax:* variableName.scroll

The Scroll property (found on the Actions panel by choosing Function > scroll) is a numeric value that represents the line number of the top-most visible line currently displayed in an input or dynamic text element. Thus, if the text field has ten lines of text and the user has scrolled to the point where Line 4 is the top-most visible line, the scroll value for this text element would be 4. This value is constantly updated as your movie plays. It can be evaluated in expressions, or you can create buttons that cause the top-most line to jump to wherever you want (see script that follows).

The following script uses an expression to evaluate the current Scroll property of the text element with a variable name of myTextBox. *If the value is greater than 3, the movie will stop playing.*

```
if (myTextBox.scroll > 3) {
    stop();
}
```

The following script shows a mouse event that will cause the text element with a variable name of myTextBox *to make Line 6 its top-most visible line.*

```
on (release) {
    myTextBox.scroll = 6;
}
```

Maxscroll Property

• *Syntax:* variableName.maxscroll

*The Maxscroll property—found on the Actions panel by choosing Function > maxscroll—is a numeric value that represents the line number of the top-most scrollable line in an input or dynamic text element. If you have a text element that is high enough only to show two lines of text even though it actually contains five, the maxscroll value is 4. This is because at its highest scroll point, Line 4 is the top-most visible line. If a text element contains ten lines of text but can only display four lines at a time, the maxscroll value for this text field would be 7. This is because at its highest scroll point, Line 7 is the top-most visible line (**Figure 12.20**).*

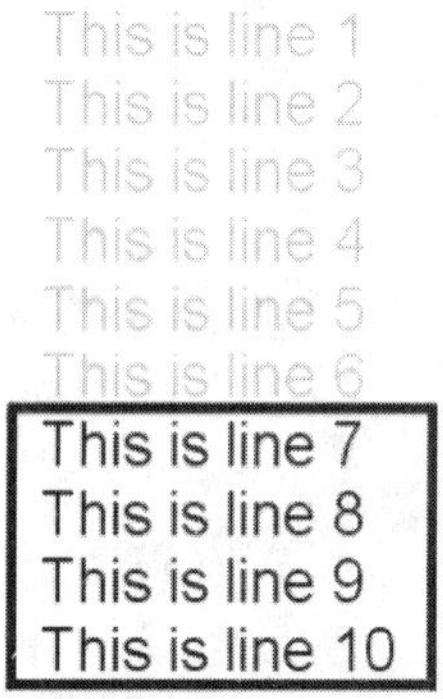

You can use the value in an expression that is attached to a button instance to create a looping scroll—that is, one in which a text element's text scrolls when the button is clicked and scrolls from the top again when it reaches its bottom-most point (see the script below).

Figure 12.20
Ten lines of text in a text field that can only display four lines at a time would make Line 7 the maxscroll value.

The following script causes the text field with the variable name myTextBox *to go to a line number based on the value of* count, *which is updated with each click of the button. Also with each button-click, the value of* count *is compared to the value of* myTextBox.maxscroll. *When the value of* count *equals the value of* myTextBox.maxscroll, *this means the end of the scroll has been reached and count is reset so that on the next button-click, the text field will display Line 1 again and start the process all over again:*

```
on (release) {
    count = count++;
    myTextBox.scroll = count;
    if (count = myTextBox.maxscroll) {
        count = 0;
    )
)
```

Using and Changing Individual Timeline Data

Just as each timeline has its own set of properties, each can also contain its own set of variables and functions. These data elements can be accessed from scripts in any timeline as long as the timeline they are a part of is present in the Player window. For example, if a particular movie clip instance is only available for 40 frames in your movie, its variable data or functions can only be accessed during those 40 frames.

How can you tell which timeline a variable or function exists on? As with other aspects of ActionScript, any variables you create and any functions you define become part of the current movie unless you specify otherwise. Thus, if you create a variable with an action inside of a movie clip instance and don't specify a target, that variable data exists in the movie clip instance, and that instance's name acts as an address for accessing that data. A single script can draw from data in multiple timelines. But don't worry: It's not as complicated as it may seem.

Setting and using variable values on different timelines

You can create, update, or access a variable's data for any movie present in the Flash Player window (including movie clips and loaded movies). Just prefix the name of the variable with the path of the timeline with which it's associated. For example, the following script creates a variable named myVariable that will exist in the movie clip instance named myMovieClip, which resides on the main timeline (_root):

```
on (release) {
    _root.myMovieClip.myVariable = 200;
}
```

Once the variable has been created, you can access its value from scripts on any time-line simply by addressing its location properly. Take a look at the following example, which will send the current movie's timeline to Frame 20 if the value of the variable on another timeline (the variable we created above) plus 50 equals 300:

```
if (_root.myMovieClip.myVariable + 50 == 300) {
    gotoAndPlay (20);
}
```

Functions and multiple timelines

Similar to variables, a function can exist on any timeline. Simply use that timeline's address to call a function. Take a look at the following example, which defines a function in the movie clip instance named myMovieClip (which resides on the main timeline):

```
function _root.myMovieClip.doStuffFunction () {
    gotoAndPlay ("myFrameLabel");
    stopAllSounds ();
    getURL ("http://www.mydomain.com");
}
```

To call this function, simply use its complete target path:

```
on (release) {
    _root.myMovieClip.doStuffFunction ();
}
```

Keep It Simple

Working with data and functions across timelines can get confusing if you're not care-ful. In some cases, you may find if helpful to use the _root timeline as a central loca-tion for most of your movie's data. This way, you only need to create or use data from a single source. Take a look at the following examples:

```
//create a variable that exists on the _root timeline.
_root.myVariable = 250 ;
```

The great thing about this technique is that regardless of which timeline you use the expression above on, it will always create (or update, if the variable already exists) the variable on the _root timeline.

Same thing with functions:

```
//define a function that exists on the _root timeline.
function _root.doStuffFunction ();
  stopAllSounds ();
  getURL ("http://www.mydomain.com");
}
```

Once again, no matter which timeline you place this function definition on, the function will exist on the _root timeline. To access variable data or call a function on the main timeline from scripts on other timelines, see the two preceding sections of this chapter, "Using and Changing Individual Timeline Data" and "Functions and Multiple Timelines."

Sure, it may take a few extra keystrokes to add _root when creating variables or defining functions, but in the end you save time by not having to guess where a particular piece of data exists.

Understanding the Context of Each Line in a Script

In the scripts we've included thus far, we've demonstrated the various ways that timelines communicate with each other. In this section, you'll learn how to put it all together in a working ActionScript.

As you've already learned, just because a script is attached to a button on the main timeline doesn't mean that it only affects or draws data from that timeline. A single script can communicate with multiple timelines simultaneously. Nearly every line in an ActionScript does something in the context of a particular timeline. To help you understand this concept, we'll decipher each line of the following script:

```
on (release) {
  myVariable = 25;
  gotoAndPlay (myVariable);
  _root.anotherMovieClip._rotation = 120;
  _root.myMessage = "The current value of myVariable is
  " + myVariable + ".";
  _level3.doStuffFunction();
}
```

The actions in this script are a bit exaggerated, but they help demonstrate how context affects the way a script works. This script is attached to a button in a movie clip instance named myMovieClip; let's examine each line.

```
myVariable = 25;
```

On this line a variable is created and assigned a value of 25. The important thing to note is that since no target is defined for this action, the target is considered the current movie (myMovieClip). Thus, the variable that's created exists on myMovieClip's timeline.

```
gotoAndPlay (myVariable);
```

Once again, since no target is defined, this action sends the current movie (myMovieClip) to a frame number based on the value of myVariable.

```
_root.anotherMovieClip._rotation = 120;
```

This action rotates the movie clip instance named anotherMovieClip by 120 degrees. Since _root prefaces the target path, it is understood that this movie clip instance is a child movie of the main movie.

```
_root.myMessage = "The current value of myVariable is "
+ myVariable + ".";
```

This action will display "The current value of myVariable is 25" in a dynamic text element named myMessage, which exists on the _root timeline.

```
_level3._alpha = _root.anotherMovieClip.anotherVariable;
```

This action will change the transparency of the movie on Level 3 based on the value of anotherVariable, which exists on _root.anotherMovieClip's timeline.

```
_level3.doStuffFunction();
```

This action calls a function that was defined in a loaded .swf file that exists on Level 3.

Objects

ActionScript is an object-oriented programming (scripting) language. Without getting too technical, this means that you use and work with *objects* to accomplish interactive tasks. Just like in the real word, objects in the programming world have characteristics that describe their make-up and unique behaviors that allow them to do certain things. In ActionScript terms, characteristics are known as *properties* and behaviors are known as *methods*. The primary benefit of object-oriented programming languages is that they allow you to program and manipulate data in a context that makes sense to *humans*. The following table should help you get a handle on this concept.

Table 12.5
Objects Defined

Object	Property	Method
Person	Height	Speak
	Gender	Walk
	Marital status	Laugh
Umbrella	Color	Open
	Material	Close
Television	Brand	On
	Size	Off
	Display type	Volume up

In object-oriented programming, objects are organized into *classes*. An instance, or *object*, has the properties and methods associated with the class that it's part of (**Figure 12.21**).

ActionScript contains several predefined object classes, some of the more common and interesting of which we'll look at next.

> **TIP** *These object classes can be found in the Objects section of the Toolbox list on the Actions panel.*

Person class

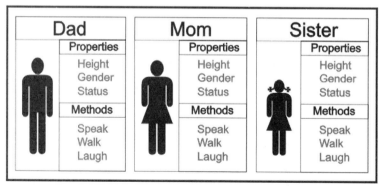

Figure 12.21
A graphical representation of the Person class. Notice that each instance of the person class shares the same types of properties and methods.

MovieClip Objects

By now, you should be fairly familiar with MovieClip objects. Each timeline in your project (including the main timeline and the timelines of your movie clip instances and loaded movies) is an instance of the MovieClip class. Each movie clip object has a set of properties and methods that are included in the MovieClip class. In the section "Using and Changing Individual Timeline Properties" earlier in this chapter, you learned how to work with the properties of movie clip objects. The following represent some of the things you can do with an instance of a movie clip using the methods available to a MovieClip object. The following interactive tutorials can be found on the CD:

- Duplicating a Movie Clip

- Dragging a Movie Clip

- Testing for Collisions

- Loading Variables into a Movie

Color Objects

To manipulate the color of a movie, you must create a Color object, then associate that Color object with a movie. Once you've done this, the color of the associated movie can be manipulated using the methods available to the Color object class. To get a handle on this, take a look at the following example:

```
on (release) {
  _//create a new Color object when this button is released.
  myColorObject = new Color (_root.myMovieClip);
  myColorObject.setRGB (0x33F366);
}
```

Now let's explain what's happening in each line of script:

```
myColorObject = new Color (_root.myMovieClip);
```

This line creates the Color object—essentially telling Flash to "create a new color object named `myColorObject` and associate it with the movie clip instance with the target path of _root.myMovieClip (**Figure 12.22**). To the left of the equal sign is the name we want to assign to our newly created Color object. (When naming objects, follow the same rules as those that apply to naming variables.) To the right of the equal sign is what's known as a *color object constructor*. This is the ActionScript syntax used to

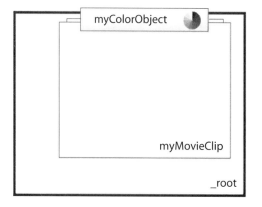

Figure 12.22
myColorObject is a color object associated with myMovieClip. Using any of the methods available to the Color object class to affect myColorObject will actually affect the movie it's associated with—in this case, myMovieClip.

create a new Color object and associate it with a particular movie. Once this object has been created and associated with a movie, we can manipulate that movie's color by addressing the name of the Color object (not the name of the movie clip instance), followed by a Color object method, which is what the next line of our script does:

```
myColorObject.setRGB (0x33F366);
```

This line of the script says, "Set the RGB value of `myColorObject` to a hex value of 33F366." This will make `_root.myMovieClip` turn green. (See the ActionScript Dictionary—which you can access by choosing Help > ActionScript Dictionary—to see what other methods are available to the Color object.)

Manipulating a movie's color via a Color object is similar to selecting an instance of a movie clip in the authoring environment and applying a tinting effect to it with the Effect panel. The difference is that the Color object lets you do it dynamically—i.e., *while* the movie is playing.

A movie can contain as many Color objects as you wish, each associated with a different movie. To get a better handle on this concept, take a look at the following interactive tutorial on the accompanying CD:

- Changing the Color of Objects Dynamically

Date Objects

Date objects allow you to work with data that pertains to time, including years, months, days, hours, minutes, seconds, and even milliseconds. This lets you display the current time and build clocks, counters, calendars, and more. You must create a Date object before you can use date data in your project. The following script creates a

Date object, then uses it to display a custom message in the dynamic text element with the variable name of myMessage:

```
on (release) {
  _//create a new Date object when this button is released.
  myDateObject = new Date ();
  myMessage = "Can you believe it's already the year " +
  myDateObject.getFullYear() + "?";
}
```

Let's look at each line of this script.

```
myDateObject = new Date ();
```

This line creates a new Date object with the name myDateObject. You'll notice that we didn't enter any parameters within the parentheses; this means that our Date object will be based on the current date and time (as defined by the computer on which Flash Player is running). More on this in a moment.

```
myMessage = "Can you believe it's already the year" +
myDateObject.getFullYear() + "?";
```

This line determines the message that will be displayed in our dynamic text element. Using the getFullYear() method (which returns the four-digit year of the associated Date object), this will display the message "Can you believe it's already the year 2000?"

A Date object doesn't always need to contain the current date and time. The following creates a Date object based on February 21, 1993:

```
myWeddingDay = new Date (1993, 1, 21);
```

The three parameters in the parentheses represent the year, month, and day of the Date object you're creating. You'll notice that the number *1* identifies February; this is because ActionScript starts the months of the year with January being *0*, February *1*, March *2*, and so on.

Creating Date objects that relate to specific dates allows you to display information about that particular date. For example, if you wanted to let your user enter his or her birth date so that you could display a custom message indicating the day of the week he or she was born, you could create three input text elements on the stage with variable names of year, month, and day, respectively. If the following values were entered:

```
year = 1966;
month = 7;
day = 27;
```

The following script would be used to display the message:

```
on (release) {
  convertMonth = month - 1;
  userBirthDate = new Date(year, convertMonth, day);
  if (userBirthDate.getDay() == 0) {
    dayOfWeek = "Sunday";
  } else if (userBirthDate.getDay() == 1) {
    dayOfWeek = "Monday";
  } else if (userBirthDate.getDay() == 2) {
    dayOfWeek = "Tuesday";
  } else if (userBirthDate.getDay() == 3) {
    dayOfWeek = "Wednesday";
  } else if (userBirthDate.getDay() == 4) {
    dayOfWeek = "Thursday";
  } else if (userBirthDate.getDay() == 5) {
    dayOfWeek = "Friday";
  } else if (userBirthDate.getDay() == 6) {
    dayOfWeek = "Saturday";
  }
  myMessage = "You were born on a " + dayOfWeek + ".";
}
```

Let's examine this script:

```
convertMonth = month - 1;
```

If our user was born in July and entered 7 as the month in which she was born, we would need to convert that 7 to a 6 to represent July correctly in a Date object. That's what this line accomplishes.

```
userBirthDate = new Date(year, convertMonth, day);
```

This line creates a new Date object and names it userBirthDate. The current values of year, convertMonth, and day are used to define it. Thus, userBirthDate is an object based on the date July 27, 1966.

```
if (userBirthDate.getDay() == 0) {
    dayOfWeek = "Sunday";
```

In this statement, the `getDay()` method is used to determine a numerical value (between 0 and 6) that denotes the day of the week for the specified Date object. Sunday is represented by 0, Monday by 1, Tuesday by 2, and so on. Thus, the `if` statement states, "If July 27, 1966, occurred on a Sunday (or 0), then `dayOfWeek` is assigned a value of 'Sunday.'" The remaining `else if` statements in this script are used in a similar fashion to the `if` statement. In the end, `dayOfWeek` will have a string value representing the name of a day in the week.

```
myMessage = "You were born on a " + dayOfWeek + ".";
```

The last line displays a custom message in the dynamic text field named `myMessage`, based on the value of `dayOfWeek`. In our example, since July 27, 1966, occurred on a Wednesday, `myMessage` displays "You were born on a Wednesday."

To learn about additional Date object methods, see the ActionScript Dictionary (which you can access by choosing Help > ActionScript Dictionary). Look for the following interactive tutorial on the CD:

- Displaying the Current Date

Sound Objects

With Sound objects, you can manipulate aspects of sound, such as volume and panning, in particular movies. Similar to the Color object, you create a Sound object, associate it with a movie, and then use Sound object methods to control the sound of that movie (**Figure 12.23**). Take a look at the following script:

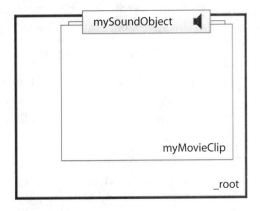

Figure 12.23
Similar to the Color object, when a new Sound object is created, it is associated with a particular movie. This lets you control the sound in that movie using the methods available to the sound object.

```
on (release) {
    _//create a new Sound object when this button is released.
    mySoundObject = new Sound (_root);
    mySoundObject.setVolume (75);
    mySoundObject.setPan (-50);

}
```

Let's now examine each line of this script.

```
mySoundObject = new Sound (_root);
```

This line creates a new Sound object with the name `mySoundObject` and attaches it to the main movie.

> **TIP** *If you don't define a specific movie when creating a Sound object, it will affect sounds that exist on all timelines in the Flash Player window.*

```
mySoundObject.setVolume(75);
```

This line reduces the overall volume of any sounds on the main timeline to 75 percent of their original volume. This means that if there are several sounds playing at different volumes on the main timeline, their relative volumes will remain the same but their overall volume will decrease to 75 percent.

```
mySoundObject.setPan(-100);
```

This line sets the pan of the sounds on the main timeline. A value of -100 means that the sound will only play in the left speaker; a value of 100 means that it will only play in the right speaker. A value of 0 will cause the sound coming out of the left and right speakers to be equal.

To learn about the other methods that are available to the Sound object, see the Action-Script Dictionary (which you can access by choosing Help > ActionScript Dictionary). Also, look for the following interactive tutorial on the CD: Changing the Sounds Dynamically.

Math Object

The Math object is the means by which you manipulate numbers with ActionScript. It is not necessary to create a Math object to use the methods and properties that are available to it.

The `Math.round()` method will round a number to the nearest integer. Thus, in the following example `myVariable` is assigned a value of 34.

```
myMathVariable = 34.365;
```

myVariable = Math.round(myMathVariable);

The `Math.ceil()` method will round a number *up* to the nearest integer. Thus, in the following example `myVariable` is assigned a value of 35.

```
myVariable = Math.ceil(34.365);
```

The `Math.floor()` method will round a number *down* to the nearest integer. Thus, in the following example `myVariable` is assigned a value of 34.

```
myVariable = Math.floor(34.945);
```

The `Math.max()` method determines which of two values is higher and returns that value. Thus, in the following example `myVariable` is assigned a value of 45.

```
mathVariable1 = 45;
mathVariable2 = 19;
myVariable = Math.max(mathVariable1, mathVariable2);
```

The `Math.min()` method determines which of two values is smaller and returns that value. Thus, in the following example `myVariable` is assigned a value of 19.

```
mathVariable1 = 45;
mathVariable2 = 19;
myVariable = Math.min(mathVariable1, mathVariable2);
```

To find out about the other methods and properties available to the Math object, see the ActionScript Dictionary (which you can find by choosing Help > ActionScript Dictionary).

Mouse Object

The Mouse object's sole purpose in ActionScript is to provide methods for making the mouse cursor invisible or visible. Take a look at the following script:

```
onClipEvent (mouseMove) {
  Mouse.hide();
  startDrag(this, true);
  updateAfterEvent();
}
```

Let's now examine each line of this script:

```
onClipEvent (mouseMove) {
```

This line shows that the script is attached to a movie clip instance and will be executed when the mouse is moved anywhere in the Flash player window.

```
Mouse.hide();
```

This line hides the mouse cursor.

```
    startDrag(this, true);
```

This line essentially states, "Start dragging the movie clip instance *this* script is attached to," and, "Yes (true), I want to lock the center of the movie clip instance to the position of the cursor."

```
    updateAfterEvent();
```

This line is a bonus action. Normally, the position of the dragged movie clip is updated at whatever frame-per-second rate your movie is set to run—however, if that number is set to, say, 12 frames per second, dragging will appear choppy at best. By using updateAfterEvent(), you can cause the movie clip's position to be updated with *every pixel* the cursor is moved, which makes for a much smoother drag. Look for the following interactive tutorial on the CD: Creating a Custom Cursor.

Array Objects

You can think of an Array object as a *supervariable:* Where a variable can only contain a single value, an Array object can contain multiple values. Similar to the Sound and Color objects, an Array object must be created using a constructor, as demonstrated by the following:

```
    directions = new Array ("North", "East", "South", "West");
```

Each value in an array is identified by an index number (0, 1, 2, and so on) that denotes its position in the array. In the array we just created, North has an index number of 0, East an index number of 1, and so on. To access a value that exists in an array, you would use the following syntax:

```
    myVariable = directions[2];
```

In this script, myVariable is assigned a value of South because this is the value that exists at Index Position 2 in our directions array. There are numerous methods available to the Array object that let you manipulate the data within the array. For example, the directions array we created currently contains data in the following order:

```
    directions[0] = "North"
    directions[1] = "East"
    directions[2] = "South"
    directions[3] = "West"
```

Using the reverse() method as follows,

```
    directions.reverse()
```

we can reverse the order of values to the following:

```
directions[0] = "West"
directions[1] = "South"
directions[2] = "East"
directions[3] = "North"
```

Or using the sort() method as follows,

```
directions.sort()
```

we can change the order of values so they exist alphabetically like the following:

```
directions[0] = "East"
directions[1] = "North"
directions[2] = "South"
directions[3] = "West"
```

Arrays help you logically store data in groups that are easy to work with. You might, for example, use an array to store user information. By creating four input text elements on the stage with the variable names name, age, phoneNumber, and email, respectively, and then entering the following values:

```
name = "Derek";
age = 20;
phoneNumber = "555-1234";
email = "derek@derekfranklin.com";
```

you could then create a user array:

```
user = new Array (name, age, phoneNumber, email);
```

Then, whenever you needed to access a particular piece of data about your user, you could easily do it by using the array's name, followed by the index number of the particular piece of data you wished to use. Take a look at the following:

```
myMessage = "Hello " + user[0] + ". You seem to be " + user[1] + "
years old.";
```

myMessage is a dynamic text element that, in this case, will display "Hello Derek. You seem to be 20 years old."

To learn about additional methods for the Array object, see the ActionScript Dictionary (which you access by choosing Help > ActionScript Dictionary).

String Objects

Using the methods available to the String object, you can manipulate string values such as those that exist in input and dynamic text elements. The following demonstrates some of the things you can do with strings:

Example 1

For demonstration purposes, assume there is a dynamic text element on the stage with a variable name of myText that contains the text "Creative Web Animation." Look at the following script:

Figure 12.24
The first character in a string value is always assigned an index value of 0 with subsequent characters numbered accordingly.

```
myVariable = myText.charAt (5);
```

In this script, the value assigned to myVariable is "i". This is because counting from the left (with *C* being 0), *i* is the fifth character in the text string "Creative Web Animation" (**Figure 12.24**).

> **TIP** *When determining the position of characters in a string (known as the index), ActionScript counts the first character as 0, the second as 1, and so forth.*

When would you use this string method? The following example demonstrates how this method could be used to check the validity of a phone number entered. Assume there are two text elements on the stage, one named phone (into which the user enters a phone number, including area code) and another named myMessage (which will display a message depending on the validity of the phone number entered). The user is asked to enter his or her phone number, then press the button that has the following script attached to it:

```
on (release) {
  if (phone.charAt(3) != "-" || phone.charAt(7) != "-") {
    myMessage = "That is an invalid phone number!";
  } else {
    myMessage = "That is a valid phone number!";
  }
}
```

The If statement in this script states that "if the fourth or eighth characters in the phone text element are not dashes, display 'That is an invalid phone number!' in the myMessage text element. Otherwise, display 'That is a valid phone number!' "

Example 2

Next, we're going to look at the substring method, which allows you to extract a portion of a string. The syntax for this method looks like this:

```
nameOfString.substring (from, to);
```

nameOfString indicates the variable name of the text element to evaluate; from represents the number of characters from the left of the string (with the first character counting as 0) to use as a *starting* point for the extraction; and to specifies the number of characters from the left of the string to use as an *ending* point for the extraction. Look at the following example, which assumes there is a dynamic text element on the stage named myText that contains a string value of Macromedia.

```
myVariable = myText.substring (3, 7);
```

In this example, *Macromedia* is the string, and the section of the string to be extracted begins with the character at Position 3 (*r*), and extends to the character at Position 7 (*e*). Thus, myVariable is assigned a value of *rome*.

You would use the substring method to isolate parts of strings so that they could be evaluated individually from the string itself.

Imagine a dynamic text element on the stage with a variable name of title. If a user were to enter the text *Dr. Frankenstein* in the field and push a button, the script below would be executed:

```
on (release) {
   if (title.substring(0, 2) == "Ms.")
   myMessage = "Hello Madam.";
   } else (title.substring(0, 2) == "Dr.") {
   myMessage = "Hello Doctor.";
   }
}
```

Based on the information entered into the text field title, when this script has executed, another text element with a variable name of myMessage will display the string "Hello Doctor."

Example 3

You can use the `toUpperCase()` and `toLowerCase()` methods to convert a string to all uppercase or all lowercase characters. Take a look at the following example:

```
myText.toUpperCase()
```

If `myText` contains a string value of `"Creative Web Animation!"` this will change it to read `"CREATIVE WEB ANIMATION!"`

To find out about the other methods available to the String object, see the ActionScript Dictionary (which you can access by choosing Help > ActionScript Dictionary).

Example 4

Strings have a single property, length. This is a numeric value based on the number of characters in a string. The string parameter indicates the string to evaluate. For example, if you had a text element that contained the string "Flash", its length would have a numeric value of 5 because the word *Flash* has five characters.

You can use this property to easily check the length of strings—for example, to verify data that must contain a specific number of characters, such as Zip codes and phone numbers.

Imagine a text field on the stage with a variable name of `zipCode` in which a user has entered the text *46293*. The user pushes a button, and the script below is executed:

```
on (release) {
  if (zipCode.length == 5) {
    myMessage = "That is a valid Zip Code.";
  } else {
    myMessage = "Please enter a valid Zip Code.";
  }
}
```

Based on the information entered into the `zipCode` text element, when this script has executed, another text element with a variable name of `myMessage` will display the string "That is a valid Zip Code."

Smart Clips

Imagine being able to use movie clips whose powerful ActionScript capabilities you could configure not by changing the script via the Actions panel but simply by altering parameter settings in a dialog box. That's what Smart Clips allow you to do. This means that even someone without scripting experience can easily configure a movie clip by simply entering custom values for those parameter settings (**Figure 12.25**).

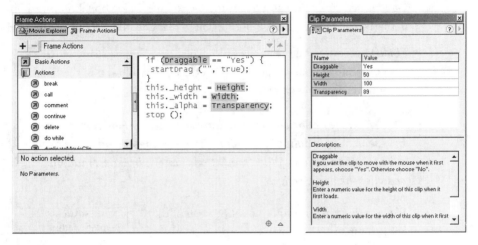

Figure 12.25
Smart Clips let you take the values that determine how a movie clip instance appears and functions (as shown by gray boxes in the Actions panel on the left) and turn them into a set of parameters that users can easily set without looking at the actual script.

Smart Clips are created from regular movie clips in the library. Apart from the fact that each Smart Clip contains an associated set of parameters, they are used in your project like any other movie clip. Your project can contain numerous instances of a single Smart Clip, each configured differently. The easiest way to understand the concept of Smart Clips is to actually create one and use a couple of instances of it in your project.

> **TIP** *A number of Smart Clips are included with Flash and can be found by choosing Window > Common Libraries > and one of the following: Learning Interactions, Learning Objects, or Smart Clips.*

The Actions Panel Options Menu

As with most panels in Flash, the Actions panel contains an Options menu with a list of commands that pertain to tasks that you perform there. These options make creating and refining your ActionScripts a bit easier. They include the following (**Figure 12.26**):

- **Normal Mode/Expert Mode.** See Chapter 13, "Creating Interactivity with Basic Actions," for a description of these options.

- **Go to Line.** This command opens the Go to Line dialog box. Entering a number in this box and clicking OK will take you to that line in the script and highlight it.

- **Find.** This command opens the Find dialog box. Enter a string of text that you wish to locate in your script and click OK. Flash will jump to the first line that contains the text you entered.

> **TIP** *When the Actions panel is in Normal mode, the Find command only searches portions of the script where Parameter fields have been used to define actions. When the Actions panel is in Expert mode, it searches the entire script.*

- **Find Again.** This is simply a continuation of the Find command. Initiating this command will jump to the next line in your script that contains the text you entered with the Find command.

- **Replace.** Similar to the Find and Replace command in most word processing programs, this command will search for a specified string of text in your script and replace it with another string of text.

- **Check Syntax.** This command will check the current script for ActionScript syntax errors. Any errors will be displayed in the Output window, which automatically opens if errors are found.

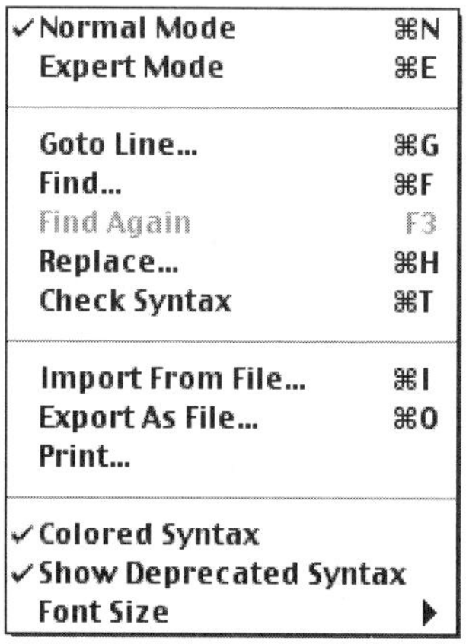

Figure 12.26
The Actions panel Options menu.

> **TIP** *Errors in your code are identified in red. When you place your mouse over an area that contains improper syntax, a Tooltip message explaining the error will appear.*

- *Import From File.* This command imports an external text file (with an .as extension) that contains ActionScript. These are simple text files created in the Actions panel, with Notepad or SimpleText.

- *Export As File.* This command saves the current script as an external text file with an .as extension. You can later import the file back into Flash (see last command) or open and edit it in an external editor such as Notepad or SimpleText.

- *Print.* This command prints the currently displayed ActionScript.

- *Colored Syntax.* This command turns color coding on or off so that you can display various syntax components (keywords, comments, properties, etc.) in different colors for easier readability. Keywords appear in blue, properties in green, strings in gray, and comments in magenta. This makes it easy to identify syntax errors in your script. For example, if a property is defined as `property`, it will not appear green (as if would had it been defined properly). Add the underscore (`_property`), and the property will appear green.

- *Show Deprecated Syntax.* Deprecated syntax is ActionScript syntax that was used in previous versions of Flash but has been replaced by new syntax in Flash 5. Selecting this command will highlight deprecated syntax in the Toolbox list window.

- *Font Size.* This command lets you choose a font size to display ActionScript code in the Actions panel.

Printing

Despite all the interactive and exciting ways you can use Flash to create powerful multimedia presentations, sometimes there's still nothing like the printed page to get your point across. In this section, we'll show you some of the many ways you can use the printed page to make your content more compelling.

Advantages Over Browser Printing

Printing content using ActionScript rather than through a browser's Print command offers the following advantages:

- *Content does not need to be visible to be printed.* For content to be printed from the browser, it must be visible from within the browser window. In contrast, from Flash, you can hide printable content from the user so that it's *only* available for printing (its purpose). For example, a small 100 x 200 pixel Flash banner ad could contain a hidden movie (see "The Power of Hidden Movies" later in this section) which is 640 x 800 pixels and contains numerous graphics that cannot be seen until printed. Thus, the physical size of the actual Flash movie has no bearing on the size of any printable material contained within it.

- *You select what's printed.* When you print an HTML page from a browser, everything you see is printed. This includes banner ads, navigation buttons, and more. When printing from Flash, this is not the case. You can select which content you wish to print, and which you don't.

- *Multipage printing.* Printing multiple HTML documents from a browser entails going to the first page and printing it, then the next page, and so on. You can avoid this tedium by printing from Flash: Since individual frames in a movie represent *pages*, you can easily tell Flash to print any number of these pages with a single action.

- *High-quality output.* Content printed from the browser sometimes suffers from being based on bitmap graphics. Although such graphics may look fine on screen, they often appear pixelated on page. Printed Flash content, in contrast, can be rendered as vector graphics to produce sharp, clear graphics.

Printing Movies Using ActionScript

Using ActionScript to print is simple if you think of every movie (including the main timeline, movie clips, and loaded movies) as a document and each frame of a movie as a printable page. When you initiate a print action with ActionScript, you define which frames to print. For example, the following script will print frames in the movie clip instance myMovieClip:

```
print ("myMovieClip", "bmovie");
```

Specifying which frames to print

By default, all frames of the specified movie will print. By using special frame labels on the printed movie's timeline, you can print content from selected frames only.

To designate specific frames as printable:

1. In the authoring environment, activate the timeline whose frames you want to make printable.

2. With the Frame panel open, select a keyframe on the timeline that you wish to designate as printable.

3. In the Frame panel, enter *#p* in the Label text box.

4. Repeat Steps 2 and 3 to specify addtional keyframes as printable (**Figure 12.27**).

When a `print` action is initiated that targets this timeline, only the frames you designated with *#p* will print.

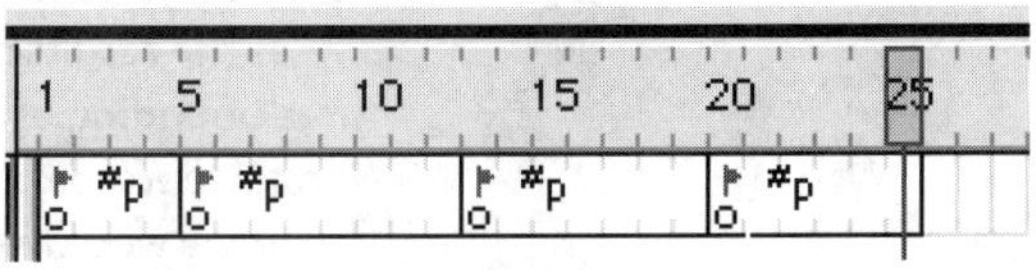

Figure 12.27
Giving a keyframe a label of *#p* designates it as printable. Content on other frames will not print.

Setting up the ActionScript

A `print` action tells Flash to send a movie's frames to the user's printer and print all frames specified as printable. The `print` action can be triggered by a mouse, movie clip, or frame event.

To set up a print action:

1. Select a button instance, a movie clip instance, or a keyframe.

2. With the Actions panel open, press the Add (+) button, and from the menu that appears choose Actions > Print.

This adds a `print` action in the Actions list window. Parameters for this action appear at the bottom of the Actions panel.

3. For the Print parameter, choose from the following:

- *As vectors.* This option will print content at a high resolution. The trade-off is that any object with a transparency will be printed opaque, and color effects applied to symbol instances will not appear—all of which may interfere with the look you want for your printed material.

- *As Bitmap.* This option prints all content as bitmaps. Transparency and color effects will print when using this setting.

4. For the Location parameter, choose from the following:

- *Level.* Choosing this option lets you specify a movie on a specific level as the movie to print.

- *Target.* Choosing this option lets you specify a target path to a movie (such as `_root.myMovieClip`) to indicate which movie to print.

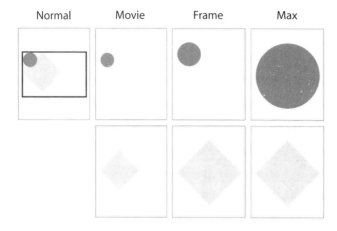

| Normal | Movie | Frame | Max |

Figure 12.28
This graphic demonstrates the results of the three bounding options. Normal represents how the movie would appear against an actual sheet of paper.

5. For the Bounding parameter, choose from the following (**Figure 12.28**):

- *Movie.* This option sets the movie's bounding box as the total area of printed content. Content is printed at actual size.

- *Frame.* This option sets the composite bounding box of the content on all printable frames as the print area. Thus, the frame that contains content with the largest bounding box will be scaled to print as large as possible on the printed page, and the content on all other printable frames will be scaled a relative amount.

- *Max.* This option will scale the content on each printable frame so that they all print the same size. Thus, the content on each frame will be scaled to fill the printed page.

Printing Tip Sheet

- *You can designate multiple movies as printable.* Your Flash movie can contain any number of printable movies in the form of movie clips or loaded movies.

- *A movie must be fully loaded to be printed.* A print action will not work on a movie that hasn't been fully loaded. Use the _framesloaded property to check whether the movie has fully loaded. Take a look at the following example:

```
if (myClip._framesloaded == myClip._totalframes) {
    print ("myClip", "bmovie");
}
```

- *A movie clip must be given an instance name to be designated as printable.*

Disabling Printing

Even though your movie may not contain any `print` actions, the user can still print content via the Print command by right-clicking (Windows) or Control-clicking (Macintosh) the Flash Player. To make this feature unavailable to the user (dimming it on the menu), select the keyframe on Frame 1 of the main timeline and give it a label of `!#p`. This will prevent users from printing from within Flash, though they can still print from their browsers.

Using Hidden Movies

Chances are, you won't want printable content cluttering your animated presentation. A movie does not need to be visible in Flash to be targeted for the `print` action. Even though invisible, when printed, its content appears normal. The idea with this technique would be to attach an `onClipEvent(load)` event to any movie clip instance that contains printable content, along with an action that makes that movie clip instance invisible upon loading. The following script, if attached to `myMovieClip`, will make it invisible upon loading.

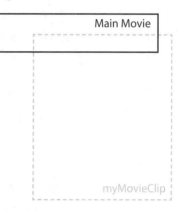

```
onClipEvent (load) {
  this._visible = 0;
}
```

While invisible, the clip can still be targeted for the `print` action (**Figure 12.29**):

```
on (release) {
  print ("myMovieClip", "bmovie");
}
```

Figure 12.29
Invisible movies (myMovieClip) can be targeted for printing, allowing you to print content that is much larger than the visible movie that contains it (Main Movie).

Obviously, this technique assumes that the content in the movie you are hiding is printable content, not content used to enhance the presentation of your overall movie.

Printing on Demand

Let's say you have five different product catalogs (movies) of 10 pages (frames) each that you would like to make available to your customers via Flash's printing feature—

a total of 50 pages of content. If you made these movies part of you main movie, however, it would take most of the day to download. A better solution would be to make each catalog a separate .swf, then use a `loadMovie()` action in your main movie to load and print the appropriate catalog movie as needed.

To set up the loaded movies that will be printable:

1. Create a new Flash authoring file (of any size that can accomodate your material) and place each page of printable content on seperate keyframes on this movie's timeline. For our demonstration, you would need ten keyframes, each of which contains a page of content from one of your calalogs.

With content in place, we need to add two actions to this movie: one to make it invisible when loaded, and one to make it print when it has fully loaded.

2. Add a new layer to your movie and name it Actions.

This layer will contain our two actions.

3. On the first frame of this new layer, add the following ActionScript:

```
this._visible = 0;
```

Because this action exists on Frame 1, this movie will be invisible when first loaded.

4. To ensure that our movie is fully loaded before we print it, add a keyframe to Frame 11 on the Actions layer, and place the following script there:

```
print ("", "bmovie");
stop();
```

The reason for placing this action on Frame 11 is simple: Our movie contains ten frames of content. By placing the action on Frame 11, we ensure that the movie will have completely loaded before the `print` action is triggered. The `stop()` action prevents the movie from looping.

5. Export this movie with a name such as catalog1.swf and save it in the directory that contains your main movie.

6. Repeat these steps to create any number of .swf files (named catalog2.swf, catalog3.swf, and so on), each of which contains a different catalog (or whatever content you want to make printable).

To set up your main movie:

1. Open the authoring file that represents your main movie.

2. If you have created five seperate .swf files that are printable documents, place five buttons in your main movie.

3. Attach the following script to each button.

```
on (release) {
  loadMovieNum ("catalog1.swf", 1);
}
```

When the button is released, `catalog1.swf` is loaded into Level 1. Once that movie has been loaded, it performs the functionality we set up earlier.

For each button you would need to change the name of the .swf file to load (as it appears in the script above) from `catalog1.swf` to `catalog2.swf`, `catalog3.swf`, and so on.

This technique can be used for any printable content that you want to make available on an as-needed basis so that its file size does not weigh down your main movie.

Interactive Tutorials

- *Using Functions.* This tutorial shows you how create and use functions in your movie to make your scripting more efficient.

- *Creating and Using Smart Clips.* Learn how to create a Smart Clip from a movie clip as well as use several instances of it in your project.

- *Dragging and Dropping.* This tutorial will show you how to use the _droptarget property to create drag-and-drop functionality in your movie.

- *Duplicating and Removing Movie Clips Dynamically.* This tutorial shows you how instances of movie clips can be replicated dynamically, then removed.

- *Creating a Mouse Tracker.* This tutorial shows you how to create a movie that contains a mouse tracker, a device that constantly displays the current *x* and *y* position of the user's pointer in a couple of text fields.

- *Creating a Custom Cursor.* In this tutorial you'll learn how to use a movie clip as a custom cursor in your project.

- **Testing for Collisions.** Detecting when one object "collides" with another is an important aspect of games. In this tutorial we'll show you how it's done.

- **Controlling Sounds Dynamically.** In this tutorial we'll show you a simple technique for adding volume and panning controls to your movie.

- **Controlling Color Dynamically.** In this tutorial you'll learn how to change the color of a movie clip instance dynamically.

- **Displaying the Current Date.** Having your movie display the current date makes your content appear fresh. In this tutorial we'll show you how it's done.

- **Creating an MP3 Jukebox.** Learn how to create your own custom MP3 jukebox with this tutorial.

- **Working with Properties.** In this tutorial we'll show you how to create and work with a movie's properties to make your presentation interactive.

- **Loading Variables from an External File.** Learn how to load variable information from an external file so that your movie can react to it.

Using the Library to Manage Your Assets

Think how difficult it would be to accomplish anything using your computer if it didn't have a built-in organizational system to help you work with and keep track of your files. Imagine trying to locate a single file among the thousands that reside on your computer's hard drive—you could spend the greater part of a week and still not find what you were looking for. Fortunately, the computer's operating system makes file management fairly painless.

Most computer operating systems allow you to organize your files in imaginary "folders" that work the same way real folders do. You can open and close them, name and rename them, reorder them, and move them around. In short, you can organize your files in a way that makes sense to *you*. The library in Flash works much the same way.

A Flash project can contain hundreds of items, or *assets*, including symbols, sounds, bitmaps, and video. Keeping track of and working with all of these items would be a daunting task without the library, which has all the functionality you need to keep your movie elements organized. You work with items in Macromedia Flash's library in much the same way you do with files on your hard drive—each asset in your project is identified by an icon representing the type of asset it is, and all assets are organized into folders.

The Interface

To begin our examination of the library, let's take a look at its interface, which can provide all kinds of information about the items in your movie. Note that because the library can contain both folders and movie assets, we use the term *item* to denote both. Where there's a need to distinguish between them, we'll point it out.

To open the library, do one of the following:

- Froms the Window menu, choose Library.

- Press the Show Library button on the Launcher bar.

    The library will remain open until you deliberately close it.

The library window is made up of the following areas **(Figure 13.1)**:

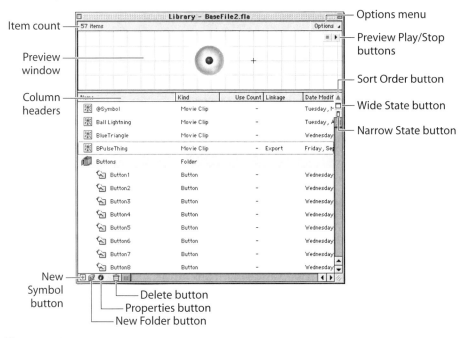

Item count

Preview window

Column headers

New Symbol button

Options menu

Preview Play/Stop buttons

Sort Order button

Wide State button

Narrow State button

Delete button

Properties button

New Folder button

Figure 13.1
The library interface.

- *Item count.* This area shows you the number of items in your library, including individual items such as symbols, sounds, and bitmaps, as well as folders.

- *Options menu.* Clicking here opens the Library Options menu, where you'll find all of the commands you need to work with library items. (We discuss these commands later in the chapter.)

- *Preview window.* This window lets you preview an asset's appearance and function.

- *Preview Play/Stop buttons.* Use these buttons to control the preview of any animated assets in your library.

- *Column headers.* The following headers describe the content in the information column beneath them:

  Name. This hierarchical list includes the names of all of the items in the library. In the case of sounds, bitmaps, and QuickTime movies, it includes the name of the symbol, folder, or imported file from which the asset was derived.

  Kind. This describes the *kind* of item (graphic, button, movie clip, bitmap, sound, video, or folder).

  Use Count. This tells you how many times your project uses an asset in the library.

  Linkage. Indicates if the asset is part of a shared library, or has been imported from or exported to a shared library. (We'll provide a more in-depth discussion of this later in the chapter.)

  Date Modified. This indicates the date and time an item was last edited or updated.

- *Sort order.* Use this button to sort your items in ascending or descending order.

- *Wide State button.* This button maximizes the library window so that all column headers are visible.

- *Narrow State button.* This button minimizes the library window so that it displays only the most pertinent information. You can use the horizontal scroll bar to scroll through the columns.

- *New Symbol button.* Use this button to create a new symbol from the library window. (It functions in the same way as the New Symbol command in the Insert menu on the Flash main menu bar.)

- *New Folder button.* Use this button to create a new folder in the library directory.

- *Properties button.* Use this button to bring up the asset's Properties dialog box so that you can adjust the selected asset's settings.

- *Delete button.* If you select an item in the library and then press this button, the item will be deleted from your project. But be careful: You cannot undo this action.

Additional Menus

The following are a couple of additional menus you'll find useful when working with the library:

- If you right-click (Windows) or Control-click (Macintosh) an item in the library window, a menu pops up offering a choice of several tasks that can be performed on that item **(Figure 13.2)**.

- If you right-click (Windows) or Control-click (Macintosh) the Preview window in the library, another menu pops up, allowing you to set how you want the background in the Preview window to appear.

Figure 13.2
An item's contextual pop-up menu.

Managing Library Assets

A library asset is any element that can be used more than once in your Flash movie. Library assets can include symbols you've created, as well as sounds, bitmaps, and video that have been imported. Each asset in the library is identified by an icon that represents the asset type **(Figure 13.3)**, as well as a name that differentiates it from the other assets.

> **TIP** *You may come across a special library asset known as a* Smart Clip. *We discuss the creation and use of Smart Clips in Chapter 12, "Using ActionScript for Advanced Interactivity."*

You can perform all sort of tasks from within the Library window, some of which pertain to the library and others (such as creating new symbols or updating imported files) that are similar to tasks you can perform elsewhere in Flash. Being able to perform such tasks from within this window is simply a matter of convenience.

Let's take a look at some of the Library window's functionality.

Figure 13.3
Library items and their identifying icons.

Selecting Items

Selecting on an item in the library allows you to move, rename, and delete the item, as well as drag it onto the stage in order to work with it there. In most cases, selecting items, in the library is no different then selecting items elsewhere in Flash. (You select folders and assets the same way.)

To select an item:

◆ Click it once. It will appear highlighted.

To select multiple items:

◆ Click an item once, hold down the Control (Windows) or Command (Macintosh) key, and then click another item.

Keep doing this to add items to the selection.

Once you've selected an item, you can drag it to the stage and add it to your movie (though you can't do this with folders). You can also drag items to a folder within the library.

The commands on the Options menu will always pertain to the selected item(s) **(Figure 13.4)**.

Figure 13.4
When you select an item in the library window, the commands on the library Option menu will pertain to that item.

Previewing Assets

When you select a graphic or sound asset, the Preview window will show you how it will appear or sound in your movie. If the asset is one that plays over a span of frames (for example, a sound, movie clip, or button), you can click the Play button in the Preview window to see or hear it played live in that window. Click the Stop button to halt it.

To resize the preview window:

◆ Place your cursor between the Preview window and column headers. When it turns into a double-sided arrow, click and drag **(Figure 13.5)**.

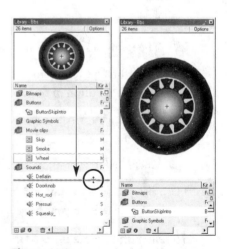

Figure 13.5
Resizing the Preview window provides a more detailed view.

Renaming Items

If you're no longer happy with an item's name, you can simply rename it.

To rename an item in the library, do one of the following:

- Double-click its name.

- Right-click (Windows) or Control-click (Macintosh), and from the contextual menu that appears, choose Rename.

- Select the item in the library, then press the Item Properties button at the bottom of the Library window.

- Select the item in the library, and from the Options menu in the Library window choose Rename.

Deleting Items

If you're like most Flash developers, not all of the symbols you create or the files you import will make it into the final product. However, Flash stores every one of those files and symbols in the library unless you deliberately delete them. Although these unused items won't affect your final exported movie's file size, they will remain part of your Flash authoring file, making that file unnecessarily large. It's a good idea to do periodic housecleaning to rid the library of all those unused files.

To delete an item from the library:

1. Select the items you wish to delete.

   The item—a symbol, sound, bitmap, video, or folder—will be highlighted.

2. From the Options menu in the Library window, choose Delete, and then click the Delete button in the dialog box that appears.

   A Delete confirmation box will appear asking if you're sure you want to delete the item.

3. Click the Delete button to complete the action.

Flash also provides a command that allows you to search and select all of the items that aren't actually used in your project. Once selected, they can be deleted simultaneously.

To select and delete unused items:

1. From the Options menu on the Library window, choose Select Unused Items.

   All unused items appear highlighted.

2. Click the Delete button at the bottom of the Library window **(Figure 13.6)**.

A delete confirmation box will appear, asking whether you're sure you want to delete.

3. Click the Delete button to complete the action.

TIP *Remember, when you delete an object from the library, it's really gone—that is, you can't undo the action—so be certain of your choice before completing the action.*

Working with Symbols in the Library Window

You can create and duplicate symbols, alter a symbol's properties, change its behavior, and even edit its content and timeline from within the Library window—functions similar to those discussed in the chapter on symbols. Being able to perform these tasks from a central location can save you considerable mouse clicks—it definitely beats having to hop around to various menus, panels, and dialog boxes to accomplish the same thing. For more information about any of the tasks that follow, see Chapter 7, "Symbols."

To create a new symbol from the Library window:

1. From the Options menu in the Library window, choose New Symbol, or click the New Symbol button at the bottom of the window.

The Symbol Properties box will appear.

2. Give your new symbol a name and assign it a behavior.

3. Click OK.

Your new symbol will be added automatically to the library, and you will be taken to its timeline and stage so that you can begin adding content. For more information about symbol creation, see Chapter 7, "Symbols."

Figure 13.6
Deleting unused items prevents your authoring file from becoming unnecessarily large.

TIP *When you create a new symbol using the library window, it is added to the currently active directory. Selecting a folder or an asset within a folder makes it the active directory. Thus, if you select a symbol that resides in a folder named My Buttons, all new symbols or folders will be placed in that folder initially since it's the active directory.*

To duplicate symbols from the Library window:

1. From the list of symbols that appears in the Library window, select the one you wish to duplicate.

   The asset will be highlighted.

2. From the Options menu in the Library window, choose Duplicate to make the Symbol Properties box appear.

3. Name your new symbol, assign a behavior to it, and click OK.

   The new symbol will be added to the library.

To view a symbol's properties from the Library window:

1. Select the symbol in the Library window.

2. From the Options menu in the Library window, choose Properties, or click the Properties button at the bottom of the window.

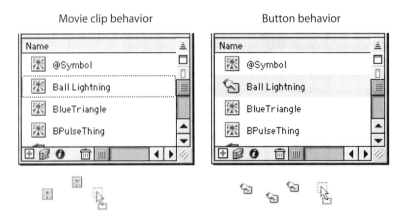

Figure 13.7
When changing a movie clip's behavior to a button behavior in the Library window, any new instances dragged onto the stage will reflect the new behavior.

To change a symbol's behavior from the Library window:

1. Right-click (Windows) or Control-click (Macintosh) the symbol whose behavior you would like to change.

2. On the menu that appears, choose Behavior and then the particular behavior you would like to change this symbol to.

Once a symbol's behavior has been changed in this manner, any new instances of it that you drag from the library will reflect the new behavior **(Figure 13.7)**.

To enter a symbol's symbol-editing mode from the Library window:

1. Select the symbol from the Library window.

2. From the Options menu in the Library window, choose Edit to open the symbol's stage and timeline for editing.

Working with Sounds, Bitmaps, and Videos in the Library Window

Working with sounds, bitmaps, and videos in the Library window varies only slightly from working with symbols. There are basically two tasks you can perform on these library assets: You can get or change their properties (for example, name, compression settings, and so on), and you can update them to reflect the most current version of the file that was used when they were imported into Flash. Both of these are tasks discussed more fully in Chapter 5, "Sound," and Chapter 6, "Bitmaps."

To get or change the properties of a sound, bitmap, or video from within the Library window:

1. Select a sound, bitmap, or video asset from the Library window; it will be highlighted.

2. From the Options menu in the Library window, choose Properties, or click the Properties button at the bottom of the Library window.

To update a sound, bitmap, or video file:

1. Select a sound, bitmap, or video asset from the Library window.

2. From the Options menu on the Library window, choose Update to update the file used in Flash to reflect any changes you made to it externally.

Viewing and Organizing Library Items

Although you can do all sorts of things from within the library, it is primarily an organizational tool that you can use to quickly locate, use, and adjust properties, as well as to view information about your project's various elements.

Creating and Working with Folders

Flash uses folders in much the same way your operating system does: to help you locate and work with files. Using folders effectively can save you a great deal of time and aggravation.

Any item in the library can be put into a folder; you can even put folders within folders.

To create a folder:

1. From the Options menu in the Library window, select New Folder, or click the New Folder button at the bottom of the Library window.

   A folder will appear on the list of library items.

2. Assign a name to the folder that will readily identify its contents, such as Backgrounds **(Figure 13.8)**.

3. To complete the operation, click outside the text box for the name. Your new folder will be added to the library directory structure.

To expand or collapse a folder, do one of the following:

- Double-click the folder's icon.

- Select the folder in the Library window, and from the Options menu choose Expand Folder or Collapse Folder.

   TIP *Use the Expand All or Collapse All commands on the Options menu to open or close all folders simultaneously.*

Figure 13.8
Click the New Folder button at the bottom of the library window to add folders to the library's directory structure.

Moving Items into Folders

As the scope of your project grows, you may need to move items into different folders to make your library's directory structure more logical.

To move an item into an existing folder:

1. Select the item(s) in the library, and begin dragging it.

As you drag the item, the cursor will turn into a circle with a line through it (indicating an area that cannot be dragged to) or an arrow with a small box in its lower right corner (indicating an acceptable area to drag to) **(Figure 13.9)**.

2. Drag the item to the folder you wish to drop it into, and then release the mouse.

> **TIP** *You cannot drag and drop items into the folder in which they already reside. You can, however, drag and drop them into parent or child folders.*

To move an item into a new folder:

1. Select the item(s) in the Library window; it will appear highlighted.

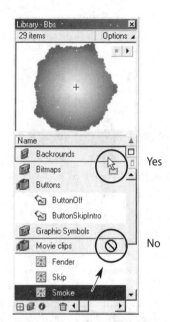

Figure 13.9
When dragging an item to a folder, the cursor will indicate where the item can be placed.

2. From the Options menu in the Library window, choose Move to New Folder.

A dialog box appears, asking you to name your new folder.

3. Give your folder a name, and then click OK.

A new folder is created in the Library window, and the item you originally selected is automatically placed inside of it.

Sorting Items

Folders are great for organizing items, but how do you locate items within folders? Say, for example, you have a folder that contains every element used in Scene 1—all 50 of them: Flash makes it easy for you to find the one you want by allowing you to view these elements in a sequential order based on criteria you've defined.

To sort items in the library:

1. Click the column header that describes how you want to sort the list of library items.

For example, if you click the Name header, library items will be sorted in alphabetical order according to their names **(Figure 13.10)**. Each folder is sorted separately.

2. Click the Sort Order button to select whether to sort your items in ascending or descending order.

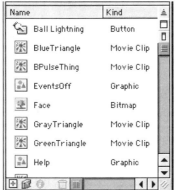

Sorting by name

Sorting by kind

Figure 13.10
Sorting by Name causes assets in the Library to be listed alphabetically. Sorting by Kind groups types of assets together.

Special Libraries

Normally, the assets that appear in the library window are only available to the movie you're working on currently—a situation that could be frustrating if you'd spent a great deal of time creating and fine-tuning an asset that would work perfectly in another project. Don't despair: Two special types of Flash libraries make it possible to use the same assets in more than one movie.

Common Libraries

Common libraries are nothing more than flash authoring files (.fla's containing library assets such as symbols, sounds, and bitmaps) that are placed in a special folder on your hard drive. By placing an .fla file in this folder, the contents of its library become available through the Flash menu bar **(Figure 13.11)**.

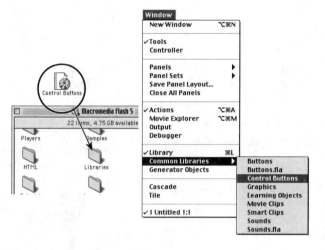

Figure 13.11
Placing an authoring file inside the Libraries folder of the Flash program folder makes the library assets of that authoring file available on the Window > Common Libraries submenu.

To create a common library:

1. Open a new Flash authoring file.

2. Create, place, or import assets into its library.

3. Save the file in the Flash 5\Libraries directory on your hard drive.

> **TIP** *Since the name you assign the saved authoring file will appear as a menu choice inside of Flash, make sure that name reflects the contents of the authoring file's library, such as Control Buttons.fla or Text Animations.fla.*

To open a common library and use its assets:

1. Choose Window > Common Libraries > and then the name of the library from the submenu.

A library window will appear containing all the assets of the common library you just selected.

2. Click and drag an asset from that library onto the stage or into the Library window of your current project.

That asset and any supporting assets will be added to your current project and become part of its authoring file. Any changes you make to that asset once you've added it to your current project will affect only that version of it, not the one in the common library.

> **TIP** *Flash contains several built-in common libraries that contain buttons, animations, and sounds you can use immediately.*

Shared Libraries

Although shared and common libraries are based on the same principle—i.e., one object, many uses—the former are more dynamic. A common library asset, when added to a movie, becomes a permanent, internal part of the authoring file. A shared library asset, in contrast, is merely *linked* to a movie, meaning it remains external from the movie in which it is used.

Shared library assets include any asset that is part of a normal library:

- Graphic, button, and movie clip symbols

- Sounds

- Bitmaps

- Font symbols

There are a couple of benefits to using shared library assets in your movies:

- Users only need to download them once—regardless of how many movies they're used in. If, for example, your site contained multiple .swf files that used a common sound, you could ensure that users would only need to download it once by making that sound a shared library asset **(Figure 13.12)**.

- When you edit or update a shared library asset, any linked movies will automatically reflect those edits **(Figure 13.13)**.

You can treat shared library assets the same way you would normal library assets, using them as animations and button states, as well as employing instances of them throughout your movie.

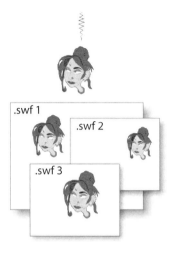

Figure 13.12
A shared library asset needs to be downloaded only once to be used across multiple .swf files.

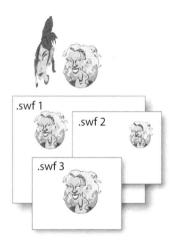

Figure 13.13
Updating a shared library asset automatically updates any .swf file linked to it.

Understanding Shared Libraries

A shared library asset is nothing more than a regular library asset within a .swf file that has been given an identifier name and can be used by other .swf files.

When another movie links to a shared asset, the link includes the URL to the .swf file containing the shared asset, as well as the shared asset's identifier. This is how the linked movie knows where to look for the shared asset **(Figure 13.14)**.

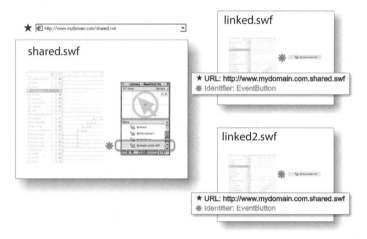

Figure 13.14
A linked movie can locate linked assets using the URL where the shared library resides and the identifier, which identifies a particular asset in a shared library.

The steps for creating a shared asset and using it in another movie are described below:

1. Open the Flash authoring file that contains the library asset you wish to turn into a shared library asset.

> **TIP** *Although a shared library asset can exist in any .fla (including full-blown Flash productions), you may find it easier to create .fla files that contain nothing but shared library assets.*

2. With the Library window open, select an asset, and from the Options menu choose Linkage.

The Symbol Linkage dialog box will appear.

3. Because you're defining a library asset that you want to designate as sharable, choose the Export This Symbol option.

4. In the Identifier field, enter a name or identifier for this symbol (the name cannot contain spaces).

The identifier label—which is required to make the process work—must be different from the asset's name (as shown in the Library window).

5. Click OK.

6. Continue performing these steps to designate other shared assets.

> **TIP** *A movie's library can contain numerous assets, any of which can be designated as* sharable. *A shared asset can be used for animation and interactivity in the same way any other asset in your movie can be used.*

7. Now it's time to define where it is that the shared asset(s) will reside. In the Library window, press the Options button and choose Shared Library Properties.

8. Define the URL where the shared library .swf file will reside.

This can be an absolute URL (http://www.mydomain.com/sharedlibrary.swf) or a relative URL (sharedlibrary.swf), depending on where the shared library will exist in relation to the .swf files that will link to it **(Figure 13.15)**.

> **TIP** *The URL you define at this point is used by Flash to automatically create links to shared assets, as described in Part 6 below. You will have to manually place the exported .swf file at this URL once it has been exported.*

9. Now you need to create the .swf file that will become the shared library and put it at the appropriate URL. First, you must save the authoring file, export it to a Flash movie, and then close it.

10. Now place the exported .swf file at the URL you chose in Step 8.

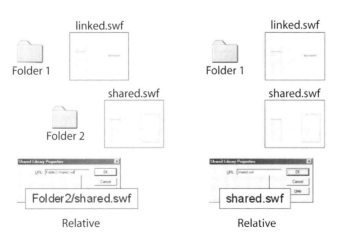

Figure 13.15 When defining a relative URL, linked and shared .swf's must reside in the proper relative position.

11. Open a different authoring file that you want to contain links to shared assets.

12. Now it's time to open the shared library you created earlier containing the assets you want to link to. From the File menu choose Open as Shared Library and navigate to the authoring file where you earlier defined shared assets.

The library for that file will appear.

13. Drag an asset that was defined as a shared asset from the Library window onto the stage of the current authoring file.

This automatically creates a link to the asset in the shared library **(Figure 13.16)**.

14. Close the Shared Library window.

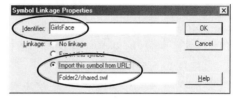

Figure 13.16
After dragging a shared library asset into your current movie, selecting it in the Library window and choosing Linkage from the Library Option menu displays the Symbol Linkage Properties box, which shows the linked asset's properties, including its identifier and the URL it links to.

Although the current authoring file contains only a link to the shared asset, that asset appears in the current movie's library as any other asset and can be used in the same way as any other asset.

15. Finally, you need to save the current authoring file that has the linked assets and export it as a Flash movie. If you defined a relative URL in Step 8 above, place this .swf file in the appropriate relative location to the .swf that contains the shared assets.

During playback, when this .swf file reaches a point where it needs an asset from a shared library, it will look for it at the URL you defined in Step 8.

If you want to update or change an asset in a shared library, reopen the authoring file in which it was defined (Step1 through Step 5 above), change or edit the asset, then re-export as a .swf file and place it back at the URL you defined in Step 8. Next time a linked movie plays, it will reflect your edits.

Caveats

Before you begin using shared library assets, you need to be aware of a couple things: First, whenever your movie requires an asset that exists in a shared library, the contents of the entire shared library will be downloaded, not just that asset. If the shared library contains a number of assets, this could slow the streaming of you movie. One way around this problem is to make shared libraries as small as possible (containing only a few assets) and use assets from several shared libraries. A second issue to be aware of is that if a shared library asset is not available for one reason or another (network problems, etc.), the movie will not play. Once again, splitting assets into several shared libraries may help resolve these issues.

Interactive Tutorials

- *Working with the Library.* This tutorial takes you through a basic tour of the library and shows you how to manage library items as well as how to organize them using folders.

- *Understanding and Using Shared Libraries.* This tutorial steps you through the process of creating a shared library and linking to assets in it.

Using Movie Explorer to Manage Structure

If you've ever worked on a large project, you've probably come to appreciate project management tools. They can help you keep track of your project's many elements within the context of the whole. And they can automate the process of locating, changing, and updating items—tasks you could spend the better part of the day on without such a tool.

In the last chapter, we showed you how to use the library to organize the many reusable elements of your project. In this chapter, we'll focus on a tool with a much broader scope—one that lets you work with, organize, and manage almost every aspect of your movie. We're talking, of course, about Flash's Movie Explorer, a project management tool new to Flash 5, designed to help you work with and dispense information about timelines, frames, layers, symbols, text blocks, ActionScripts, and more.

Understanding the Display List

Understanding Movie Explorer's interface is the key to using this tool effectively. Just a quick glance provides an abundance of information about the overall makeup of your movie and its many parts.

To open Movie Explorer, do one of the following:

- Click the Show Movie Explorer button on the Launcher bar.

- Choose Window > Movie Explorer.

    The Movie Explorer window will appear.

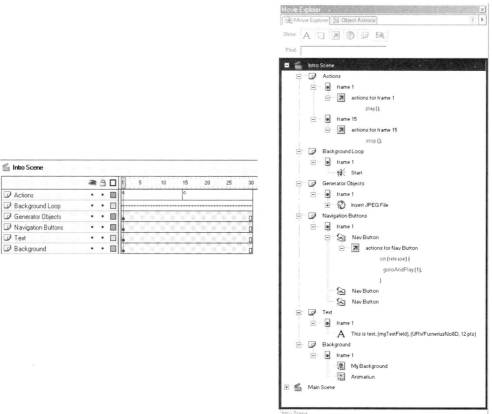

Figure 14.1
Items in the Display List window correspond to items on the timeline, identifying the hierarchical structure of your movie.

The Display List window in Movie Explorer **(Figure 14.1)** contains a hierarchical tree of your movie's content. This tree displays individual elements within the context of the whole movie, providing specific information about each.

To understand this hierarchical tree, you need to know something about its structure. You also need to be familiar with the terms used to describe that structure: The term, *branch,* for example, denotes a level in the tree. Thus, if the universe were your tree, galaxies would represent a branch of that tree, solar systems would represent a branch of the galaxies, and planets would represent a branch of solar systems. Each step is another level, or branch, in the universe (the hierarchical tree). Since a galaxy is a part of the universe, it can be considered a *child* branch of the universe. At the same time, because it is a level higher than a solar system, it is considered the *parent* branch of the solar system.

A movie's hierarchical tree contains the following parent and child branches **(Figure 14.2)**:

- *Scene.* As a section of your movie's overall timeline, a scene is a child branch of the overall movie but a parent branch of layers.

- *Layers.* Each scene is made up of layers—which makes them child branches of a scene but parent branches of frames.

- *Frames.* These are keyframes that exist on the individual layers. A frame is a child branch of a layer but the parent branch of frame actions and movie elements.

- *Frame actions.* These are actions attached to keyframes. A frame action is a child branch of a keyframe.

- *Graphics, button, and movie-clip instances.* These elements exist at a particular keyframe on a layer and include instances of graphic, button, and movie-clip

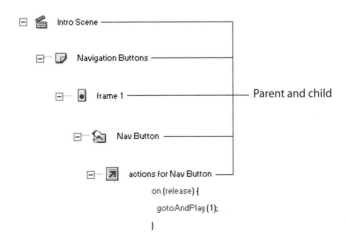

Figure 14.2
Each branch of the hierarchical tree in this case is a child of the branch above it and a parent of the branch or branches below it. (Intro Scene is a child branch of the overall movie.)

symbols. A graphic, button, or movie-clip instance is a child branch of a frame and the parent branch of object actions.

- *Object actions.* These actions are attached to instances of buttons or movie clips. An object action is a child branch of a button or movie-clip instance.

- *Video, sounds, and bitmaps.* These imported elements exist at a particular keyframe on a layer and include instances of videos, sounds, and bitmaps. A video, sound, or bitmap instance is a child branch of a frame.

- *Text.* These text elements exist at a particular keyframe on a layer. A text element is a child branch of a frame.

- *Generator.* These are Generator objects that exist at a particular keyframe on a layer. A Generator object is a child branch of a frame.

Filtering the View

A project can contain hundreds of elements, which means that attempting to view them simultaneously in the Display List window can be a dizzying experience. Fortunately, Movie Explorer lets you choose which content you wish to view.

Setting the Context of the Display List Window

By setting the context of the Display List window, you can choose the level of detail you would like to see within Movie Explorer. Normally, the Display List window shows the hierarchical tree of your entire movie as well as the *symbol definitions*, which represent hierarchical trees of each symbol **(Figure 14.3)**. However, if you want to view only the hierarchical tree of the movie or only the symbol definitions, you can do that as well.

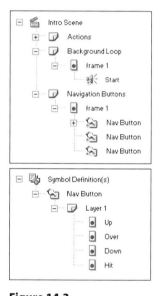

Figure 14.3
You can view the Display List window in the context of your overall movie or its symbol definitions.

To set the context of the Display List window:

1. Press the Customize button.

   The Movie Explorer Settings dialog box will appear **(Figure 14.4)**.

2. Check the appropriate boxes in the Context section of this dialog box, then click OK.

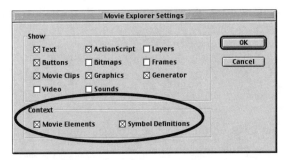

Figure 14.4
Pressing the Customize button lets you set the context of the Display List window.

Figure 14.5
The Options button.

A quicker alternative is to press the Options button on the top-right corner of Movie Explorer **(Figure 14.5)**, and then from the menu that appears select Show Movie Elements, Show Symbol Definitions, or both.

Showing and Hiding Filters

Movie Explorer's Show and Hide filters let you choose which elements you want to see in the Display List window. For example, if you're only interested in viewing the ActionScripts in your movie, you can hide buttons, layers, frames, and so forth so that they won't distract you.

To show or hide particular elements in the Display List window:

1. Click the Customize button.

   The Movie Explorer Settings dialog box will appear.

2. Check or uncheck the appropriate boxes in the Show section of this dialog box.

   A quicker alternative is to click one of the Show/Hide buttons at the top of the Movie Explorer interface **(Figure 14.6)**.

Figure 14.6
The Show/Hide buttons.

Choosing the Scene Mode

Because Flash uses scenes to break timelines into logical chunks, you may sometimes want to see content pertaining only to the current scene, while at other times you may want to view all of the content of every scene simultaneously.

To choose a scene mode:

◆ Press the Options button on the top-right corner of Movie Explorer. From the menu that appears, choose Show All Scenes.

Since this is a toggle command, choosing it from the menu again will cause it to revert to the previous mode.

Collapsing Branches

By expanding and collapsing branches on the tree, you can focus on sections of your movie without being distracted by multiple open branches.

To expand or collapse a branch, do one of the following:

• Click the + and – icons (Windows) or the small twirly arrow (Macintosh) where a branch stems to open or close that branch and its child branches.

• Press the Options button on the top-right corner of the Movie Explorer. From the menu that appears, choose from the following options:

Expand Branch. Expands the tree at the selected branch, making all of its child branches visible.

Collapse Branch. Collapses the tree at the selected branch, thus hiding its child branches.

Collapse Others. Collapses all branches of the tree that do not contain the selected element.

Getting Information from the Display List

Each branch of the hierarchical tree has an associated icon that helps you identify its function in the movie. (For example, a button instance is identified in the Display List window by a button icon.) To the right of the icon is text describing that branch. The following information is included for each type of branch **(Figure 14.7)**:

• *Scene.* The name of the scene.

• *Layers.* The name of the layer.

• *Frames.* The frame number where the keyframe exists. Any label or comments assigned to the keyframe will appear in parentheses.

• *Frame actions.* The code for the ActionScript assigned to the keyframe.

• *Graphics, button, and movie-clip instances.* The name of the symbol from which the instance is derived. If the instance is a movie clip that has been assigned an instance name, that name will also appear in parentheses.

- *Object actions.* Indicates the name of the object that has the action attached to it. For example, if the action is attached to a button named "myButton," this area will read "actions for myButton." Also shown is the code for the ActionScript that has been assigned to the object.

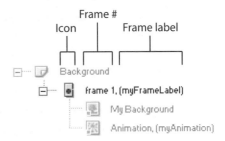

Figure 14.7 The type of information available for items in the Display List window.

- *Video, sounds, and bitmaps.* The name of the element as it appears in the library.

- *Text.* The text contained in the element, followed by the font face and size (shown in parentheses). If the text element has a variable name, the name will appear in parentheses as well.

- *Generator.* The type of Generator object and its attributes.

Viewing and Editing Assets from Movie Explorer

When you select a branch in the hierarchical tree, several things happen to Flash's overall interface that allow you to immediately view and edit selected items.

The following describes how Flash's main interface responds when a branch of Movie Explorer's hierarchical tree is highlighted (if the display-list context is set to Movie Elements):

- *Scene.* The interface goes to the selected scene. If the Scene panel is open, the scene will be highlighted.

- *Layers.* The interface goes to that layer's scene.

- *Frames.* The interface goes to the selected keyframe. The keyframe sequence is highlighted on the timeline, as are all graphical elements on the stage that are included in the sequence. This activates open panels, enabling you to edit highlighted graphical elements. You can even add or edit ActionScript on the selected keyframe via the open Actions panel.

- *Frame actions.* The interface goes to the keyframe on which the action is based. The keyframe sequence is highlighted on the timeline, as are all graphical elements on the stage that are part of that sequence. This activates any open panels, enabling you to edit highlighted graphical elements. In addition, you can add or edit ActionScript on the selected keyframe via the open Actions panel.

- *Graphics, button, and movie-clip instances.* Oddly enough, the playhead's position on the timeline determines how Flash reacts when you select a symbol instance. If the instance is visible on the stage, it becomes highlighted on the stage and the open panels become active, allowing you to edit it. You can even add or edit ActionScript attached to the selected instance, as long as the Actions panel is open **(Figure 14.8)**. If the instance isn't visible on stage, the interface takes you to the instance's scene.

- *Object actions.* Once again, the playhead's position on the timeline determines what happens when an object action is selected on the tree. If the instance to which the action is attached is visible on the stage, it will be highlighted and the open Actions panel will be active, allowing you to edit the attached ActionScript. If the instance is not visible on the stage, the interface takes you to the scene containing the relevant instance.

    TIP *An instance must be selected on the stage for the Action panel to be active.*

- *Video, sounds, and bitmaps.* If a sound is selected, the interface takes you to the keyframe where the sound resides and the Sound panel becomes active. When selecting a bitmap or video, if the element is visible, it will be selected on the stage and the open panels will become active, allowing you to edit the element. If the element is not visible, the interface takes you to the relevant scene.

- *Text.* When selecting a text element on the tree, if it is visible on the stage, the element will be selected and the open text panels will become active, allowing you to edit it. If it is not visible, the interface will take you to the relevant scene.

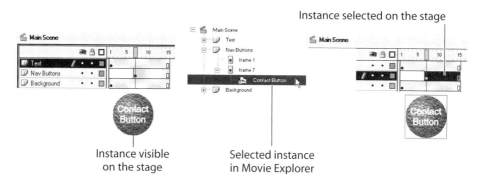

Instance selected on the stage

Instance visible on the stage

Selected instance in Movie Explorer

Figure 14.8
If an instance is visible when it is selected in the Display List Window, the instance is highlighted on the stage and several panels become active.

- *Generator.* If you select a Generator object on the tree and it is visible on the stage, it becomes highlighted and the open Generator panel becomes active, allowing you to edit it. If it is not currently visible on the stage, the interface takes you to the relevant scene.

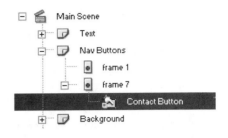

TIP *When selecting a movie element, the complete path in the movie is displayed at the bottom of the Movie Explorer window (Figure 14.9).*

Figure 14.9
When selecting a movie element, you can see its path at the bottom of the Movie Explorer window.

Double-Clicking

The following describes what happens when you double-click any of these branch types:

- *Scene.* Allows you to change the name of the scene.

- *Layers.* Allows you to change the name of the layer.

- *Frames.* Opens the Actions panel where you can add or edit an ActionScript attached to the frame.

- *Frame actions.* Opens the Actions panel where you can edit the ActionScript attached to the frame.

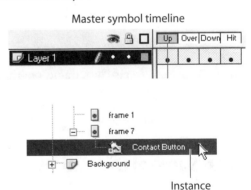

- *Graphics, button, and movie-clip instances.* Opens the master symbol of the instance in symbol-editing mode so that it can be edited (**Figure 14.10**).

Figure 14.10
Double-clicking an instance of a symbol in the Display List window opens the timeline of the master symbol it is based on.

- *Object actions.* Opens the Actions panel where you can edit the action attached to the object.

- *Video, sounds, and bitmaps.* Double-clicking a sound will open the Actions panel, where you can add or edit an ActionScript attached to the relevant keyframe. Double-clicking a bitmap or video will make it visible as well as automatically select it on the stage.

- *Text.* Allows you to edit the text in the element.

- *Generator.* Opens the Generator panel so that you can set the attributes for the Generator object.

Movie Explorer Tasks

In addition to the wealth of information Movie Explorer provides in the Display List window, it also automates several tasks that can help you locate and edit movie elements, spell-check your movie's text, and more.

Go to Location

Although Flash's interface will not always automatically jump to the location of the element selected in the display list (for example, in the case of layers and frames that are part of a symbol definition), you can use the Go to Location command to do so manually. This command causes Flash to jump to the frame (on any timeline) that contains the selected element.

To go to a location:

1. Select a scene, layer, frame, or other movie element in the Display List window.

2. Press the Movie Explorer Options button, and choose Go to Location from the menu that appears.

Go to Symbol Definition

When you select a symbol instance in the Display List window, you may want to look at the definition of the symbol on which the instance is based so that you can understand its structure.

To go to a symbol definition:

1. Select a symbol instance in the Display List window.

2. Press the Movie Explorer Options button, and choose Go to Symbol Definition from the menu that appears.

Opening Panels

Being able to quickly find and edit elements selected in the Display List window is one of biggest advantages of Movie Explorer. Because you do most of your editing in Flash's panels, it's important that the appropriate panels be open and available when you select an element. Movie Explorer makes this easy by offering a command that allows you to automatically open all of the panels relevant to the element selected on the hierarchical tree.

To open all pertinent panels:

1. Select an element on the hierarchical tree in the Display List window.

2. Press the Movie Explorer Options button, and choose Panels from the menu that appears **(Figure 14.11)**.

   TIP *Because layers do not have associated panels, selecting a layer and then invoking this command opens the Layer Properties box instead.*

Editing

When you select a symbol instance or definition in the Display List window, you can immediately open its timeline for editing.

To edit a symbol:

1. Select a symbol instance or definition on the hierarchical tree in the Display List window.

2. Press the Movie Explorer Options button, and choose Edit in Place or Edit in New Window from the menu that appears.

Figure 14.11
Choosing Panels from the Movie Explorer Options menu opens all pertinent panels.

Searching

As your project grows to contain hundreds of symbols, sounds, and other movie elements, finding any one of these elements can be a time-consuming task. Fortunately, Movie Explorer allows you to locate specific items using a keyword search. If you type a string of characters, numbers, or both in the Find box, the Display List window will display only those branches that contain that string. The more text you enter into the Find box, the more detailed your search will be. Any text associated with an element in the Display List window is searched, including branches of the hierarchical tree that are closed **(Figure 14.12)**. To narrow your search further, filter the view in the Display List window as described earlier in this chapter.

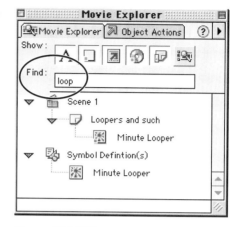

Figure 14.12 When you enter a string of text in the Find box, Movie Explorer searches all open and closed branches in the Display List window for that text.

Find in Library

Because you can work with elements in the library in ways that are not available to you in the Movie Explorer window, Flash offers a command that will let you select an instance of a symbol, sound, bitmap, or video in the Movie Explorer window and then open the master symbol on which it is based in the Library window.

To find a symbol in the library:

1. Select a symbol definition or instance of a symbol, sound, bitmap, or video on the hierarchical tree in the Display List window.

2. Press the Movie Explorer Options button in the upper right corner, and choose Find in Library from the menu that appears.

This opens the Library window (if it's not already open), where the appropriate master symbol is selected and appears in the Preview window of the library **(Figure 14.13)**.

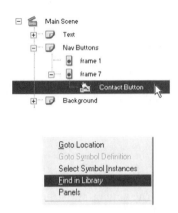

Figure 14.13 When you use the Find in Library command, the library is automatically opened, and the selected symbol is highlighted and appears in the Preview window.

Selecting Symbol Instances

Knowing where instances of a symbol are used in your movie can help you understand the movie's overall structure. If you select a symbol on the Symbol Definition hierarchical tree and then choose Select Symbol Instances from the Movie Explorer options menu, any instances of the selected symbol that are used in your movie will be highlighted in the Display List window.

> **TIP** *The Show Movie Elements option must be selected (on the Movie Explorer options menu) for the action to have an effect.*

Spell-Checking

Although Flash doesn't include a built-in spell-checker, it provides a workaround to this dilemma by allowing you to copy all of the text in your movie to the system clipboard so that you can paste it into another application for spell-checking. But be forewarned: There's no automated process for selecting all spell-checked text from the external application and pasting it back into the appropriate text elements. You must instead select each section of spell-checked text and then paste it back into the appropriate text element in Flash.

To spell-check text:

1. Filter the Display List window view so that only text elements are visible.

2. Press the Movie Explorer Options button, and choose Copy Text to Clipboard from the menu that appears.

3. Open an application with spell-checking capabilities, and use the Paste command to paste the text onto the clipboard.

   All text that was visible in the Display List window will be pasted into the application window of the spell-checking program (for some reason, this text will include scene names, font face names, and so forth). Locate any misspelled words, then return to Flash and make any needed adjustments.

Cutting, Copying, and Clearing

You can cut, copy, or delete graphical elements that appear on the stage right from Movie Explorer, which has the same effect as clicking the item on the stage and selecting the respective command from the Edit menu.

To cut, copy, or clear a graphical element:

1. Select a graphical element in the Display List window.

2. Press the Movie Explorer Options button, then choose Cut, Copy, or Clear from the menu that appears.

Printing

You may sometimes need a hard copy of the hierarchical structure of your movie—to study when you're away from your computer or to hand out at team project meetings. To print only the currently configured hierarchical list in the Display List window, select Print from the Movie Explorer options menu.

> **TIP** *Most of the Options menu commands discussed in this section are also available by right-clicking (Windows) or Control-clicking (Macintosh) an item on the hierarchical tree in the Display List window.*

Interactive Tutorial

 Using the Movie Explorer. This tutorial takes you through a basic tour of the Movie Explorer and reviews many of the concepts you've learned in this chapter.

Testing

CHAPTER 15

What you'll learn…

Using Flash's testing tools

Testing download speeds

Although it's natural to dread tests, they can actually be a good thing. Sure, we can "burn the midnight oil," sweat blood studying, or even write the answers on the palms of our hands, but all of these efforts are pointless if we can't make something work in real life. That's where testing can help.

In computer-driven interactive content, mistakes are referred to as *bugs*—and they can be as ugly and bothersome as their name implies. Although your project is probably not as complex as a major piece of software, you're still likely to discover some glitches. If you don't want to scare off your audience, you'll need to exterminate them.

One of the keys to becoming a Flash master is understanding the need for testing. It doesn't matter how good your project is: If you don't test it, you're putting your reputation (not to mention your neck) on the line. But testing is about more than simply eliminating mistakes; it's also about optimizing your movie so that it plays back in the most efficient manner. Lucky for you, because of the powerful testing tools in Macromedia Flash, this process is relatively quick and easy.

Getting Ready to Test

The following are some tips to get you started:

- *Plan.* Don't even approach a project until you've created a basic outline.

- *Test everything.* Never assume something works—even if it seems like a trivial part of your project. All it takes is one mistake to bring your movie to a screeching halt.

- *Test often.* Don't wait until your project is nearing completion—test at every opportunity. It's much easier to isolate problems if you know your movie was working five minutes ago.

439

- *Fix bugs in an orderly fashion.* Don't attempt to fix a bunch of bugs at the same time. It's best to fix one or two problems at a time, and then test after each. After all, you don't want to create any new bugs in the process.

- *Get a second opinion.* Sometimes you're too close to a project to spot problems. One of the best things you can do is have someone else test your project. Because this person doesn't know what to expect, he or she may stumble upon problems you might have otherwise overlooked. Encourage your testers to be brutal and diligent—and don't get upset if they provide some unsolicited opinions about design and functionality along the way. Swallow your pride and listen: Their opinions may be those of your target audience.

Testing Within the Flash Authoring Environment

Although it shouldn't be your first choice for heavy-duty project testing, the Flash authoring environment does accommodate some minor testing. Within the authoring environment you can test the following:

- *Button states.* You can test the way buttons look in their up, down, over, and hit states.

- *Sounds on the main timeline.* You can listen to sounds placed along the main timeline (including those that are synchronized with on-stage animations) when the timeline is played.

- *Frame actions along the main timeline.* You can test any Go To, Play, and Stop actions attached to frames or buttons on the main timeline when that timeline is played (see below for actions that won't work within the authoring environment).

- *Animation along the main timeline.* Although you can test animation along the main timeline (including shape and motion tweens), this does not include animation within movie clips or buttons (see below for more information).

To preview the current scene:

- Choose Control > Play.

- Press Enter/Return on your keyboard.

- Choose Window > Toolbars > Controller (Windows) or Window > Controller (Macintosh); then click the Play button when the Controller appears.

TIP *To preview all of the scenes in your movie in succession, choose Control > Preview All Scenes, and then play your movie.*

To test a button's visual functionality:

◆ Choose Control > Enable Simple Buttons.

With buttons enabled, they'll react the same way (visually) as they will in your final movie when a user puts the cursor over them. Disable this feature to edit instances of buttons.

To test frame actions such as Go To, Stop, and Play:

◆ Choose Control > Enable Simple Frame Actions.

With frame actions enabled, Go To, Stop, and Play actions will respond accordingly when the timeline is played within the authoring environment (as long as they don't rely on ActionScript expressions or point to URLs).

Within the authoring environment you *cannot* test the following:

- *Movie clips.* Sounds, animation, and actions that are part of movie clips will not be visible or function within the authoring environment. (Only the first frame of a movie clip will appear.)

- *Actions.* Go To, Play, and Stop are the only actions that work in the authoring environment. This means you can't test interactivity, mouse events, or functionality that relies on any other actions.

- *Movie speed.* Playback within the Flash authoring environment is slower than it will be in your final optimized and exported movie.

- *Download performance.* From within the authoring environment, you can't gauge how well your movie will *stream,* or download, over the Web.

The important thing to remember here is that the above-described limitations are only limitations *within the authoring environment.* Just a couple clicks away are commands you can employ to fully test your movie. Let's take a closer look at them.

The Test Movie and Test Scene Commands

As you just saw, testing *within* the authoring environment is limited. To evaluate movie clips, ActionScripts, and other important movie elements, you must move outside the authoring environment. This is where the Test Scene and Test Movie commands— both located on the Control menu—can help: They automatically create working versions of the current scene or entire movie and open them in a window where you can test nearly every aspect of their interactivity, animation, and functionality.

The Test Scene and Test Movie commands generate actual .swf files and place them in the same directory as the authoring file. If your test file works as it should and you wish to use it as your final file, locate it on your hard drive and upload it to your server.

The export settings used when creating .swf files with the Test Scene and Test Movie commands are based on the settings on the Flash tab in the Publish Settings dialog box (for more information, see Chapter 16, "Publishing"). To change these settings, from the File menu choose Publish Settings and make the necessary adjustments under the Flash tab.

To test the current scene:

◆ From the Control menu, choose Test Scene.

Flash automatically exports the current scene and opens it in a new window ready for you to test it.

To test the entire movie:

◆ From the Control menu, choose Test Movie.

Flash automatically exports all of the scenes within the current project and opens the file in a new window ready for you to test it.

The Testing Environment

When using the Test Scene or Test Movie command, you'll notice that although you're still within Flash, the interface has changed. This is because you're now in the testing environment rather than the authoring environment, though both look similar. The differences are as follows (**Figure 15.1**):

- Tool bars appear but do not function.

- The menu bar has changed, as have many of the menu choices.

- The Timeline has been replaced with the Bandwidth Profiler, which itself includes a timeline, graph, and number of other features (see "Understanding the Bandwidth Profiler" later in this chapter.)

- The stage and work area have been replaced with a fully functional copy of the scene or movie you are testing.

Unless otherwise stated, the following information and instructions assume you are working in the testing environment.

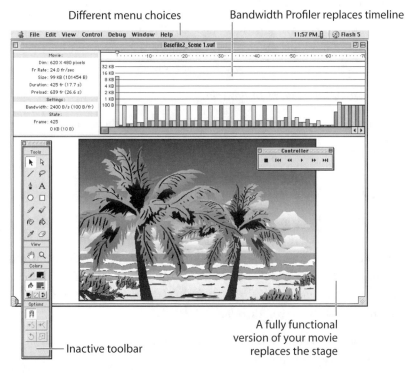

Different menu choices   Bandwidth Profiler replaces timeline

Inactive toolbar

A fully functional version of your movie replaces the stage

Figure 15.1
The Test Movie environment.

Viewing Options

You can change your movie's magnification and quality while it's playing within the testing environment. By changing the view, you can get a more detailed look at the movie; by changing the quality, you can improve playback. Both of these settings only affect the movie's appearance within the testing environment.

To set the magnification of the movie in the testing environment:

- From the View menu, choose Zoom In/Zoom Out.

- Choose View > Magnification > 100%.

To set the quality of playback:

- Choose View > Quality > then Low, Medium or High.

> **TIP** *Any time you wish to close this window and return to the Flash authoring environment, from the File menu choose Close.*

Controlling Playback

Within the testing environment, you have full control over your movie's playback. You can play and test your movie from beginning to end, rewind it, fast-forward it, and more. In this way, you can view certain sections or frames.

To control your movie's playback:

- Use the Controller that appears when you enter the testing environment.

- Choose Control > and then one of the playback options.

Testing Functionality

You may find that you enjoy testing your movie's functionality since it gives you an opportunity to see how your work is coming together—and the process itself is not very difficult. During this phase of testing, you check animation for mistakes, press buttons, and run through your movie. Leave nothing unchecked—mistakes in animation and interactivity should be easy to spot at this point. And remember: If your movie doesn't work here, it won't work *period*.

The testing environment offers the following additional commands on the menu bar to help you track down problems.

List Objects command

The List Objects command provides a complete tally of all of the objects in a given frame, including type, level, frame, and—if it's a target—its name and path. This will help you to determine whether all the necessary objects are present in a particular frame the way they should be.

To list objects for a particular frame:

1. Move the playhead to a frame.

2. From the Debug menu, choose List Objects.

A dialog bog will appear with a list of all objects present on the current frame (**Figure 15.2**).

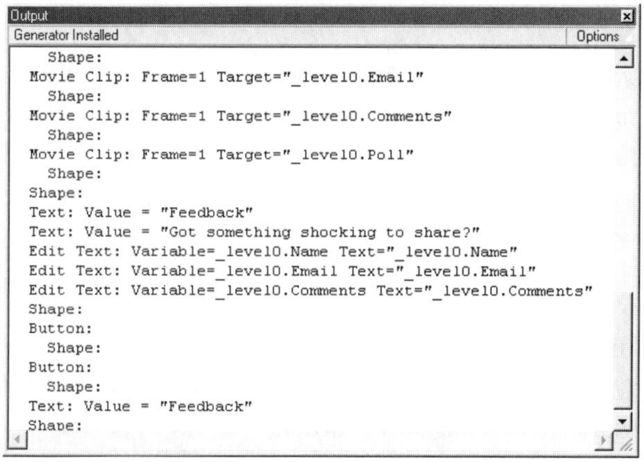

Figure 15.2
The List Objects command provides a list of objects on the current frame.

List Variables command

The List Variables command provides a complete tally of all of the variables (and their values) in a given frame. This will help ensure that variables are created and updated properly as the timeline plays.

To list variables for a particular frame:

1. Move the playhead to a frame.

2. From the Debug menu choose List Variables.

A dialog box will appear with a list of all variables present on the current frame, along with their current values.

Output

The Output command on the Window menu opens the Output window, which is always used in conjunction with the Trace action (see sidebar that follows). It's easy to use the Trace action to ensure that your movie's ActionScripting logic flows in the proper manner. For more information, see Chapter 11, "Basic Actions for Building Interactivity."

Every time a Trace action is encountered in your movie, the Output window displays a Trace message.

To display the Output window:

♦ From the Window menu, choose Output to bring up the Output window.

Using the Trace Action

The Trace action allows you to output a custom message to the Output window—which does not appear in your final movie and has no effect on the rest of the script. This is useful to get a behind-the-scenes look at how your script is functioning—primarily to test interactivity and to output custom messages that tell you what's happening with the data in your movie at any point in time.

The following script shows a mouse event that causes the Count *variable to be updated by a value of 1 each time the mouse event occurs and (if testing in Flash's testing environment) the message associated with the* trace() *action to be output to the Output window:*

```
on (release) {
  Count = ++Count;
  trace ("Count is now " + Count);
}
```

To see a Trace action output to the Output window, choose Control > Test Scene or Test Movie. Whenever the trace() *action is encountered, the Output window in the testing environment will open automatically and display the message associated with the action.*

Figure 15.3
The Output window in the testing environment will display any Trace messages you have set up to help test the flow and execution of your ActionScript.

In the testing environment, the trace() *action in the script above will output the set of messages shown in **Figure 15.3**.*

Debugging

Normally, you cannot see either the data in variables or the values associated with movie properties while your movie is playing. However, this data plays a crucial role in determining how your interactive movie looks and works. Visual bugs are easy to spot, but bugs in ActionScripts can be trickier to track down and correct: Not only is the data usually invisible, it can also be constantly changing. This is where Flash's Debugger comes in: With it, you can view the real-time values of variables and properties while your movie is playing, as well as change values at will to see how such alterations will affect the flow of an individual script or your movie as a whole. By taking control of your movie's logic, you can often pinpoint problems in your scripts.

If you're creating simple presentations, however, chances are you'll never have to touch the Debugger—it's primarily a tool for more complex projects. If, however, you do need to use the Debugger, don't be intimidated: It's very intuitive.

Preparing Your Movie for Debugging

By default, SWF files cannot be debugged—the assumption being that you don't necessarily want people to know how your movie is assembled. To allow your movie to be debugged, you must do two things:

- Enable debugging in the .swf file

- View your movie through a special Debug Flash player (which is installed with the program)

You use the Publish Settings dialog box to enable debugging as well as to assign a password (if you want to control who can view your movie's internal workings).

To enable debugging and password protect your movie:

1. In the authoring environment, Choose File > Publish Settings.

2. Click the Flash tab.

3. Select Debugging Permitted.

4. To set a password that must be entered before debugging the movie, enter a password into the Password box (**Figure 15.4**).

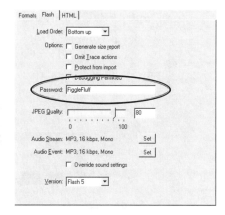

Figure 15.4

The debug settings on the Flash tab of the Publish Settings dialog box let you choose whether or not the exported .swf file is debug-enabled.

If you leave the password field blank, you can debug the movie without first providing a password.

To debug the movie from within Flash:

◆ In the authoring environment, choose Control > Debug Movie.

This opens your movie as a debug-enabled .swf file in the testing environment. The Debugger appears automatically, ready to debug.

To debug from a browser or projector:

1. Right-click (Windows) or Control-click (Macintosh) a movie as it plays in the Flash Player window.

2. Choose Debugger from the menu that appears.

Flash must be open to activate the Debugger in this manner. If the movie is password protected, you will need to enter the appropriate password before debugging can commence.

Using the Debugger

The Debugger's interface is made up of the following areas (**Figure 15.5**):

• **Display list.** The Display list shows the hierarchical structure of the movies in the movie window, including the main movie, movie clips, and any movies that have been loaded. This list is updated in real time as various clips and loaded movies are added and removed from the Player window. Selecting a movie from the Display list causes the Properties and Variable tabs to reflect that movie's current properties and variables.

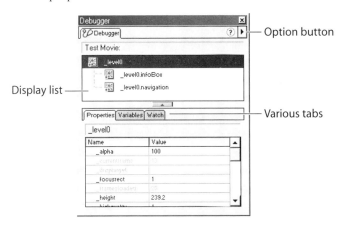

Figure 15.5
The Debugger interface.

- **Properties tab.** Clicking this tab displays the names and current values of the properties of the movie selected in the Display list. Some of the properties here are grayed out, meaning you can view but not change them. If you double-click a value that's *not* grayed out, you can change that value and immediately see the effect of those changes in your movie while it plays. Because your movie may contain scripts with conditional statements based on the current value of a specific property of a particular movie, you can make sure these conditional statements are working properly by changing a property value on this tab. Keep in mind, however, that you cannot use expressions when entering new property values from the Debugger: New values can be strings (use quotes), numbers, or a Boolean (true or false).

- **Variables tab.** Clicking this tab displays the names and current values of the variables included in the movie that's selected in the Display list. Double-clicking a value allows you to change it and view the immediate results of that change in your movie. Because variables provide the foundation of most Action-Scripts, using the Debugger to change individual values can help you track down the problems that might occur when your movie is fed a certain piece of data. Although you can see the values of Object and Array variables on this tab, you cannot change them, nor can you use expressions when entering new variable values from the Debugger. New values can be strings (use quotes), numbers, or a Boolean (true or false).

- **Watch list tab.** The Watch list tab contains a list of variables that you've designated to be "watched," meaning that their values are constantly monitored on this tab. You can add variables from different movies to this list so that you can manage all of them from a single tab. To add a variable to this tab, see below.

- **Options button.** Pressing this button displays a menu of commands pertaining to the Debugger. It also contains commands for controlling playback and view quality of the movie being debugged.

To add a variable to the Watch list do one of the following:

- Right-click (Windows) or Control-click (Macintosh) a variable on the Variables tab, and choose Watch from the menu that appears (**Figure 15.6**).

   or

- Select a variable on the Variables tab, and from the Options menu choose Add Watch.

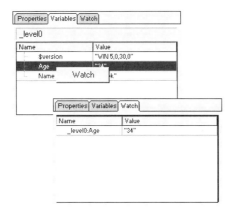

Figure 15.6
Right-clicking a variable on the Variable tab and choosing Watch from the menu that appears adds the selected variable to the Watch list tab so that it can be easily monitored.

To remove a variable from the Watch list do one of the following:

- Right-click (Windows) or Control-click (Macintosh) a variable on the Watch list tab, and choose Remove from the menu that appears.

  or

- Select a variable on the Watch list tab, and from the Options menu choose Remove Watch.

Testing Download Performance

Testing your movie's functionality is only half the battle. Because the majority of Flash movies are delivered over the Web, you need to plan, design, and create your movie with bandwidth limitations in mind.

To test how well your movie will stream over the Web:

1. With the testing environment open, from the Debug menu choose a bandwidth for testing the download performance, also known as the streaming performance, of your movie (**Figure 15.7**).

2. Make sure your movie has been rewound to its beginning; then from the View menu, choose Show Streaming.

Your movie will begin to play as it would over the Web at the connection speed you chose in the previous step.

```
Debug
  List Objects        ⌘L
  List Variables      ⌥⌘V

  14.4 (1.2 KB/s)
✓ 28.8 (2.3 KB/s)
  56K (4.7 KB/s)
  User Setting 4 (2.3 KB/s)
  User Setting 5 (2.3 KB/s)
  User Setting 6 (2.3 KB/s)
  Customize...
```

Figure 15.7
Choosing the bandwidth for testing from the Control menu.

Although this method can be helpful for locating specific problem areas in the streaming process, sometimes more information can make troubleshooting easier. This is where the Bandwidth Profiler can help.

Understanding the Bandwidth Profiler

The Bandwidth Profiler is one of your most important sources of information for testing download performance (**Figure 15.8**). At a glance it can provide you with vital statistics that help you pinpoint problem areas in streaming, including information about the size of individual frames and the amount of time that will elapse between when streaming begins and your movie can begin playing.

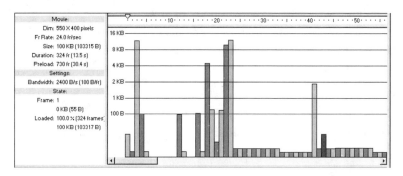

Figure 15.8 The Bandwidth Profiler.

Using the Bandwidth Profiler, you can simulate the download experience of someone using a 28.8-Kbps, 33.6-Kbps, or 56-Kbps modem. You can even use a custom setting to simulate the streaming process of an ISDN, DSL or LAN connection. By simulating a particular modem speed, you can detect pauses in streaming caused by content-heavy frames so that you can reedit them to achieve acceptable performance. Perhaps most important, the Profiler saves you the hassle of uploading your movie to the Web and testing it over an actual Web connection.

To display the Bandwidth Profiler:

◆ From the View menu choose Bandwidth Profiler.

To resize the Bandwidth Profiler:

◆ Place your cursor over the horizontal bar that separates the Bandwidth Profiler from your movie. When the cursor changes to a double-sided arrow, click and drag to resize.

To help you get the most from the Bandwidth Profiler, let's take a look at its parts.

The Information Bar section of the Bandwidth Profiler provides all sorts of vital information about the movie or scene you're testing (**Figure 15.9**), including the following:

- *Dim.* Your movie's dimension.

- *Fr Rate.* The speed, based on frames per second, at which your movie plays.

- *Size.* The file size of the entire movie (or if testing a scene, its contribution to your movie's overall file size). The number in parentheses represents the exact amount.

- *Duration.* The number of frames in the movie (or if testing a scene, the number of frames in the scene). The number in parentheses represents the duration of the movie or scene (in seconds as opposed to frames).

- *Preload.* The number of frames and seconds (based on the current frame rate) between the point at which the movie begins to download and the point at which it's ready to begin playing.

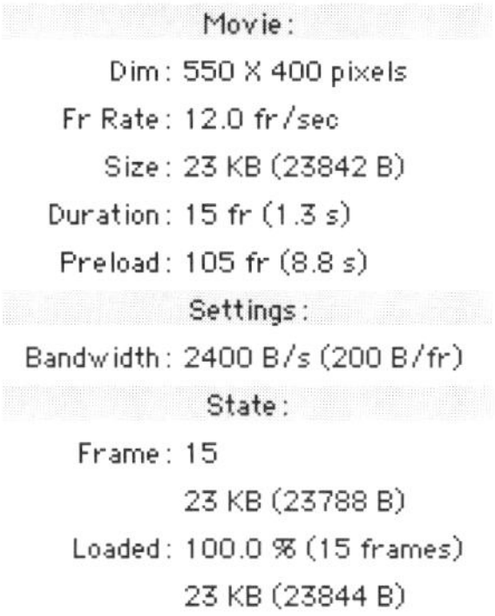

```
             Movie:
   Dim:  550 X 400 pixels
Fr Rate:  12.0 fr/sec
   Size:  23 KB (23842 B)
Duration: 15 fr (1.3 s)
Preload:  105 fr (8.8 s)
            Settings:
Bandwidth: 2400 B/s (200 B/fr)
              State:
  Frame: 15
         23 KB (23788 B)
 Loaded: 100.0 % (15 frames)
         23 KB (23844 B)
```

Figure 15.9
The Information Bar section of the Bandwidth Profiler.

- *Bandwidth.* The bandwidth speed used to simulate an actual download. This figure is only meaningful when it's used in conjunction with the Control > Show Streaming command.

- *Frame.* Displays two numbers: The top one indicates the frame number at which the timeline playhead is currently positioned in the testing environment, and the bottom one indicates the current frame's contribution to your movie's overall file size. The number in parentheses represents the exact file size. If you move the playhead on the timeline, the statistics for the individual frames will appear here. This information is useful for detecting particularly large frames.

   TIP *You can also navigate to different frames along the timeline by simply clicking the gray bars that represent the frames in the Streaming/Frame-by-Frame graph area.*

- *Loaded.* The information in this area only makes sense when used in conjunction with the Control > Show Streaming command. This area shows two numbers: The top one indicates the percentage (or number of frames) of the movie that have downloaded in the background at any given point during playback. The bottom number indicates the total amount, in file size, that has been streamed in the background. Watch these figures closely to evaluate your movie's streaming.

Figure 15.10
The Streaming bar.

- *Testing Timeline.* The testing timeline looks and functions like the one in the authoring environment, with one notable exception—the Streaming bar (**Figure 15.10**). When used in conjunction with the View > Show Streaming command, the Streaming bar shows how much of the of the movie has downloaded in the background, and the playhead reflects the current playback position. By observing how much the Streaming bar is ahead of actual playback, you can pinpoint areas or frames that may be causing glitches in streaming. Remember, however, that the testing environment merely *simulates* download and streaming; actual conditions may vary.

- *Streaming Graph/Frame-by-Frame Graph.* Depending on the option you choose (View > Streaming Graph or View >Frame by Frame Graph), you are presented with a graphical representation of your movie's frames. The gray blocks represent the different frames in your movie; the height of these blocks indicates frame size. Areas where no blocks appear indicate frames that do not add to your movie's overall file size (empty frames or frames with no movement or interactivity). Each graph has its own advantages:

  Streaming graph. This graph (**Figure 15.11**) is helpful for determining where pauses will occur when the movie is being downloaded over the Web. Each colored block represents a frame. A block above the red line indicates an area where a pause in the streaming process may occur.

  Frame-by-frame graph. This graph (**Figure 15.12**) gives you a graphical representation of the size of individual frames along the timeline.

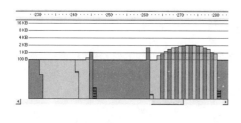

Figure 15.11
The Streaming graph provides a graphical representation of how you movie will stream. In this example, bars above the 100B line indicate areas where streaming could be interrupted during playback.

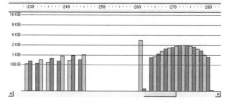

Figure 15.12
The Frame-by-Frame graph provides a graphical representation of the size of various frames in you movie. Areas where no bars appear represent frames in your movie where nothing changes.

Creating custom streaming speeds

With the Web, you must always contend with varying conditions when creating content—one of which is bandwidth. When delivering streamed content, bandwidth issues become even more important. Fortunately, Flash allows you to test your movie's Web delivery at different modem speeds, including the most common speeds of 14.4 Kbps, 28.8 Kbps, and 56 Kbps. It also allows you to test at less common speeds, or speeds you determine, so that you have complete control over the testing process.

To create custom modem speeds to test streaming:

1. From the Debug menu, choose Customize to bring up the Custom Modem Settings dialog box (**Figure 15.13**).

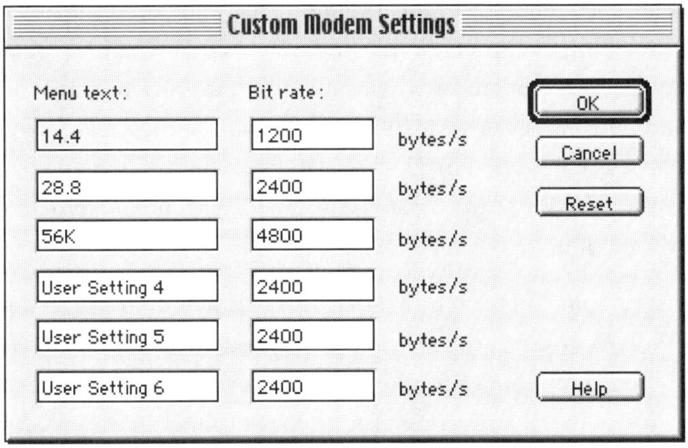

Figure 15.13
The Custom Modem Settings dialog box.

2. In one of the available Menu Text boxes, enter the text you want to appear on the Control menu as a modem speed choice.

3. In the accompanying Bit Rate box, enter the bit rate you want this choice to simulate.

4. Click OK.

The custom speed you created will now be available on the Debug menu.

Planning Your Project

Maximizing Streaming

Despite the benefits of streaming, many Flash developers fail to make use of it. You've probably encountered the infamous "Now Loading…" sequence that sometimes plays when a page with Flash content begins to load into your browser. Affectionately referred to as preloaders, *these sequences are actually animations that are displayed before your main movie has loaded. In other words, the animation is* preloaded. *(An interactive tutorial explaining how to create a preloader is included on the accompanying CD-ROM.) Such preloaders are not bad in and of themselves. However, there is a problem if you have to wait 5 to 10 minutes for the main content to begin. Where was streaming utilized? You might as well put a 1-MB video file on the page, and have your visitors download that.*

To reap the benefits of streaming, you need to consider a few things in the planning process.

Imagine the parking nightmare that would occur at the Indianapolis 500 if the parking lot gates didn't open until all 250,000 spectator cars were lined up and waiting. Talk about road rage! Fortunately, the gate opens early, so some cars are being parked as others are filing in. This continues at an even pace so that when the last car shows up, the previous 249,999 cars are already parked.

In much the same way, streaming delivers part of your movie over the Web while the rest continues to download in the background. If you plan it right, you can usually have your preload sequence play for just a short time before the main section of your movie begins.

The difference between the car analogy and streaming is that cars are generally all about the same size, whereas the frame sizes in your movie can vary wildly: While some may have 20 KB of content, others may have none, so it takes some frames longer to download than others. For your movie to stream as seamlessly as possible, you need to apply a few basic "buffering" techniques when planning your presentation's flow.

If you've downloaded all of your movie's 80 frames in the background but have only actually viewed the first 50 of them, this means that 30 frames are buffered, *or already downloaded but waiting to be played. The trick to maintaining a smooth streaming presentation is to keep this buffer amount as high as possible. In the above example, the buffer amount is 30 frames. Although this may seem like a lot, if your movie is playing at 15 frames per second, that buffer amount will be deplete in just 2 seconds. If zero frames are buffered, your presentation will come to a screeching halt at that point—and stay that way until the streaming process builds the buffer back up.*

Things that can quickly eat away at your buffer include sections of your movie that contain bitmaps, sounds, or a section of frames (in a row) that has a lot of content that changes or moves within a short period of time.

To maintain a reasonable buffer, you need to do the following:

- **Use offsetting.** Include reasonably long stretches where your animation changes very little. Make creative use of vector graphics or text as well as previously used symbols over a long stretch of frames as a prelude to a section that introduces a lot of new content.

- **Use bitmaps and sounds sparingly; use symbols generously.** Symbols, symbols, symbols: Use them whenever you can.

- **Use a preloader.** This is the most common way to maintain a decent buffer. Preloaders usually contain little content and are often simple. This means that a good deal of your movie can download in the background while the preloader is keeping your audience occupied. The buffer amount will usually increase substantially during this process. Remember: You don't need to buffer, or download, the whole movie before it plays. Use a preloader simply to get the streaming process going and working smoothly.

First impressions are important, and on the Web one of the things people hate most is waiting. If it takes too long for action to occur on a Flash-enhanced page, viewers may get frustrated and go elsewhere. However, all Web content takes some time to download and display. With Flash, you can make this process a lot less tedious by making it seem like "part of the show."

You should never create preloaders that display the Now Loading message for more than 5 percent to 10 percent of the movie's duration. But pay attention: Your preloader can actually stretch as long as necessary to create a decent-sized buffer—you simply need to make it look like an interesting part of the overall presentation.

You accomplish this by starting simple: Use creatively animated vector graphics rather than bitmaps. If you must use bitmaps, use them sparingly and make sure they're small. Text, on the other hand, can be used generously in the form of quotes or short bits of information that the viewer can read while the movie is downloading in the background. And finally, use short sounds, if any.

Publishing Your Work

As much as we may deny it, many of us are egomaniacs at heart. When you've worked hard to perfect your Flash movie, few things are as rewarding as having others view and praise it. Whatever the *stated* purpose of our Flash movies, we all share at least one goal: to get our movies into the hands of as many people as possible.

Whether you distribute your movie via a Web page or as a standalone application, video, or still image, Flash offers ways to automate the process. Let's take a look at the delivery modes and the final production process, so that you can finally begin to experience the joy of a job well done.

Delivery Methods

With Flash's Publish feature, you simply choose the formats in which you want your authoring file delivered, adjust the settings for that format, click Publish, and—voilà—Flash converts your authoring file to the selected formats and creates the files based on the settings you selected for that format.

Most of what we're going to be talking about next involves the Publish Settings dialog box.

To open the Publish Settings dialog box:

◆ Choose File > Publish Settings.

Publish Settings

With Flash, you control the way your movie is delivered: You can choose a single method of delivery (such as on an HTML page), or multiple delivery modes (for example, on an HTML page, as a QuickTime movie, and as a Projector). In the latter case, the Publish feature creates all of the files simultaneously.

Let's take a look at the options available through the Publish Settings dialog box.

Formats

Choosing the format for movie delivery is the first task in the publishing process. The Formats tab (**Figure 16.1**) provides you with several selections:

- *Type.* Checking a format (other than Projector) causes a new tab to appear in the Publish Settings dialog box. By clicking that tab, you make all of that format's settings available for adjusting.

- *Filename.* You can name any file you create with the Publish feature. If you check "Use default names," the newly created files will have the same name as the authoring file (but with the appropriate file extensions). If you leave this option unchecked, you can specify file names.

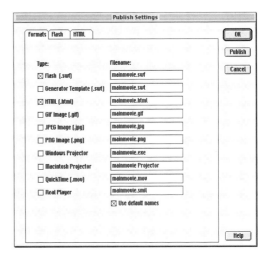

Figure 16.1
The Formats tab.

Depending on the template you choose on the HTML tab (see "HTML" later in this section), you may actually need to select more than one format from the Formats tab. For example, if you choose an HTML template that detects whether Flash Player is installed on the viewer's computer, your actual Flash movie will be displayed if the player is installed, but a bitmap image (GIF, JPEG, or PNG) will be displayed if the player is not installed. This type of functionality requires three elements: an HTML page, a Flash movie file, and an image file. So, on the Formats tab, you must select Flash, HTML, and GIF, JPEG, or PNG (the choice of image is up to you). This will allow the Publish feature to create all of the files (.swf, .html, .gif, .jpeg, or .png) needed for the player detection template to work (**Figure 16.2**).

To use any of the files created by the Publish feature, you must place them in the same directory as your authoring file and upload them to your server. When uploading a set of files that are intended to work together, make sure they all reside in the same folder on your server and that they retain their relative positions after uploading. For example, if your authoring file resides on your hard drive in a folder named Awesome Flash Project, all new files created by the Publish feature will initially reside there as well.

Figure 16.2

If viewers have Flash Player, they'll see the Flash movie on an HTML page (left). If Flash Player isn't installed, a .gif file will be displayed instead (right).

Flash (.swf)

Creating a .swf file is the most common way of delivering a Flash movie. It is also the first step toward getting your movie on the Web (see "HTML" below). When you place your movie on an HTML page in this format, users can view it through a Web browser such as Microsoft's Internet Explorer or Netscape's Navigator or Communicator—as long as the browser has the Flash Player installed. You can also use Flash movies in this format with Macromedia Director and Authorware or any program that can host the Flash Player ActiveX control.

When you export your project to a Flash movie, all interactivity and functionality remain intact.

The following settings are available when exporting in this format (**Figure 16.3**):

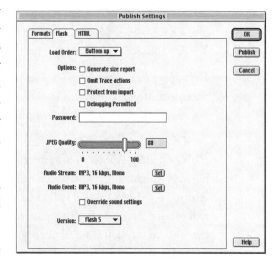

Figure 16.3

The Flash format tab.

- **Load Order.** When your movie is being downloaded over the Web, the first frame is visually "constructed" a layer at a time as information arrives in the viewer's browser. This option allows you to set the order in which layers are loaded (**Figure 16.4**).

  Bottom Up. Causes the bottom layer to load first, with all subsequent layers following.

  Top Down. Causes the top layer to load first, with all subsequent layers following.

- **Generate Size Report.** Creates a text file (with a .txt extension) that contains information about individual frame sizes in your movie. The text file also contains a list of imported files and fonts. This text file has the same name as the exported movie, and it resides in the same directory.

- **Omit Trace Actions.** Removes Trace actions from the exported Flash movie, thus preventing others from viewing your code.

- **Protect from Import.** Prevents your final exported movie from being reimported into Flash—i.e., it prevents anyone else from claiming your work as their own. This option does not affect the authoring file, just the resulting Flash movie.

- **Debugging Permitted.** Lets you choose whether the exported movie can be debugged. If you check this box, the Password field becomes active so that you can specify a password for debugging purposes. See Chapter 15, "Testing" for more information.

- **JPEG Quality.** Allows you to set a default for the amount of compression of all bitmaps in your movie that have not been optimized individually (see Chapter 6, "Bitmaps"). A setting of 0 will export the bitmaps at their lowest quality (which will produce a movie with a smaller file size), whereas a setting of 100 will export them at their highest quality (and consequently produce a movie with a larger file size).

- **Audio Stream.** Lets you set a default for the amount of compression of all streamed sounds in your movie that have not been optimized individually (see Chapter 5, "Sound"). The amount shown represents the settings that will be used. To change the settings, click the accompanying Set button. The available settings are the same as those in the Sound Properties dialog box.

Top down

Bottom up

Figure 16.4
The Load Order setting determines how layers are loaded on the first frame as the movie is downloaded.

- *Audio Event.* Allows you to set a default for the amount of compression of all event sounds in your movie that have not been optimized individually (see "Optimizing Sounds" in Chapter 5). The amount shown represents the settings that will be used. To change the settings, click the accompanying Set button. The available settings are the same as those in the Sound Properties dialog box.

- *Override Sound Settings.* If you optimized sounds individually in the Sound Properties dialog box, this option overrides any of those settings with the settings you define in the Audio Stream and Audio Event areas of this dialog box. You might want to do this if you wished to produce a version of your movie with higher-quality sound for distribution on CD.

- *Version.* Allows you to export your movie so that a previous version of Flash Player can view it. Version-specific features will not work when exporting to an earlier version.

Generator (.swt)

When you install Flash 5, you have the option of installing the authoring extensions for Macromedia Generator. Generator is a server-based program that greatly extends the capabilities of Flash by dynamically generating up-to-the-minute content, including text, graphics, and sounds, based on an external data source such as a text file or database. This type of functionality provides for a unique user experience, since content in the movie can be generated based on personal information or other data-driven factors.

While Generator itself is an add-on, the authoring extensions that are a part of Flash 5 give you access to Generator objects within the Flash authoring environment. You can use these objects in your project to indicate places where you want content to be dynamically generated. Generator can dynamically generate SWFs, GIFs, JPGs, PNGs, QuickTime movies, and Flash projectors. When you export your movie, you export it as a Generator template (as this tab allows you to do) and place it on a server that has Generator installed. The Generator objects in the template are then replaced by actual media prior to the movie being sent to the user.

A practical discussion of the options on the Generator tab within Flash is beyond the scope of this book. For more information, go to http://www.macromedia.com/software/generator/

Macromedia recently made the Generator server application more affordable, but you may still find that it is a product well beyond your needs, especially for sites that do not require constant updating.

HTML (.html or .htm)

The HTML format tab (**Figure 16.5**) allows you to choose settings that will automatically generate an HTML page containing your Flash movie. You simply upload the generated HTML page and exported movie file to your server to make it available on the Web.

Publishing to HTML is done in conjunction with publishing your movie to the SWF format (see "Flash" above) because the exported Flash movie is placed on the generated HTML page at the same time.

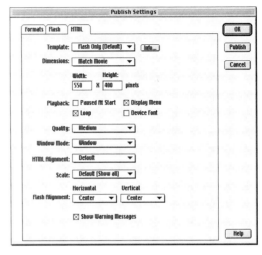

Figure 16.5
The HTML format tab.

The HTML code generated by this feature includes the `<object>` and `<embed>` tags, which enable your movie to be viewed in Microsoft's Internet Explorer and Netscape's Navigator and Communicator Web browsers. It also generates the code needed to set your movie's parameters within the HTML page, including alignment, size, automatic play, and more (for additional information, see "Flash and HTML" later in this chapter).

The following settings are available when exporting in this format:

- *Template.* Flash provides templates for generating the HTML pages produced from this dialog box. Different templates offer specific functionality. For example, one template simply places your Flash movie on the generated HTML page so that users can view it through a Web browser only if the Player is already installed. Another template allows you to do the same thing, except that it will first detect whether the Flash Player has been installed; if it hasn't, the template will automatically install it. Other templates employ JavaScript for such functions as player detection and cookie creation and detection. For more on templates, see "Understanding Templates" later in this chapter.

    Ad 3 Banner. Creates an HTML page that uses JavaScript to determine whether version 3 of Flash Player has been installed on the user's machine. If it has, your movie will show up on the Web page. If it hasn't, Internet Explorer users will get the newest player automatically downloaded and installed; Netscape users will see an image map instead (see "Player Issues" later in this chapter). Any keyframe with buttons that have Get URL actions attached can be used as a basis for the generated image map. To specify which keyframe you wish to use for the image map, label it "#Map"; if you fail to do this, Flash will automatically create the image map using buttons on the last frame of the movie. You must select Flash 3 as the version number to export to (on the Flash tab), and GIF, JPEG, or PNG on the Format tab for the necessary image map to be generated (see "Flash Movie" later in this chapter).

Ad 4 Banner. Generates an HTML page that uses JavaScript to detect whether version 4 of Flash Player has been installed on the user's machine. Besides needing to select Flash 4 as the version number to export to (on the Flash tab), this template performs the same actions as the Ad 3 Banner option.

Ad 5 Banner. Generates an HTML page that uses JavaScript to detect whether version 5 of Flash Player has been installed on the user's machine. Besides needing to select Flash 5 as the version number to export to (on the Flash tab), this template performs the same actions as the Ad 3 Banner option.

Ad All Banner. Generates an HTML page that uses JavaScript to detect whether any version of Flash Player has been installed on the user's machine. Then it performs the same actions as the Ad 3 Banner option.

Flash Only (Default). Generates an HTML page with the Flash movie embedded. This template does not include Flash Player detection.

Flash with FS Command. Builds an HTML page with your Flash movie embedded. This option also includes the necessary code for enabling FS Commands to work on the page (see the "Actions" section in Chapter 11, "Using Basic Actions for Building Interactivity"). This template does not include Flash Player detection.

Image Map. Creates an HTML page with an image map embedded. Any keyframe with buttons that have Get URL actions attached can be used as a basis for the generated image map. To specify which keyframe to use for the image map, label it "#Map." If you fail to do this, Flash will automatically create the image map using buttons on the last frame of the movie. This option generates only an embedded image map, not an embedded Flash movie. The image generated can be a GIF, JPEG, or PNG, depending on the format you chose on the Format tab of the Publish Settings dialog box.

Java Player. Generates an HTML page that displays a Java-based version of your movie. All the necessary Java classes are created and should be placed in the same directory as the accompanying HTML page. Flash 2 must be selected as the version to export to (see "Flash Movie" in this section).

QuickTime. Makes an HTML page that displays a QuickTime 4 version of your movie. Flash 3 must be selected as the version number to export to on the Flash dialog box, and QuickTime must be selected on the Format tab for the necessary QuickTime movie to be generated.

User Choice. Creates an HTML page with links that let users decide how they want to view your movie—as a Flash movie or as an image—and then creates a cookie based on that choice. This cookie serves as the basis for the way each user will view other Flash-enhanced pages (that is, as movies or images). The Flash movie generated for this option is based on your Flash tab settings (see "Flash Movie" in this section). The image generated can be GIF, JPEG, or PNG, depending on the format you chose on the Format tab of the Publish Settings dialog box.

TIP *Selecting a template and then clicking the Info button opens a small dialog box that displays information about the currently selected template, including name, function, and the formats that must be selected and adjusted for it to output properly (**Figure 16.6**). To scroll through the dialog box, press the up- or down-arrow keys on your keyboard.*

- *Dimensions.* Lets you set the horizontal and vertical dimensions of the window in which your movie appears within the HTML page. You can make your movie and movie window proportionately different sizes and shapes. Depending on the dimensions you specify here, your movie may not fit precisely edge to edge within the movie window (see "Scale" setting in this section). This setting does not affect the authoring file, just the exported movie as it will appear within the movie window on the HTML page.

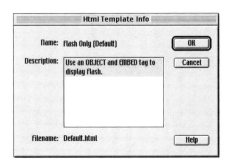

Figure 16.6
The Info box provides information about the selected template.

- *Match Movie.* Sets the dimensions of your movie window on the generated HTML page to match the dimensions specified in the Movie Properties dialog box.

- *Pixels.* Sets the dimensions of your movie window on the generated HTML page to a specific pixel amount.

- *Percent.* Sets the dimensions of your movie window on the generated HTML page to a percentage amount relative to the browser window through which it is viewed.

TIP *A common practice is to enter percentage values of 100 in each of these boxes so that your Flash movie will appear full screen in the browser.*

- *Playback.* Provides options that determine what happens at the start and during playback of your movie on the generated HTML page.

  Paused at Start. Your movie will not play back on the HTML page until the user clicks a button within your movie or selects the Play option from the Flash Player shortcut menu (see "Display Menu" in this section).

  Loop. Your movie will automatically begin to play again after the last frame.

  Display Menu. The Display menu, which provides options that let the user stop, play, and rewind your movie, will appear in the browser window when a user right-clicks (Windows) or Control-clicks (Macintosh) your movie. If you uncheck this option, you eliminate all of these options, and the menu will only display information about Flash Player.

  Device Font (Windows only). If users' computers do not have the necessary fonts when the movie is played, antialiased system fonts will be substituted.

- *Quality.* Because users who view your movie have computers with varying processor speeds, this option lets you determine how processor limitations will affect your movie's playback in terms of speed and visual quality.

  Low. This sacrifices visual quality for playback speed. Your movie will never be antialiased.

  Autolow. Antialiasing is turned off initially, but if the user's processor is fast enough to handle it, it will be turned on to improve visual quality.

  Autohigh. Antialiasing is turned on initially but if the frame-per-second rate drops below the amount set in the Movie Properties dialog box, antialiasing will be turned off to improve playback speed.

  Medium. Antialiasing on bitmaps is turned off and other elements are slightly antialiased.

  High. Skips frames during playback to maintain visual quality on computers with slower processors. Antialiasing is always on when this option has been selected. If your movie is animated, bitmaps will not be smoothed; if it is not animated, they will be.

  Best. Bitmaps are always smoothed; antialiasing is always on; and frames are never skipped due to processor limitations.

- **Window Mode (Windows only).** Allows you to take advantage of capabilities only available in a Windows version of Internet Explorer with the Flash Player ActiveX control installed.

  Window. Providing the best playback performance, this option plays your movie within its own rectangular area on the HTML page. For more information on this and the next two options, see "Flash and HTML" later in this chapter.

  Opaque. Allows you to move elements on the HTML page behind the rectangular area of the movie without having them show through. Use this option in conjunction with dynamic HTML layers.

  Transparent Windowless. Causes the background color of your Flash movie (as set in the Movie Properties dialog box) to become transparent so that the background of the HTML page on which your movie is embedded will show through. This setting, though interesting, provides the slowest playback performance, so use it sparingly.

- **HTML Alignment.** Determines the alignment of your movie in relation to other elements on the page. It will not have any visible effect unless you re-edit the generated HTML page and place other elements, such as text or graphics, alongside your movie. The available options are Default, Left, Right, Top, and Bottom.

- **Scale.** If you've selected width and height settings for the actual movie window in the Dimensions setting that differ from those in the Movie Properties dialog box, your movie elements may not fit perfectly within the dimensions of your movie window. This setting determines how the movie will look within the boundaries of the movie window you have specified (**Figure 16.7**).

  Default (Show All). Makes your entire movie visible within the movie window. All elements are scaled proportionately to fill the movie window. Borders may appear between movie elements and the movie window if the window's proportions differ from the movie's original size.

  No Border. Scales your movie proportionately so that it fills the movie window and no borders appear. As a result, elements of your movie may be cropped and not visible within the movie window.

  Exact Fit. Disproportionately scales your movie to fit the dimensions of the movie window. Thus, your movie may appear squashed or bloated, depending on how the movie window's proportions differ from the movie itself.

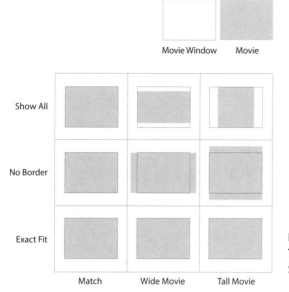

Movie Window   Movie

Show All

No Border

Exact Fit

Match   Wide Movie   Tall Movie

Figure 16.7
The effect of different
Scale settings.

- *Flash Alignment.* These options—which are used in conjunction with the Show All and No Border settings described above—determine your movie's alignment within the movie window (**Figure 16.8**). With Show All, borders may appear between the movie and the movie window—this option affects which borders appear. For example, if you use vertical/horizontal alignment settings of center/center, the movie will be placed in the center of the movie window, and borders will appear on all four sides of the movie window. If, however, you use vertical/horizontal alignment settings of top/left, the movie will be placed in the top left portion of the movie window, and borders will only exist on the bottom and right sides of the movie window. Remember, these borders exist only if the dimensions of the movie window differ from those of the actual movie.

  With the No Border setting, your movie is scaled proportionately to fill the movie window, becoming larger than the movie window and possibly forcing parts of your movie to be hidden. The Flash alignment settings let you determine which areas are visible. For example, if you use vertical/horizontal alignment settings of bottom/right, the movie will be placed in the bottom right corner of the movie window, and sections of the top left portion of the movie will not be visible. If, however, you choose vertical/horizontal alignment settings of top/center, the movie will be placed in the top center portion of the movie window, and sections of the bottom, left, and right portions of the movie will not be visible.

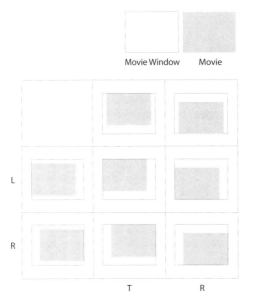

Movie Window   Movie

L

R

T   R

Figure 16.8
The effect different Alignment settings will have if the movie doesn't completely fill the movie window.

- *Show Warning Messages.* When using templates, a warning message displays indicating the template in use requires you to select additional publish formats or to adjust publish settings.

GIF (.gif)

GIFs are the most popular form of graphics used on the Web today—primarily because they can be compressed and animated (unlike JPEGs and PNGs). There are basically two scenarios in which you would create a GIF from the Flash authoring file: If you simply wanted to use Flash as a GIF creation tool for regular HTML pages, or if you wanted to use a GIF file as a replacement for a Flash movie on a Web page because the user didn't have the proper Flash Player. Either way, Flash makes it simple. The following options are available when creating GIFs (**Figure 16.9**).

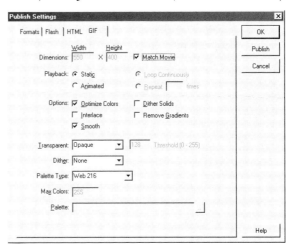

Figure 16.9
The GIF format tab.

- **Dimensions.** Lets you set the vertical and horizontal dimensions (in pixels) of the GIF that is created. "Match movie" creates a GIF that has the same dimensions as those of the movie in the Movie Properties box. If you check this option, the Width and Height boxes will have no effect (and thus will be grayed out). If you leave this option unchecked, you can enter a new size for the exported GIF. You only need to enter either the width or the height because Flash will always export an image that maintains the aspect ratio of the original.

- **Playback.** Lets you choose whether the exported GIF will be static or animated and, if animated, how it will play.

  Static. Creates a nonanimated GIF based on a single keyframe in your movie. You need to label a keyframe "#Static" to make it the one that is exported. If you don't do this, Flash will use the first frame of the movie.

  Animated. Creates an animated GIF based on your movie or a section of it. You can specify the range of frames exported by labeling the first and last keyframe of the range "#First" and "#Last," respectively. If you do not do this, the entire movie will be exported, which could result in a huge file. Interactivity and sound are lost when exporting to GIF.

  Loop Continuously. Your animated GIF will automatically, and continuously, replay after it has played its last frame.

  Repeat Times. If you check this, your animated GIF will automatically begin to play again—as many times as you specify—when it has reached the last frame during playback.

The following options determine the visual appearance of your GIF:

- **Optimize Colors.** Can reduce the file size of the resulting GIF by removing any unused colors from its color table. When using an Adaptive palette, this option has no effect.

- **Dither Solids.** Dithers solid colors, gradients, and images. For more information, see "Dither," below.

- **Interlace.** Causes the GIF to be displayed in stages—as if it's coming into focus—when it is downloaded over a slow connection.

- **Remove Gradients.** Gradients can increase the size of the exported GIF and are usually poor quality. Selecting this will convert all gradients to solid colors based on the first color of the gradient. This means that if an area is filled with a gradient going from white to blue, selecting this option will convert that filled area to white only.

- *Smoothing.* Antialiases the exported GIF. This creates a slightly larger file, but elements of the image, especially text, appear smooth instead of jaggy. If your exported GIF has a transparent background, turning this off can eliminate the halo effect that sometimes appears around the edges of the image when it is placed on a multicolored background.

- *Transparency.* When a transparent GIF is placed on a Web page, that page's background can be seen through any area of the GIF that is transparent. The following transparency settings determine which parts of the exported GIF are transparent.

    Opaque. Makes the entire rectangular area of the image opaque. The exported image will appear on the HTML page the way it does in Flash.

    Transparent. Makes the background of the exported GIF transparent. This means that any portion of the movie's background that can be seen in Flash will now become transparent.

    Alpha. This deals with colors in your movie to which an alpha value has been applied (that is, semitransparent colors). In the Threshold box enter a number between 0 and 255 (which corresponds to the 0–100% alpha slider in the Color window; thus, a value of 128 for this setting is equal to 50 percent in the color window). Any colors with alpha values higher than the amount you entered will be exported as opaque; any colors with alpha settings lower than the amount you entered will be exported as transparent.

- *Dither.* A GIF file, by nature, has a limited color palette (256 colors, max). If the GIF you are exporting uses colors not available on the current palette, dithering can help approximate those colors by mixing available colors. This process tricks the eye into believing that more colors are shown than actually are. Before you use dithering, though, be aware of two things: It can increase the file size of your exported image, and it can, in some cases, look bad on low-resolution monitors.

    If you do not use dithering, any colors that are not available on the current palette will be replaced with the closest available color. If you go with this option, be sure to check the exported file because you can get unexpected results.

    None. Exports your image without using dithering.

    Ordered. Dithers the exported image at a reasonable quality with minimal effect on file size.

    Diffused. Creates the highest-quality dithering, and also the biggest increase in file size.

- *Palette Type.* Because GIF files have limited color palettes, you must choose the right palette if you want the color of your exported file to be as accurate as possible. The following options provide a great deal of control in palette selection.

  Web 216. If you've used mostly Web-safe colors in your project, this will provide the best results. It produces a GIF file based on the 216-color palette used by Microsoft and Netscape browsers.

  Adaptive. Creates a custom palette based on the colors in the image—the result is more accurate colors (than those produced by the Web 216 palette) but a bigger image file. By decreasing the maximum number of colors available (see the Max Colors option below), you can minimize file size.

  Web Snap Adaptive. Combines the best parts of the two previous palette options by creating a custom palette based on the image's colors but substituting Web-safe colors (for custom ones) whenever possible.

  Custom. If you created a custom palette (with an .act file extension) in another application (such as Macromedia's Fireworks), you can use this palette when exporting your image to GIF. Choosing this option activates the Palette option beneath it. Press the button with the ellipsis (…) to locate the palette you wish to use.

  Max Colors. When using an Adaptive or Web Snap Adaptive palette option, a custom palette is created when the image is exported. This allows you to set the maximum number of colors that will be created. Fewer colors result in a smaller image file but less accurate colors. More colors result in truer colors but a larger file.

JPEG (.jpeg or .jpg)

GIFs are great for creating simple, small images with few colors. However, if you want to export an image that renders gradients well and is not hindered by a limited color palette, JPEGs are the way to go. The JPEG format tab (**Figure 16.10**) gives you the ability to export photographic-quality images that are compressed to maintain a relatively small file size. The main difference between JPEGs and GIFs is that JPEGs can't be exported as animated graphics. In addition, JPEGs aren't very good at exporting images with few colors.

JPEG images can only be exported as *static,* or nonanimated, images. Label a keyframe "#Static" to make it the keyframe that is exported; if you fail to do this, Flash will use the first frame of the movie.

- **Dimensions.** Lets you set the vertical and horizontal dimensions, in pixels, of the JPEG that's created. "Match movie" will create a JPEG with the same dimensions as those set for the movie in the Movie Properties dialog box. If you check this option, the Width and Height boxes will have no effect (and thus will be grayed out). If you leave this option unchecked, you can enter a new size for the exported JPEG.

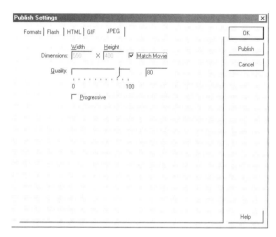

Figure 16.10
The JPEG format tab.

- **Quality.** Allows you to set the amount of compression that will be applied to the exported JPEG. A setting of 0 will export the JPEG at its lowest visual quality, which will produce an image with the smallest file size; a setting of 100 will export the JPEG at its highest visual quality, which will result in an image with the largest file size.

- **Progressive.** Similar to the Interlace option for GIFs, this will cause the JPEG to be displayed in stages—as if it's coming into focus—when it is downloaded over a slow connection.

PNG (.png)

The PNG format tab (**Figure 16.11**) allows you to export an image to a relatively new standard in graphics that offers numerous advantages over GIFs— especially when it comes to compression, color capabilities, and transparency. (For more information, see "Using PNGs" in Chapter 6.) Keep in mind, however, that PNGs are not yet widely used or supported, so use discretion when exporting to this format.

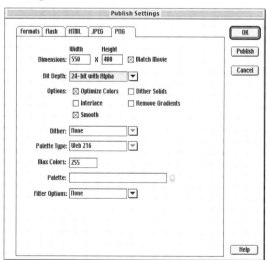

Figure 16.11
The PNG format tab.

Like JPEGs, PNG images can only be exported as static images. Label the keyframe that you wish to import as "#Static" so that Flash will use it rather than the first frame of the movie.

- **Dimensions.** Lets you set the vertical and horizontal dimensions, in pixels, of the PNG that is created. "Match movie" will create a PNG with the same dimensions as those set for your movie in the Movie Properties box. If you check this option, the Width and Height boxes will be grayed out. If you leave it unchecked, you can enter a new size for the exported PNG.

- **Bit Depth.** Bit depth determines the number of colors that will be used in the exported image. The lower the bit depth, the smaller the resulting file.

  8-bit. Produces an image file with a maximum palette of 256 colors. Dithering options are only available when this setting is selected (otherwise, they are grayed out).

  24-bit. Produces an image file with a maximum palette of more than 65,000 colors. Highly accurate color is achieved at a cost of increased image file size.

  24-bit with Alpha. Produces an image file with a maximum palette of more than 65,000 colors as well as 256 values of transparency. Highly accurate color and transparency effects are achieved at a cost of increased file size.

You can use the following options to adjust your PNG's appearance.

- **Optimize Colors.** This option can reduce the file size of the resulting PNG by removing any unused colors from the PNG's color table. When using an Adaptive palette, this option has no effect.

- **Dither Solids.** Dithers solid colors, gradients, and images.

- **Interlace.** Lets the PNG display in stages when it is downloaded over a slow connection.

- **Remove Gradients.** Gradients can increase the size of the exported PNG and are usually poor quality. Selecting this option will convert all gradients to solid colors based on the first color of the gradient.

- **Smoothing.** Antialiases the exported PNG. This creates a slightly larger file, but elements of the image appear smooth rather than jaggy.

- **Dither.** If you choose a bit depth of 8 bits (see "Bit Depth" earlier in this section), the available palette can contain a maximum of 256 colors. If the PNG you're exporting uses colors not available on the current palette, dithering can mix available colors to approximate those that aren't available. The following options are available for dithering:

None. Will export your image without dithering.

Ordered. Will dither the exported image at a reasonable quality but have little impact on its file size.

Diffused. Will produce the highest-quality dithering but also the greatest impact on file size.

- *Palette Type.* When exporting your image using a bit depth of 8 bits, your color palette is limited; thus, it's important that you choose the right palette so that the colors in your exported file are as accurate as possible. The following options provide a great deal of control in color palette selection.

Web 216. If you've used mostly Web-safe colors in your project, this option will provide the best results. It produces a PNG file based on the 216-color palette used by Internet Explorer and Netscape browsers.

Adaptive. Creates a custom palette based on the colors in the image—the result is more accurate colors (than those produced by the Web 216 palette) but a larger image file. By decreasing the maximum number of colors available (see the Max Colors option below), you can minimize file size.

Web Snap Adaptive. Uses the best parts of the two previous palette options by creating a custom palette based on the image's colors but substituting Web-safe colors (for custom ones) whenever possible.

Custom. If you created a custom palette (with an .act file extension) in another application, you could use it when exporting your image to PNG. Press the button with the ellipse (…) to locate the palette you wish to use.

Max Colors. When using an Adaptive or Web Snap Adaptive palette option, a custom palette is created when the image is exported. This option allows you to set the maximum number of colors that will be created. Fewer colors result in a smaller image file but less accurate colors. More colors result in truer colors but also a larger file size.

- *Filter Options.* During compression, a PNG image goes through a filtering process that enables it to be compressed in the most efficient manner. Choose a filter that provides the best results in terms of both image quality and file size—a process that may require some experimentation. The available options include None, Sub, Up, Average, and Paeth.

QuickTime (.mov)

You can now combine the interactive features of Flash with the multimedia and video features of QuickTime to produce a single QuickTime 4 movie that anyone with the QuickTime 4 plug-in can view.

> **TIP** *You can only combine Flash and QuickTime content when exporting to the QuickTime 4 format, not when creating Flash movies. The Flash 5 Player cannot read or play back QuickTime movies or content. Also, be aware that only Flash 3–specific functionality is available when using Flash in a QuickTime movie. When exporting to QuickTime, make sure you have selected Version 3 from the Version drop-down on the Flash tab of the Publish Settings dialog box. For more information, see "Using QuickTime Video" in Chapter 10.*

Any Flash content you export to a QuickTime video is known as the Flash track. No matter how many layers are in your actual Flash project, they are all considered part of a single Flash track.

The following options are available in the QuickTime format tab (**Figure 16.12**):

- *Dimensions.* Lets you set the vertical and horizontal dimensions, in pixels, of the PNG that is created. "Match movie" will create a QuickTime movie with the same dimensions as those set for your movie in the Movie Properties box. If you check it, the Width and Height boxes will be grayed out. If you leave it unchecked, you can enter a size for the QuickTime movie.

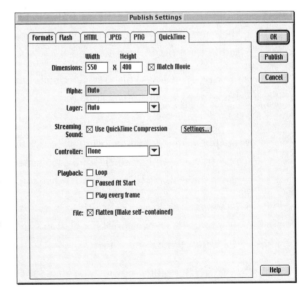

Figure 16.12
The QuickTime format tab.

- *Alpha.* Determines the transparency mode of the Flash track in the QuickTime movie. Alpha settings used within the Flash movie are not affected by this setting.

  Auto. With this option, if the Flash track appears over other tracks, it becomes transparent; if it's the bottom or only track in the movie, it becomes opaque.

  Alpha Transparent. Makes the Flash track transparent (so that you can see content beneath).

  Copy. Makes the Flash track opaque, obscuring any content beneath it.

- *Layer.* Lets you set where the Flash track will appear in relation to other tracks in the QuickTime movie.

  Top. Places the Flash track above other tracks in the QuickTime movie.

  Bottom. Places the Flash track below other tracks in the QuickTime movie.

  Auto. Detects whether Flash content has been placed in front of imported QuickTime content and, if so, places the Flash track on top. (If not, the Flash track is placed on bottom.)

- *Streaming Sound.* Converts streaming audio in the Flash move to a QuickTime sound track using the settings available through the Settings button. (Because these are QuickTime settings, you'll need to refer to the QuickTime documentation for more information.)

- *Controller.* Allows you to select which QuickTime controller will be used to play back the exported QuickTime movie; your choices are None, Standard, or QuickTime VR.

- *Looping.* Allows you to specify whether the exported QuickTime movie will play from beginning to end and then start over. Deselecting this option will cause the exported QuickTime movie to play once and stop.

- *Pause at Start.* If you check this option, your QuickTime movie will not begin to play until the viewer presses a button within your movie or the Play button on the QuickTime control panel.

- *Play Every Frame.* Slower machines sometimes skip frames of your movie to maintain the timeline's flow. By selecting this option, you cause every frame to be seen, regardless of the effect on playback. This option also disables any sound in the exported QuickTime movie.

- *Flatten (Make Self-Contained).* If you select this option, the Flash content and imported video content will be combined in a self-contained QuickTime 4 movie. Otherwise, the QuickTime movie will reference any imported video files externally.

Projectors (.exe or .hqx)

Projectors are stand-alone files (and applications in and of themselves) that can play on just about any computer, regardless of whether the Flash Player is installed. The projector file contains not only your Flash movie but everything needed to play it. This means you can create a Flash movie, turn it into a projector, and then distribute it widely. To view the movie, all users need to do is start it (like any other application), and the projector will open in its own application window and begin to play (**Figure 16.13**).

A projector can open URLs, load and unload movies, update variables, and more. You don't need much marketing savvy to understand the potential they provide—full multimedia business presentations, Web sites on-a-disk, "Flashmercials." The list goes on and on.

No settings are available when creating projectors using the Publish Settings dialog box; however, this doesn't mean you can't

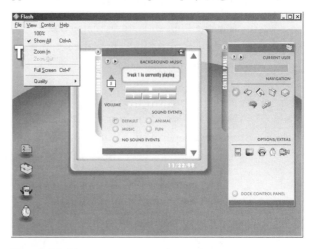

Figure 16.13
A Projector is a stand-alone application with its own menu bar—in other words, a self-contained version of your movie.

configure projectors. Using button and frame actions such as Toggle High Quality and (especially) FS Commands, you can tailor your projector to your needs. For more information, see "FS Command" in Chapter 11.

You create both Windows and Macintosh projectors from either operating system. However, be aware that when creating a Macintosh projector from a Windows machine, you will need to convert the Mac projector file you create from its initial exported form to an application file that a Macintosh can read. This is easy to do on a Macintosh using a file-encoding program (Macromedia recommends BinHex). Once converted, your projector/movie is ready for distribution.

Previewing Your Settings

If you want to create the best Flash presentation possible, testing is a necessary evil. Thank goodness, then, for the Publish Preview command, which allows you to preview what you have exported, or created, based on the settings you selected in the Publish Settings dialog box.

The Publish Preview command creates and places temporary preview files into the same directory as your Flash authoring file. However, it does not automatically delete them when you've finished previewing; they remain on your drive until you manually remove them.

To preview your settings using Publish Preview:

1. From the Publish Settings dialog box, select the formats and adjust the settings according to your needs.

2. Click OK.

3. From the File menu choose Publish Preview to open a submenu with the following options (**Figure 16.14**):

   - *Default ().* This varies depending on the settings you select in the Publish Settings dialog box.

   - *Flash.* Opens your movie in Flash's own testing environment (see Chapter 15, "Testing").

Figure 16.14 The Publish Preview menu provides options for previewing the settings you selected in the Publish Settings dialog box.

   - *HTML.* Opens your default browser with a preview of the Web page that will be created when you publish your project. It contains all the HTML required to make the movie look and work as it should, based on the settings and template you chose.

   - *GIF.* Opens your default browser with a preview of the GIF image that will be generated based on the settings you selected in the Publish Settings dialog box.

   - *JPEG.* Opens your default browser with a preview of the JPEG image that will be generated based on the settings you made in the Publish Settings dialog box.

- **PNG.** Opens your default browser with a preview of the PNG image that will be generated based on the settings you made in the Publish Settings dialog box.

- **Projector.** Opens your Flash movie in its own Projector window.

- **QuickTime.** Opens a QuickTime version of your movie inside the QuickTime player.

TIP *For a QuickTime preview to work, you must have QuickTime 4 or greater installed on your machine. For more information, visit Apple's Web site at* http://www.apple.com/quicktime/.

Exporting

Using the Publish feature is not the only way to create images or movies from your authoring file. Exporting allows you to accomplish almost the same thing, though it's designed for using Flash-created content in other applications such as a photo editor or vector drawing program.

Exporting as a movie

Exporting your authoring file to a movie allows you to do one of two things: You can convert your animation to an animation file format such as Flash, QuickTime, Windows AVI, or an animated GIF. (Yes, this is the same thing that you can do with the Publish feature—you're not confused.) Or you can export each frame of your animation as a separate static image file. When exporting in this manner, each file you create is given a name you assign appended by a number indicating its position in the sequence. So, if you provide a file name such as "myimage" for a JPEG sequence and your movie consists of 10 frames, the resulting files would be named"myimage1.jpg through myimage10.jpg.

To export your animation as a movie or sequence:

1. From the File menu choose Export Movie to bring up the Export Movie dialog box.

2. Name the exported movie and choose a file type to save as.

3. Click OK.

   Depending on the file type you selected, an additional Export dialog box may appear. For information on these settings, see "Export Settings" in this section.

4. Adjust any of the settings in this dialog box, and click OK.

Exporting as an image

Exporting as an image allows you to create a single image file based on the currently displayed frame. If exported in a vector format, you can open this image in a drawing program such as Macromedia Freehand or Adobe Illustrator for further editing. If exported as a bitmap, you can open the image in a photo-editing program such as Macromedia Fireworks or Adobe Photoshop for further editing.

To export a single frame as an image:

1. From the File menu choose Export Movie to bring up the Export Image dialog box.

2. Name the exported image and choose a file type to save as.

3. Click OK.

Depending on the file type you selected, an additional Export dialog box may appear. For information on these settings, see "Export Settings" in this section.

4. Adjust any of the settings in this dialog box, and click OK.

Export Settings

As you've probably figured out by now, when exporting to most file types, you have several configuration options. The file types discussed here are those found in the Save as Type pop-up menu on the Export Movie/Export Image dialog boxes **(Figure 16.15)**.

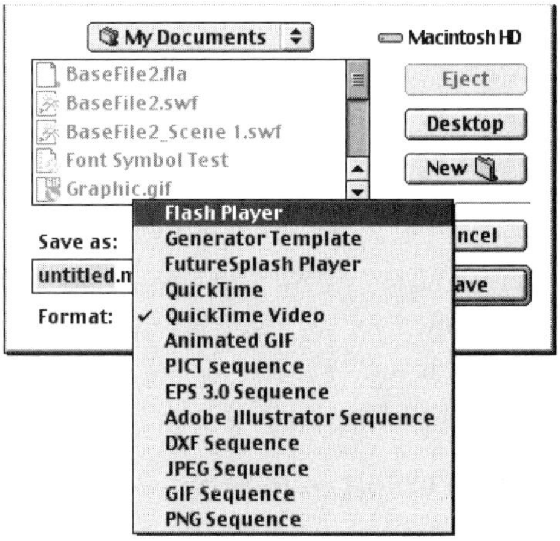

- *Flash Player (*.swf).* The settings here are the same as those available from the Flash tab on the Publish Settings dialog box.

- *Generator template (*.swt).* With one exception, the settings here are the same as those available from the Flash tab on the Publish Settings dialog box:

Figure 16.15
The Export Movie dialog box with a list of supported export file types.

Create External Font Files. Because a Generator template is dynamic (that is, it can be changed on the fly), creating external font files allows sets of fonts to be created externally from the Generator template and then loaded as needed. This helps reduce the overall size of the template file.

- *FutureSplash Player (*.spl).* This is the file format that was used by Flash prior to Macromedia's acquisition. The settings here are the same as those available from the Flash tab on the Publish Settings dialog box.

- *Windows AVI (*.avi) (Windows only).* This format will export your movie as a Windows video; however, all interactivity will be lost, and the Mac OS does not support this format. The following options are available (**Figure 16.16**):

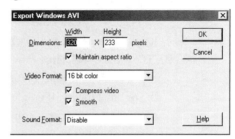

Figure 16.16
The Export Windows AVI dialog box.

Dimensions. Lets you set the vertical and horizontal dimensions, in pixels, of the AVI. If the Maintain Aspect Ratio option is checked, you must enter the width or the height dimension, and Flash will export the AVI so that it maintains the aspect ratio of the original movie. If you leave the option unchecked, you can enter values that change the proportions of the exported AVI.

Video Format. Lets you set the color depth of the exported movie. A lower color depth results in a smaller exported file but at a cost to image quality.

Compress Video. If you select this, you can set additional compression options for the exported file.

Smooth. Antialiases the exported AVI, creating a slightly larger file but one in which image elements—especially text—will appear smooth rather than jaggy.

Sound Format. Lets you set the sample rate and size of the sound track as well as whether it will be exported in mono or stereo (see "Understanding Sound" in Chapter 5). The smaller the sample rate and size, the smaller the exported file—though sound quality will be sacrificed.

- *QuickTime (*.mov).* The settings here are the same as those available from the Flash tab on the Publish Settings dialog box.

- *QuickTime video (*mov) (Macintosh Only).* Allows you to export your movie in the older QuickTime 3 format. Be aware, however, that exporting to this format is not the same as exporting to QuickTime 4: All Flash interactivity will be lost, and Flash elements will be converted from vector graphics to bitmaps. The following options are available (**Figure 16.17**):

Size. Lets you set the vertical and horizontal dimensions, in pixels, of the QuickTime movie that is created. If you check the Maintain Aspect Ratio option, you need only enter the width or height dimension, and Flash will export the QuickTime movie so that it retains the aspect ratio of the original movie. If you leave this option unchecked, you can enter values that will change the proportions of the exported QuickTime movie.

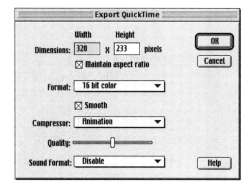

Figure 16.17
The Export QuickTime Video dialog box.

Format. Lets you set the color depth of the exported movie.

Smooth. Selecting this option antialiases the exported QuickTime movie.

Compressor. Allows you to select the standard QuickTime compressor.

Quality. Allows you to set the amount of compression that will be applied to your movie when it is exported to the QuickTime format.

Sound Format. Lets you set the sample rate and size of the sound track as well as whether it is exported in mono or stereo (see "Understanding Sound" in Chapter 5). The smaller the sample rate and size, the smaller the exported file—though sound quality will be sacrificed.

- **Animated GIF (*.gif).** With two exceptions, the settings here are the same as those available from the GIF tab on the Publish Settings dialog box:

  Resolution. Resolution is the size of the image based on its width in pixels (dots per inch, or dpi). Obviously, changing the resolution affects the pixel size of your movie, so if you adjust one setting, the other will reflect the change. Click the Match Screen button to make the exported images match the size of the movie as it appears on your screen. A resolution of 72 dpi is usually sufficient for most graphics you can view on your computer.

  Colors. Allows you to set the number of colors that will be used to create the exported image. Although fewer colors create a smaller file, image quality suffers. The Standard Colors option, which uses the Web-safe 216-color palette, usually provides the best results.

- **WAV Audio (*.wav) (Windows only).** If you export your movie in this format, only the sound file will be exported. There are two definable options:

    Sound Format. Lets you set the sample rate and size of the soundtrack and whether it's exported in mono or stereo.

    Ignore Sound Events. Checking this will exclude Event sounds from the exported sound file.

- **EMF Sequence/Enhanced Metafile (*.emf) (Windows only).** This format allows you to export both vector and bitmap information in a single file, so that it can be imported into other applications. This format has no adjustable settings.

- **WMF Sequence/Windows Metafile (*.wmf) (Windows only).** This Windows-native format for importing and exporting graphics among applications does not include any adjustable settings.

- **EPS 3.0 Sequence/EPS 3.0 (*.eps).** EPS is a popular format for placing image files within page-layout programs. The current frame is exported when using this option, which does not include any adjustable settings.

- **Adobe Illustrator Sequence/Adobe Illustrator (*.ai).** This vector format allows you to export vector elements of your movie so that they can be brought into a vector drawing program to be edited further. When exporting using this format, you are prompted for which version of Illustrator you would like to export to.

- **DXF Sequence/DXF (*.dxf).** This 3D format allows you to export elements of your movie so that they can be brought into a DXF-compatible program for further editing. It does not include any adjustable settings.

- **PICT Sequence/PICT (*.pict) (Macintosh Only).** This format allows you to export vector or bitmap information in a file so that it can be imported into other applications. The following options are available:

    Dimensions. Lets you set the dimensions, in pixels, of the PICT. Enter only the width or the height, and Flash will retain the aspect ratio of the original image in the exported image.

    Resolution. Click the Match Screen button to make the exported images match the size of the movie as it appears on your screen.

    Include. Allows you to choose which elements of your movie will be included in the exported PICT file. If you choose Minimum Image Area, the exported PICT file will be just big enough to include the graphic elements in the current frame. If you choose Full Document Size, the entire movie will be exported so that the PICT file dimensions match those found in the Movie Properties dialog box. You can use this setting as an alternative to the above-described Dimension setting.

Color Depth. This pop-up box serves two purposes: It allows you to determine whether the PICT graphic will be object based (a vector) or bitmap based. And if it is bitmap based, it allows you to set color depth.

Include PostScript. If you choose to export a PICT file as object based, including PostScript information will optimize the graphic for PostScript printing.

- ***Bitmap Sequence/Bitmap (*.bmp).*** This format allows you to create bitmapped images for use in other programs. The following options are available:

    Dimension. Lets you set the vertical and horizontal dimensions, in pixels, of the bitmap that is created. You can enter either the width or the height because Flash will retain the aspect ratio of the original image in the exported image.

    Resolution. Click the Match Screen button to make the exported images match the movie as it appears on your screen.

    Include. Pick which elements of your movie will be included in the exported bitmap. Note that the Minimum Image Area option has no effect when exporting as a bitmap sequence.

    Color Depth. Lets you set the color depth of the exported bitmap. A lower color depth results in a smaller exported file but at a cost in image quality.

    Smooth. Antialiases the exported bitmap, creating a slightly larger file but one in which image elements—especially text—will appear smooth rather than jaggy.

- ***JPEG Sequence/JPEG (*.jpeg).*** With one exception, this option includes the same settings as those found on the JPEG tab in the Publish Settings dialog box:

    Resolution. Click the Match Screen button to make the exported images match the size of the movie as it appears on your screen.

- ***GIF Sequence/GIF (*.gif).*** With two exceptions, the settings here are the same as those available on the GIF tab in the Publish Settings dialog box:

    Resolution. If you click the Match Screen button, the exported image matches the size of the movie as it appears on your screen.

    Colors. Allows you to set the number of colors that can be used to create the exported image.

- *PNG Sequence/PNG (*.png).* With two exceptions, the settings here are the same as those available on the PNG tab in the Publish Settings dialog box:

  Resolution. Click the Match Screen button to make the exported images match the movie as it appears on your monitor.

  Include. Pick which elements of your movie will be included in the exported bitmap.

Flash and HTML

You can normally place a Flash movie on an HTML page automatically by using the Publish feature. However, if you wish to make your pages manually or are interested in creating custom templates, you should know how Flash integrates with HTML.

HTML Tags

As with most things browser related, Microsoft's Internet Explorer and Netscape's Communicator/Navigator each has its own tag requirements that you must follow to display your movie properly on an HTML page. To place a movie on a page so that Internet Explorer can interpret it correctly, use the <OBJECT> tag; for Communicator, use the <EMBED> tag. You can use these tags separately or together on the same page, and you can also use them in conjunction with other HTML content. Each of these tags has additional attributes, or parameters, that affect the look and playback of your movie. The following describes how to place your movie on an HTML page using each tag on separate pages first, then both tags on the same page.

<OBJECT> tag

If you were to place your movie on an HTML page using the <OBJECT> tag, it would look something like this:

```
<HTML>
<HEAD>
<TITLE>Using the Object Tag</TITLE>
</HEAD>
<BODY>

<OBJECT CLASSID="clsid:D27CDB6E-AE6D-11cf-96B8-44553540000" WIDTH="400"
HEIGHT="400" CODEBASE="http://download.macromedia.com/pub/shockwave/cabs/
flash/swflash.cab#version=5,0,0,0">
```

```
<PARAM NAME="MOVIE" VALUE="coolflashmovie.swf">

<PARAM NAME="PLAY" VALUE="true">

<PARAM NAME="QUALITY" VALUE="best">

<PARAM NAME="LOOP" VALUE="false">

</OBJECT>

</BODY>

</HTML>
```

Now, let's take a closer look. Within the opening <OBJECT> tag, we find four attributes in the form of ATTRIBUTE="value". These include the CLASSID, WIDTH, HEIGHT, and CODEBASE attributes. Once again, these attributes are contained within the opening <OBJECT> tag and are all required for your movie to appear on the page. After the opening <OBJECT> tag, we find a set of <PARAM> tags. Although the <OBJECT> tag actually places your movie on the page, the <PARAM> tags affect the way it looks and plays. For more information about all of these attributes as well as the <PARAM> tags, see "HTML Tag Reference" later in this chapter.

<EMBED> tag

If you were to place your movie on an HTML page using the <EMBED> tag, it would look similar to this:

```
<HTML>

<HEAD>

<TITLE>Using the Embed Tag</TITLE>

</HEAD>

<BODY>

<EMBED SCR="coolflashmovie.swf" WIDTH="400" HEIGHT="400" PLAY="true"
QUALITY="best" LOOP="false" PLUGINSPAGE="http://www.macromedia.com/
shockwave/download/index.cgi?P1_Prod_Version=ShockwaveFlash">

</EMBED>

</BODY>

</HTML>
```

You will notice two differences in the way the <OBJECT> and <EMBED> tags are used:

• The <EMBED> tag consists of only ATTRIBUTE="value" settings, which are within the opening <EMBED> tag. These are equivalent to the <OBJECT> tag's <PARAM> settings.

- There are no CLASSID or CODEBASE attributes because these are unique to the <OBJECT> tag. Instead, the <EMBED> tag includes a PLUGINSPAGE attribute, which is unique to it. For more information about all these attributes as well as <PARAM> tags, see "HTML Tag Reference" later in this chapter.

<OBJECT> and <EMBED> tags together

Chances are you'll want both Microsoft and Netscape browser users to be able to view your movie from the same page. You can facilitate this by using the <OBJECT> and <EMBED> tags in tandem. The following example illustrates how to do so:

```
<HTML>

<HEAD>

<TITLE>Using the Object and Embed Tags Together</TITLE>

</HEAD>

<BODY>

<OBJECT CLASSID="clsid:D27CDB6E-AE6D-11cf-96B8-44553540000" WIDTH="400"
HEIGHT="400" CODEBASE=" http://download.macromedia.com/pub/shockwave/cabs/
flash/swflash.cab#version=5,0,0,0">

<PARAM NAME="MOVIE" VALUE="coolflashmovie.swf">

<PARAM NAME="PLAY" VALUE="true">

<PARAM NAME="QUALITY" VALUE="best">

<PARAM NAME="LOOP" VALUE="false">

<EMBED SCR="coolflashmovie.swf" WIDTH="400" HEIGHT="400" PLAY="true"
QUALITY="best" LOOP="false" PLUGINSPAGE="http://www.macromedia.com/
shockwave/download/index.cgi?P1_Prod_Version=ShockwaveFlash">

</EMBED>

</OBJECT>

</BODY>

</HTML>
```

When using the <OBJECT> and <EMBED> tags together on the same page, it's a good idea to enter the same values for both. This will ensure that your movie looks and plays the same in most major browsers.

HTML Tag Reference

The following key will help you to understand the various tags and parameter settings that can affect the way your movie looks and acts on an HTML page.

MOVIE

Required. This value indicates the directory path to the Flash movie that is to be loaded; it can be either a relative or an absolute path. An <OBJECT>-only attribute.

Possible values: YourMoviesName.swf or
http://www.yourdomain.com/YourMoviesName.swf

Sample: <PARAM NAME="MOVIE" VALUE="coolflashmovie.swf"> or <PARAM NAME="MOVIE" VALUE="http://www.derekfranklin.com/coolflashmovie.swf">

Template variable: $MO

SCR

Required. This value indicates the directory path to the Flash movie that is to be loaded; it can be either a relative or an absolute path. An <EMBED>-only attribute.

Possible values: YourMoviesName.swf or
http://www.yourdomain.com/YourMoviesName.swf

Sample: SCR="coolflashmovie.swf" or SCR ="http://www.derekfranklin.com/coolflashmovie.swf">

Template variable:$MO

WIDTH

Required. This value indicates the width of your movie window within the browser. You may enter a specific pixel amount or a percentage of the browser window.

Possible values: 18–2880 pixels or 0%–100%

Sample: WIDTH="400" or WIDTH="75%"

Template variable: $WI

HEIGHT

Required. This value indicates the height of your movie window within the browser. You may enter a specific pixel amount or a percentage of the browser window.

Possible values: 18–2880 pixels or 0%–100%

Sample: HEIGHT="400" or HEIGHT="75%"

Template variable: $HE

CLASSID

Required. The Flash Player ActiveX control identification number, which tells Internet Explorer which ActiveX control to initiate. An <OBJECT>-only attribute.

Possible values: D27CDB6E-AE6D-11cf-96B8-44553540000
(must be entered exactly as shown).

Sample: CLASSID="D27CDB6E-AE6D-11cf-96B8-44553540000"
(must be entered exactly as shown).

Template variable: not applicable.

CODEBASE

Required. The URL where the Flash Player ActiveX control can be downloaded if it is not already installed on your user's Internet Explorer browser. An <OBJECT>-only attribute.

Possible values:
http://download.macromedia.com/pub/shockwave/cabs/flash/swflash.cab#version=5,0,0,0
(must be entered exactly as shown).

Sample:
CODEBASE="http://download.macromedia.com/pub/shockwave/cabs/flash/swflash.cab#version=5,0,0,0" (must be entered exactly as shown).

Template variable: not applicable.

PLUGINSPAGE

Required. The URL where the Netscape Player can be downloaded if it is not already installed on your user's Netscape browser. An <EMBED>-only attribute.

Possible values: `http://www.macromedia.com/shockwave/download/index.cgi?` `P1_Prod_Version=ShockwaveFlash` (must be entered exactly as shown).

Sample: `PLUGINSPAGE="http://www.macromedia.com/shockwave/download/index.cgi?` `P1_Prod_Version=ShockwaveFlash"` (must be entered exactly as shown).

Template variable: not applicable (value is not configurable).

ID

Optional. A name that identifies your movie on the page for use in scripting. If no scripting is used in conjunction with Flash, you don't need to fill in this attribute. An <OBJECT>-only attribute.

Possible values: Any name you choose. May not include spaces. When using a template variable, this value is derived from the name of the authoring file.

Sample: `ID="MyMovie"`

Template variable: `$TI`

NAME

Optional. A name that identifies your movie on the page for use in scripting. If no scripting is used in conjunction with Flash, you don't need to fill in this attribute. An <EMBED>-only attribute.

Possible values: Any name you choose. May not include spaces. When using a template variable, this value is derived from the name of the authoring file.

Sample: `NAME="MyMovie"`

Template variable: `$TI`

SWLIVECONNECT

Optional. When using FS Commands in conjunction with JavaScripting within a Netscape browser, Java must be turned on for these FS Commands to work. This attribute either enables (true) or disables (false) Java. Java does not need to be enabled for normal JavaScripting purposes on pages that do not pertain to FS Commands. Enabling it can increase the time it takes for your movie to begin playing. The default setting is "false." An <EMBED>-only attribute.

Possible values:

- *True.* Enables Java.

- *False.* Disables Java.

Default setting: False.

- *Sample:* SWLIVECONNECT="false"

Template variable: not applicable (must be set in the template code).

PLAY

Optional. Controls whether your movie begins playback immediately upon being loaded or waits for user interaction.

Possible Values:

- *True.* Your movie will begin playing as soon as the first frame has loaded completely.

- *False.* Your movie will wait for user interaction to begin playing.

Default setting: True.

Sample for <\OBJECT> tag: <PARAM NAME="PLAY" VALUE="true">

Sample for <\EMBED> tag: PLAY="true"

Template variable: $PL

LOOP

Optional. Controls your movie's behavior once it reaches the last frame during playback.

Possible values:

- *True.* Your movie will return to the first frame and begin playing again.

- *False.* Your movie will play once and then stop at the last frame.

Default setting: True.

Sample for <\OBJECT> tag: `<PARAM NAME="LOOP" VALUE="true">`

Sample for <\EMBED> tag: `LOOP="true"`

Template variable: `$LO`

QUALITY

Optional. Lets you determine how certain processor limitations will affect your movie's playback in terms of speed and visual quality.

Possible values:

- *Low.* Sacrifices visual quality to maintain playback speed. With this option, your movie will never be antialiased.

- *Autolow.* Although initially turned off, antialiasing will be turned on to improve visual quality if the user's processor is fast enough to handle it.

- *Autohigh.* Although initially turned on, antialiasing will be turned off to improve playback speed if the frame-per-second rate drops below the amount set in the Movie Properties dialog box.

- *High.* Skips frames during playback to maintain visual quality on computers with slower processors. Antialiasing is always on when this option has been selected. If your movie is animated, bitmaps will not be smoothed; if it is not, they will be.

- *Best.* Bitmaps are always smoothed; antialiasing is always on; and frames are never skipped due to processor limitations.

Default setting: High.

Sample for <OBJECT> tag: `<PARAM NAME="QUALITY" VALUE="best">`

Sample for <\OBJECT> tag: `QUALITY="best"`

Template variable: `$QU`

BGCOLOR

Optional. Sets the background color of the movie window, overriding the color assigned to your movie in the Movie Properties dialog box.

Possible values: any RGB hexadecimal value.

Default setting: the color of the movie background as assigned in the Movie Properties dialog box.

Sample for <\OBJECT> tag: `<PARAM NAME="BGCOLOR" VALUE="#0099ff">`

Sample for <\EMBED> tag: `BGCOLOR="#0099ff"`

Template variable: `$BG`

SCALE

Optional. If the width and height settings you selected for the actual movie window differ from those set for the movie in the Movie Properties dialog box, movie elements (which were designed for a specific size) may not fit perfectly within the new dimensions you set for the movie window. This option determines how the movie will look within the boundaries of the movie window as you specified.

Possible values:

- **Showall.** This makes your movie completely visible within the area you defined for the movie window. All elements are scaled to fit within the movie window. Borders may appear between movie elements and the movie window if the movie window's dimensions differ from the movie's original size.

- **Noborder.** This scales your movie proportionately so that it fills the entire area of the movie window—no borders appear. As a result, movie elements may be cropped and not visible from within the movie window.

- **Exactfit.** This disproportionately scales your movie to fit exactly the dimensions of the movie window. Your movie may appear squashed or bloated depending on how much the movie window's dimensions differ from the actual movie.

Default setting: Showall.

Sample for <\OBJECT> tag: `<PARAM NAME="SCALE" VALUE="showall">`

Sample for <\EMBED> tag: `SCALE="showall"`

Template variable: `$SC`

SALIGN

Optional. This attribute allows you to set the alignment of your movie within the movie window if their dimensions differ.

Possible values:

- **T.** Aligns your movie vertically to the top edge of the movie window and centers it horizontally.

- **B.** Aligns your movie vertically to the bottom edge of the movie window and centers it horizontally.

- **L.** Aligns your movie horizontally to the left edge of the movie window and centers it vertically.

- **R.** Aligns your movie horizontally to the right edge of the movie window and centers it vertically.

- **TL.** Aligns your movie to the top left corner of the movie window.

- **TR.** Aligns your movie to the top right corner of the movie window.

- **BL.** Aligns your movie to the bottom left corner of the movie window.

- **BR.** Aligns your movie to the bottom right corner of the movie window.

Default setting: If this attribute is not specified, your movie will be placed in the center of the movie window.

Sample for <\OBJECT> tag: `<PARAM NAME="SALIGN" VALUE="tl">`

Sample for <\EMBED> tag: `SALIGN="tl"`

Template variable: `$SA`

BASE

Optional. Allows you to set the URL that serves as the basis for relative links within your movie. Thus, if your movie resides in a directory such as `http://www.yourdomain.com/flash/` and you want all relative links in the movie to be referenced from `http://www.adifferentdomain.com/`, you would enter the latter domain as the BASE attribute's value.

Possible values: any URL.

Default setting: same directory as the movie.

Sample for <\OBJECT> tag: `<PARAM NAME="BASE" VALUE="http://www.adifferentdomain.com/">`

Sample for <\EMBED> tag: `BASE="http://www.adifferentdomain.com/"`

Template variable: `$SA`

MENU

Optional. Allows you to determine which options are available on the Flash Player pop-up menu that appears when the user right-clicks (Windows) or Control-clicks (Macintosh) the movie in the browser window.

Possible values:

- *True.* Displays all available menu items.
- *False.* Displays only the About Flash menu item.

Default setting: True.

Sample for <\OBJECT> tag: `<PARAM NAME="MENU" VALUE="true">`

Sample for <\EMBED> tag: `MENU="true"`

Template variable: `$ME`

WMODE

Optional. Allows you to take advantage of capabilities available only on a Windows version of Internet Explorer that has the Flash Player ActiveX control installed. This attribute is not available for the `<EMBED>` tag.

Possible values:

- *Window.* Plays your movie within its own rectangular area on the HTML page, providing the best playback performance.

- *Opaque.* Allows you to move elements on the HTML page behind the rectangular area of the movie without having them show through. Use this option in conjunction with dynamic HTML layers.

- *Transparent.* Causes the background color of your Flash movie (as set in the Movie Properties dialog box) to become transparent so that the background of the HTML page on which your movie is embedded will show through. This setting, though cool, provides the slowest playback performance. Use it sparingly.

Default setting: Window.

Sample for <\OBJECT> tag: `<PARAM NAME="WMODE" VALUE="opaque">`

Template variable: `$WM`

Setting Up the Server

When your movie is downloaded over the Web, two things are sent over the connection that enable viewers to see your movie: The first, and most obvious, is the movie file itself. The second is the movie's MIME type, which Communicator needs to determine which Player to use to play your movie. Without this MIME type, your movie may not be displayed properly—or at all—in a Netscape browser. (This is not an issue with Internet Explorer.) It may even cause the browser—and your computer—to crash, so be sure to take the proper steps to avoid this.

You set the MIME type on the server that delivers your movie. Thus, unless you're the administrator of your own server, you'll probably never need to do this yourself. You will, however, need to call your ISP or talk to the server administrator so that they can set the MIME type for your site.

When setting up the MIME type for Flash content, you need to know the MIME type itself (application/x-shockwave-flash) and the Flash file extension (.swf). For Mac servers, the following parameters must also be set:

- Action: Binary
- Type: SWFL
- Creator SWF2

Player Issues

To see Flash content, you need the Flash Player. And with each new version of Flash, comes a new version of the Player. Now, this is not to say that you can't view a Flash 5 presentation using the Flash 4 Player. It just means that if you want to use all of the groovy new features included in Flash 5, you must have the Flash 5 Player installed.

Currently, more than 250 million users—or more than 90 percent of those online— have the Flash Player installed. However, because it's so new, relatively few people have the *latest version* (Flash 5) installed. Your hurdle is convincing users that it's worth their time to download and install it.

The Front-Door Approach

Figure 16.18
The Get Flash Player button.

One of the best ways to tackle this problem is right from your site's front door—i.e., its home page. This is an effective place to notify users that they need the Flash 5 Player to truly experience the wonders of your site. Place the Get Flash button (**Figure 16.18**) somewhere on that page and link it to Macromedia's download site at http://www.macromedia.com/shockwave/download/index.cgi?P1_Prod_Version=ShockwaveFlash. Clicking the button will take users to a well-executed page that explains the Player's benefits and its download procedure. It will also include a link so that the user can download the Player immediately. Once a user has downloaded and installed the Player, he or she can return to your site and view it in all its glory.

Go with What Works

If you want to have an interesting Flash-driven site yet keep Player downloads to a minimum, the solution is simple: Design for Flash 4—at least until most users have made the transition to Flash 5. This, of course, means avoiding the features that are unique to Flash 5.

Keep in mind, however, that you can export Flash 5–created content using the Flash 4 format. Even though the Flash 5–specific features won't work in Flash 4, everything else—including Mouse Events, Tell Targets, and more—will.

Provide an Alternative

Maybe you only want to provide Flash content for those who have the Player installed, though you don't want to require it for Web users to visit your site. If that's the case, provide an alternative: You can create a Flash-driven version of your site *and* an HTML version. This way, if the Player is not installed on your user's computer, he or she can still visit the HTML version without a hitch.

However, we don't really recommend this approach because maintaining two sites can be a headache. If you think you're up to it, though, don't let us stop you.

Bold and Beautiful

If you truly don't care about potentially annoying your users, go ahead and set up your Flash 5 site so that it automatically installs the latest version of the Player. Your users will thank you for it in the end!

What's more, by taking the "who cares" approach, you help Flash 5 proliferate—benefiting all of us who don't have the guts to force it down users' throats! After all, the more people who have the Flash 5 Player installed, the more people who can enjoy Flash 5 content on the rest of our sites.

Understanding Templates

You need to set numerous HTML settings and parameters if you want your movie to look and function properly. There are width and height settings, playback options, and even JavaScript in some cases. Some of us use custom HTML pages (with custom JavaScript perhaps) to place our Flash content. With the exception of a few changing attributes, these custom HTML pages could be used for many Flash movies. After all, writing Player detection scripts and filling in parameters every time you want to place a Flash movie on a Web page—especially if you only want to change a few things—quickly becomes tedious. However, by using templates in conjunction with the Publish feature, you can easily fill in attributes that affect not only what movie goes on the page but also how your movie will look and play back in the Web browser. You can even eliminate the need to edit an HTML page that contains a Flash movie. This is because the template is created once with variables placed in specific places within the template. Using the Publish feature, you then fill in specific information (<OBJECT> and <EMBED> attributes) about the way you want this movie to appear and play back in the browser window. When you publish to HTML, the variables in the template you select are replaced with the information you entered. The resulting document is an HTML page with your movie embedded. You could easily use the same template, enter different settings in the HTML tab of the Publish settings dialog box, and output a new HTML page.

The Process

There are essentially three stages in creating and using templates:

- Creating the template

- Filling in the settings on the various tabs of the Publish Settings dialog box

- Publishing from Flash (which generates an HTML page based on your template and settings)

Creating a template

A Flash template is simply a text file that contains both HTML code (which never changes) and template code, or variables (which are not the same as the variables used in ActionScripts). Flash includes pre-built templates, which are sufficient for most users' needs; however, you can also build your own.

Creating a template is very similar to creating a standard HTML page. The only difference is that you replace the values pertaining to a Flash movie with variables that begin with a dollar sign. If you need to use the dollar sign for something other than a template variable, prefix it with a backslash (\$). For a complete list of template variables, see Table 16.1 at the end of this section.

In the meantime, take a look at the following sample template code:

```
$TTCool Template
$DS
This Cool Template
is to help you understand
how to use variables.
$DF
<HTML>
<HEAD>
<TITLE>$TI</TITLE>
```

```
</HEAD>

<BODY bgcolor=$BG>

$MU

$MT

<OBJECT CLASSID="clsid:D27CDB6E-AE6D-11cf-96B8-44553540000"
WIDTH="$WI" HEIGHT="$HE" CODEBASE=" download.macromedia.com/
pub/shockwave/cabs/flash/swflash.cab#version=5,0,0,0">

<PARAM NAME="MOVIE" VALUE="$MO">

<PARAM NAME="PLAY" VALUE="$PL">

<PARAM NAME="QUALITY" VALUE="$QU">

<PARAM NAME="LOOP" VALUE="$LO">

<EMBED SCR="$MO" WIDTH="$WI" HEIGHT="$HE" PLAY="$PL" QUALITY="$QU"
LOOP="$LO" PLUGINSPAGE="http://www.macromedia.com/shockwave/download/
index.cgi?P1_Prod_Version=ShockwaveFlash">

<NOEMBED><IMG SRC=$IS WIDTH=$IW HEIGHT=$IH usemap=$IU
BORDER=0></NOEMBED>

</EMBED>

</OBJECT>

</BODY>

</HTML>
```

Now let's take a closer look at each section of this template.

```
$TTCool Template
```

The name Cool Template will appear in the template drop-down box on the HTML tab of the Publish Settings dialog box.

```
$DS
This Cool Template
is to help you understand
how to use variables.
$DF
```

Anything between $DS and $DF will be what appears in the Info box that you access by clicking the Info button on the HTML tab of the Publish Settings dialog box.

```
<HTML>
<HEAD>
<TITLE>$TI</TITLE>
</HEAD>
```

This is the standard way of beginning an HTML document. The $TI variable between the <TITLE> tags represents the page title as it will appear on the Web browser. This is derived from the file name of the movie placed on the page. Thus, if your movie is named CoolFlashMovie.swf, your page will be entitled CoolFlashMovie.

```
<BODY bgcolor=$BG>
```

This will cause the generated HTML page to have the same background color as your movie.

```
$MU
```

This template variable will place a list of the URLs used in your movie on the generated HTML page.

```
$MT
```

This template variable will place a list of text used in your movie on the generated HTML page so that search engines can index your movie's content. This is output between HTML comment tags.

```
<OBJECT CLASSID="clsid:D27CDB6E-AE6D-11cf-96B8-44553540000"
WIDTH="$WI" HEIGHT="$HE" CODEBASE=" download.macromedia.com/pub/
shockwave/cabs/flash/swflash.cab#version=5,0,0,0">
```

You will notice that the WIDTH and HEIGHT parameters of the <OBJECT> tag have been replaced with template variables.

```
<PARAM NAME="MOVIE" VALUE="$MO">
<PARAM NAME="PLAY" VALUE="$PL">
<PARAM NAME="QUALITY" VALUE="$QU">
<PARAM NAME="LOOP" VALUE="$LO">
```

Different attributes, or parameters, of the <OBJECT> tag have been substituted with template variables.

```
<EMBED SCR="$MO" WIDTH="$WI" HEIGHT="$HE" PLAY="$PL" QUALITY="$QU"
LOOP="$LO" PLUGINSPAGE="http://www.macromedia.com/shockwave/download/
index.cgi?P1_Prod_Version=ShockwaveFlash">
```

The different attributes of the <EMBED> tag have been replaced with template variables.

```
<NOEMBED><IMG SRC=$IS WIDTH=$IW HEIGHT=$IH usemap=$IU
BORDER=0></NOEMBED>
```

For browsers that don't support the Player, the <NOEMBED> tag provides an alternative image that Flash automatically generates when you publish. You'll notice the template variables that are used.

```
</EMBED>
</OBJECT>
</BODY>
</HTML>
```

Figure 16.19 Place all custom templates in the HTML folder of the Flash 5 directory.

These are the tags you need to finish creating your template. While this template does not use every possible template variable, it should still give you a pretty good idea of how template variables are used in conjunction with HTML.

Template variables can be used in conjunction with other HTML content, including JavaScript, Cold Fusion, Active Server Pages, and more. Any template variables used within the syntax of these programming languages will be replaced with actual movie and image values when you publish your movie, based on the values you've entered on the HTML tab of the Publish Settings dialog box.

Save your template (as an HTML document if you wish; see "The Published HTML Page" later in this section for information about file extensions) and place it in the HTML folder of the Flash 5 program directory (**Figure 16.19**). Once you have created a template and placed it in this folder, it becomes available from the template pop-up box on the HTML tab of the Publish Settings dialog box.

Entering Publish settings

Now that you've created a template, you can use it for any movie in conjunction with the Publish feature.

Using an example authoring file (MapUSA.fla) that we wish to publish to HTML, we'll adjust the settings for our demonstration (**Figure 16.20**). All of these settings relate to a template variable that, when published, will be replaced with the values you set. Once you have entered all of the necessary values, click the Publish button to complete the process.

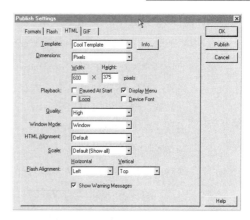

Figure 16.20 The values entered on the HTML format tab of the Publish Settings dialog box are the values that will replace corresponding template variables when you publish.

The published HTML page

When publishing your movie, you need to be aware of two things: the name of the published HTML that is created and its location.

The name of the published HTML page will be a combination of your movie's file name and the file extension you gave the template. For example, if your movie's file name is MapUSA.swf and the file name of your template is cooltemplate.html, the file name of the published HTML page will be MapUSA.html. If the template's file extension were .cfm (Cold Fusion), the resulting file name of the published HTML page would be MapUSA.cfm.

The published HTML page and all of its associated files can be found in the same directory as the authoring file that was used at the time of publishing.

The HTML of the published HTML page will appear similar to the following. Compare it to the HTML of the original template to help understand how the template itself and the settings adjusted in the Publish Settings dialog box merge to become the final HTML document:

```
<HTML>

<HEAD>

<TITLE>MapUSA</TITLE>

</HEAD>

<BODY bgcolor=#FFFFFF>
```

```
<A HREF="http://www.usa.com"></A>

<A HREF="http://www.america.com"></A>

<!-This is a map of the USA -->

<OBJECT CLASSID="clsid:D27CDB6E-AE6D-11cf-96B8-44553540000" WIDTH="600"
HEIGHT="375" CODEBASE=" download.macromedia.com/pub/shockwave/cabs/flash/
swflash.cab#version=5,0,0,0">

<PARAM NAME="MOVIE" VALUE="MapUSA.swf">

<PARAM NAME="PLAY" VALUE="true">

<PARAM NAME="QUALITY" VALUE="high">

<PARAM NAME="LOOP" VALUE="false">

<EMBED SCR="MapUSA.swf" WIDTH="600" HEIGHT="375" PLAY="true" QUALITY=
"high" LOOP="false" PLUGINSPAGE="http://www.macromedia.com/shockwave/
download/index.cgi?P1_Prod_Version=ShockwaveFlash">

<NOEMBED><IMG SRC="MapUSA.gif" WIDTH=600 HEIGHT=375 usemap="#MapUSA"
BORDER=0></NOEMBED>

</EMBED>

</OBJECT>

</BODY>

</HTML>
```

Template Variables

This is a complete list of the variables you can use in creating your own templates. Keep in mind that template variables are case sensitive; thus, "$tt" will not work, but "$TT" will.

Table 16.1
Template Variables

Parameter	Variable
Template title	$TT
Template description start	$DS
Template description finish	$DF
Width	$WI
Height	$HE
Movie	$MO
Name, ID, or Title	$TI
HTML alignment	$HA
Looping	$LO
Play	$PL
Quality	$QU
Scale	$SC
Salign	$SA
Wmode	$WM
Devicefont	$DE
Bgcolor	$BG
Movie text	$MT
Movie URLs	$MU
Parameters for <OBJECT>	$PO
Parameters for <EMBED>	$PE
Image width (unspecified image type)	$IW
Image height (unspecified image type)	$IH
Image file name (unspecified image type)	$IS
Image map name	$IU

continued

Table 16.1
Template Variables (continued)

Parameter	Variable
Image map tag location	$IM
QuickTime width	$QW
QuickTime height	$QH
QuickTime file name	$QN
GIF width	$GW
GIF height	$GH
GIF file name	$GS
JPEG width	$JW
JPEG height	$JH
JPEG file name	$JN
PNG width	$PW
PNG height	$PH
PNG file name	$PN
Generator variables <OBJECT>	$GV
Generator variables <EMBED>	$GE

Interactive Tutorial

 Publishing Your Movie. This tutorial will guide you through the steps of publishing your movie, including setting values in the Publish Settings dialog box, previewing the settings, and doing a final publish.

On the CD

Using the Tutorials and Source Files

The video tutorials on the accompanying CD-ROM are in QuickTime format. To view them, you must have Quick-Time 4 installed on your computer. (Since this is a common piece of software, you may have it on your machine already.) For your convenience, we've included the QuickTime 4 installer on this CD-ROM.

Most of the tutorials consist of a QuickTime video tutorial and a source file. To view a video tutorial, simply double-click its name. The QuickTime Player will start up, and the tutorial will begin to play. Use the QuickTime Player controls to play, stop, rewind, fast-forward, and skip to specific parts of the tutorial.

To open a Flash source file in the Flash authoring environment, simply double-click it. The source files are compatible only with Flash 5 and will not open properly in older versions of the program.

The CD-ROM includes a 30-day trial version of Flash 5, along with trial versions of other Macromedia applications.

Enjoy!

Ultimate Arcade Games

Our friends at Ultimate Arcade *(www.ultimatearcade.com)* have generously provided a couple of games for inclusion in this CD (which you'll find in the Ultimate Arcade Games directory). Included are exported movies as well as source files that you can open in the Flash authoring environment to get a feel for how they were put together. Some of the world's most accomplished Flash developers created these games; they were gracious to provide us with a glimpse of their secrets.

★★★★★★★★★★★★

Keyboard Shortcuts

FILE MENU

Command	Windows	Macintosh
New	Control-N	Command-N
Open	Control-O	Command-O
Open as Library	Control-Shift-O	Command-Shift-O
Close	Control-W	Command-W
Save	Control-S	Command-S
Save as	Control-Shift-S	Command-Shift-S
Import	Control-R	Command-R
Export Movie	Control-Alt-Shift-S	Command-Shift-Option-S
Publish Settings	Control-Shift-F12	Command-Shift-F12
Publish	Shift-F12	Shift-F12
Print	Control-P	Command-P
Quit	Control-Q	Command-Q

PUBLISH SUBMENU

Command	Windows	Macintosh
Default	F12	F12

EDIT MENU

Command	Windows	Macintosh
Undo	Control-Z	Command-Z
Redo	Control-Y	Command-Y
Cut	Control-X	Command-X
Copy	Control-C	Command-C
Paste	Control-V	Command-V
Paste In Place	Control-Shift-V	Command-Shift-V
Clear	Delete	Delete
Duplicate	Control-D	Command-D
Select All	Control-A	Command-A
Deselect All	Control-Shift-A	Command-Shift-A
Cut Frames	Control-Alt-X	Command-Option-X
Copy Frames	Control-Alt-C	Command-Option-C
Paste Frames	Control- Alt-V	Command-Option-V
Edit Symbols	Control-E	Command-E

VIEW MENU

Command	Windows	Macintosh
Zoom In	Control-=	Command-=
Zoom Out	Control- -	Command- -
Outlines	Control-Alt-Shift-O	Shift-Option-Command-O
Fast	Control-Alt-Shift-F	Shift-Option-Command-F
Antialias	Control-Alt-Shift-A	Shift-Option-Command-A
Antialias Text	Control-Alt-Shift-T	Shift-Option-Command-T
Timeline	Control-Alt-T	Command-Option-T
Work Area	Control-Shift-W	Command-Shift-W
Rulers	Control-Alt-Shift-R	Shift-Option-Command-R
Snap to Objects	Control-Shift-/	Command-Shift-/
Show Shape Hints	Control-Alt-H	Command-Option-H
Hide Edges	Control-H	Command-H
Hide Panels	Tab	Tab

GO TO SUBMENU

Command	Windows	Macintosh
First	Home	Home
Previous	Page Up	Page Up
Next	Page Down	Page Down
Last	End	End

MAGNIFICATION SUBMENU

Command	Windows	Macintosh
100%	Control-1	Command-1
Show Frame	Control-2	Command-2
Show All	Control-3	Command-3

GRID SUBMENU

Command	Windows	Macintosh
Show Grid	Control-'	Command-'
Snap to Grid	Control-Shift-'	Command-Shift-'
Edit Grid	Control-Alt-G	Command-Option-G

GUIDE SUBMENU

Command	Windows	Macintosh
Show Guides	Control-;	Command-;
Lock Guides	Control-Alt-;	Command-Option-;
Snap to Guides	Control-Shift-;	Command-Shift-;
Edit Guides	Control-Alt-Shift-G	Command-Option-Shift-G

INSERT MENU

Command	Windows	Macintosh
Convert to Symbol	F8	F8
New Symbol	Control-F8	Command-F8
Frame	F5	F5
Remove Frames	Shift-F5	Shift-F5
Key Frame	F6	F6
Blank Key Frame	F7	F7
Clear Key Frame	Shift-F6	Shift-F6

MODIFY MENU

Command	Windows	Macintosh
Instance	Control-I	Command-I
Frame	Control-F	Command-F
Movie	Control-M	Command-M
Optimize	Control-Alt-Shift-C	Command-Option-Shift-C
Group	Control-G	Command-G
Ungroup	Control-Shift-G	Command- Shift-G
Break Apart	Control-B	Command-B

TRANSFORM SUBMENU

Command	Windows	Macintosh
Scale and Rotate	Control-Alt-S	Command-Option-S
Remove Transform	Control-Shift-Z	Command-Shift-Z
Add Shape Hint	Control-Shift-H	Command-Shift--H

ARRANGE SUBMENU

Command	Windows	Macintosh
Bring To Front	Control-Shift-Up	Command-Shift-Up
Bring Forward	Control-Up	Command-Up
Send Backward	Control-Down	Command-Down
Send To Back	Control-Shift-Down	Command-Shift-Down
Lock	Control-Alt-L	Command-Option-L
Unlock All	Control-Alt-Shift-L	Command-Option-Shift-L

TEXT MENU

Command	Windows	Macintosh
Character	Control-T	Command-T
Paragraph	Control-Shift-T	Command-Shift-T

STYLE SUBMENU

Command	Windows	Macintosh
Plain	Control-Shift-P	Command-Shift-P
Bold	Control-Shift-B	Command-Shift-B
Italic	Control-Shift-I	Command-Shift-I

ALIGN SUBMENU

Command	Windows	Macintosh
Align Left	Control-Shift-L	Command-Shift-L
Align Center	Control-Shift-C	Command-Shift-C
Align Right	Control-Shift-R	Command-Shift-R
Justify	Control-Shift-J	Command-Shift-J

TRACKING SUBMENU

Command	Windows	Macintosh
Decrease	Control-Alt-Left	Command-Option-Left
Increase	Control-Alt-Right	Command-Option-Right
Reset	Control-Alt-Up	Command-Option-Up

CONTROL MENU

Command	Windows	Macintosh
Play	Enter	Enter
Rewind	Control-Alt-R	Command-Option-R
Step Forward	.	.
Step Backward	,	,
Test Movie	Control-Enter	Command-Enter
Debug Movie	Control-Shift-Enter	Command-Shift-Enter
Test Scene	Control-Alt-Enter	Command-Option-Enter
Enable Simple Buttons	Control-Alt-B	Command-Option-B
Mute Sounds	Control-Alt-M	Command-Option-M

WINDOW MENU

Command	Windows	Macintosh
New Window	Control-Alt-N	Command-Option-N
Actions	Control-Alt-A	Command-Option-A
Movie Explorer	Control-Alt-M	Command-Option-M
Library	Control-L	Command-L

PANELS SUBMENU

Command	Windows	Macintosh
Info	Control-Alt-I	Command-Option-I
Align	Control-K	Command-K
Character	Control-T	Command-T
Paragraph	Control-Shift-T	Command-Shift-T
Instance	Control-I	Command-I
Frames	Control-F	Command-F

HELP MENU

Command	Windows	Macintosh
Using Flash	F1	

DRAWING SHORTCUTS

To	Windows	Macintosh
Set fill and line attributes for all tools	Shift-click with the Dropper tool	Shift-click with the with the Dropper tool
Create a new corner handle	Control-drag a line	Control-drag a line
Move a selected element by 1 pixel	Arrow keys	Arrow keys
Move a selected element by 8 pixels	Shift-Arrow keys	Shift-Arrow keys
Toggle between zoom in and zoom out while the magnifier tool is selected	Alt	Option
Drag a copy of the selected element	Control-drag	Option-drag
Drag the stage with the Hand tool	Press Spacebar and drag	Press Spacebar and drag

SPRING-LOADED TOOLS

Hold down the keys below to temporarily activate certain tools. When the key is released, the previous tool is reactivated.

To temporarily activate this tool	Windows	Macintosh
Arrow	Control	Command
Hand	Spacebar	Spacebar
Magnifier zoom-in	Control-Spacebar	Command-Spacebar
Magnifier zoom-out	Control-Shift-Spacebar	Command-Shift-Spacebar

SWITCHING TOOLS

To switch to this tool	Press
Arrow	V
Subselect	A
Line	N
Lasso	L
Pen	P
Text	T
Oval	O
Rectangle	R
Pencil	Y
Brush	B
Ink Bottle	S
Paint Bucket	K
Dropper	I
Eraser	E
Hand	H
Zoom	M, Z

Resource Sites

derekfranklin.com

http://www.derekfranklin.com

This site, by one of this book's authors, offers a wealth of tools that tie directly to this book, including tips and how-to's, tutorials, a testing module (with references to specific pages), and other powerful learning aids. Armed with this book and the support you'll find at derekfranklin.com, you should be ready to tackle the most ambitious Flash projects.

Flash Kit

http://www.flashkit.com

As one of the largest resource sites for Flash developers, Flash Kit offers comprehensive tutorials, forums, open sources, links, sounds, and games. It also includes official forums for Swish, Swift 3d, OpenSWF, and swift generator.

Flash Academy

http://www.enetserve.com/tutorials

Flash Academy is designed for Flash developers of all levels. Although many of the tutorials developed by Flash Academy can now be found on other Flash resource sites as well (for example, Virtual-FX and Flashzone), the difference here is that Bill Tagliaferro, the programmer behind the tutorials, is always ready to help Flash developers get answers to tough questions.

FlashChallenge

http://www.flashchallenge.com

FlashChallenge, developed by the wddg *(www.wddg.com)*, is one of the premier sites for rating, commenting on, and reviewing other Flash sites. Its huge database of Flash sites allows users to rate these sites in any of six categories. Users can also nominate sites for the Challenge and vote on which sites are included.

FlashFever.com

http://www.flashfever.com

FlashFever.com continues to evolve as a resource for information about Flash technology as well as tips, tricks, and news about the program. Tyler Reichert *(ty@flashfever.com)*, an avid Flash supporter and evangelizer, created the site.

Flashmagazine

http://www.flashmagazine.com

A good place to get information about Flash, Adobe LiveMotion, Swift3D, Swish, and other Vector-based products for the Web.

FlashMove

http://www.flashmove.com

Founded by Ryan Tan of *www.ryanosure.com,* this site lets you search for information about Flash animation and game development, share resources and ideas, and interact with fellow members. Its Members' Forum provides real-time discussions, employment resources, and a chat area. The site also provides downloads on source files and links to developer, ActionScript, software, audio, and user group sites.

FlashPlanet.com

http://www.flashplanet.com

FlashPlanet.com offers free tutorials and a variety of downloadable movie sources for Flash developers. The site also offers original vector clip art, articles, interviews, extensive links to other Flash sites, a Flash site directory, and a custom-built Resource Search Engine, which allows users to search multiple sites for tutorials and source files.

Flashsound

http://www.flashsound.com

This is a good place for Flash developers to get music for their projects. This site's developers have created something called Grooveloops, which are songs that have been broken into 6 to 12 loops that can be chained together or used seamlessly for different scenes within Flash.

SoundShopper.com

http://www.soundshopper.com

A popular source for royalty-free music and sounds on the Web. Users can hear previews of different sound categories and—if interested—download sounds for a fee. Categories include Business, Vibes, Party Zone, Urban Grooves, Effects, and Button Sounds.

Ultrashock.com

http://www.ultrashock.com

Ultrashock contains content from some of the most well-known Flash developers in the world, offering a mix of educational content, resources, and entertainment for Flash developers.

Virtual-FX Flash Resources

http://www.virtual-fx.net

This site specializes in Flash tutorials for beginners to experts. It even includes gaming tutorials and tutorials for third-party tools.

Third-Party Software

Swift 3D

http://www.swift3d.com

Electric Rain's Swift 3D is a 3D authoring tool that enables designers to quickly create 3D text, simple models, and animations for export to either the SWF file format for Macromedia Flash or as sequential EPS files for use with Adobe LiveMotion. The program also easily imports and converts 3D models and animations in the 3DS file format, in addition to extrusion and beveling of 2D artwork in the AI or EPS format.

Swish

http://www.swishzone.com

Swish allows users to obtain sophisticated text animation effects without having to manually construct them letter by letter. Swish will appeal to both professional designers, who can expect to significantly cut production times, and hobbyists, who can now add animated elements to their Web sites cheaply, quickly, and easily.

Moho 2.0

http://www.lostmarble.com

As a 2D vector-based cartoon animation application, Moho provides a complete set of tools for creating animated cartoons. Moho facilitates everything from drawing and painting to keyframe animation and multilayer compositing and final output of Quick-Time, AVI, and Flash movie files. Moho contains a vector-based drawing component, making it suitable for illustration tasks as well. The animation tools include manipulators for controlling skeletons, which are extremely useful for working with characters.

KoolMoves

http://www.koolmoves.com

KoolMoves Web animation authoring software makes creating Flash movies simple. Use this program to add text effects, import vector clip art, attach wav audio, fill shapes with color gradients or bitmaps, transform text and graphic elements, and add actions to text buttons and frames.

SwiffTools

http://www.swifftools.com

Screenweaver 2.05

Use this program to create customizable screen savers from Flash files instantly. Screenweaver also allows you to convert various other media types into a "single installer file" screen saver.

SwiffCanvas 1.0

This easy-to-use tool helps you prepare your Flash Projector files for final distribution over the Internet or on CD-ROM. With SwiffCanvas, you can create organically shaped, printable, and date/time–sensitive projectors. It also lets you save and retrieve movie variables to or from the user's registry or to a file.

SwiffPeg 1.0

SwiffPeg enables you to convert an MP3-fomat file into a SWF-format file instantly. You can then use the resulting file as a stand-alone movie or incorporate it into an existing Web page or application by using the Load Movie ActionScript command. By providing batch processing for multiple MP3s, SwiffPeg can save lots of time if you do much audio-related Flash work.

SWF Browser 2.93

The SWF-Browser's Explorer-like interface makes it possible for you to quickly browse through all the .SWF files on your hard drive or network. You can also extract elements from these files, such as bitmaps, sounds, and movie clips. It's important to note, however, that although SWF-Browser can extract movie clips and unlock SWF files, Flash provides limited support for importing SWFs.

FlashJester Creator

http://www.flashjester.com/software/creator/index.htm

FlashJester allows you to use your Flash Projector files to produce unique screen savers. Using this suite of programs, you can make a fully customized set-up box that molds to the shape of your bitmap.

FlashJester Jugglor

http://www.flashjester.com/software/jugglor/index.htm

Jugglor allows you to turn your Flash Projector files into full-fledged stand-alone programs.

FlashJester JTools

http://www.flashjester.com/software/jtools/index.htm

JTools makes up for the lack of plug-ins in Flash 3 and Flash 4 with a line of useful utilities that add functionality to your Projector files.

FlashJester Woof

http://www.flashjester.com/software/woof/index.htm

Use this program to retrieve viewed Shockwave movies from your cache. Woof will search your local drives and your Netscape or Internet Explorer folders for Shockwave movies (.swf's) and then list them so that you can browse through them at your leisure.

FlashJester Entertainor

http://www.flashjester.com/software/woof/index.htm

Entertainor can play your Projector files as screen savers, allowing you to turn on or off sound, interaction, and more.

Index